1 MONTH OF
FREE
READING

at
www.ForgottenBooks.com

By purchasing this book you are eligible for one month membership to ForgottenBooks.com, giving you unlimited access to our entire collection of over 1,000,000 titles via our web site and mobile apps.

To claim your free month visit:
www.forgottenbooks.com/free1086587

ISBN 978-0-331-48293-5
PIBN 11086587

ALPHABETICAL CATALOGUE

OF

THE LIBRARY

OF THE

United States

DEPARTMENT OF THE INTERIOR, *—Library*

INCLUDING THE

ADDITIONS MADE FROM DECEMBER 31, 1874, TO MAY 31, 1877.

———◆———

WASHINGTON:

OVERNMENT PRINTING OFFICE.

1877.

1877. Sept 3,
Gift of
The Dept. of the Interior.

SECRETARY OF THE INTERIOR,

CARL SCHURZ.

ASSISTANT SECRETARY,

ALONZO BELL.

CHIEF CLERK,

GEORGE M. LOCKWOOD.

LIBRARIAN AND SUPERINTENDENT OF PUBLIC DOCUMENTS,

JOHN G. AMES.

ASSISTANT LIBRARIAN,

WILLIAM P. SEVILLE.

EXPLANATIONS.

The plan on which this catalogue is arranged is very simple. It is, more correctly speaking, an alphabetical index to the Library, rather than a catalogue. The principal object had in view in adopting this method was, more especially, to furnish a comprehensive list of the books in the Library, in as compact a form as possible, and to facilitate the search for any particular work or volume, rather than to adhere to the established rules of cataloguing generally followed by bibliographers.

Every book has been entered twice: once under the name of the author, when known, and again under the leading word in its title; which latter, also, to a great extent, has collected the titles into a classification according to subject. In the entry of each work by its title, brevity has been consulted, with a view to economizing space; but it has, in all cases, been made sufficiently full to afford a correct general idea of the work, to give the name of the author, and to indicate its place in the Library. If it should be desired to learn more of the nature and scope of the work sought than is supplied in the title thus epitomized, by reference to the name of the author an extended abstract of the title-page may be found.

The imprint of the work is given under both the title and the author, and the number of volumes indicated. The abbreviation "illus." signifies that the work is illustrated with cuts and plates; and an editor or translator is designated by the abbreviation "ed." or "tr." following the name. The case and shelf marks are given in figures at the end of each entry; the first or left-hand number indicating the case, and those following the dash-mark the shelf or shelves. Cases designated alphabetically are indicated by their respective letters. Books deposited in the document-room are marked D. R.

All books marked with an asterisk, thus (*), are regarded as works of reference, volumes of plates, or rare books, and are not to be taken from the Library.

DEPARTMENT OF THE INTERIOR,
May 31, 1877.

RULES OF THE LIBRARY.

1. Only the employés of this Department are entitled to borrow books from the Library.

2. No book must be taken until its title and the name of the borrower have been registered by the Librarian.

3. Of works in single volumes, only one at a time may be borrowed; when of two or more volumes, two may be taken.

4. Books usually called "Works of Reference" are not to be taken from the Library.

5. Books must not be kept longer than *two weeks*, and must not be lent by those who take them from the Library.

6. If it is desired to retain books longer than two weeks, the loan must be renewed at the end of that time.

7. The loan of a book can be renewed but once.

8. When books are injured while in the possession of a borrower, they must be replaced by perfect copies.

9. Those wishing to borrow books must apply for them and return them *in person*, excepting in cases of sickness or absence from the city.

10. No book will be re-issued by the Librarian until it has been examined and restored to its proper shelf.

11. When books are detained beyond two weeks without renewal, their value will be stated to the disbursing-clerk to be deducted from the salary of the person so detaining them.

12. The Library will be open on Wednesday and Saturday of each week, and books can be taken from and returned to the Library only on those days.

13. Writing in and folding the leaves of books are strictly prohibited, and the name of any person detected in a breach of this rule will be stricken from the register.

14. In selecting books care will be used to replace them on the same shelf from which they were taken; the number of the shelf may be ascertained by turning to the label inside the cover of the book.

15. Persons desiring to enjoy the privilege of using the Library will present to the Librarian evidence from the *Chief Clerk of their Bureau*, showing that they are employed in the Department.

16. Employés on quitting service in the Department must be careful to return books borrowed from the Library, and final payment of salary will not be made to them until they satisfy the disbursing-clerk that they have surrendered all books charged to their account.

17. For non-compliance with any of the foregoing rules the Librarian is authorized to refuse to lend books.

By order of the Secretary.

GEO. M. LOCKWOOD,
Chief Clerk.

CATALOGUE.

Abbot, The. Sequel to "The monastery." Scott, *Sir* W. Bost., 1868. 3—17.

Abbott, Jacob. Gentle measures in the management and training of the young. Illus. N. Y., 1872. 2—11.

—— Science for the young: water and land. Illus. N. Y., 1872. 38.

Abel Drake's wife: a novel. Saunders, J. N. Y., 1863. 5—29.

Abell, *Mrs.* L. G. Woman in her various relations; containing practical rules for American females. N. Y., 1860. P—2.

Abode of snow, The. Wilson, A. N. Y., 1875. 10—57.

About, Edmond. The king of the mountains. Mary L. Booth, tr. Bost., 1861. 6—40.

—— Tolla: a tale of modern Rome. Bost., 1856. 6—40.

—— The man with the broken ear. Henry Holt, tr. N. Y., 1872. 6—40.

—— Germaine. Mary L. Booth, tr. Bost., 1860. 6—40.

—— Rouge et noir. Phil., 1873. 6—40.

—— The Roman question. Annie T. Wood, tr. *Rev.* E. N. Kirk, ed. Bost., 1859. 40—222.

—— The notary's nose. H. Holt, tr. N. Y., 1874. 41—226.

—— The Fellah. *Sir* R. Roberts, tr. Lond., 1870. 6—40.

About men and things. Henry, C. S. N. Y., 1873. 19—114.

Abrantes, Laure Permon Junot, *duchess d'.* Memoirs of Napoleon; his court and family. Illus. N. Y., 1854. 2 v. 11—61.

Ab-sa-ra-ka; home of the Crows. Illus. Carrington, M. J. Phil., 1868. 17—103.

Acadia; or, a month with the Blue Noses. Cozzens, F. S. N. Y., 1870. 28—169.

Actors and the art of acting, On. Lewes, G. H. Leipzig, 1875. 40—221.

Across the continent. Bowles, S. Springfield, 1869. 17—103.

Acta Touiciana; 1507-13. 2 v. D. R.

Adam Bede. "George Eliot." N. Y., 1870. 6—36.

Adams, Abigail, *wife of* John Adams, Letters of, with a memoir by her grandson, Charles Francis Adams. Bost., 1840. 2 v. 27—162.

Adams, John, The works of; with a life of the author, notes, and illustrations by his grandson, Charles Francis Adams. Bost., 1856. 10 v. 25—147.

—— Familiar letters of John Adams and his wife, Abigail Adams, during the revolution; with a memoir of Mrs. Adams by Charles Francis Adams. N. Y., 1876. 40—222.

Adams, John Quincy. Dermot Mac-Morrogh; or, the conquest of Ireland; an historical tale of the twelfth century, in four cantos. Columbus, 1834. 16—100.

Adams, W. H. Davenport. The land of the Nile; or, Egypt, past and present. Illus. Lond. and N. Y., 1871. 9—53.

Adeler, Max, *pseud.* See Clark, C. H.

Addison, Joseph, The works of. G. W. Greene, ed. N. .Y., 1853. 5 v. 2—11.

Contents.

Vol. 1. Biographical sketches of the author; Translations; Miscellaneous poems; Rosamond; The drummer; Cato; Poemata.

Vol. 2. Dialogues of medals; Remarks on Italy; Miscellaneous prose; Letters; Political writings.

Vol. 3. The freeholder; The plebeian; The old whig; The tatler; The guardian; The lover.

Vols. 4-5. The spectator.

Adèle: a tale. Kavanagh, J. N. Y., 1873. 7—41.

Adler, G. J. *A dictionary of the German and English languages. Phil., 1849. 22—131.

Administrations of Washington and Adams, Memoirs of the. Gibbs, G. N. Y., 1846. 2 v. 25—149.

Adventures of a brownie. Illus. Muloch, D. M. N. Y., 1872. 39.

—— of a young naturalist. Illus. Biart, L. N. Y., 1872. 38.

—— of a roving diplomatist, The. Wikoff, H. N. Y., 1857. O—3.

—— on the Columbia River. Cox, R. N. Y., 1832. R—2.

—— of Caleb Williams. Godwin, W. N. Y., 1870. P—2.

—— of Captain Bonneville. Irving, W N. Y. and Lond., 1850. 3—19.

—— of Signor di Lucca, The. Balt., 1800. 8—50.

—— of Philip, The. Illus. Thackeray, W. M. Lond., 1869. 2 v. 5—31.

—— in the Apache country. Illus. Browne, J. R. N. Y., 1869. 17—101.

—— in the wilderness. Illus. Murray, W. H. H. Bost., 1869. 17—102.

—— on the great hunting-grounds of the world. Illus. Meunier, V. N. Y., 1873. 28—169.

—— of a marquis. Dumas, A. D. Phil., 1864. 3—20.

—— of Capt. Mago; or, a Phœnician expedition B. C. 1000. Illus. Cahun, L. N. Y., 1876. 10—57.

—— of Mr. Verdant Green, an Oxford freshman. Illus. "Bede, Cuthbert." Lond., n. d. 2—8.

—— of Tom. Sawyer, The. " Mark Twain." Toronto, 1876. 2—9.

Advice to a young gentleman on entering society. Phil., 1839. E.

Aerial world, The. Illus. Hartwig, G. N. Y., 1875. 40—225.

Æschylus, Works of. R. Potter, tr. Lond., 1833. 17—107.

Contents.

Essay on the Grecian drama, etc. ; Prometheus chained; The suppliants; The seven chiefs against Thebes; Agamemnon; The Choephoræ; The Furies; The Persians.

Æsop's fables, literally translated. Illus. Townsend, G. T. Lond., 1871. 38.

Afloat and ashore. Illus. Cooper, J. F. N. Y., 1871. 3—14.

.frica and the American flag. Illus. ᵀoote, A. H. N. Y., 1854. 9—54.

Africa, The heart of. Illus. Schweinfurth, G. N. Y., 1874. 2 v. 10—56.

——, Voyage to the west coast of. Carnes, J. A. Boston, 1852. 9—53.

African travel, Four thousand miles of. Illus. Southworth, A. S. N. Y. and Lond. 1875. 10—57

Afrique, D'Avezac ; Carthage, La Malle et Yanoski ; Numidie et Mauritanie, Lacroix; L'Afrique chrétienne, Yanoski. (L'Univers.) Paris, 1844. D. R.

—— australe, orientale et centrale, et l'empire de Maroc. (L'Univers.) Hoefer, F. Paris, 1848. D. R.

After dark. Collins, W. W. Lond., 1870. 6—38.

Aftermath. Longfellow, H. W. Bost., 1874. 17—106.

Against the stream. Charles, E. N. Y., 1874. 2—11.

—— the world. Hadermann, J. R. Bost., 1873. 4—22.

Agassiz, Louis. Contributions to the natural history of the United States of America. Illus. Bost., 1857-60. 3 v. V.

—— Études sur les glaciers; ouvrage accompagné d'un atlas de 32 planches. Neuchâtel, 1840. D. R.

—— Études sur les glaciers; planches. Neuchâtel, 1840. U.

Agatha's husband. Muloch, D. M. N. Y., 1871. 4—23.

Age of chivalry. Illus. Bulfinch, T. Bost., 1867. 2—10.

—— of fable, The. Illus. Bulfinch, T. Bost., 1869. 3—19.

Agnes of Sorrento. Stowe, H. B. Bost., 1869. 6—35.

Agricultural chemistry, Lectures to farmers on. Petzholdt, A. N.Y.,1846. (Farmers' library, vol. 1.) S.

Agriculture, A treatise on. Illus. Sproule, J. Dub., 1842. 15—90.

——, The year-book of. Illus. Wells, D. A. Phil., 1856. D. R.

——, The monthly journal of. Illus. Skinner, J. S. N. Y., 1846-48. 3 v. S.

——, Library of practical. Baxter. Lond., 1846. 2 v. T.

Aguilar, Grace. Home scenes and heart studies. N. Y., 1870. 5—34.

—— Woman's friendship: a story of domestic life. N. Y., 1871. 5—34.

Aguilar, Gràce. The women of Israel. N.Y.,1871. 2 v. 5—34.
—— The vale of Cedars; or, the martyr. N.Y.,1872. 5—34.
—— Home influence : a tale for mothers and daughters. N. Y., 1872. 5—34.
—— The mother's recompense: a sequel to "Home influence." N. Y., 1872. 5—34.
—— The days of Bruce: a story from Scottish history. N. Y., 1872. 2 v. 5—34.

Aikin, John. The works of the British poets, selected and chronologically arranged, from Ben Jonson to Sir Walter Scott; with biographical and critical notices. Illus. N. Y., 1856. 3 v. 16—94.
Aileen Ferrers: a novel. Morley, S. N.Y., 1875. 6—35.
Ainslie, Herbert. The pilgrim and the shrine. Lond. and N. Y., 1871. 2—10.
Akenside, Mark, Poetical works of; with a life, by the *Rev.* A. Dyce. Bost., 1864. 16—97.
Akerman, John Yonge. Ancient coins of cities and princes geographically arranged and described. Lond., 1846. 15—88.
—— An introduction to the study of ancient and modern coins. Lond , 1848. 15—88.

Alaska, Travel and adventure in the territory of. Whymper, F. Illus. N. Y., 1871. 17—102.

Albany penitentiary, History of the. Dyer, D. Albany, 1867. D. R.
Albert N'Yanza great basin of the Nile, The. Illus. Baker, *Sir* S. W. Phil. 1870. 17—101.

Alcedo, *Don* Antonio de. The geographical and historical dictionary of America and the West Indies. G. A. Thompson, tr. Lond., 1812-15. 5 v. 32—192.
Alchemist, The. Balzac, H. de. N. Y., 1841. 7—46.
Alchemy of happiness, The. Al-Ghazzali, M. Albany, 1873. 19—116.
Alcock, *Sir* Rutherford. The capital of the Tycoon : a narrative of a three years' residence in Japan. Illus. N. Y., 1863. 2 v. 17—103.

Alcott, A. Bronson. Concord days. Bost., 1872. 2—12.

Alcott, Louisa M. Moods. Bost., 1864. 5—31.
—— Little women; or, Meg, Jo, Beth, and Amy. Illus. Bost., 1869. 2 v. 5—31.
—— An old-fashioned girl. Illus. Bost., 1872. 5—31.
—— Little men : life at Plumfield with Jo's boys. Bost., 1871. 5—31.
—— Morning glories, and other stories. Illus. N. Y., 1871. 5—31.
—— My boys. (Aunt Jo's scrap-bag, vol. 1.) Bost., 1872. 5—31.
—— Hospital sketches, and camp and fireside stories. Illus. Bost., 1872. 5—31.
—— Shawl-straps. (Aunt Jo's scrap-bag, vol. 2.) Bost., 1872. 5—31.
—— Work: a story of experience. Illus. Bost., 1873. 5—31.
—— Eight cousins; or, the aunt-hill. Illus. Bost., 1875. 5—31.
—— Cupid and chow-chow, etc. (Aunt Jo's scrap-bag, vol. 3.) Bost., 1874. 5—31.
—— Silver pitchers, and other stories. Bost., 1876. 5—31.
—— Rose in bloom: a sequel to "Eight Cousins." Bost., 1876. 5—31.
Alderbrook : a collection of Fanny Forrester's village sketches, poems, etc. Chubbuck, E. Bost., 1856. 2—10.
Aldrich, Thomas Bailey. Marjorie Daw, and other people. Bost., 1873. 39.
—— Cloth of gold, and other poems. Bost., 1874. 17—106.
—— Prudence Palfrey : a novel. Bost., 1874. 6—35.

Alec Forbes of Howglen : a novel. MacDonald, G. N. Y., 1874. 6—35. •
Alexander, *Mrs.* The wooing o't : a novel. N. Y., 1873. 7—44.
—— Which shall it be? a novel. N. Y., 1874. 7—44.
—— Ralph Wilton's weird : a novel. N. Y., 1875. 7—44.
—— Her dearest foe : a novel. N. Y., 1876. 7—44.

Alford, Henry. A plea for the Queen's English : stray notes on speaking and spelling. N. Y., n. d. 27—160.
Alger, William Rounseville. The poetry of the orient. Bost., 1866. 16—98.

Algeria and the French conquest. Illus. Pulazky, F. N. Y., 1855. 35—213.

Algérie. (L'Univers.) Du génie, Rozet et Carette; États tripolitains, Hoefer; Tunis, Frank. Paris, 1850. D. R.

Al-Ghazzali, Mohammed. The alchemy of happiness. H. A. Homes, tr. Albany, 1873. 19—116.

Algiers, The journal of a residence in. Illus. Campbell, T. Lond., 1842. 2 v. 17—102.

Alhambra, The. Irving, W. N. Y., 1853. 3—19.

—— and the Kremlin, The. Illus. Prime, S. I. N. Y., 1873. 17—101.

Alice; or, the mysteries; sequel to "Ernest Maltravers." Bulwer-Lytton, Sir E. Phil., 1869. 5—33.

—— Brand : a romance of the capital. Riddle, A. G. N. Y., 1875. 4—24.

—— Lorraine. Blackmore, R. D. N. Y., 1875. 5—28.

Alicia Warlock, a mystery, and other stories. Illus. Collins, W. W. Bost., 1875. 6—38.

Alison, Sir Archibald. History of Europe. N. Y., 1850. 8 v. 1st and 2d series. 32—192.

—— Military life of John, Duke of Marlborough. N. Y., 1848. 11—61.

——, Miscellaneous essays of. (Modern British essayists.) Bost., 1854. 27—159.

All in the dark : a novel. Le Fanu, J. S. N. Y., 1866. 5—29.

Allen, Ethan, Life of. (Library of American biography, vol. 1.) 11—65.

Allen, Z. Philosophy of the mechanics of nature, and the source and modes of action of natural motive power. Illus. N. Y., 1852. 15—89.

Allibone, S. Austin. *A critical dictionary of English literature and British and American authors. Phil., 1871. 3 v. 23—137.

*—— Poetical quotations from Chaucer to Tennyson; with copious indexes. Phil., 1874. 17—105.

Allworth Abbey. Southworth, E. D. E. N. Phil., 1865. 6—37.

*Almanach de Gotha. Illus. 1852-77. 18—112 and 15—93.

Alroy; Ixion in heaven; The infernal marriage; and Popanilla. Disraeli, B. Lond., 1871. 4—24.

Alton Locke. Kingsley, C. N. Y., n. d. 7—43.

Amelia. Fielding, H. N. Y., 1861. 5—34.

America, Impressions of. Power, T. Phil., 1836. 2 v. in 1. 9—53.

——, History of the discovery and settlement of. Robertson, W. N. Y., 1839. 29—176.

——, The progress of. Macgregor, J. Lond., 1847. 2 v. 8.

—— and the West Indies, The geographical and historical dictionary of. Alcedo, Don A. de. Lond., 1812-15. 5 v. 32—191.

——. Illus. Buckingham, J. S. Lond., 1841. 9 v. 29—175.

——, Annals of. Holmes, A. Cambridge, 1829. 2 v. 29—176.

——, The discovery of, by the Northmen. Beamish, N. L. Lond., 1841. 29—176.

——, Researches on. M'Culloh, J. H. Balt., 1817. 30—178.

—— and the American people. Raumer, F. L. G. von. N. Y., 1846. 8—49.

——, Thoughts on the future civil policy of. Draper, J. W. N. Y., 1865. 26—155

—— : the origin of her present conflict. Massie, J. W. Lond., 1864. L.

——, The stranger in. Lieber, F. Phil., 1835. 26—155.

——, Teresina in. Yelverton, T. Lond., 1875. 2 v. 10—57.

American. The (a novel.) James, H. Bost., 1877. 41—228.

*——, almanac and repository of useful knowledge. Bost., N. Y., and Phil., 1829 to 1862. 20 v. 24—144.

—— Association for the Advancement of Science, Proceedings of the. Phil., 1849-56. 5 v. T.

—— architect, The. Illus. Ritch, J. W. N. Y., n. d. V.

—— among the orientals, An. Boulden, J. E. P. Phil., 1855. 17—102.

—— annual register, The. 1825-33. N. Y. 6 v. R—1.

—— antiquities and researches into the origin and history of the red race. Bradford, A. W. N. Y., 1843. 20—176.

—— baron, The. Illus. De Mille, J. N. Y., 1872. 6—35.

—— biography, Library of. Sparks, J. N. Y., 1834-48. 25 v. 11—65.

Ancient history, A manual of. Heeren, A. H. L. Lond., 1847. 32—193.

—— history, A manual of. Illus. Thalheimer, M. E. Cin., 1872. 32—193.

—— history from the monuments:— Egypt. Illus. Birch, S. N. Y., 1875. 14—85.

—— law. Maine, H. S. N. Y., 1867. 26—157.

—— monuments of the Mississippi Valley. Illus. Squier, E. G., and E. H. Davis. N. Y., 1848. 14—80.

—— mythology, A new system of. Bryant, J. Lond., 1807. 6 v. 27—163.

—— painted glass of Winchester Cathedral. Illus. Carter, O. B. Lond., 1845. 14—80.

—— regime, The. Taine, H. A. N. Y., 1876. 40—224.

—— Spanish ballads. Lockhart, J. G. Bost., 1861. 17—105.

Andersen, Hans Christian. Only a fiddler: a Danish romance. N. Y., 1871. 6—39.

—— The story of my life: author's edition, containing chapters additional to those published in the Danish edition, bringing the narrative down to the Odense festival of 1867. N. Y., 1871. 13—76.

—— Stories for the household. Illus. H. W. Dulcken, tr. Lond., 1872. 38.

—— What the moon saw, and other tales. Illus. H. W. Dulcken, tr. Lond., 1871. 38.

—— Wonder stories told for children. Illustrated by V. Pedersen and M. L. Stone. N. Y., 1875. 39.

—— The two baronesses: a romance. N. Y., 1873. 4—25.

—— The improvisatore. Mary Howitt, tr. N. Y., 1873. 4—25.

—— Stories and tales. Illustrated by M. L. Stone and V. Pedersen. N.Y., 1875. 39.

Anderson, Rufus. The Hawaiian islands; their progress and condition under missionary labors. Illus. Bost., 1864. 17—101.

Anderson, R. B. Norse mythology; or, the religion of our forefathers, containing all the myths of the Eddas, systematized and interpreted, with an intro-

duction, vocabulary, and index. Chicago, 1876. 40—224.

Andes and the Amazon, The. Illus. Orton, J. N. Y., 1872. 17—102.

Andreana: containing the trial, execution, and various matter connected with the history of Major John Andre, adjutant-general of the British army in America. Illus. Phil., 1865. V.

Andreas Hofer. Illus. Mühlbach, L. N. Y., 1868. 4—21.

Andree de Taverney. Dumas, A. D. Phil., 1875. 3—20.

Andrews, C. C. Minnesota and Dacotah; in letters descriptive of a tour through the Northwest in the autumn of 1856; with information relative to public lands, and a table of statistics. Wash., 1857. 8—50.

Andrews, Fanny, (*Elzey Hay.*) A family secret: a novel. Phil., 1876. 41—230.

Andrews, John. History of the war with America, France, Spain, and Holland. Illus. Lond., 1785-86. 4 v. 33—199.

Andrews, Joseph. Journey from Buenos Ayres, through the provinces of Cordova, Tucman, and Salta, to Potosi, Arica, Santiago de Chili, and Coquimbo, in the years 1825-26. Lond., 1827. 2 v. 17—104.

Andrews, Stephen Pearl. Discoveries in Chinese; or, the symbolism of the primitive characters of the Chinese system of writing. Illus. N. Y., 1854. 28—166.

Anecdote biographies of Thackeray and Dickens. (Bric-a-brac series.) Richard H. Stoddard, ed. N, Y., 1874. 19—114.

——, The world of: a collection of facts, incidents, and illustrations of the ways of doing good, adventure, science, things clerical, lawyers, human folly, martyrs, the Bible, prayer, Christian life, preachers and preaching, noble women, etc., etc. Collected and arranged by Edwin Paxton Hood. Phil., 1874. 4 v. 2—7.

Anecdotes, poetry, and incidents of the war, north and south. Illus. Moore, F. N. Y., 1866. 2—7.

—— of distinguished persons. Illus. Seward, W. Lond., 1798. 4 v. Q—2.

Anecdotes of public men. Forney, J. W. N. Y., 1874. 11—60.

Angelo, Michael, Life of. Grimm, H. Bost., 1869. 2 v. 12—69.

Angleterre. (L'Univers.) Galibert et Pellé. Paris, 1842-44. 4 v. D. R.

———, Histoire d'. Millot, C. F. Paris, 1820. 2 v. D. R.

Anglo-Saxon derivatives, A hand-book of. N. Y., 1855. Q—2.

Anglo-Saxons, History of. Illus. Palgrave, F. Lond., 1867. 36—219.

———, History of the. Turner, S. Phil., 1841. 2 v. 36—219.

Animals, The geographical distribution of. Illus. Wallace, A. R. N. Y., 1876. 2 v. 24—141.

Anna Clayton; or, the mother's trial: a tale of real life. Bost., 1856. O—3.

Annales antiquitatis: chronological tables of ancient history, synchronistically and ethnographically arranged. Oxford, 1835. V.

Annals of a quiet neighborhood. Illus. MacDonald, G. N. Y., 1874. 7—45.

—— of the English stage. Doran, J. N. Y., 1865. 2 v. 19—114.

*—— of Congress. 42 v. D. R.

Annapolis, Annals of. Ridgely, D. Balt., 1841. 31—189.

Anne Boleyn: a tragedy. Boker, G. H. Phil., 1850. 16—100.

Anne Judge, spinster. Robinson, F. W. N. Y., n. d. 5—29.

Annette; or, the lady of the pearls. Dumas, A. D. Phil., n. d. 3—20.

Annis Warleigh's fortunes: a novel. "Holme Lee." N. Y., 1867. 4—24.

Annual of scientific discovery; or, yearbook of facts in science and art. D. A. Wells, ed. Bost., 1853-57 and 1865-71. 10 v. Q—1.

Annual report of the Board of Regents of the Smithsonian Institution, showing the operations, expenditures, and condition of the institution for the years 1863 to 1875. Wash., 1863-76. 13 v. D. R.

Anson, The life of George, Lord. Barrow, Sir J. Lond., 1839. 13—75.

Ansted, David Thomas. The geologist's text-book. Lond., 1845. T.

Anthon, Charles. *A classical dictionary; containing an account of the prin-

cipal proper names mentioned in ancient authors, and intended to elucidate all the important points connected with the geography, history, biography, mythology, and fine arts of the Greeks and Romans; together with an account of coins, weights, and measures, with tabular values of the same. N. Y., 1860. 22—132.

Antiquary, The. Scott, Sir W., Bost., 1869. 3—17.

Antiquities of Mexico. Illus. Kingsborough, E. K. Lond., 1830—48. 9 v. U.

Antiquity of man, The geological evidences of the. Illus. Lyell, Sir C. Lond., 1863. 14—81.

Anti-slavery conference, held in Paris in the salle Herz on the 26th and 27th August, 1867, Special report of the. Lond., n. d. T.

Antonia: a novel. "George Sand." Bost., 1870. 7—41.

Antonina; or, the fall of Rome. Collins, W. W. N. Y., 1871. 5—28.

A—y Brade. Lowell, R. Bost., 1874. O—1.

Apocalypse revealed, The. Swedenborg, E. N. Y., 1873. 2 v. 1—3.

Appleton's cyclopædia of drawing. Worthen. N. Y., 1866. 15—87.

*—— cyclopædia of biography. Illus. N. Y., 1856. 23—138.

*—— dictionary of machines, mechanics, engine-work, and engineering. Illus. N. Y., 1861. 2 v. 21—125.

*—— new American cyclopædia: a popular dictionary of general knowledge. George Ripley and Charles A. Dana, eds. N. Y., 1861-63. 16 v. 22—130.

*—— American cyclopædia, and register of important events. N. Y., 1861-76. 16 v. 23—136.

—— journal of literature, science, and art. Illus. 1870-72. N. Y. 6 v. 20—118.

—— new American cyclopædia, A general index to; embracing Volumes I to XV, inclusive, and the years 1861 to 1875. N. Y., 1876. 23—136.

Aquatic rights, An essay on. Schultes, H. Lond., 1811. T.

Arabia, ancient and modern, History of. Crichton, A. Edin., 1833-34. 2 v. 36—217.

Arabian days' entertainments. Illus. Hauff, W. Bost., 1871. 6—38.

—— nights' entertainment, The. Illus. Phil., 1873. 7—41.

Arabie. (L'Univers.) Desvergers. Paris, 1847. D. R.

Ararat, Journey to. Parrot, F. Illus. N. Y., 1846. 10—57.

Arblay, Frances Burney, Madame d'. Camilla; or, a picture of youth. Lond., 1796. 5 v. 7—46.

—— The wanderer; or, female difficulties. Lond., 1814. 5 v. 7—46. \

—— Cecilia; or, memorials of an heiress. Lond., 1786. 5 v. 7—46.

—— Evelina; or, the history of a young lady's entrance into the world. Lond., 1791. 2 v. 7—46.

—— Same. N. Y., 1873. 2 vols in one. 41—227.

Arboretum et fruticetum Britannicum. Illus. Loudon, J. C. Lond., 1844. 8 v. 15—90.

Arcana cœlestia. Swedenborg, E. N. Y., 1870-73. 10 v. 1—1 and 2.

Archæologia; or, miscellaneous tracts relating to antiquity. Illus. Lond., 1860. Vol. 38. 14—80.

—— Americana: transactions and collections of the American Antiquarian Society. Worcester, Mass., 1820. 3 v. 29—176.

Archie Lovell: a novel. Edwards, A. N. Y., n. d. 6—39.

Architect, The. Illus. Ranlett, W. H. N. Y., 1849. 2 v. V.

*Architecture, An encyclopædia of. Illus. Gwilt, J. Lond., 1842. 15—90.

—— and painting, Lectures on. Illus. Ruskin, J. N. Y., 1864. 26—158.

—— civile. Krafft, J. Ch. Paris, 1829. V.

—— of country houses. Illus. Downing, A. J. N. Y., 1866. 15—90.

——, Principles of. Illus. Nicholson, P. Lond., 1848. T.

——, Wonders of. Illus. Lefèbre, M. N. Y., 1875. 28—169.

Arctic boat journey, An. Illus. Hayes, I. I. Bost., 1871. 9—53.

—— explorations. Illus. Kane, E. K. Phil., 1857. 2 v. 9—52.

—— experiences: containing Captain George E. Tyson's wonderful drift on the

ice-floe, a history of the Polaris expedition, the cruise of the Tigress, and rescue of the Polaris survivors; to which is added a general Arctic chronology. Illus. E. Vale Blake, ed. N. Y., 1874. 17—102.

—— land expedition. Illus. Back, G. Lond., 1836. 8—48.

—— regions, Voyages of discovery and research within the. Barrow, Sir J. Lond., 1846. 10—58.

—— searching expedition. Illus. Richardson, Sir J. Lond., 1851. 2 v. 9—51.

Argyll, Duke of. The reign of law. Illus. N. Y., 1873. 19—114.

Ariadne: the story of a dream. "Ouida." Phil., 1877. 7—44.

Ariosto, Ludovico. Orlando Furioso. J. Hoole, tr. Lond., 1799. 5 v. 16—95.

Aristotle. Treatise on poetry, with two dissertations on poetical and musical imitation. T. Twining, tr. Lond., 1812. 2 v. R—2.

—— Ethics and politics. Gillies, J. Lond., 1813. 2 v. 28—170.

Armadale. Collins, W. W. N. Y., 1871. 5—28.

Armes défensives et offensives des Grecs, des Romains et autres peuples de l'antiquité d'après les monumens antiques. V.

Armitage, John. The history of Brazil, from the period of the arrival of the Braganza family in 1808 to the abdication of Don Pedro the first in 1831; a continuation of Southey's history. Lond., 1836. 2 v. 35—209.

Army life in a black regiment. Higginson, T. W. Bost., 1870. 19—115.

*—— register of the volunteer force of the U. S. Army for the years 1861-65. Wash., 1865. 8 v. 24—145.

*—— regulations of the U. S., revised. Wash., 1863. R—2.

Arnold, Benedict, The life and treason of. (Library of American biography, vol. 3.) 11—65.

Arnold, Arthur. Through Persia by caravan. N. Y., 1877. 10—57.

Arnold, Frederick. Turning-points in life. N. Y., 1873. 28—169.

Arnold, Matthew. Essays in criticism. Bost., 1869. 27—159.

—— Culture and anarchy; an essay in political and social criticism. N. Y., 1875. 18—108.

Arnold, Thomas. History of Rome. N. Y., 1851. 35—212.

—— History of the later Roman commonwealth, from the end of the second Punic war to the death of Julius Cæsar, and of the reign of Augustus. N. Y., 1846. 35—212.

—— Introductory lectures on modern history. N. Y. 1847. 32—193.

—— The life and correspondence of. Stanley, A. P. 2 vols. in one. N. Y., 1877. 11—60.

Arnott, Neil. On warming and ventilating; with directions for making and using the thermometer stove, or self-regulating fire, and other new apparatus. Lond., 1838. T.

Around the world. Illus. Prime, E. D. G. N. Y., 1872. 17—103.

Arp, Bill, *pseud*. See Smith, C. H.

Arrowsmith, John. The London atlas of universal geography. Lond., 1842. U.

Art, Monuments of; showing its development and progress from the earliest artistic attempts to the present period. *Prof.* Wm. Lübke and *Dr.* Chas. Fr. A. von Lützow, eds. N. Y., n. d. 1 vol. of text and 2 vols. of plates. V.

—— of war in Europe, in 1854-56; a report by *Major* Richard Delafield, *corps of engineers*. Wash., 1860. X.

* —— journal, The. New series. Illus. N. Y., 1875-76. 2 v. M.

* —— journal, The London. 1867-68. 2 v. 26—153.

Arthur Bonnicastle: an American novel. Illus. Holland, J. G. N. Y., 1874. 3—18.

Arthur O'Leary. Lever, C. J. Phil., n. d. 5—29.

Arthur, William. The tongue of fire: or, the true power of Christianity. T. O. Summers, ed. Nashville, 1856. E.

Article 47. Belot, A. Phil., 1873. 5—29.

Arts, The handmaid to the. Lond., 1758. 2 v. Q—2.

Ascanio. Dumas, A. D. Lond. and N. Y., n. d. 5—31.

Ashango-land. A journey to. Illus. Du Chaillu, P. B. N. Y., 1874. 40—225.

Asie centrale. Humboldt, A. *von.* Paris, 1843. 3 v. W.

Askaros Kassis, the Copt. Leon, E. de. Phil., 1870. 7—44.

Assistant engineer's railway guide in boring. Illus. Haskoll, W. D. Lond., 1846. T.

Assyrian discoveries. Illus. Smith, G. N. Y., 1875. 10—56.

Astoria. Irving, W. N. Y. and Lond., 1852. 3—19.

Astrea; the balance of illusions: a poem. Holmes, O. W. Bost., 1850. 16—100.

Astrology, Illustration of the celestial science of. Sibly, E. Lond., 1784. 28—165.

Astronomical observations at the U. S. Naval Observatory. Wash., 1846, 51, 52, 68, and 69. 5 v. D. R.

Astronomy, Elements of. Guy, J. Phil., 1853. 14—82.

—— of the Bible, The. Mitchel, O. M. N. Y., 1868. 14—82.

——, Popular. Illus. Mitchel, O. M. N. Y., 1867. 14—82.

——, Essays on. Illus. Proctor, R. A. Lond. and N. Y., 1874. 14—82.

——, The romance of. Miller, R. K. Lond., 1875. 14—83.

At Capri: a story of Italian life. Bauer, C. Phil., 1875. 41—229.

—— home and abroad; first and second series. Taylor, J. B. N. Y., 1869. 2 v. 17—103.

—— last: a Christmas in the West Indies. Illus. Kingsley, C. Lond., 1874. 17—102.

—— odds. Tautphœus, J. M. Phil., 1872. 6—36.

—— the altar. "E. Werner." Phil., 1872. 5—34.

—— the councillors; or, a nameless history. "E. Marlitt." Phil., 1876. 7—42.

—— the sign of the silver flagon. Farjeon, B. L. N. Y., 1875. 6—35.

Athenian empire, The. (Epochs of Ancient History.) N. Y., n. d. 35—209.

Athens: its rise and fall. Bulwer-Lytton, *Sir* E. Lond., 1837. 35—210.

Athern, Anna. Here and hereafter; or, the two altars. Bost. and Lond., 1858. 4—26.

Atlantic essays. Higginson, T. W. Bost., 1871. 19—115.

*****Atlas.** Bradford, T. G. Bost., 1835. X.

*——, General. Colton, G. W. and C. B. N. Y., 1871. R.

*Atlas, New· general. Mitchell, S. A. Phil., 1874. R.

*——, The universal historical. Sheahan, J. W. N. Y., 1873. R.

—— de l'exploration du territoire de l'Orégon. Duflot de Mofras. Paris, 1844. Texte, D. R.

—— géographique et physique du royaume de la, Nouvelle-Espagne. Humboldt, A. *von.* Paris, 1812. X. Texte, case U.

—— para el viage de las goletas, sutil y Mexicana, al reconocimiento del estrecho de Juan de Fuca, en 1792; publicado en 1802. V.

——, traité d'exploitation des mines. Combes, Ch. Paris, 1844-46. U. Texte, D. R.

—— of classical geography, An. Hughes, W. N. Y., 1856. 19—113.

——, Physical. Johnston, A. K. Lond., 1849. R.

Atonement of Leam Dundas, The. Illus. Linton, E. L. Phil., 1876. 41—230.

Attaché, The. Haliburton, T. C. N. Y., n. d. 3—20.

Attic philosopher in Paris. Souvestre, E. N. Y., 1869. 2—9.

Aubrey, John. Miscellanies upon various subjects. Lond., 1857. 27—162.

Aubuisson de Voisins, J. F. D. A treatise on hydraulics, for the use of engineers. Jos. Bennett, tr. Bost., 1852. 15—92.

Auer, Adelheid von. It is the fashion. Phil., 1872. O—1.

Auerbach, Berthold. Villa Eden, the country-house on the Rhine. C. C. Shackford, tr. Bost., 1870. 6—35.

—— Black Forest village stories. C. Goepp, tr. Illus. N. Y., 1871. 7—46.

—— German tales: with an introduction by C. C. Shackford. Bost., 1869. 2—13.

—— The little barefoot: a tale. Illus. Eliza B. Lee, tr. Bost., 1867. 7—46.

—— Edelweiss: a story. Ellen Frothingham, tr. Bost., 1871. 7—46.

—— Waldfried: a novel. Simon Adler Stern, tr. N. Y., 1874. 7—46.

—— On the heights: a novel. Bost., 1874. 7—46.

—— The villa on the Rhine. J. Davies, tr. With a biographical sketch by Bayard Taylor. N. Y., 1874. 2 v. 41—226.

Aunt Jo's scrap-bag. Alcott, L. M. Bost. 1872. 2 v. 5—31.

Aunt Judy's Christmas volume for 1874. H. K. F. Gatty and J. H. Ewing, eds. Illustrated by W. H. Petherick, H. Paterson, J. Temple, and A. S. Gatty. Lond., 1874. 38.

Aurora Floyd. Braddon, M. E. N. Y., 1871. 5—29.

Austen, Jane. Sense and sensibility: a novel. Lond., 1870. 4—27.

—— Emma: a novel. Lond., 1870. 4—27.

—— Northanger Abbey: a novel, Lond., 1870. 4—27.

—— Mansfield Park: a novel. Lond., 1870. 4—27.

—— Pride and prejudice: a novel. Lond., 1870. 4—27.

——, A memoir of. By her nephew, J. E. Austen Leigh. To which is added Lady Susan and fragments of two other unfinished tales by *Miss* Austen. Lond., 1872. 4—27.

—— Persuasion. Lond., 1870. 4—27.

Austin Elliot. Kingsley, H. Bost., 1863. 7—43.

Austin, James T. The life of Elbridge Gerry, with contemporary letters to the close of the American revolution. Bost., 1828. 2 v. 12—68.

Austria in 1848 and 1849. Stiles, W. H. N. Y., 1852. 2 v. 36—218.

Autobiography of an actress; or, eight years on the stage. Ritchie, A. C. M. Bost., 1854. 11—64.

Autocrat of the breakfast-table, The. Holmes, O. W. Bost., 1865. 2—13.

Avenger, The. DeQuincey, T. Bost., 1859. 2—12.

Avillion, and other tales. Muloch, D. M. N. Y., 1870. 5—28.

Aytoun, William Edmondstoune. The book of ballads, edited by Bon Gaultier; and Firmilian, a spasmodic tragedy, by T. Percy Jones. Illus. N. Y., n. d. 17—106.

—— Lays of the Scottish cavaliers, and other poems. N. Y., n. d. 17—106.

Bachelder, John B. Illustrated tourist's guide of the United States. Popular resorts and how to reach them; including Gettysburg; what to see, and how to see it. Bost., 1873. 10—57.

Back, George. Narrative of the Arctic land expedition to the mouth of the Great Fish River, and along the shores of the Arctic Ocean, in the years 1833-35. Illus. Lond., 1836. 8—48.

Bacon, Lord Francis, the works of; with a life of the author. Basil Montagu. Phil., 1857. 3 v. 27—159.

Bacon, Leonard. The genesis of the New England churches. Illus. N. Y., 1874. 32—195.

Bacon, Nathaniel, Life of. (Library of American biography, vol. 13.) 11—65.

Bad habits of good society, The. Baker, G. A. N.Y., 1876. 41—226.

Badeau, Adam. Military history of Ulysses Grant, from April, 1861, to April, 1865. N. Y., 1868. Vol. 1. 11—59.

Baffin's Bay, A voyage of discovery to. Illus. Ross, Sir J. Lond., 1819. 9—51.

Bailments, An essay on the law of. Jones, Sir W. Lond., 1833. T.

Bailey, James M. Life in Danbury: being a brief but comprehensive record of the doings of a remarkable people, under more remarkable circumstances, and chronicled in a most remarkable manner, by the author, and carefully compiled with a pair of eight dollar shears, by the compiler. Illus. Bost., 1874. 2—11.

Baily, Francis. A catalogue of 2,381 principal fixed stars. Drawn up at the request of the council of the Astronomical Society of London. Lond., 1825. T.

Baird, Henry M. Modern Greece; a narrative of a residence and travels in that country; with observations on its antiquities, literature, language, politics, and religion. Illus. N. Y., 1856. 17—101.

Baird, Spencer Fullerton, T. M. Brewer, and R. Ridgway. A history of North American birds. Illus. Bost., 1874. 3 v. N.

Baker, George A. The bad habits of good society. N. Y., 1876. 41—226.

Baker, Sir Samuel W. The Nile tributaries of Abyssinia, and the sword-

2 I

hunters of the Hamran Arabs. Illus. Phil., 1871. 17—101.

—— The Albert N'Yanza great basin of the Nile, and exploration of the Nile sources. Illus. Phil., 1870. 17—101.

—— Cast up by the sea. Illus. Phil., 1871. 39.

Baker, William M. Mose Evans: a simple statement of the singular facts of his case. N. Y., 1874. 7—43.

—— The new Timothy. N. Y., 1870. 7—43.

—— Carter Quarterman : a novel. Illustrated by Elias J. Whitney. N. Y., 1876. 41—230.

Bakewell, Robert. An introduction to geology; intended to convey a practical knowledge of the science, and comprising the most important recent discoveries, with explanations of the facts and phenomena. Prof. B. Silliman, ed. New Haven, 1839. 15—91.

Baldwin, John D. Pre-historic nations; or, inquiries concerning some of the great peoples and civilizations of antiquity, and their probable relation to a still older civilization of the Ethiopians or Cushites of Arabia. N.Y., 1871. 14—81.

—— Ancient America, in notes on American archæology. Illus. N. Y., 1872. 14—81.

Baldwin, Thomas, and J. Thomas. *A new and complete gazetteer of the United States. Phil., 1854. 21—124.

Ballads and tales. Illus. Thackeray, W. M. Lond., 1870. 5—32.

——, lyrics, and hymns. Cary, A. N. Y., 1876. 17—105.

Ballantyne, Robert Michael. The Norsemen in the West; or, America before Columbus: a tale. Illus. Lond. and N. Y., 1872. 6—38.

Ballou, Maturin M. Treasury of thought ; forming an encyclopædia of quotations from ancient and modern authors. Bost., 1872. 2—7.

Balzac, Honoré de, Œuvres complètes de. Illus. Paris, 1853-55. 20 v. W.

—— The alchemist ; or, the house of Claes. O.W. Wight and F. B. Goodrich, trs. N. Y., 1841. 7—46.

Bancroft, George. History of the United States, from the discovery of the

American continent. Bost., 1850. 10 v. 2 copies. 29—174.

Bancroft, Hubert Howe. The native races of the Pacific States of North America. N. Y., 1874. 5 v. 19—115.

Banking, A practical treatise on. Gilbart, J. W. Phil., 1860. 15—88.

Baptist denomination, A general history of the. Illus. Benedict, D. N. Y., 1848. 32—195.

Barbara's history: a novel. Edwards, A. B. N. Y., 1875. 6—38.

Barbary States, History and condition of. Illus. Russell, M. Edin., 1835. 36—217.

Barber, John Warner. Historical collections of the State of New York. Illus. N. Y., 1851. 31—190.

—— Historical collections of history and antiquities of every town in Massachusetts. Illus. Worcester, 1844. 30—183.

—— Connecticut historical collections. Illus. New Haven, 1838. 30—181.

—— and Henry Howe. Historical collections of the State of New Jersey. Newark, 1844. 31—189.

Barbour, John. The Bruce; or, the metrical history of Robert I, king of Scots; published from a manuscript dated 1489, with notes and a memoir of the life of the author, by John Jamieson, D. D. Glas., 1869. 17—105.

Barchester towers. Trollope, A. Phil., n. d. 7—43.

Barclay, Sidney. Personal recollections of the American revolution: a private journal. N. Y., 1859. 30—179.

Barham, Richard Harris, (*Thomas Ingoldsby.*) The Ingoldsby legends; or, mirth and marvels, by Thomas Ingoldsby. Illustrated by Crqikshank. N. Y., 1872. 17—105.

Baring-Gould, Sabine. In exitu Israel: an historical novel. N. Y., 1870. P—2.

—— Curious myths of the middle ages. Illus. Lond., 1872. 3—19.

—— Legends of the patriarchs and prophets; and other Old Testament characters; from various sources. N.Y., 1872. 27—161.

—— Gabrielle André: an historical novel. N. Y., 1871. 5—29.

Barker, Edmond Henry. The claims of Sir Philip Francis, K. B., to the author-

ship of Junius's letters; with some inquiry into the claims of the late Charles Lloyd, esq., etc. Lond., 1828. 19—117.

Barlow, Peter. A treatise on the strength of timber, cast and malleable iron, and other materials. Illus. Lond., 1851. 15—88.

Barnaby Rudge. Illus. Dickens, C. N. Y., 1868. 2 v. 3 copies. 3—15 and 16.

Barnard, Henry. National education in Europe: an account of the organization, administration, instruction, and statistics of public schools of different grades in the principal states. Hartford, 1854. L.

Barnard, Jonathan G. A report on the defenses of Washington, to the chief of engineers, U. S. Army. Wash., 1871. V.

Barnes, William Horatio. History of the Thirty-ninth Congress of the United States. Illus. N. Y., 1868. 31—186.

—— History of Congress; the Fortieth Congress of the United States. 1867-69. Illus. N. Y., 1871. 2 v. 31—186.

Barney, Joshua, A biographical memoir of. Mary Barney, ed. Bost., 1832. 12—68.

Barnum, Samuel W. *A comprehensive dictionary of the Bible. Illus. N. Y., 1871. 23—140.

Barrera, *Madame* A. de. Memoirs of Rachel. N. Y., 1858. 11—60.

Barrett, Bryant. The code Napoléon; with an introductory discourse, containing a succinct account of the civil regulations comprised in the Jewish law; the ordinances of Menu; the Ta-Tsing Leu Lee; the Zend Avesta; the laws of Solon; the twelve tribes of Rome; the laws of the Barbarians; the assises of Jerusalem, and the Koran. Lond., 1811. 2 v. 26—157.

Barrett, Joseph H. Life of Abraham Lincoln, presenting his early history, political career, and speeches in and out of Congress; also, a general view of his policy as President of the United States; with his messages, proclamations, letters, etc., and a history of his eventful administration, and of the scenes attendant upon his tragic and lamented demise. Illus. Cin., 1865. 12—66.

Barriers burned away. Roe, E. P. N. Y., 1875. 6—38.

Barrington. Lever, C. J. Lond., n. d. 7—44.

Barrington, Sir Jonah. Personal sketches of his own times. N. Y., 1853. 3—20.

Barrow, Sir John. Voyages of discovery and research within the Arctic regions, from the year 1818 to the present time. Lond., 1846. 10—58.

—— The life of George, Lord Anson. Lond., 1839. 13—75.

Bart Ridgeley. Riddle, A. G. Bost., 1873. 4—24.

Barstow, George. The history of New Hampshire, from its discovery, in 1614, to the passage of the toleration act, in 1819. Concord, 1842. 30—183.

Barth, Henry. Travels and discoveries in North and Central Africa, under the auspices of H. B. M.'s government, in the years 1849-55. Illus. N. Y., 1857-59. 3 v. 10—56.

Barthélemy, Jean Jacques. Travels of Anacharsis the younger, in Greece, during the middle of the fourth century before the Christian era. Lond., 1794. 7 v. 8—48.

—— Maps, plans, views, and coins illustrative of the travels of Anacharsis the younger. Lond., 1793. 9—51.

Bartlett, John. *Familiar quotations: being an attempt to trace to their source, passages and phrases in common use. Bost., 1871. 16—96.

Bartlett, John Russell. Personal narrative of explorations and incidents in Texas, New Mexico, California, Sonora, and Chihuahua, connected with the United States and Mexican boundary commission. Illus. N. Y., 1854. 2 v. 10—56.

—— Dictionary of Americanisms: a glossary of words and 'phrases usually regarded as peculiar to the United States. Bost., 1860. 23—137.

—— A collection of college words and customs. Cambridge, 1851. 2—13.

—— Records of the colony of Rhode Island and Providence plantations. Prov., 1856-62. 7 v. 30—182.

Barton, Edward H. The cause and prevention of yellow fever at New Orleans, and other cities in America. N. Y., 1857. L.

Barton, William. Memoirs of the life of David Rittenhouse, late president of the American Philosophical Society. Phil., 1813. 12—68.

Barton, experiment, The. Habberton, J. N. Y., 1877. 41—227.

Bascom, John. Science, philosophy, and religion: lectures delivered before the Lowell Institute, Boston. N. Y., 1872. 14—85.

—— A philosophy of religion; or, the rational grounds of religious belief. N. Y., 1876. 14—85.

Bastile and its principal captives, The history of the. Illus. Davenport, R. A. Lond. and N. Y., 1875. 40—223.

Bates, Samuel P. *History of Pennsylvania volunteers, 1861-65; prepared in compliance with acts of the legislature. Harrisburgh, 1869-71. 5 v. X.

Battle of Dorking: the German conquest of England in 1875; or, reminiscences of a volunteer. By an eye-witness, in 1925. Chesney, G. Phil., n. d. 2—12.

Bauer, Clara. (Carl Detlef.) At Capri: a story of Italian life. M. S., tr. Phil., 1875. 41—229.

—— Dead to the world; or, sin and atonement. M. S., tr. Bost., 1875. 41—228.

—— Valentine, the countess; or, between father and son. M. S., tr. Phil., 1874. 5—30.

—— Must it be? a romance. Illus. M. S., tr. Phil., 1873. 4—21.

Baxter's library of practical agriculture; with memoirs of the Duke of Richmond and John Ellman, esq. Lond., 1846. 2 v. T.

Bayne, Peter. The life and letters of Hugh Miller. Bost., 1871. 2 v. 13—76.

—— Essays in biography and criticism. Bost., 1867. 2 v. 27—159.

Bay-path, The. Holland, J. G. N. Y., 1872. 3—18.

Beamish, North Ludlow. The discovery of America by the Northmen in the tenth century; with notices of the early settlements of the Irish in the western hemisphere. Lond., 1841. 29—176.

Beattie, James. Poetical works of, with a memoir. Bost., 1866. 16—97.

Beatrice. Kavanagh, J. N. Y., 1872. 7—41.

Beatrice Boville. "Ouida." Phil., 1868. 7—44.

Beaumarchais: an historical novel. Illus. Brachvogel, A. E. N.Y., 1868. 5—28.

—— and his times. Loménie, L. de. N. Y., 1857. 11—64.

Beauties of modern architecture. Illus. Lafever, M. N. Y., 1849. T.

—— of the English annuals, The. Hartford, 1846. O—3.

Beautiful thoughts from Greek authors. Ramage, C. T. Liver., 1864. 16—96.

—— thoughts from Latin authors. Ramage, C. T. Liver., 1869. 16—96.

—— thoughts from French and Italian authors. Ramage, C. T. Liver., 1866. 16—96.

—— thoughts from German and Spanish authors. Ramage, C. T. Liver., 1868. 16—96.

—— fiend, A. Southworth, E. D. E. N. Phil., 1873. 6—36.

Beauty and the beast, and tales of home. Taylor, J. B. N. Y., 1872. 5—34.

Beckett, Gilbert Abbott à. The comic history of England. Illus. Lond., n. d. 2—9.

—— The comic history of Rome. Illus. Lond., n. d. 2—9.

Beckett, Sylvester B. Guide-book of the Atlantic and St. Lawrence and St. Lawrence and Atlantic railroads, including a full description of all the interesting features of the White Mountains. Illus. Portland, 1853. 8—50.

Beckmann, John. A history of inventions, discoveries, and origins. W. Johnston, tr. Lond., 1846. 2 v. 19—117.

Bede, Cuthbert, pseud. See Bradley, Rev. E.

Bed-time stories. Illus. Moulton, L. C. Bost., 1874. 39.

Beechcroft. Yonge, C. M. N. Y., 1871. 5—30.

Beecher, Henry Ward. Lectures to young men on various important subjects. N. Y., 1851. E.

—— Norwood; or, village life in New England. Illus. N. Y., 1874. 7—42.

Beecher's recitations and readings; humorous, serious, and dramatic. N. Y., 1874. 40—221.

Beechey, Frederick William. Narrative of a voyage to the Pacific and Behr-

ing's Strait to co-operate with the polar expeditions, performed under the command of Captain F. W. Beechey, R. N., in the years 1825-28. Phil., 1832. 8—47.

—— Same. Lond., 1831. 2 v. 8—47.

Beethoven, Ludwig von, Letters of, from 1790 to 1826, from the collection of Dr. Ludwig Nohl. Lady Wallace, tr. N. Y., 1868. 27—162.

Before the footlights and behind the scenes. Illus. Logan, O. Phil., 1870. 2—9.

Belcher, Sir Edward. Narrative of a voyage round the world during the years 1836-42. Illus. Lond., 1843. 2 v. 8—49.

Belden, E. Porter. New York, past, present, and future; comprising a history of the city of New York, a description of its present condition, and an estimate of its future increase. Illus. N. Y., 1850. 31—190.

Belgique et Hollande. (L'Univers.) Hasselt, A. van. Paris, 1844. D. R.

Bell, Acton, pseud. See Brontë, Anne.

Bell, Currer, pseud. See Brontë, Charlotte.

Bell, Ellis, pseud. See Brontë, Emily.

Bell, John. New pantheon; or, historical dictionary of the gods, demi-gods, heroes, and fabulous personages of antiquity. Illus. Lond., 1790. 2 v. 23—137.

Bell, Robert. The life of the Right Hon. George Canning. N. Y., 1846. 13—79.

—— A history of Russia. Lond., n. d. 3 v. 36—220.

Bell's new pantheon; or, historical dictionary of the gods, etc. Illus. Lond., 1790. 2 v. 23—137.

Belot, Adolphe. Article 47 : a romance. James Furbish, tr. Phil., 1873. 5—29.

Below the salt: a novel. Wood, Lady E. Lond., 1876. 3 v. 4—27.

Belton estate, The. Trollope, A. Phil., 1866. 7—43.

Ben Asaph. The Moriad; or, the end of the Jewish state. From the Syriac Hebrew, by Anselm Koristoff. Nashville, 1857. 16—100.

Bench and bar. Illus. Bigelow, L. J. N. Y., 1871. 2—9.

—— and bar of South Carolina. Biographical sketches of the. O'Neall, J. B. Charleston, 1859. 2 v. 2—9.

Bench and bar of Georgia. Miller, S. F. Phil., 1858. 2 v. 2—9.

Benedict, David. A general history of the Baptist denomination in America. and other parts of the world. Illus. N. Y., 1848. 32—195.

Benedict, Frank Lee. Miss Dorothy's charge: a novel. N. Y., 1874. 5—28.

—— John Worthington's name: a novel. N. Y., 1874. 5—28.

—— Miss Van Kortland: a novel. N. Y., 1874. 5—28.

—— My daughter Elinor: a novel. N. Y., 1869. 6—35.

—— Mr. Vaughan's heir: a novel. N. Y., 1875. 6—35.

Benton, Thomas H. *Abridgment of the debates in Congress. 1789-1856. N. Y., 1856-58. 9 v. D. R.

—— Thirty years' view; or, a history of the working of the American government for thirty years, from 1820 to 1850. N. Y., and Lond., 1854. 2 v. 28—165.

Beppo, the conscript. Trollope, T. A. Phil., n. d. 7—43.

Berber, The. Mayo, W. S. N. Y. and Lond., 1850. 6—39.

Berguin-Duvallon, M. Vue de la colonie espagnole du Mississipi, ou des Provinces de Louisiane et Floride occidentale, en l'année, 1802. Paris, 1804. W.

Berlin and Sans-Souci. Illus. "L. Mühlbach." N. Y., 1873. 4—21.

Bernan, Walter. On the history and art of warming and ventilating rooms and buildings. Illus. London., 1845. 15—88.

Bernard, Charles de. A fatal passion; or, "Gerfaut." O. Vibeur, tr. N. Y. and Paris, 1874. 5-30.

Bernard, Frédéric. Wonderful escapes. Illus. R. Whiteing, tr. N. Y., 1871. O—3.

Bersier, *Madame* Eugène. Micheline: a tale. Illus. *Mrs.* Carey Brock, tr. N. Y., 1876. 41—228.

Berthoud, Henry. Stories of bird life: a book of facts and anecdotes illustrative of the habits and intelligence of the feathered tribes. Illus. Lond., 1875. 3-.

Bertram family, The. Charles, E. N. Y.. n. d. 3—20.

Bertrams, The. Trollope, A. N. Y., 1871. 7—43.

Berzelius, Johann Jacob. The use of the blow-pipe in chemistry and mineralogy. J. D. Whitney, tr. Bost., 1845. T.

Bessie: a novel. Kavanagh, J. N. Y., 1872. 6—35.

Bessy Rane: a novel. Wood, E. P. Phil., n. d. 41—230.

Best of all good company, The. Illus. Jerrold, B. Bost., 1874. 28—169.

Bethune, Maximillian de, Memoirs of. Lond., 1761. 3 v. 13—73.

Betrothed, and the Highland widow. Scott, *Sir* W. Bost., 1868. 3—17.

Better self, The. Friswell, J. H. Phil., 1875. 19—116.

Beulah: a novel. Evans, A. J. N. Y. and Lond., 1874. 7—44.

Bewick's select fables of Æsop and others, to which are prefixed the life of Æsop, and an essay upon fable by Oliver Goldsmith; faithfully reprinted from the rare New-Castle edition published by T. Saint in 1784; with the original wood engravings by Thomas Bewick, and an illustrated preface by Edwin Pearson. Lond., n. d. 38.

Beyond the breakers. Illus. Owen, R. D. Phil., 1874. 5—28.

—— the Mississippi. Illus. Richardson, A. D. Hartford, 1867. 17—101.

Biart, Lucien. Adventures of a young naturalist. Illus. P. Gillmore, ed. N.Y., 1872. 38.

Bible, The superhuman origin of the. Rogers, H. N. Y., 1875. 40—224.

—— the Koran, and the Talmud. Weil, G. N. Y., 1846. E.

Bibles, A century of; from 1611 to 1711. Loftie, W. J. Lond., 1872. 15—88.

Biblical archæology. Jahn, J. N. Y., 1849. 23—140.

—— legends: the Bible, the Koran, and the Talmud. Weil, G. N. Y., 1846. E.

Bibliographer's manual of English literature. Lowndes, W. T. Lond. and N. Y., 1869. 6 v. 28—166.

Bibliography, An introduction to the study of. Illus. Horne, T. H. Lond., 1814. 2 v. 28—170.

Bibliotheca Americana nova. Rich, O. Lond., 1846. 2 v. D. R.

Bibliotheca Americana, and supplement to the. Roorbach, O. A. N. Y., 1855. 2 v. T.

*—— classica; or, a dictionary of all the principal names and terms relating to the ancients. Lempriere, J. Phil., 1856. 22—132.

Bibliothèque américaine. Ternaux, H. Paris, 1837. X.

Bickersteth, Edward Henry. Yesterday, to-day, and forever: a poem in twelve books. N. Y., 1876. 17—105.

Bigelow, L. J. Bench and bar: a complete digest of the wit, humor, asperities, and amenities of the law. Illus. N. Y., 1871. 2—9.

Bill Arp. Illus. Smith, C. H. N. Y., 1866. 0—3.

* Biographical annals of the civil government of the United States during its first century. Lanman, C. Wash., 1876. 22—132.

—— sketches. Martineau, H. N.Y., 1869. 13—76.

—— essays. De Quincey, T. Bost., 1860. 2—12.

—— sketches of distinguished Marylanders. Boyle, E. Balt., 1877. 24—143.

Biography and criticism, Essays in. Bayne, P. Bost., 1867. 2 v. 27—159.

Biology, The principles of. Spencer, H. N. Y., 1868. 2 v. 14—84.

Bion, Poetical works of. F. Fawkes, tr. Lond., 1832. 17—107.

Birch, Samuel. Ancient history from the monuments:—Egypt from the earliest times to B. C. 300. Illus. N. Y., 1875. 14—85.

Birch, Thomas. The court and times of James the first. Lond., 1849. 2 v. 34—205.

Bird, Robert Montgomery. Peter Pilgrim; or, a rambler's recollections. Phil., 1838. 2 v. in one. P—2.

—— Nick of the woods; or, the Jibbenainosay: a tale of Kentucky. N. Y., n. d. 3—16.

Birds, A history of North American. Illus. Baird, S. F., Brewer, F. M., and R. Ridgway. Bost., 1874. 3 v. N.

——, North American, A key to. Illus. Coues, E. Salem, 1872. 14—80.

—— of prey. Illus. Braddon, M. E. N. Y., 1870. 5—29.

Birth and education. Schwartz, M. S. Bost., 1871. 5—28.

Births, marriages, and deaths in Massachusetts. Warner, O. Bost., 1866. D. R.

Bishop, Nathaniel H. The Pampas and Andes: a thousand miles' walk across South America: with an introduction by E. A. Samuels. Bost., 1869. 17—102.

Bisset, Robert. History of the reign of George the third. Lond., 1803. 6 v. 34—206.

Bits of talk about home matters. Hunt, H. Bost., 1873. 19—114.

—— of travel. Illus. Hunt, H. Bost., 1874. 40—221.

Bitter-sweet: a poem. Holland, J. G., N. Y., 1868. 16—96.

Björnson, Björnstjerne. The fisher-maiden: a Norwegian tale. M. E. Niles, tr. N. Y., 1874. 5—30.

Black dwarf. Scott, Sir W. Bost., 1868. 3—17.

—— Forest village stories. Illus. Auerbach, B. N. Y., 1871. 7—46.

—— gauntlet, The. Schoolcraft, M. H. Phil., 1860. P—2.

—— prince, The. Illus. Jones, M. Lond. and N. Y., n. d. 38.

—— tulip, The. Dumas, A. D. Phil., n. d. 3—20.

Black, William. Love or marriage: a novel. N. Y., 1868. 5—29.

—— The monarch of Mincing Lane: a novel. Illus. N. Y., 1871. 5—29.

—— A daughter of Heth: a novel. N. Y., 1871. 5—29.

—— Kilmeny. N. Y., 1870. 5—29.

—— In silk attire: a novel. N. Y., 1869. 5—29.

—— A princess of Thule: a novel. N. Y., 1874. 5—29.

—— The maid of Killeena, and other stories. N. Y., 1875. 5—29.

—— Three feathers: a novel. Illus. N. Y., 1875. 5—29.

—— The strange adventures of a phaeton: a novel. N. Y., 1876. 5—29.

—— Madcap violet: a novel. N. Y., 1877. 4—26.

Blackie, John Stuart. On self-culture, intellectual, physical, and moral: a vade-mecum for young men and students. N. Y., 1874. 19—114.

Blackie, John Stuart. Four phases of morals: Socrates, Aristotle, Christianity, Utilitarianism. N. Y., 1874. E.

Blackie, W. G. * The imperial gazetteer: a general dictionary of geography, physical, political, statistical, and descriptive. Lond., 1855. 2 v. 21—124.

Blackmore, Richard Doddridge. The maid of Sker: a novel. N. Y., 1872. 5—28.

—— Cradock Nowell: a tale of the New Forest. N. Y., 1866. 5—28.

—— Clara Vaughan: a novel. Lond., 1864. O—2.

—— Lorna Doone: a romance of Exmoor. N. Y., 1875. 5—28.

—— Alice Lorraine: a tale of the South Downs. N. Y., 1875. 5—28.

Blackstone, Sir William. Commentaries on the laws of England, with additional notes by George Sharswood Phil., 1866. 2 v. 21—123.

Blackwood, Tales from. Edin. and Lond. 6 v. O—2.

Blackwood's Edinburgh magazine. 44 v. 29—171 to 173.

Blade-o'-grass. Farjeon, B. L. Illus. N. Y., 1872. 6—35.

Blair, Hugh. Lectures on rhetoric and belles-lettres; with a memoir of the author's life. Phil., 1860. Q—2.

Blair, John. *Chronological and historical tables from the creation. Lond., 1851. 32—192.

Blake, John S. *A general biographic dictionary. Bost., 1848. 23—138.

Blake, William J. The history of Putnam County, New York; with an enumeration of its towns, villages, rivers, creeks, lakes, ponds, mountains, hills, and geological features, local traditions, and short biographical sketches of early settlers, etc. N. Y., 1849. 31—189.

Blanc, Jean Joseph Louis. The history of ten years, 1830-40. Lond., 1844-45. 2 v. 35—213.

Blanchard, Claude, Journal of, during the American revolution—1780-1783. W Duane, tr. T. Balch, ed. Albany, 1876. 12—70.

Bleak House. Illus. Dickens, C. N. Y., 1868. 2 v. 2 copies. 3—15 and 16.

Bledsoe, Albert Taylor. An essay on liberty and slavery. Phil., 1856. 27—161.

Blessington, Countess. of. See Gardiner, Margaret.

Blindpits: a story of Scottish life. Gardiner, M. N. Y., 1870. 7—41.

Blithedale romance, The. Hawthorne, N. Bost., 1852. 3—18.

Blitz, Antoine, Signor. Fifty years in the magic circle. Illus. Hartford, 1871. 2—8.

Blockade of Phalsburg, The. Illus. Erckmann, E., and A. Chatrian. N. Y., 1872. 5—31.

Bloodgood, S. De Witt. A treatise on roads, their history, character, and utility. Albany, 1838. T.

Blowpipe, A practical treatise on the use of the. Griffin, J. J. Glasgow, 1827. 15—93.

——, The use of the. Berzelius, J. J. Bost., 1845. T.

——, The use of the. Plattner, C. F. Lond., 1845. T.

Bluebeard's keys, and other stories. Thackeray, A. I. N. Y., 1875. 4—21.

Boaden, James. Memoirs of Mrs. Siddons, interspersed with anecdotes of authors and actors. Lond., 1831. 2 v. 11—60.

Boat life in Egypt and Nubia. Illus. Prime, W. C. N. Y., 1872. 8—49.

Boccaccio, Giovanni. The decameron; or, ten days' entertainment. W. R. Kelly, tr. Lond., 1841. 1—4.

Bogen, Frederick W. von. The German in America; or, advice and instruction for German emigrants in the United States of America; also, a reader for beginners in the English and German languages. German and English text. N.Y., 1856. 27—164.

Bohn, Henry G. A polyglot of foreign proverbs; comprising French, Italian, German, Dutch, Spanish, Portuguese, and Danish; with English translations. Lond., 1857. 16—96.

Boies, Henry L. History of De Kalb County, Illinois. Illus. Chicago, 1868. 31—186.

Boileau-Despréaux, Nicolas, Œuvres de, précédés des œuvres de Malherbe, suivies des œuvres poétiques de J. B. Rousseau. Paris, 1861. W.

Boker, George H. Anne Boleyn: a tragedy. Phil., 1850. 16—100.

Bolingbroke, Henry St. John, *Lord Viscount,* The works of; with a life of the author. Phil., 1841. 4 v. 25—152.

Bolivar, Simon, Memoirs of. Holstein, H. L. V. D. Bost., 1829. 12—68.

Boller, Henry A. Among the Indians: eight years in the far West ; 1858-1866 : embracing sketches of Montana and Salt Lake. Phil., 1868. 17—101.

Bölte, Amely. Madame de Staël: an historical novel. T. Johnson, tr. N. Y., 1869. 6—39.

Bombaugh, Charles C. Gleanings from the harvest-fields of literature, science, and art : a melange of excerpta, curious, humorous, and instructive. Balt., 1860. 2—10.

Bonaparte, Louis Napoleon. History of Julius Cæsar. N. Y., 1865-67. 3 v. 35—213.

—— Atlas to the above. V.

Bond, John Wesley. Minnesota and its resources; with camp-fire sketches. Illus. Chicago, 1856. 31—187.

Boniface, Xavier, (*X. B. Saintine.*) Pic-ciola,—the prisoner of Finestrella; or, captivity captive. Illus. N. Y., 1871. 4—23.

Bonney, Catharina V. R. A legacy of historical gleanings, with illustrations and autographs. Albany, 1875. 2 v. 40—224.

Bonney, Henry Kaye. The life of the right reverend father in God, Jeremy Taylor, D. D. Lond., 1815. 12—70.

Bonnie Scotland: tales of her history, heroes, and poets. Illus. Lippincott, S. J. Bost., 1872. P—3.

Bonnycastle, *Sir* Richard H. Canada as it was, is, and may be. Lond., 1852. 9—54.

—— Canada and the Canadians in 1846. Lond., 1846. 9—54.

Book of ballads, The. Illus. Aytoun, W. E. N. Y., n. d. 17—106.

—— of days, The. Chambers, W. and R. Edin., 1864. 2 v. 2—7.

—— of songs. Heine, H. N. Y., 1874. 17—106.

—— of snobs, The. Illus. Thackeray, W. M. Lond., 1869. 5—32.

—— of archery, The. Illus. Hansard, G. A. Lond., 1841. 2—9.

—— of golden deeds. Yonge, C. M. Bost.. 1871. 39.

Book of vagaries. Paulding, J. K. N. Y., 1868. 2—10.

—— of worthies. Yonge, C. M. Lond., 1869. 39.

—— of the world, The. Fisher, R. S. N. Y., 1850. Vol. 2. 2—7.

—— of the farm. Illus. Stephens, H. N. Y., 1847. 2 v. (Farmers' library, vols. 2 and 3.) S.

Books published in Great Britain, London catalogue of, with classified index. 1816-51. Lond., 1851. T.

Boone, Daniel, Life of. (Library of American biography, vol. 23.) 11—65.

Booth, John. Epigrams, ancient and modern; humorous, witty, satirical, moral, panegyrical, and monumental. Lond., 1863. 16—96.

Borcke, Heros von. Memoirs of the confederate war for independence. Phil., 1867. 30—180.

Borderland of science, The. Proctor, R. A. Phil. and Lond., 1874. 14—82.

Border lines of knowledge. Holmes, O. W. Bost., 1862. 15—89.

—— reminiscences. Illus. Marcy, R. B. N. Y., 1872. 2—12.

Borrow, George. Lavengro: the scholar, the gypsy, the priest. N. Y., 1857. 5—28.

—— The Romany Rye: a sequel to "Lavengro." N. Y., 1857. 5—28.

Bossange, Hector. Catalogue de livres. Paris, 1845. D. R.

—— Supplement. Paris, 1847. D. R.

Bossu, J. A. Travels through that part of North America formerly called Louisiana. J. R. Forster, tr. Lond., 1771. 2 v. 10—58.

Bossuet, Jacques Bénigne. Œuvres de. Paris, 1841. 4 v. W.

Boston, Analytical and sanitary observations on the census of, in May, 1855. Curtis, J. Bost., 1856. L.

—— massacre, History of the. Kidder, F. Albany, 1870. 30—182.

Boswell, James. The life of Samuel Johnson, LL. D.; comprehending an account of his studies and numerous works, in chronological order. Lond., 1811. 5 v. 13—78.

Bosworth, Joseph. *A compendious Anglo-Saxon and English dictionary. Lond., 1849. 23—137.

Botany, Outlines of. Illus. Burnett, G. T. Lond., 1835. 2 v. 15—90.

—— of the Northern United States, Manual of. Illus. Gray, A. N. Y., 1867. 15—90.

Botta, Charles. History of the war of the independence of the United States of America. G. A. Otis, tr. New Haven, 1838. 2 v. 30—179.

Bottom of the sea, The. Illus. Sonrel, L. N. Y., 1872. 28—169.

Bouchette, Joseph. The British dominions in North America. Lond., 1832. 3 v. 33—197.

Boulden, James E. P. An American among the orientals; including an audience with the Sultan, and a visit to the interior of a Turkish harem. Phil., 1855. 17—102.

Bouligny, Mrs. M. E. Parker. Bubbles and ballast; being a description of life in Paris during the brilliant days of the empire, a tour through Belgium and Holland, and a sojourn in London. Balt., 1871. 2—8.

Bound to John Company; or, the adventures and misadventures of Robert Ainsleigh. Illus. Braddon, M. E. N. Y., 1869. 5—28.

—— to the wheel: a novel. Saunders, J. N. Y., 1866. 5—29.

Boundary survey between the United States and Mexico, made under the direction of the Secretary of the Interior, by Wm. H. Emory, major First cavalry and U. S. Commissioner. Wash., 1859. 3 v. X.

Bourdaloue, Louis, Œuvres de. Paris, 1865. 3 v. W.

Bourrienne, Louis, Antoine Fauvelet de. Memoirs of Napoleon Bonaparte. Illus. Edin., n. d. 2 v. 11—61.

Bouton, Nathaniel. The history of Concord, from its first grant, in 1725, to 1853; with a history of the ancient Penacooks. Illus. Concord, 1856. 30—183.

Bouverie, J. Fortrey. Her good name: a novel. Lond., 1875. 3 vols. in one. 6—40.

Bouvier, John. *A law dictionary adapted to the Constitution and laws of the United States of America and of the

several States of the Union. Phil., 1867. 2 v. 21—123.

Bowen, Francis. The principles of political economy, applied to the condition, the resources, and the institutions of the American people. Bost., 1856. 15—88.

—— Virgil, with English notes. Bost., 1860. T.

Bowen, T. J. Adventures and missionary labors in several countries in Central Africa, from 1849 to 1856. Charleston, 1857. 8—49.

Bowles, Samuel. Across the continent: a stage-ride over the plains to the Rocky Mountains, the Mormons, and the Pacific States, in the summer of 1865. Springfield, 1869. 17—103.

Boy in grey, The. Illus. Kingsley, H. Lond., 1871. 39.

Boyd, Andrew Kennedy Hutchinson. Recreations of a country parson. 1st and 2d series. Bost., 1869. 2 v. 2—12.

Boyesen, Hjalmar Hjorth. A Norseman's pilgrimage. N. Y., 1875. 41—227.

Bcyle, Esmeralda. Biographical sketches of distinguished Marylanders. Balt., 1877. 24—143.

Boynton, Charles B. The history of the navy during the rebellion. Illus. N. Y., 1867-68. 2 v. 30—179.

Boynton, Henry V. Sherman's historical raid: the memoirs in the light of the record; a review based upon compilations from the files of the war office. Cin., 1875. 40—224.

Boys in white, The. Wheelock, J. S. N. Y., 1870. 2—13.

—— of '76. Illus. Coffin, C. C. N. Y., 1877. 40—225.

Bozman, John Leeds. The history of Maryland, from its first settlement, in 1633, to the restoration, in 1660. Balt., 1837. 31—189.

Bracebridge Hall. Irving, W. N. Y., 1853. 3—19.

Brachvogel, A. Emil. Beaumarchais: an historical novel. Illus. Thérèse J. Radford, tr. N. Y., 1868. 5—28.

Brackenridge, Henry M. History of the late war between the United States and Great Britain. Phil., 1846. 30—179.

Brackenridge, Henry M. Voyage to South America in the years 1817–18 Balt., 1819. 2 v. 33—201.

Brackenridge, Hugh H. Incidents of the insurrection in the western parts of Pennsylvania, in the year 1794. Phil., 1795. 31—189.

Bradford, Alden. History of Massachusetts, from 1764 to 1820. Bost., 1822–29. 3 v. 30—182.

—— history of the federal government for fifty years; from March, 1789, to March, 1839. Bost., 1840. 29—176.

Bradford, Alexander W. American antiquities and researches into the origin and history of the red race. N. Y., 1843 29—176.

Bradford, Thomas Gamaliel. A comprehensive atlas: geographical, historical, and commercial. Bost., 1835. X.

Braddon, Mary Elizabeth. The doctor's wife: a novel. N. Y., n. d. 5—29.

—— Lady Audley's secret. Illus. N. Y., n. d. 6—38.

—— Henry Dunbar, the outcast. Illus., N. Y., n. d. 5—29.

—— Rupert Godwin: a novel. N. Y., n. d. 5—29.

—— Only a clod : a novel. N. Y., n. d. 5—29.

—— Charlotte's inheritance: a novel. Sequel to "Birds of prey." N. Y., 1868. 5—29.

—— Birds of prey : a novel. Illus. N. Y., 1870. 5—29.

—— John Marchmont's legacy : a novel. N. Y., 1863. 5—29.

—— Eleanor's victory: a novel. Illus. N. Y., 1870. 5—29.

—— Darrell Markham ; or, the captain of the Vulture. N. Y., n. d. 5—29.

—— Diavola; or, nobody's daughter. N. Y., n. d. 5—29.

—— The Lady Lisle: a novel. N. Y., n. d. 5—29.

—— The Lovels of Arden : a novel· Illus. N. Y., 1872. 5—29.

—— Aurora Floyd : a novel. N. Y. 1871. 5—29.

—— Fenton's quest : a novel. Illus. N. Y., 1871. 5—29,

—— Dead Sea fruit: a novel. Illus. 1872. 5—29.

Braddon, Mary Elizabeth. Bound to John Company. Illus. N.Y.,1869. 5—28.

—— The factory girl ; or, all is not gold that glitters : a romance of real life. N. Y., n. d. 5—29.

—— The white phantom : a romance. N. Y., 1868. 5—29.

—— Publicans and sinners ; or, Lucius Davoren : a novel. N. Y., 1874. 5—29.

—— Strangers and pilgrims : a novel. Illus. N. Y., 1874. 5—29.

—— Taken at the flood : a novel. N. Y., 1874. 5—29.

—— A strange world : a novel. N. Y., 1875. 5—29.

—— Lost for love : a novel. Illus. N. Y., 1875. 5—29.

—— Dead men's shoes : a novel. N. Y., 1876. 5—29.

—— Hostages to fortune : a novel. N. Y., 1875. 5—29.

—— Milly Darrell and other tales. Lond., 1873. 3 v. 41—227.

Bradley, Rev. Edward, (Cuthbert Bede.) The adventures of Mr. Verdant Green, an Oxford freshman. Illus. Lond. n. d. 2—8.

Bragelonne, the son of Athos. Dumas, A. D. Phil., n. d. 3—20.

Brainerd, David, Life of. (Library of American biography, vol. 8.) 11—65.

Braman, D. E. E. Information about Texas. Phil., 1857. 31—187.

Bramleighs of Bishop's Folly, The. Lever, C. J. N. Y.,1871. 5—29.

Brand, John. Observations on the popular antiquities of Great Britain. Lond., 1853-55. 3 v. 27—163.

Brandon, Raphael, and J. Arthur. Parish churches ; being perspective views of English ecclesiastical structures, accompanied by plans drawn to a uniform scale and letter-press description. Illus. Lond., 1848. 40—225.

Brannan, John. Official letters of the military and naval officers of the United States during the war with Great Britain, in the years 1812-15. Wash., 1823. 30—179.

Brant, Joseph, Life of. Stone, W. L. N. Y., 1838. 2 v. 12—68.

Brave hearts: a novel. Illus. Gray, R. N. Y., 1873. 7—42.

Brave lady, A. Illus. Muloch, D. M. N. Y., 1872. 4—23.

Bravo, The. Illus. Cooper, J. F. N. Y., 1873. 3—14.

Brazil, History of. Armitage, J. Lond., 1836. 2 v. 35—209.

——, History of. Southey, R. Lond., 1822. 3 v. 35—209.

——, A history of. Illus. Henderson, J. Lond., 1821. 35—209.

——, Travels in. Illus. Spix, J. B. von, and C. F. P. von Martius. Lond., 1824. 2 v. 10—58.

——, Sketches of a residence and travels in. Illus. Kidder, D. P. Phil., 1845. 2 v. 10—58.

——, The empire of, at the universal exhibition of 1876 in Philadelphia. Rio de Janeiro, 1876. D. R.

Bread and cheese and kisses. Illus. Farjeon, B. L. N. Y., 1874. 6—35.

Breezie Langton. Smart, H. N. Y., 1870. 5—28.

Bremer, Fredrika. The neighbors: a story of every-day life. Mary Howitt, tr. Phil., n. d. P—1.

—— Same. Lond., 1870. P—1.

—— Father and daughter: a portraiture from the life. Mary Howitt, tr. Phil., n. d. P—1.

—— The home; or, family joys and family cares. Mary Howitt, tr. Phil., n. d. P—1.

—— The four sisters: a tale of social and domestic life in Sweden. Mary Howitt, tr. Phil., n. d. P—1.

—— A dairy; the H—— family; Axel and Anna, and other tales. Mary Howitt, tr. Lond., 1853. P—1.

—— The president's daughters: including Nina. Mary Howitt, tr. Lond., 1852. P—1.

—— The home; or, life in Sweden; and Strife and peace. Mary Howitt, tr. Lond., 1853. P—1.

Bressant: a novel. Hawthorne, J. N. Y., 1873. 3—14.

Brevia: short essays and aphorisms. Helps, Sir A. Bost., 1871. 28—165.

Brewer, E. Cobham. *Dictionary of phrase and fable. Lond., n. d. 16—96.

Brewster, Sir David. The martyrs of science: lives of Galileo, Tycho Brahe, and Kepler. Illus. Lond., 1874. 11—64.

Bric-a-brac series. Personal recollections of Lamb, Hazlitt, and others. Illus. R. H. Stoddard, ed. N. Y., 1875. 11—61.

—— Personal reminiscences by Moore and Jerdan. Illus. N. Y., 1875. 11—61.

—— Personal reminiscences by O'Keefe, Kelly, and Taylor. Illus. N. Y., 1875. 11—61.

—— Personal reminiscences by Cornelia Knight and Thomas Raikes. Illus. N. Y., 1875. 11—61.

—— Personal reminiscences by Barham, Harness, and Hodder. R. H. Stoddard, ed. N. Y., 1875. 11—61.

—— Personal reminiscences by Chorley, Planché, and Young. R. H. Stoddard, ed. N. Y., 1874. 11—61.

—— Anecdote biographies of Thackeray and Dickens. R. H. Stoddard, ed. N. Y., 1874. 11—61.

—— A journal of the reigns of King George the fourth and King William the fourth. N. Y., 1875. 11—61.

Bridal eve, The. Southworth, E. D. E. N. Phil., 1864. 6—37.

Bride of Lammermoor. Scott, Sir W. Bost., 1868. 3—17.

—— of Lewellyn, The. Southworth, E. D. E. N. Phil., 1866. 6—37.

Brides and bridals. Jeaffreson, J. C. Lond., 1872. 2 v. 3—20.

Bride's fate, The: a sequel to the "Changed brides." Southworth, E. D. E. N. Phil., 1869. 6—36.

Bridge construction, General theory of. Haupt, H. N. Y., 1851. 15—87.

—— of glass. Robinson, F. W. N. Y., 1872. 5—29.

Bridge-building, A practical treatise on. Illus. Cresy, E. Lond., 1839. U.

Bridges, George Wilson. The annals of Jamaica. Lond., 1828. 2 v. 33—200.

Bridges executed in stone, iron, timber, and wire, and on the principle of suspension, Illustrations of. Lond., 1847. V.

——; in theory, practice, and architecture. Weale, J. Lond., 1839. 2 v. T.

Bridgewater treatises, on the power, wisdom, and goodness of God, as manifested in the creation. Lond., 1852. 5 v. 14—85.

Contents.

Vol. 1. Astronomy and general physics, by Wm Whewell.

Vol. 2. On the adaptation of external nature to the moral and intellectual constitution of man, by Thomas Chalmers.
Vols. 3 and 4. On the history, habits, and instincts of animals, by Rev. Wm. Kirby.
Vol. 5. On the adaptation of external nature to the physical condition of man, by John Kidd.

Brightwell, D. Barron. A concordance to the entire works of Alfred Tennyson. Lond., 1869. 16—100.

Bristed, Charles Astor. Five years in an English university. N. Y., 1852. 2—12.

British America. McGregor, J. Edin., 1833. 2 v. 33—200.

—— America, An historical and descriptive account of. Murray, H. N. Y., 1848. 2 v. 30—184.

—— almanac, from 1827 to 1860. Lond., n. d. 21 v. D. R.

—— Cicero, The. Browne, T. Lond., 1813. 3 v. 26—156.

—— colonies in the West Indies, History of the. Edwards, B. Phil., 1806. 4 v. 32—191.

—— colonial library. Martin, R. M. Lond.. 1844. 10 v. 33—201.

—— Columbia and Vancouver's Island. Macdonald, D. G. F. Lond., 1862. 33—200.

—— dominions in North America. Bouchette, J. Lond., 1832. 3 v. 33—197.

—— dominions in North America, The history of the, from the first discovery by Sebastian Cabot, in 1497, to its establishment in 1763. Lond., 1773. 29—175.

—— drama: comprehending the best plays in the English language; operas and farces. Lond., 1804. 16—94.

—— empire, A statistical account of the. McCulloch, J. R. Lond., 1837. 2 v. 18—109.

—— historians, Lives of. Lawrence, E. N. Y., 1855. 2 v. Q—2.

—— history, chronologically arranged. Wade, J. Lond., 1848. 32—192.

—— India, The history of. Mill, J., and H. H.Wilson. Lond., 1848. 9 v. 33—200.

—— monachism. Illus. Fosbroke, T. D. Lond., 1843. 28—165.

—— North American colonies. Young, G. R. Lond., 1834. 33—200.

—— Plutarch, The. Wrangham, F. Lond., 1816. 6 v. 11—63.

British poets, The works of the. Illus. Aikin, J. N. Y., 1856. 3 v. 16—94.

Britton, John. The authorship of the letters of Junius elucidated; including a memoir of *Lieut. Col.* Isaac Barré, *M. P.* Lond., 1848. 19—117.

Brock, Sallie A. Kenneth, my king: a novel. N. Y. and Lond., 1873. 6—38.

Broken chains. "E. Werner." Bost., 1875. 41—230.

Brontë, Anne, (*Acton Bell.*) Tenant of Wildfeld Hall. N. Y., 1868. 2 copies. 7—45.

—— Anne and Emily. Wuthering Heights and Agnes Grey; with a preface and memoir of both authors, by Charlotte Brontë. Lond., 1870. 7—45.

Brontë, Charlotte, (*Currer Bell.*) Villette. N. Y., n. d. 2 copies. 7—45.

—— Shirley: a tale. N. Y., 1868. 2 copies. 7—45.

—— The professor: a tale. N. Y., 1868. 2 copies. 7—45.

—— Jane Eyre: an autobiography. N. Y., n. d. 2 copies. 7—45.

—— , Life of. Mrs. E. C. Gaskell. N. Y., 1868. 13—76.

Brontë, Emily, (*Ellis Bell,*) and Anne. Wuthering Heights and Agnes Grey. Lond., 1870. 7—45.

Brooke, Spofford A. Theology in the English poets, Cowper, Coleridge, Wordsworth, and Burns. N. Y., 1875. 28—166.

Brookes of Bridlemere, The. Melville, G. J. W. N. Y., 1872. 6—40.

Brooklyn, A history of the city of. Illus· Stiles, H. R. Brooklyn, 1867-70. 3 v. 31—188.

Brooks, James. A seven-months' run up and down and around the world, written in letters to the N. Y. Evening Express. N. Y., 1874. 10—57.

Brooks, Charles Shirley. Sooner or later. Illus. N. Y., 1868. 6—35.

—— The silver cord: a novel. Illus. N. Y., 1871. 6—35.

—— The Gordian knot: a story of good and of evil. N. Y., 1868. 5—28.

Brougham, Henry, *Lord.* Lives of men of letters and science who flourished in the time of George the third. Illus. Lond., 1845. 11—63.

—— Political philosophy. Second edition. Lond., 1849. 3 v. 15—92.

Brougham, Henry, *Lord.* Historical sketches of statesmen who flourished in the time of George the third. Lond., 1853. 3 v. 12—72.

Broughton, Rhoda. Cometh up as a flower: an autobiography. N. Y., 1872. 4—23.

—— Red as a rose is she: a novel. N. Y., 1872. 4—23.

—— "Good-bye, sweetheart!" a novel. N. Y., 1872. 4—23.

—— Nancy: a novel. N. Y., 1874. 5—29.

—— Not wisely, but too well: a novel. N. Y., 1871. 6—35.

Broussais, François Joseph Victor. On irritation and insanity: a work wherein the relations of the physical with the moral conditions of man are established on the basis of physiological medicine. T. Cooper, tr. To which are added two tracts on materialism, and an outline of the association of ideas, by T. Cooper. Lond., 1833. 15—92.

Brown, Jones, and Robinson, The foreign tour of. Illus. Doyle, R. N. Y., 1871. 17—101.

Brown, Charles Brockden, Life of. (Library of American biography, vol. 1.) 11—65.

Brown, Henry. The history of Illinois, from its first discovery and settlement to the present time. N. Y., 1844. 31—186.

Brown, John, *M. D.* Spare hours. First and second series. Bost., 1869. 2 v. 2—13.

Brown, John P. The Dervishes; or, oriental spiritualism. Illus. Phil., 1868. 28—169.

Brown, Jonathan. The history and present condition of Saint Domingo. Phil., 1837. 2 v. 36—217.

Brown, Thomas N. The life and times of Hugh Miller. N. Y., 1859. Q—2.

Brown, Thurlow W. Minnie Hermon; or, the night and its morning: a tale for the times. N. Y., 1855. P—3.

Browne, Charles F., (*Artemus Ward.*) The complete works of. Lond., n. d. 2—8.

Browne, James. A history of the Highlands and of the Highland clans. Illus. Glas., 1838. 4 v. 34—203.

Browne, John Ross. The land of Thor. Illus. N. Y., 1867. 17—104.

Browne, John Ross. Yusef; or, the journey of the Frangi: a crusade in the east. Illus. N. Y., 1872. 17—104.

—— Adventures in the Apache country: a tour through Arizona and Sonora; with notes on the silver regions of Nevada. Illus. N. Y., 1869. 17—101.

—— An American family in Germany. Illus. N. Y., 1866. 17—104.

Browne, Robert W. A history of classical literature. Lond., 1851. 2 v. 27—159.

Browne, Thomas. The British Cicero; or, a selection of the most admired speeches in the English language; to which is prefixed an introduction to the study and practice of eloquence. Lond., 1813. 3 v. 26—156.

Browning, Elizabeth Barrett. Poems. N. Y., 1862. 3 v. 16—97.

—— Last poems; with a memorial, by Theodore Tilton. N. Y., 1862. 16—97.

Browning, Robert, Poems by. Bost., 1866. 2 v. 16—96.

—— Fifine at the fair, and other poems. Bost., 1872. 16—96.

Bruce; (The) or, the metrical history of Robert I, King of Scots. Barbour, J. Glas., 1869. 17—105.

Bryant, Edwin. What I saw in California: journal of a tour in the years 1846-47. N. Y., 1848. 17—103.

Bryant, Jacob. New system; or, an analysis of antient mythology. Lond., 1807. 6 v. 27—163.

Bryant, William Cullen. Letters from the east. N. Y., 1869. 17—104.

—— Letters of a traveler; or, notes of things seen in Europe and America. N. Y., 1870. 17—104.

—— A library of poetry and song, being choice selections from the best poets. Illus. N. Y., 1872. 16—94.

——, Poems by. Illus. N. Y. and Lond. 1872. 16—96.

Bubbles and ballast. Bouliguy, M. E. P. N. Y., 1871. 2—8.

Buchanan, George. History of Scotland, in twenty books, containing an account of its several situations and the nature of its soil and climate; the ancient names, manners, laws, and customs of the country, and what people inhabited the island from the very beginning;

a chronicle of all its kings, in an exact series of succession, from Fergus, the first founder of the Scottish monarchy, to the reign of King James VI. Aberdeen, 1771. 2 v. 34—204.

Buchanan, James. Sketches of the history, manners, and customs of the North American Indians. Lond., 1824. 30—178.

Buchanan's administration, on the eve of rebellion. N. Y., 1866. 29—177.

Büchner, Louis. Man in the past, present, and future: a popular account of the results of recent scientific research as regards the origin, position, and prospects of the human race. W. S. Dallas. tr. Lond., 1872, 14—80.

—— Force and matter: empirico-philosophical studies, intelligibly rendered. J. F. Collingwood, ed. Lond., 1864. 14—81.

Buck, George Watson. A practical and theoretical essay on oblique bridges. Lond., 1839. T.

Buckingham, James Silk. America: historical, statistical, and descriptive. Illus. Lond., 1841. 3 v. 29—175.

—— The slave States of America. Illus. Lond., 1842. 2 v. 29—175.

—— The eastern and western States of America. Illus. Lond., 1842. 3 v. 29—175.

—— Canada, Nova Scotia., New Brunswick, and the other British provinces in North America. Illus. Lond., 1843. 29—175.

Buckingham, Joseph T. Personal memoirs and recollections of editorial life. Bost., 1852. 2 v. 11—64.

Buckland, William. Geology and mineralogy, considered with reference to natural theology. Illus. Lond., 1837. 2 v. 15—91.

Buckle, Henry Thomas. History of civilization in England. N. Y., 1858-64. 2 v. 28—166.

Budge, John. The practical miner's guide, comprising a set of trigonometrical tables, adapted to all purposes of oblique or diagonal, vertical, horizontal, and traverse dialing. Lond., 1845. T.

Buffum, Edward Gould. Six months in the gold mines: from a journal of three years' residence in Upper and

Lower California, 1847-49. Phil., 1850. 17—101.

Bulfinch, Thomas. Age of chivalry; or, legends of king Arthur. Illus. Bost., 1867. 2—10.

—— The age of fable; or, beauties of mythology. Illus. Bost., 1869. 3—19.

—— Oregon and Eldorado; or, romance of the rivers. Bost., 1866. 31—187.

Bullock, William. Six months' residence and travels in Mexico, containing remarks on the present state of New Spain. Illus. Lond., 1824. 9—52.

Bulls and the Jonathans, The. Paulding, J. K. N. Y., 1867. 2—8.

Bulwer-Lytton, Sir Edward. Athens: its rise and fall; with views of the literature, philosophy, and social life of the Athenian people. Lond., 1837. 35—210.

—— Novels. Lond. and N. Y., n. d. 22 v. 5—33.

Contents.

Godolphin.
Ernest Maltravers; or, the Eleusinia. 2 v.
Pelham; or, adventures of a gentleman.
Paul Clifford.
Eugene Aram: a tale.
Devereux: a tale.
Harold, the last of the Saxon kings.
Zanoni.
Lucretia; or, the children of night.
The last days of Pompeii.
Rienzi, the last of the Roman tribunes.
The disowned.
The last of the barons.
Night and morning: a novel.
A strange story; and The haunted and the haunters.
What will he do with it? By Pisistratus Caxton. 2 v.
My novel; or, varieties in English life. By Pisistratus Caxton. 2 v.
Leila, or, the siege of Granada; Calderon, the courtier; and The pilgrims of the Rhine.
The Caxtons.

—— The lost tales of Miletus. N. Y. 1872. 17—105.

—— Caxtoniana: a series of essays on life, literature, and manners. N. Y., 1868. 3—20.

—— The student: a series of papers. N. Y., 1860. 2 v. in one. 2—13.

—— The Caxtons: a family picture. Phil., 1870. 5—33.

—— The Parisians. Illus. N. Y., 1874. 2 v. in one. 5—31.

Bulwer-Lytton, *Sir* Edward. Kenelm Chillingly: his adventures and opinions: a novel. N. Y., 1873. 5—31.

——, The poetical works of. Lond. and N. Y., n. d. 17—107.

——, The dramatic works of. Lond. and N. Y., n. d. 17—107.

—— The coming race. N. Y., 1873. 2—13.

—— The new Timon: a poetical romance; and The lady of Lyons, or, love and pride: a play. Leipzig, 1849. 17—105.

—— The Siamese twins; a satirical tale of the times, with other poems. N. Y., 1831. 17—105.

—— King Arthur: a poem. N. Y., 1871. 17—105.

—— Pausanias, the Spartan: an unfinished historical romance, by the late *Lord* Lytton, edited by his son. Tauchnitz edition. Leipzig, 1876. 5—33.

Bunyan, John. The pilgrim's progress from this world to that which is to come; with a life of the author, by the *Rev.* Robert Philip. Illus. Lond., 1845. 28—167.

—— The holy war made by king Shaddai upon Diabolus, for the regaining of the metropolis of the world; or, the losing and taking of the town of Mansoul. Illus. N. Y., 1866. 28—167.

——, Select life of. Southey, R. Lond., 1849. 12—71.

Burch, Samuel. *A digest of the laws of the corporation of the city of Washington to the 1st of June, 1823. Wash., 1823. T.

Burdett, Charles. Margaret Moncrieffe, the first love of Aaron Burr: a romance of the revolution; with an appendix containing the letters of Colonel Burr to "Kate" and "Eliza," and from "Leonora," etc., etc.; with a fac-simile of the celebrated cipher letter and key. N. Y., 1860. 3—19.

Bureau County, Illinois, Map of, with sketches of its early settlement. Illus. Matson, N. Chicago, 1867. 31—186.

Burgomaster's family, The. "C. Muller," Lond., 1872. 6—39.

Burk, John. The history of Virginia, from its first settlement to the present

day. Petersburgh, 1804-05. 3 v. 31—188.

—— Same, commenced by John Burk and continued by Skelton Jones and Louis Huc Girardin. Petersburgh, 1816. 31—188.

Burke, Edmund. Reflections on the revolutions in France. Lond., 1790. 35—213.

——, Memoirs of the political life of. Croly, G. Edin., 1840. 2 v. 13—77.

——, Memoir of the life and character of; with specimens of his poetry and letters. Prior, J. Bost., 1854. 2 v. 13—77.

——, Works of. Lond., 1826-27. 16 v. 25—151.

Burke, John Bernard. *A genealogical and heraldic dictionary of the peerage and baronetage of the British empire. Lond., 1853. 11—59.

Burlesques. Illus. Thackeray, W. M. Lond., 1869. 5—32.

Burnaby, Frederick. A ride to Khiva: travels and adventures in Central Asia; with maps, and an appendix, containing, among other information, a series of march-routes, compiled from a Russian work. N. Y., 1877. 10—57.

Burnand, Francis Cowley. My health. Bost., 1872. 2—13.

—— Happy thoughts. Bost., 1872. 2—13.

—— Out of town. Lond., 1870. 2—13.

—— More happy thoughts. Bost., 1871. 2—13.

—— Happy-thought Hall. Illus. Bost., 1872. 2—13.

—— The new history of Sandford and Merton; being a true account of the adventures of masters Tommy and Harry, with their beloved tutor, Mr. Barlow. Illus. Bost., 1872. 39.

Burnet, Gilbert. The history of the reformation of the Church of England. Lond., 1850. 2 v. 32—196.

Burnet, Jacob. Notes on the early settlement of the Northwestern territory. Cin., 1847. 29—177.

Burnett, Frances Hodgson. That lass o' Lowrie's. Illustrated by Alfred Fredericks. N. Y., 1877. 4—26.

Burnett, Gilbert T. Outlines of botany; including a general history of the vegetable kingdom, in which plants are arranged according to the system of natural affinities. Illus. Lond., 1835. 2 v. 15—90.

Burney, Frances. See Arblay, F. B. *Mme. d'*.

Burnham, George P. History of the hen fever: a humorous record. Illus. Bost., 1855. 2—10.

Burns, Robert, The complete works of: containing his poems, songs, and correspondence; with a new life of the poet, and notices, critical and biographical, by Allen Cunningham. Illus. Lond., n. d. 16—94.

—— The genius and character of. Wilson, J. N. Y., 1845. 11—63.

Burr, Aaron, The private journal of, during his residence of four years in Europe; with selections from his correspondence. M. L. Davis, ed. N. Y., 1856. 2 v. 13—75.

——, Memoirs of. Davis, M. S. N. Y., 1855. 2 v. 13—75.

—— The life and times of. Parton, J. Bost., 1872. 2 v. 40—224.

Burr, Enoch Fitch. Ecce cœlum; or, parish astronomy in six lectures, by a Connecticut pastor. Bost., 1872. 14—82.

Burton, Richard Francis. The lake regions of Central Africa: a picture of exploration. Illus. N. Y., 1860. 17—102.

—— Vikram and the vampire; or, tales of Hindu devilry. Illus. N. Y., n. d. P—2.

Burton, Robert. Anatomy of melancholy; what it is; with all the kinds, causes, symptoms, prognosticks, and several cures of it, by Democritus, jr. Phil., 1854. 28—166.

Burton, William E. The cyclopædia of wit and humor; containing choice and characteristic selections from the writings of the most eminent humorists of America, Ireland, Scotland, and England. Illus. N. Y., 1872. 2—7.

Busby, Thomas. Arguments and facts demonstrating that the letters of Junius were written by John Lewis De Lolme, *LL. D.* Lond., 1816. 19—117.

Bush, Richard J. Reindeer, dogs, and snow-shoes: a journal of Siberian travel

and explorations in the years 1865-67. Illus. N. Y., 1871. 17—103.

Bushnell, Horace. Nature and the supernatural, as together constituting the one system of God. N. Y., 1859. 15—92.

Bussey, George Moir, and Thomas Gaspey. The pictorial history of France and the French people, from the establishment of the Franks in Gaul to the period of the French revolution. Lond., 1843. 2 v. 35—214.

Butler, Mann. A history of the commonwealth of Kentucky. Louisville, 1834. 31—186.

Butler, Samuel. Hudibras, and other poems. Lond., 1835. 2 v. 17—107.

Butler, Samuel, *D. D.* Geographia classica; or, the application of antient geography to the classics, with Atlas. Phil., 1835. V.

Butler, W. F. The wild North land; being a story of a winter journey, with dogs, across Northern North America. Illus. Phil., 1874. 17—101.

Butt, Beatrice May. Miss Molly. N. Y., 1876. 41—227.

Butterworth, John. A new concordance to the Holy Scriptures. Bost., 1858. E.

By his own might. Hillern, A. *von* Phil., 1872. 6—38.

—— still waters. Illus. " Edward Garrett." N. Y., 1874. 3—15.

Byr, Robert. Sphinx; or, striving with destiny: a novel. Illus. A. Forestier, tr. Phil., 1871. O—1.

Byron, George Gordon Noël, *Lord,* The poetical works of. Bost., 1864. 10 v. 16—99.

Contents.

Vol. 1. Life of Lord Byron; Hours of idleness; Article from the Edinburgh review; Occasional pieces.

Vol. 2. English bards and Scotch reviewers; Hints from Horace; The curse of Minerva; The waltz; Ode to Napoleon Bonaparte; Hebrew melodies; Domestic pieces; Monody on the death of the Right Hon. R. B. Sheridan; The dream; The lament of Tasso; Ode on Venice.

Vol. 3. Beppo; The prophecy of Dante; Francesca of Rimini; The Morgante Maggiore of Pulci; The blues; The vision of judgment; The age of bronze.

Vol. 4. Manfred; Marino Faliero, doge of Venice.

Vol. 5. Childe Harold.

|Vol. 6. Giaour; Bride of Abydos; Corsair; Lara;

Siege of Corinth; Parisina; Prisoner of Chillon; Mazeppa.
Vol. 7. Sardanapalus; The two Foscari; Cain.
Vol. 8. Heaven and earth; The deformed transformed; Werner, or, the inheritance.
Vols. 9 and 10. Don Juan.

—— Same; complete in 1 vol., with notes. Illus. N. Y., 1859. 16—94.

—— The letters and journals of. Illus. Moore, T. N. Y., 1875. 40—222.

By-ways of Europe. Taylor, J. B. N.Y., 1869. 17—103.

Cabot, Sebastian, Life of. (Library of American biography, vol. 9.) 11—65.

Cæsar, Caius Julius, Works of. W. Duncan, tr. Lond., 1832. 2 v. 13—79.

——, Commentaries of; to which is prefixed a discourse concerning the Roman art of war, with A. Hirtius Pansa's commentaries on the Alexandrian, African, and Spanish wars. W. Duncan, tr. Phil., 1837. 35—212.

——, History of. Napoleon the third. N. Y., 1865-67. 3 v. 35—213.

—— Atlas to the above. V.

Cæsars, The. De Quincey, T. Bost., 1858. 2—12.

Cahun, Léon. The adventures of Captain Mago; or, a Phœnician expedition B. C. 1000. Illus. N. Y., 1876. 10—57.

Cairnes, John E. Some leading principles of political economy newly expounded. N. Y., 1874. 15—88.

—— The slave power; its character, career, and probable designs; being an attempt to explain the real issues involved in the American contest. N. Y., 1862. 19—117.

Calamities and quarrels of authors, The. Disraeli, I. Lond. and N.Y., 1859. O—3.

Caldwell, Charles. Memoirs of the life and campaigns of the Hon. Nathaniel Greene. Phil, 1819. 12—70.

Calendar of victory, The. Being a record of British valour and conquest. Johns, R. Lond., 1855. 21—128.

Calhoun, John C., The works of. R. K Cralle, ed. Columbia, S. C., 1851-55. 6 v. 25—149.

California, A natural and civil history of. Venegas, M. Lond., 1759. 2 v. 31—187.

3 I

California, A tour of duty in. Illus. Revere, J. W. N. Y., 1849. 17—101.

——, Life in. Illus. Robinson, A. N. Y., 1846. R—2.

—— and Oregon trail, The. Parkman, F. N. Y. and Lond., 1849. 31—187.

—— in-doors and out. Farnham, E. W. N. Y., 1856. 17—102.

——, Upper and Lower, A history of. Illus. Forbes, A. Lond., 1839. 31—187.

—— for health, pleasure, and residence. Illus. Nordhoff, C. N. Y., 1874. 17—101.

Callan, John F. The military laws of the United States, relating to the army, marine corps, volunteers, militia, and to bounty lands and pensions; from the foundation of the Government to 1858. Balt., 1858. 18—109.

Called to account. Thomas, A. N. Y., 1867. 5—28.

Calmet, Augustin. * Dictionary of the Holy Bible, historical, critical, geographical, and etymological. Taylor's edition. Illus. Charlestown, 1812. 5 v. 21—127.

—— The phantom world. The history and philosophy of spirits, apparitions, etc. Rev. H. Christmas, tr. Phil., 1850. 15—88.

Caloric, Metcalfe, S. L. Phil., 1859. 2 v. 15—88.

Calverly, C. S. Fly leaves by C. S. C., with additions from the author's earlier volume of "Verses and translations." N. Y., 1872. 17—106.

Calvert, Leonard, Life of. (Library of American biography, vol. 19.) 11—65

Cambridge essays, contributed by members of the university. Lond., 1855. 27—159.

Camilla; or, a picture of youth. Burney, F. Lond., 1796. 5 v. 7—46.

Camille. Dumas, A. Phil., n. d. 5—34.

Campaign against Quebec. Henry, J. J. Lancaster, 1812. 30—179.

Campaigning on the Oxus. Illus. MacGahan, J. A. N. Y., 1874. 17—101.

Campaigns of the British army at Washington and New Orleans in the years 1814-15. Gleig, G. R. Lond., 1847. 30—179.

Campbell, Charles. Introduction to the history of the colony and ancient dominion of Virginia. Rich., 1847. 31—188.

Campbell, Duncan, The life and adventures of. De Foe, D. Oxford, 1841. 27—163.

Campbell, John. Naval history of Great Britain, including the history and lives of the British admirals. Lond.. 1813. 8 v. 33—199.

Campbell, Lord John. The lives of the chief justices of England, from the Norman conquest till the death of Lord Mansfield. Second American edition. Phil., 1853. 3 v. 11—62.

—— Lives of the lord chancellors and keepers of the great seal of England, from the earliest times till the reign of King George the fourth. Lond., 1847-49. 7 v. 13—73.

Campbell, Robert Allen. Gazetteer of Missouri, from articles contributed by prominent gentlemen in each county of the State, and information collected and collated from official and other authentic sources, by a corps of experienced canvassers. Illus. St. Louis, 1875. 31—186.

Campbell, Thomas. The journal of a residence in Algiers. Illus. Lond., 1842. 2 v. 17—102.

—— Frederick the Great: his court and times. Lond., 1842-43. 4 v. 12—71.

——, The poetical works of, with a memoir. Bost., 1874. 17—106.

Campbell, William W. Annals of Tryon County; or, the border warfare of New York during the revolution. N. Y., 1831. 31—189.

Can you forgive her? Illus. Trollope, A. N. Y., n. d. 5—28.

Canada as it was, is, and may be. Bonnycastle, Sir R. H. Lond., 1852. 2 v. 9—54.

—— and the Canadians in 1846. Bonnycastle, Sir R. H. Lond., 1846. 9—54.

——, Historie du. Garneau, F. X. Quebec, 1852. 3 v. W.

Canadian scenery. Illustrated by W. H. Bartlett; description by N. P. Willis. Lond., 1842. 2 v. 17—101.

—— Red River exploring expedition of 1857. Illus. Hind, H. Y. Lond., 1860. 2 v. 8—48.

Canning, George, The life of. Bell, R. N. Y., 1846. 13—79.

Canoe voyage up the Minnay Sotor. Illus.

Featherstonhaugh, G. W. Lond., 1847. 2 v. 10—58.

Canterbury tales. Illus. Chaucer, G. N. Y., 1867. 16—100.

Cantero, J. G. Los ingenios. Coleccion de vistas de los principales ingenios de azúcar de la isla de Cuba. Habana, n. d. V.

Capacity and genius, An essay on, with an enquiry into the nature of ghosts and other appearances supposed to be supernatural. Lond., n. d. 15—92.

Cape Cod. Thoreau, H. D. Bost., 1865. 17—104.

Caper-sauce : a volume of chit-chat about men, women, and things. "Fanny Fern." N. Y., 1872. 2—8.

Capes, W. W. Roman history : the early empire. (Epochs of ancient history.) N. Y., n. d. 35—212.

Capital of the Tycoon, The. Illus. Alcock, Sir R. N. Y, 1863.. 2 v. 17—103.

Captain Brand of the "Centipede." Illus. "Harry Gringo." N. Y., 1871. 5—28.

Captains of the old world, The. Herbert, H. W. N. Y., 1852. 13—76.

Captivity among the Indians, Memoirs of a. Hunter, J. D. Lond., 1823. 10—58.

Cardinal de Richelieu, Mémoires du. Petitot, C. B. Paris, 1823. 10 v. D. R.

—— Mazarin. Sequel to the "Three musketeers." Dumas, A. D. Lond. and N. Y., n. d. 5—31.

Carey, Henry C. Letters to the President on the foreign and domestic policy of the Union, and its effects, as exhibited in the condition of the people and the state. Phil. and Lond., 1858. L.

—— Principles of political economy ; of the laws of the production and distribution of wealth. Phil., 1837. 3 v. R—1.

—— Principles of social science. Phil. and Lond., 1858-59. 3 v. 15—92.

—— The unity of law, as exhibited in the relations of physical, social, mental, and moral science. Phil., 1872. 15—87.

Carey, William. The queen : the conspiracies of 1806 and 1813 against the princess of Wales, with that of 1820 against the queen of England. Lond., 1820. 34—208.

Caricature and grotesque in literature and art, A history of. Illus. Wright, T. Lond,. 1875. 2—7.

Carleton, *Capt.* George, Memoirs of. De Foe, D. Oxford, 1840. 27—163.
Carleton, Will. Farm ballads. Illus. N. Y., 1873. 16—95.
—— Farm legends. Illus. N. Y., 1876. 16—95.
Carlyle, Thomas. French revolution : a history. N. Y., 1871. 2 v. 35—213.
—— History of Friedrich the second. called Frederick the Great. N. Y., 1863-71. 6 v. 12—71.
—— Oliver Cromwell's letters and speeches, including the supplement to the first edition, with elucidations. N Y., 1871. 2 v. 12—71.
—— Sartor Resartus : the life and opinions of Herr Teufelsdröckh : in three books. Lond., 1831. 28—169.
—— Past and present. Bost., 1843. 28—169.
Carlyle, Thomas, *Advocate.* Pleadings with my mother, the church in Scotland; the substance of four lectures delivered in Edinburgh, May, 1854. Edin., 1854. E.
Carmen's inheritance. Illus. "Christian Reid." Phil., 1873. 5—28.
Carne, John. La Syrie, la Terre-Sainte, l'Asie-Mineure, etc. Illustrées. Une série de vues dessinées d'après nature, par W. H. Bartlett et William Purser. Lond. et Paris, 1836. 9—55.
Carnes, J. A. Journal of a voyage from Boston to the west coast of Africa : with a full description of the manner of trading with the natives on the coast. Bost., 1852. 9—53.
Carpentry, Elementary principles of. Illus. Tredgold, T. Phil, 1847. T.
——, Comprehensive guide-book for. Illus. Nicholson, P. Lond., 1852. 2 v. T.
Carrington, *Mrs.* Margaret J. Ab-sa-ra-ka, home of the Crows, being the experience of an officer's wife on the plains. Illus. Phil., 1868. 17—103.
Carroll, Lewis, *pseud.* See Dodgson, C. L.
Carry's confession. Robinson, F. W. N. Y., 1871. 5—29.
Carter, Owen B. *A series of the ancient painted glass of Winchester Cathedral. Illus. Lond., 1845. 14—80.
Carter Quarterman : a novel. Illus. Baker, W. M. N. Y., 1876. 41—230.

Carver, Jonathan. Travels through the interior parts of North America in the years 1766-68. Lond., 1778. 8—49.
Cary, Alice. Snow-berries : a book for young folks. Illus. Bost., 1867. 39.
—— Ballads, lyrics, and hymns. N. Y., 1876. 17—105.
—— A memorial of. Illus. Ames, M. C. N. Y., 1875. 17—105.
Cary, Phœbe. Poems of faith, hope, and love. N. Y., 1874. 17—105.
—— A memorial of. Illus. Ames, M. C. N. Y., 1875. 17—105.
Casimir Maremma. Helps, *Sir* A. Bost., 1871. O —1.
Casket of reminiscences. Foote, H. S. Wash., 1874. 11—60.
Cast away in the cold. Illus. Hayes, I. I. Bost., 1872. 39.
—— up by the sea. Illus. Baker, *Sir* S. W. Phil., 1871. 39.
Castelar, Emilio. Old Rome and new Italy,(recuerdos de Italia.) *Mrs.* Arthur Arnold, tr. N. Y., 1874. 17—104.
Cast-iron beams and columns, A treatise on. Turnbull, W. Lond., 1832. T.
Castilian days. Hay, J. Bost., 1872. 17—102.
Castle Daly ; the story of an Irish home thirty years ago. Keary, A. Phil., n. d. 7—42.
—— Richmond. Trollope, A. N.Y., 1862. 7—43.
—— Wafer. Wood, E. P. N. Y., n. d. 5—29.
Castle's heir, The. Illus. Wood, E. P. Phil., n. d. 41—230.
Castleton, D. R. Salem : a tale of the seventeenth century. N.Y., 1874. P—2.
* **Catalogue** of the Library of Congress, (authors.) Wash., 1864. 1—4.
* —— of books added to the Library of Congress, 1867-75. 6 v. 1—4.
* —— of the Mercantile Library of Philadelphia, 1870. 1—4.
* —— de livres. Bossange. Paris, 1845. D. R.
* —— Supplement. Paris, 1847. D. R.
Cathedral, The. Lowell, J. R. Bost., 1870. 17—106.
Catherine. Illus. Thackeray, W. M. Lond., 1869. 5—32.
Catlin, George. Illustrations of the manners, customs, and conditions of the

W. **Chambers**, ed. Lond. and Edin., 1871. 13—76.

Chambers, William and Robert. The book of days: a miscellany of popular antiquities in connection with the calendar. Illus. Edin., 1864. 2 v. 2—7.

—— Information for the people. Illus. Phil., 1860. 2 v. 27—160.

—— Miscellany of useful and entertaining tracts. Edin., 1847. 10 v. 27—162.

—— Memoir of Robert Chambers, with autobiographic reminiscences of William Chambers. N. Y., 1872. 11—65.

Chance acquaintance, A. Howells, W. D. Bost., 1873. 5—34.

—— for himself, A. Illus. Trowbridge, J. T. Bost., 1872. 39.

Chandos. "Ouida." Phil., 1874. 7—44.

Changed brides, The. Southworth, E. D. E. N. Phil., 1869. 6—37.

Channings, The. Wood, E. P. Phil., n. d. 41—230.

Chaplet of pearls, The. Illus. Yonge, C. M. Lond, 1868. 41—230.

Chapman, Edward J. Practical mineralogy; or, a compendium of the distinguishing characters of minerals. Illus. Lond. and Paris, 1843. 15—91.

Chapman, Isaac A. A sketch of the history of Wyoming; to which is added a statistical account of the valley and adjacent country, by a gentleman of Wilkesbarre, *Pa.* Wilkesbarre, 1830. 31—189.

Chapters on animals. Illus. Hamerton, P. G. Bost., 1874. 39.

Character. Smiles, S. N. Y., 1872. O—3.

—— sketches. Illus. Macleod, N. N. Y., n. d. P—3.

—— and characteristic men. Whipple, E. P. Bost., 1871. 41—228.

Characteristics of women. Jameson, A M. Bost., 1866. 2—13.

Characters of Theophrastus, The. Illus. La Bruyère, J. de. Lond., 1831. 27—162.

Charles, Elizabeth. Chronicles of the Schonberg-Cotta family, by two of themselves. N. Y., 1869. 2—10.

—— Diary of Mrs. Kitty Trevylyan : a story of the times of Whitefield and the Wesleys. N. Y., 1868. 2—11.

—— The martyrs of Spain, and the liberators of Holland. N. Y., 1865. 13—76.

Charles, Elizabeth. The early dawn ; or, sketches of Christian life in England in the olden time, with introduction by *Prof.* Henry B. Smith, *D. D.* N. Y., n. d. 3—20.

—— The Draytons and the Davenants ; a story of the civil wars. N. Y., n. d· 3—20.

—— On both sides of the sea; a story of the commonwealth and the restoration : a sequel to "the Draytons and the Davenants." N. Y., n. d. 3—20.

—— The victory of the vanquished; a story of the first century. N. Y., n. d. 3—20.

—— Winifred Bertram and the world she lived in. N. Y., n. d. 3—20.

—— The Bertram family. N. Y., n. d. 3—20.

—— Against the stream: the story of a heroic age in England. N. Y., 1874. 2—11.

Charles O'Malley. Lever, C. J. Phil., n. d. 5—29.

Charles the first, Commentaries on the life and reign of. Disraeli, I. Lond., 1828-31. 5 v. 34—205.

—— the first memoirs of the reign of. Warwick, *Sir* P. Lond., 1701. 11—65.

—— the fifth, The cloister life of. Stirling, W. Bost., 1853· 11—64.

—— the fifth, History of the reign of the emperor. Robertson, W. N. Y., 1839. 36—218.

—— the twelfth, Discourse on the history of. Voltaire, F. A. Lond., 1732. 11—60.

Charlotte's inheritance. Sequel to "Birds of prey." Braddon, M. E. N. Y., 1868. 5—29.

Charpente, Traité sur l'art de la. Krafft, J. Ch. Paris, 1840. 2 v. V.

Charteris : a romance. Meline, M. M. Phil., 1874. 3—18.

Chartism ; Past and present ; and Sartor Resartus. Carlyle, T. N. Y., 1871. 28—169.

Chase, Salmon Portland, The private life and public services of. Warden, R. B. Cin., 1874. 11—59.

——, The life and public services of. Schuckers, J. W. N. Y., 1874. 11—59.

Chattanooga. Cin., 1858. 4—25.

Chatterton, Thomas, Poetical works of; with notices of his life. Bost., 1857. 2 v. 16—99.

Chaucer, Geoffrey. The Canterbury tales; from the text, and with the notes and glossary, of Thomas Tyrwhitt. Illus. N. Y., 1867. 16—100.

Checkmate. Illus. Le Fanu, J. S. Bost., n. d. 5—29.

Chedayne of Kotono: a story of the early days of the republic. Towner, A. N. Y., 1877. 3—17.

Chemistry, Elements of. Illus. Miller, W. A. N. Y., 1864. 15—87.

—— complete works on. Liebig, J. von. Phil., n. d. 15—87.

Cherbuliez, Victor. Joseph Noirel's revenge. W. F. West, tr. N. Y., 1872. 7—46.

—— Count Kostia: a novel. O. D. Ashley, tr. N. Y., 1873. 7—46.

—— Prosper: a novel. Carl Benson, tr. N. Y., 1874. 7—46.

Chesney, George. The battle of Dorking: the German conquest of England in 1875; or, reminiscences of a volunteer. By an eye-witness, in 1925. Phil., n. d. 2—12.

Chesterfield, Philip Dormer Stanhope, earl of. Letters to his son. Phil., 1868. P—2.

Chevalier, Michel. Historie et description des voies de communication aux États-Unis, et des travaux d'art qui en dépendent. Paris, 1840. 2 v. 11—49. Atlas, W.

—— L'isthme de Panama. Paris, 1844. D. R.

Chevalier, The. Dumas, A. D. Phil., 1864. 3—20.

—— D'Harmental; or, the conspirators. Dumas, A. D. Lond. and N. Y., n. d. 5—31.

Chicot, the jester. Dumas, A. D. Lond. and N. Y., n. d. 5—31.

Chief of the pilgrims; or, the life and time of William Brewster. Illus. Steele, A. Phil., 1857. Q—2.

—— justices of England, The lives of the. Campbell, J. Phil., 1853. 3 v. 11—62.

—— justices of the Supreme Court of the United States, Lives of the. Van Santvoord, G. N. Y., 1854. 12—69.

Child life in prose. Illus. Whittier, J. G. ed. Bost., 1874. 39.

—— world. Illus. "Gail Hamilton." Bost., 1873. 2 v. 39.

Childhood. (Little classics, vol. 10.) Bost., 1875. 5—33.

Children of the abbey, The. Roche, R. M. Phil., 1869. 6—38.

—— of the New Forest, The. Illus. Marryat, Capt. F. Lond. and N. Y., n. d. 5—30.

Children's treasury of English songs, The. Palgrave, F. T. N. Y., 1875. 17—106.

Chili, History of. Molina, J. I. Middletown, Conn., 1808. 2 v. 36—216.

Chimney corner, The. Stowe, H. B. Bost., 1868. 6—35.

Chimneys, A practical treatise on. Eckstein, G. F. Lond., 1852. T.

China. Martin, R. M. Lond., 1847. 2 v. 36—216.

——, Five years in. Illus. Forbes, F. E. Lond., 1848. 8—49.

——, General history of. Illus. Du Halde, P. Lond. 1741. 4 v. 36—216.

Chinese, Discoveries in. Illus. Andrews, S. P. N. Y., 1854. 28—166.

—— empire, A journey through the. Huc, E. R. N. Y., 1855. 2 v. 9—54.

—— social life of the. Illus. Doolittle, J. 2 v. in one. N. Y., 1876. 9—52.

Chris and Otho; sequel to "Widow Goldsmith's daughter." Smith, J. P. N. Y. and Lond., 1875. 5—30.

Christ and other masters. Hardwick, C. Lond., 1874. E.

Christian names, History of. Yonge, C. M. Lond., 1863. 2 v. 26—156.

—— commission, Incidents of the United States. Illus. Smith, Rev. E. P. Phil., 1871. 2—7.

—— revelation viewed in connection with the modern astronomy, Discourses on the. Chalmers, T. N. Y., 1871. 19—116.

Christianity and modern infidelity. Morgan, R. W. N. Y., 1859. E.

Christian's mistake. Muloch, D. M. N. Y., 1871. 4—23.

Christie's faith. Robinson, F. W. N. Y., 1867. O—3.

Christmas eve and Christmas day. Hale, E. E. Bost., 1874. 5—34.

Christmas guest, The. Southworth, E. D. E. N., and F. H. Baden. Phil., 1870. 6—36.
—— books. Illus. Thackeray, W. M. Lond., 1871. 5—32.
—— books. Illus. Dickens, C. N. Y., 1868. 2 copies. 3—15 and 10.
Chronicle of Florence of Worcester, The. Lond., 1854. 33—201.
Chronicles of the Bastile. Illus. N.Y., 1859. 2—9.
—— of the Schönberg-Cotta family. Charles, E. N. Y., 1869. 2—10.
—— of Cartaphilus, the wandering Jew. Hoffman, D. Lond., 1853. 2 v. 26—156.
—— of the tombs. Pettigrew, T. J. Lond., 1857. 27—163.
—— of England, France, Spain, and the adjoining countries. Illus. Froissart, Sir J. T. Johnes, tr. Lond., 1852. 33—197.
—— of Monstrelet. Illus. T. Johnes, tr. Lond., 1849. 2 v. 33—197.
* Chronological and historical tables. Blair, J. Lond., 1851. 32—192.
Chubbuck, Emily, (Fanny Forrester.) See Judson, E. C.
Church, Florence, (formerly Florence Marryat.) Woman against woman. Bost., n. d. 4—22.
—— The prey of the gods: a novel. Leipzig, 1872. 4—22.
—— Gerald Estcourt; his confessions. Lond. and N. Y., n. d. 4—22.
—— The girls of Feversham. Lond. and N. Y., n. d. 4—22.
—— Nelly Brooke: a homely story. Lond. and N. Y., n. d. 4—22.
—— "Too good for him." Lond. and N. Y., n. d. 4—22.
—— Love's conflict. Lond. and N. Y., n. d. 4—22.
—— Petronel: a novel. Lond. and N. Y., n. d. 4—22.
—— Her lord and master: a tale. Leip., 1871. 2 v. in one. 4—22.
—— Véronique: a romance. Lond. and Bost., n. d. 4—22.
—— No intentions: a novel. Leip., 1874. 2 v. in one. 4—22.
—— Hidden chains. Lond., 1876. 3 v. 4—22.
—— For ever and ever: a drama of life. Leip., 1866. 2 v. in one. 4—22.

Church, Florence, (formerly Florence Marryat.) Mad Dumaresq: a novel. Leip., 1873. 2 v. in one. 4—22.
—— A star and a heart. Bost., n. d. 41—230.
—— Fighting the air: a novel. Leip. 1875. 2 v. in one. 41—226.
Churchill, Charles, Poetical works of; with a life of the author, by W. Tooke. Bost., 1864. 3 v. 16—99.
Churton, Henry. Toinette: a tale of transition. N. Y., 1875. 3—16.
Chynoweth, W. Harris. The fall of Maximilian, late emperor of Mexico; with an historical introduction, the events immediately preceding his acceptance of the crown, and a particular description of the causes which led to his execution; together with a correct report of the able defence made by his advocates before the court-martial, and their persevering efforts on his behalf at the seat of the republican government. Lond., 1872. 32—192.
Cicero, Marcus Tullius, Works of. Duncan, Cockman, and Melmoth, trs. Lond., 1833. 2 v. 11—64.
——, Life of. Illus. Forsyth, W. N. Y., 1869. 2 v. 11—64.
Circle of the sciences: a series of treatises on the principles of science, with their application to practical pursuits. Lond., 1854-60. 9 v. 14—84.

Contents.

Vol. 1. Organic nature:—Principles of physiology, by the editor; Structure of the skeleton and teeth, Prof. Owen; Varieties of the human race, R. G. Latham.
Vol. 2. Organic nature:—Botany, structural and systematic, Edward Smith; Zoology, invertebrated animals, W. S. Dallas.
Vol. 3. Organic nature:—Vertebrated animals, W. S. Dallas.
Vol. 4. Inorganic nature:—Geology and physical geography, Prof. Ansted; Mineralogy and crystallography, Prof. Tennant and Rev. W. Mitchell.
Vol. 5. Navigation:—Nautical astronomy, Prof. Young; Practical astronomy, H. Breen; Meteorology, Dr. Scoffern and E. J. Lowe.
Vol. 6. Elementary chemistry:—Imponderable agents, light, heat, electricity, simple chemical bodies, and their inorganic compounds, J. Scoffern.
Vol. 7. Practical chemistry:—Electro-deposition, G. Gore; Photographic art, M. Sparling; Chemistry of food and of artificial illumination, Dr. Scoffern.

Vol. 8. Mathematical sciences: — Simple arithmetic, algebra, and the elements of Euclid. Prof. Young; Planes, spherical trigonometry. series, logarithms, and mensuration, J. F. Twisden; Practical geometry, A. Jardine. Vol. 9. Mechanical Philosophy: — Properties of matter, elementary statics, dynamics, hydrostatics, hydrodynamics, pneumatics, practical mechanics, and the steam-engine, Rev. W. Mitchell, J. R. Young, and John Imray.

Circuit rider, The. Illus. Eggleston, E. N. Y., 1874. 7—45.

Civil Engineers, Transactions of the Institution of the. Lond., 1842. 3 v. T.

—— engineering, A complete course of. Gregory, J. Lond., n. d. 15—87.

—— institutions of the U. S., The Christian life and character of. Morris, B. F. Phil., 1864. 2 copies. T.

—— wars of Ireland. History of the. Taylor, W. C. Edin., 1831. 2 v. 34—205.

—— war in the United States of America, Pictorial history of the. Lossing, B. J. 1866-68. 3 v. 30—178.

—— war in America, History of the. Orleans, L. P. d'. Phil., 1875. Vol. 1. 30—181. ·

Civilization in England, History of. Buckle, H. T. N. Y. 1858-64. 2 v. 28—166.

—— The history of. Dean, A. Albany, 1868-69. 7 v. 36—215.

Clara Vaughan. Blackmore, R. D. Lond., 1864. O—2.

Clare, Israel Smith. The centennial universal history: a clear and concise history of all nations, with a full history of the United States to the close of the first one hundred years of our national independence. Illus. Phil., 1876. 30—181. .

Clarendon, Edward, earl of. History of the rebellion and civil war in England, from 1641. Oxford, 1717. 7 v. 34—204.

Clarissa Harlowe. Richardson, S. N. Y., 1874. 4—24.

Clark, Charles Heber, (Max Adler.) Out of the hurly-burly; or, life in an odd corner. Illustrated by Frost, Schell, Sheppard, and Bensell. Phil., 1874. 2—4.

—— Elbow-room: a novel without a plot. Illustrated by A. B. Frost. Phil., 1876. 2—8.

Clark, Thomas. Naval history of the United States, from the commencement of the revolutionary war to the present time. Phil., 1814. 2 v. 30—179.

Clarke, Edward Hammond. Sex in education; or, a fair chance for girls. Bost., 1874. 40—222.

Clarke, Marcus. His natural life: a novel. N. Y., 1876. 41—230.

Clarke, Mary Cowden. World-noted women ; or, types of womanly attributes of all lands and all ages. Illus. N. Y., 1857. 11—59.

—— The complete concordance to Shakespeare. Bost, 1853. 16—94.

—— A rambling story. Bost., 1875. 3—15.

—— The iron cousin; or, mutual influence. N. Y., 1875. 41—229.

Clarkson, Thomas. Memoirs of the public and private life of William Penn ; with a reply to Macaulay's charges against his character, by W. E. Forster. Lond. and Phil., 1849. 11—63.

Classical literature, A history of. Browne, R. W. Lond., 1851. 2 v. 27—159.

Claverings, The. Trollope, A. N. Y., 1871. 5—22.

Clavigero, D. Francesco Saviero. History of Mexico. Lond., 1787. 2 v. 32—191.

Clay, Henry, the works of. C. Colton, ed. N. Y., n. d. 6 v. 25—150.

Clegg, Samuel, jr. A practical treatise on the manufacture and distribution of coal-gas. Illus. Lond., 1853. D. R.

Clemency Franklyn. Keary, A. Lond. and N. Y., 1871. P—3.

Clemens, Samuel L., (Mark Twain.) The innocents abroad ; or, the new pilgrim's progress. Illus. Hartford, 1871. 2—9.

—— Roughing it. Illus. Lond., n. d. 2—9.

—— The gilded age ; a tale of to-day, by Mark Twain and Charles Dudley Warner. Illus. Hartford, 1874. 2—9.

—— The adventures of Tom Sawyer. Toronto, 1876. 2—9.

Cleveland, Ohio, Early history of. Illus. Whittlesey, C. Cleveland, 1867. 31—186.

Clever women of the family, The. Yonge, C. M. Lond. and N. Y., 1871. 5—30.

Climate and time in their geological relations. Croll, J. N. Y., 1875. 40—224.

Climbing plants, The movements and habits of. Illus. Darwin, C. N. Y., 1876. 14—81.

Clinton, De Witt, Tribute to the memory of: being a comprehensive sketch of his life. Albany, 1828. Q—2.

——, Life of. Renwick, J. N. Y., 1840. 13—79.

Clockmaker, The. Haliburton, T. C. Phil., 1838. 2—13.

Cloister and the hearth, The. Reade, C. Bost., 1871. 7—42.

Cloth of gold, and other poems. Aldrich, T. B. Bost., 1874. 17—106.

Cloverly. Higham, M. R. N. Y., 1875. 41—226.

Clunes, G. C. The story of Pauline: an autobiography. Lond., 1870. 2 v. in one. P—3.

Cluskey, Michael W. The political text-book, or encyclopædia; containing everything necessary for the reference of the politicians and statesmen of the United States. Wash., 1857. 18—108.

Clyde, Alton. Under foot: a novel. Illus. N. Y., 1870. 6—35.

Coal, Statistics of. Taylor, R. C. Phil., 1848. 19—113.

Coal-gas, Manufacture and distribution of. Illus. Clegg, S. Lond., 1853. D. R.

Coal mines, Treatise on the working and ventilation of. Hedley, J. Lond., 1851. T.

—— trade, A historical, geological, and descriptive view of the. Dunn, M. Newcastle-upon-Tyne, 1844. T.

—— regions of America, The. Illus. Macfarlane, J. N. Y., 1873. V.

Coast survey of the United States; 1861-67. 4 v. D. R.

Cobb, James F. Stories of success as illustrated by the lives of humble men who have made themselves great. Lond. and N. Y., n. d. 40—222.

Cobbe, Frances Power. The hopes of the human race, here and hereafter. N. Y., 1876. 40—222.

Cobbett, William. The pride of Britannia humbled; or, the queen of the ocean unqueened, by "the American cock-boats," and "the fir-built things, with bits of striped bunting at their mast-heads." N. Y., 1815. 33—201.

—— Political register; 1801 to 1813. Lond. 21 v. S.

—— Porcupine's works; containing various writings and selections, exhibiting a faithful picture of the United States of America, from the end of the war, in 1783, to the election of the President, in 1801. Lond., 1801. 12 v. X.

Cobden, Richard; his political career and public services. McGilchrist, J. N. Y., 1865. 13—79.

Cockton, Henry. Valentine Vox, the ventriloquist; with his life and adventures. Phil., n. d. 6—35.

—— Stanley Thorn. Lond. and N. Y., n. d. 6—40.

—— The love match: a novel. Phil., n. d. 6—35.

—— Sylvester Sound, the somnambulist: a novel. Illus. Phil., n. d. 41—230.

—— The fatal marriages. Phil., n. d. 41—230.

—— The steward; a romance of real life. Illus. Phil., n. d. 41—230.

—— Percy Effingham: a novel. Phil., n. d. 41—230.

Code Napoleon, The. Barrett, B. Lond., 1811. 2 v. 26—157.

Codman, John. Ten months in Brazil; with incidents of voyages and travels, descriptions of scenery and character, notices of commerce and productions, etc. Illus. Bost., 1867. 17—102.

Cœlebs in search of a wife. More, H. Phil., 1866. O—3.

Coffin, Charles Carleton. Winning his way. Bost., 1866. 7—46.

—— Our new way round the world. Illus. Bost., 1869. 17—101.

—— The boys of '76: a history of the battles of the revolution. Illus. N. Y., 1877. 40—225.

Coffin, James Henry. The winds of the globe; or, the laws of atmospheric circulation over the surface of the earth. The tables completed on the author's decease, and maps drawn by S. J. Coffin; with a discussion and analysis of the tables and charts by Alexander Wœikof. Wash., 1875. Smithsonian contributions to knowledge. D. R.

Coggeshall, George. History of the American privateers and letters of marque, during our war with England, in the years 1812-14. N. Y., 1856. 30—179.

Coggeshall, William T. Poets and poetry of the West; with biographical and critical notices. Columbus, O., 1860. 16—94.

Coin book, comprising a history of coinage; a synopsis of the mint laws of the U.S.; statistics of the coinage, from 1792 to 1870; list of current gold and silver coins, and their custom-house values; a dictionary of all coins known in ancient and modern times, with their values; the gold and silver product of each State to 1870; list of works on coinage; the daily price of gold from 1862 to 1871. Illus. Phil., 1872. 15—88.

Coke, Sir Edward, The life of. Woolrych, H. W. Lond., 1826. 11—62.

Colange, L. Zell's popular encyclopedia: a universal dictionary of English language, science, literature, and art. Illus. 2 v. Phil., 1876. 36—215.

Colden, Cadwallader. The history of the five nations of Canada. Lond., 1747. 29—177.

Colden, Cadwallader D. The life of Robert Fulton. N. Y., 1817. 13—74.

Coleridge, Samuel Taylor, The complete works of: with an essay upon his philosophical and theological opinions. *Prof.* Shedd, ed. N. Y., 1856. 7 v. 28—167.

——, Poetical works of: with a memoir. 16—94.

Coleridge, Sara, Memoir and letters of,—edited by her daughter. N. Y., 1874. 11—64.

Coles, Miriam, *pseud.* See Harris, M. C.

Coleccion de los viages y descubrimientos. Navarrete, M. F. de. Mad., 1825-37. 5 v. W.

College words and customs, A collection of. Bartlett, J. R. Cambridge, 1851. 2—13.

Collieries, A treatise on the winning and working of. Dunn, M. Lond., 1852. T.

Collins, Lewis. Historical sketches of Kentucky. Illus. Maysville, Ky., 1850. 31—186.

Collins, Mortimer. Marquis and merchant: a novel. N. Y., 1871. 5—28.

—— Two plunges for a pearl: a novel. Illus. N. Y., 1872. 5—28. '

Collins, William Wilkie. The crossed path; or, Basil: a story of my life. Phil., n. d. 6—38.

—— Poor Miss Finch: a novel. Illus. N. Y., 1872. 5—28.

—— The moonstone: a novel. Illus. N. Y., 1874. 6—38.

—— The woman in white: a novel. Illus. N. Y., 1873. 6—38.

—— Man and wife. N. Y., 1871. 5—28.

—— No name: a novel. Illus. N. Y., 1874. 6—38.

—— Armadale: a novel. N. Y., 1871. 5—28.

—— After dark. Lond., 1870. 6—38.

—— Hide and seek: a novel. Phil., n. d. 5—28.

—— The dead secret: a novel. Phil., n. d. 5—28.

—— Antonina; or, the fall of Rome: a romance of the fifth century. N. Y., 1871. 5—28.

—— The queen of hearts. N. Y., 1874. 5—28.

—— The dead alive. Illus. Bost., 1874. 6—38.

—— Miss, or Mrs.? and other stories. Phil., n. d. 5—28.

—— Sights a-foot. Phil., n. d. 17—101.

—— Mad Monkton, and other stories. Phil., n. d. 5—28.

—— The queen's revenge, and other stories. Phil., n. d. 5—28.

—— The frozen deep. Illus. Bost., 1875. 6—38.

—— My miscellanies. N.Y., 1874. 6—38.

—— Alicia Warlock, a mystery, and other stories. Illus. Bost., 1875. 6—38.

—— The new Magdalen: a novel.' Illus. N. Y., 1874. 6—38.

—— The law and the lady: a novel. Illus. N. Y., 1875. 6—38.

Collins, William, Poetical works of, with a memoir. Bost., 1865. 16—97.

Colman, Henry. European life and manners, in familiar letters to friends. Bost. and Lond., 1849. 2 v. 8—49.

Colorado river of the west and its tributaries, Exploration of. Illus. Powell, J. W. Wash., 1875. L.

Colton, G. Woolworth and C. B. General atlas. N. Y., 1871. R.

Colton, Walter. Three years in California. Illus. N. Y., 1851. 17—103.

Columbus, Christopher, Select letters of; with other original documents relating to his four voyages to the new world. R. H. Major, tr. Lond., 1847. 26—157.

—— Life and voyages of. Irving, W. N. Y., 1849. 3 v. 12—69.

Combe, George. The constitution of man considered in relation to external objects. Phil., 1865. 15—89.

Combe, William. Doctor Syntax's three tours in search of the picturesque, consolation and a wife. Illus. Lond., n. d. 16—96.

Combes, Ch. Traité de l'exploitation des mines. Paris, 1844-45. 3 v. D. R.

—— Atlas to the above. Paris, 1844-46. D. R.

Comedy. (Little classics, vol. 9.) Bost., 1875. 5—33.

—— of terrors, A. De Mille, J. Bost., 1872. 6—35.

Cometh up as a flower. Broughton, R. N. Y., 1872. 4—23.

Comic almanac. Illustrated by G. Cruikshank. 1835-53. Lond. 2 v. 2—8.

Coming race, The. Bulwer-Lytton, Sir E. N. Y., 1873. 2—13.

Commentaries on American law. Kent, J. N. Y., 1848. 21—128.

—— on the laws of England. Blackstone, Sir W. Phil., 1866. 2 v. 21—123.

—— of Cæsar. Phil., 1837. 35—212.

Commerce of the United States, A statistical view of. Pitkin, T. N. Y., 1817. 18—109.

—— of the prairies. Illus. Gregg, J. N. Y., 1864. 2 v. 2—13.

Commercial statistics. Macgregor, J. Lond., 1850. 5 v. R—1.

—— review of the South and West. De Bow, J. D. B. N. O., 1847-53. 14 v. D. R.

—— relations of the United States with England, Memoir concerning the. Talleyrand, C. M. de. Lond., 1806. 29—177.

—— and statistical register of the United States. Hazard, S. Phil., 1840-41. 5 v. 18—108.

Commercial and business anecdotes, Cyclopædia of. Illus. Kirkland, F. N. Y., 1864. 2 v. 2—7.

Common-place book. Southey, R. N. Y., 1860. 2 v. 27—159.

—— book of thoughts, memories, and fancies. Jameson, A. N. Y., 1855. 2—13.

Companions of my solitude. Helps, Sir A. Bost., 1870. 28—165.

Complete English tradesman, The. De Foe, D. Oxford, 1841. 2 v. 27—163.

Comte, August, The positive philosophy of. Mill, J. S. Bost., 1866. 14—34.

Concord, The history of. Illus. Bouton, N. Concord, 1856. 30—183.

—— days. Alcott, A. B. Bost., 1872. 2—12.

—— and Merrimack Rivers, A week on the. Thoreau, H. D. Bost., 1868. 9—53.

*Concordance to the Old and New Testaments. Cruden, A. Lond. and N. Y., n. d. E.

Condensed classics. Ivanhoe: a romance by Sir Walter Scott. Condensed by Rossiter Johnson. N. Y., 1876. 5—33.

—— Our Mutual Friend, by Charles Dickens. Condensed by Rossiter Johnson. N. Y., 1876. 5—33.

Condensed novels. Illus. Harte, F. B. Bost., 1873. 3—19.

Conduct of life, The. Emerson, R. W. Bost., 1875. 40—222.

Confederate States of America, Statutes at large of the. James M. Matthews, ed. Richmond, 1862-64. 2 v. 19—113.

—— war for independence, Memoirs of the. Von Borcke, H. Phil., 1867. 30—180.

Confessions of Con Cregan, The. Lever, C. J. Lond. and N. Y., n. d. 7—44.

—— of an English opium-eater. De Quincey, T. Bost., 1862. 2—12.

—— of Jean Jaques Rousseau. Illus. Lond., 1874. 20—122.

Confucius, The life and teachings of. Legge, J. Phil., 1874. 13—76.

*Congress, Annals of. 42 v. D. R.

* ——, Abridgment of the debates in: 1789-1856. Benton, T. H. N. Y., 1856-58. 9 v. D. R.

* ——, Journals of; from 1774 to 1785. 6 v. D. R.

Congress, Biographical and political history of. Wheeler, H. G. N. Y., 1848. 31—186.

——, History of the thirty-ninth. Illus. Barnes, W. H. N. Y., 1868. 31—186.

——, History of the fortieth. 1867-69. Illus. Barnes, W. H. N. Y., 1871. 2 v. 31—186.

Conjugial love. Swedenborg, E. N. Y., 1871. 1—3.

Connecticut, The history of. Dwight, jr., T. N. Y., 1840. 30—181.

——, The public records of the colony of. Hoadly, C. J. Hartford, 1868-73. 3 v. 30—181.

——: historical collections. Illus. Barber, J. W. New Haven, 1838. 30—181.

Conover, James F. A digested index of all the reported decisions in law and equity of the supreme courts of the States of Ohio, Indiana, and Illinois. Phil., 1834. T.

Conscript, The. Illus. Erckmann, E. and A. Chatrian. N. Y., 1872. 5—31.

——, The. Dumas, A. D. Phil., 1874. 5—31.

Conservation of energy, The. Stewart, B. N. Y., 1876. 40—224.

Consolations in travel; or, the last days of a philosopher. Davy, Sir H. Lond., 1830. 27—164.

Conspiracy of Pontiac, The. Parkman, F. Bost., 1870. 2 v. 28—166.

—— of Catiline, and the Jugurthine war, The history of. Sallustius, C. C. W. Rose, tr. Phil., 1837. 35—212.

Constitution of the United States, defined and annotated. Paschal, G. W. Wash., 1868. 21—125.

—— of the United States of America, The. Hickey, W. Phil., 1854. 21—125.

—— of man, The. Combe, G. Phil., 1865. 15—89.

Constitutions of the several States of the Union and United States. N. Y., 1853. 21—123.

—— des treize États-Unis de l'Amérique. La Rochefoucauld, F. de. Phil. et Paris, 1783. W.

Consuelo. "George Sand." Phil., 1870. 7—41.

Contarini Fleming. Disraeli, B. Lond., 1871. 4—24.

Contributions to the Edinburgh Review. (Modern British essayists.) Jeffrey, F. Bost., 1854. 27—159.

Conquest of Granada. Irving, W. N. Y., 1851. 3—19.

Conversations on war and general culture. Helps, Sir A. Bost., 1871. 28—165.

Cooke, John Esten. Fairfax; or, the master of Greenway court: a chronicle of the valley of the Shenandoah. N. Y., 1868. 4—26.

—— Her majesty the queen: a novel. Phil., 1873. 4—26.

—— Justin Harley: a romance of old Virginia. Illustrated by W. L. Sheppard. Phil., 1874. 4—25.

—— Pretty Mrs. Gaston, and other stories. N. Y., n. d. 4—26.

Cooley, Arnold James. A cyclopædia of six thousand practical receipts and collateral information in the arts, manufactures, and trades, including medicine, pharmacy, and domestic economy; designed as a compendious book of reference for the manufacturer, tradesman, amateur, and heads of families. N. Y., 1875. 40—225.

Coolidge, Susan. What Katy did: a story. Illus. Bost., 1873. 38.

—— What Katy did at school. Illus. Bost., 1874. 38.

—— The new-year's bargain. Illus. Bost., 1874. 38.

—— Nine little goslings. Illus. Bost., 1875. 38.

Cooper, James Fenimore. The history of the navy of the United States of America. Lond., 1839. 2 v. 30—179.

—— Afloat and ashore: a sea tale. Illus. N. Y., 1871. 3—14.

—— The Bravo: a tale. Illus. N. Y., 1873. 3—14.

—— The Chainbearer; or, the Littlepage MSS. Illus. N. Y., 1866. 3—14.

—— The Crater; or, Vulcan's peak: a tale of the Pacific. Illus. N. Y., 1866. 3—14.

—— The Headsman; or, the Abbaye des Vignerons. Illus. N. Y., 1864. 3—14.

—— The Heidenmauer; or, the Benedictines: a legend of the Rhine. Illus. N. Y., 1867. 3—14.

—— Homeward bound; or, the chase. Illus. N. Y., 1865. 3—14.

Cooper, James Fenimore. Home as found: sequel to "Homeward bound." Illus. N. Y., 1870. 3—14.

—— Jack Tier; or, the Florida reef. Illus. N. Y., 1873. 3—14.

—— Last of the Mohicans: a narrative of 1757. Illus. N. Y., 1874. 3—14.

—— Lionel Lincoln; or, the leaguer of Boston. Illus. N. Y., 1864. 3—14.

—— Mercedes of Castile; or, the voyage to Cathay. Illus. N. Y., 1864. 3—14.

—— Miles Wallingford: sequel to "Afloat and ashore." Illus. N. Y., 1870. 3—14.

—— The Monikins. Illus. N. Y., 1873. 3—14.

—— Oak-openings; or, the bee-hunter. Illus. N. Y., 1864. 3—14.

—— The Pathfinder; or, the inland sea. Illus. N. Y., 1864. 3—14.

—— The Pioneers; or, the sources of the Susquehanna: a descriptive tale. Illus. N. Y., 1864. 3—14.

—— The Prairie: a tale. Illus. N. Y., 1870. 3—14.

—— Precaution: a novel; with a discourse on the life, genius, and writings of the author, by Wm. Cullen Bryant. Illus. N. Y., 1871. 3—14.

—— The Red rover: a tale. Illus. N. Y., 1870. 3—14.

—— The Redskins; or, Indian and Injin; conclusion of the Littlepage MSS. Illus. N. Y., 1864. 3—14

—— Satanstoe; or, the Littlepage MSS.; a tale of the colony. Illus. N. Y., 1867. 3—14.

—— The Sea lions; or, the lost sealers. Illus. N. Y., 1864. 3—14.

—— The Spy: a tale of the neutral ground. Illus. N. Y., 1870. 3—14.

—— Two admirals: a tale. Illus. N. Y., 1861. 3—14.

—— The Water-witch; or, the skimmer of the seas. Illus. N. Y., 1871. 3—14.

—— Ways of the hour: a tale. Illus. N. Y., 1870. 3—14.

—— The Wept of the Wish-ton-wish. Illus. N. Y., 1864. 3—14.

—— The Wing and wing; or, le feu-follet. Illus. N. Y., 1864. 3—14.

—— Wyandotte; or, the hutted knoll. Illus. N. Y., 1864. 3—14.

Cooper, James Fenimore. The deer-slayer; or, the first war-path: a tale. Phil., 1841. 2 v. in one. 3—14.

NOTE.—The "Leatherstocking" series of tales consist of the following-named books, and take precedence in the order here given, viz: The Deerslayer, The last of the Mohicans, The Pathfinder, The Pioneers, and The Prairie.

Cooper, Thompson. Men of the time: a dictionary of cotemporaries; containing biographical notices of eminent characters of both sexes. Lond. and N. Y., 1875. 23—139.

Cooper, William M. Flagellation and the flagellants: a history of the rod in all countries, from the earliest period to the present time. Illus. Lond., 1869. 2—10.

Co-operation in England, The history of. Holyoake, G. J. Phil., 1875. Vol. 1. 18—108.

Coppée, Henry. Grant and his campaigns: a military biography. Illus. N. Y., 1866. 11—59.

Copper, The chemistry and metallurgy of. Piggot, A. S. Phil., 1858. V.

Corals and coral islands. Illus. Dana, J. D. N. Y., 1872. 14—83.

Cord and Creese. Illus. De Mille, J. N. Y., 1873. 6—35.

Cordery, B. Meriton, and J. Surtees Phillpotts. King and commonwealth: a history of Charles I and the great rebellion. Phil., 1876. 34—206.

Cordova, J. de. Texas; her resources and her public men; a companion for De Cordova's new and correct map of the State of Texas. Phil., 1858. 31—187.

Corinne; or, Italy. De Staël, A. L. G. N. Isabel Hill, tr. N. Y., n. d. 7—41.

Corneille, Pierre, Œuvres complètes de, suivies des œuvres choisies de Th. Corneille, avec les notes de tous les commentateurs. Paris, 1862. 2 v. W.

Corneille and his times. Guizot, F. P. G. N. Y., 1852. Q—2.

Correlation and conservation of forces, The. Youmans, E. L. N. Y., 1868. 15—88.

Correspondence with a child. Goethe, J. W. von. Bost., 1863. 2—12.

Corsican brothers, The. Dumas, A. D. Phil., n. d. 3—20.

Cortes, Hernando. The despatches of Hernando Cortes, the conqueror of Mex-

Cox, Edward W. The arts of writing, reading, and speaking. N. Y. and Lond., 1873. 19—114.

Cox, George W. The crusades. (Epochs of history.) Bost., 1874. 36—215.

Cox, Ross. Adventures on the Columbia River. N. Y., 1832. R—2.

Cox, Samuel Sullivan. Search for winter sunbeams in the Riviera, Corsica, Algiers, and Spain. Illus. N. Y., 1870. 17—103.

—— Why we laugh. N. Y., 1876. 19—116.

Coxe, William. History of the house of Austria, from the foundation of the monarchy by Rodolph of Hapsburgh to the death of Leopold the second, 1218 to 1792. Lond., 1847. 3 v. 36—218.

—— Memoirs of the Duke of Marlborough; with his original correspondence; a new edition, by John Wade. Lond., 1847—48. 3 v. 11—61.

Cozzens, Frederic S. Acadia; or, a month with the Blue Noses. N. Y., 1870. 28—169.

—— The Sparrowgrass papers; or, living in the country. Phil., 1869. 28—169.

—— The sayings and doings of Dr. Bushwhacker, and other learned men; with an autobiographic sketch, and several papers now first collected. N. Y., 1871. 28—169.

Crabb, George. *A universal technological dictionary; or, familiar explanation of the terms used in all arts and sciences. Lond., 1823. 2 v. 21—126.

Crackers for Christmas. Illus. Knatchbull-Hugessen, E. H. N. Y., 1872. 39.

Cradle of rebellions, The. La Hodde, L. de. N. Y., 1864. 35—214.

Cradock, Nowell. Blackmore, R. D. N. Y., 1866. 5—28.

Craik, Dinah Maria, (formerly D. M. Muloch.) John Halifax, gentleman. Illus. N. Y., 1872. 4—23.

—— The woman's kingdom: a love story. Illus. N. Y., 1870. 5—26.

—— Hannah. N. Y., 1872. 4—23.

——, Poems of. Bost., 1869. 16—100.

—— A life for a life: a novel. N. Y., 1870. 4—23.

—— Studies from life. N. Y., 1861. 4—

Craik, Dinah Maria, (formerly D. M. Muloch.) The Ogilvies: a novel. N. Y., 1871. 4—23.

—— Olive: a novel. N. Y., 1871. 4—23.

—— Christian's mistake. N. Y., 1871. 4—23.

—— A noble life. N. Y., 1871. 4—23.

—— The unkind word, and other stories. N. Y., 1872. 4—23.

—— A hero, and other tales. N. Y., 1872. 4—23.

—— A brave lady. Illus. N. Y., 1872. 4—23.

—— Agatha's husband: a novel. N. Y., 1871. 4—23.

—— Mistress and maid: a household story. N. Y., 1872. 4—23.

—— Two marriages. N. Y., 1867. 4—23.

—— The head of the family: a novel. N. Y., 1873. 5—28.

—— The fairy book: the best popular stories, selected and rendered anew. N Y., 1872. 38.

—— Little Sunshine's holiday: a picture from life. Illus. (Books for girls.) N Y., 1871. 39.

—— Twenty years ago: from the journal of a girl in her teens. (Books for girls.) N. Y., 1872. 39.

—— Is it true? Tales curious and wonderful. (Books for girls.) N. Y., 1872. 39.

—— Fair France: impressions of a traveler. N. Y., 1871. O—3.

—— The adventures of a brownie, as told to my child. Illus. N. Y., 1872. 39.

—— Nothing new: tales. N. Y, 1870. 5—28.

—— Avillion, and other tales. N. Y., 1870. 5—28.

—— My mother and I: a love story. Illus. N. Y., 1874. 4—23.

—— Sermons out of church. N. Y., 1875. 40—222.

—— The laurel bush: an old-fashioned love story. N. Y., 1876. 4—23.

Craik, George Lillie. The romance of the peerage; or, curiosities of family history. Lond., 1848—50. 4 v. 11—63.

—— and Charles Macfarlane. Pictorial history of England. N. Y., 1846—48. 4 v. 33—197.

Craik, Georgiana M. The cousin from India: a book for girls. Illus. N. Y., 1872. 39.

Cudlip, *Mrs.* Pender, (formerly Annie Thomas.) On guard: a novel. N. Y., 1867. 5—28.

—— Played out: a novel. N. Y., 1867. 5—28.

—— Playing for high stakes: a novel. Illus. N. Y., 1868. 5—28.

—— The Dower house: a story. N. Y., 1868. 5—28.

—— Dennis Donne: a novel. N. Y., 1865. 5—28.

—— Walter Goring: a story. N. Y., 1866. 5—28.

—— Maud Mohan: a novel. (Same as "The Maskleynes.") N. Y., 1872. 5—28.

—— Only herself: a novel. N. Y., 1870· 5—28.

—— False colors: a novel. N. Y., 1869. 5—28.

—— Called to account: a novel. N. Y., 1867. 5—28.

—— No alternative: a novel. Phil., n. d. 5—31.

—— "He cometh not, she said :" a novel. N. Y., 1875. 5—28.

—— The two widows: a novel. N. Y., 1874. 5—28.

—— The Maskleynes : a novel. (Same as "Maud Mohan.") Lond., 1875. 2 v. 41—227.

Cullum, George W. * Register of the officers and graduates of the U. S. Military Academy at West Point, N. Y., from March 16, 1802, to Jan. 1, 1850. N. Y., 1850. R— 2.

Culprit fay: a poem. Illus. Drake, J. R. N. Y., 1871. 16—100.

Culture and anarchy: an essay in political and social criticism. Arnold, M. N. Y., 1875. 40—222.

—— and religion in some of their relations. Shairp, J. C. N. Y., 1873. 19—114.

Cumberland, Richard. John de Lancaster: a novel. 2 v. N. Y., 1809. P—3.

——, Memoirs of, written by himself; containing an account of his life and writings, interspersed with anecdotes and characters of several of the most distinguished persons of his time. N. Y., 1806. Q—2.

Cummins, Maria Susanna. The lamplighter. Bost., 1870. 6—38.

4 I

Cummins, Maria Susanna. Haunted hearts. Bost., 1869. 6—38.

Cupid and chow-chow, etc. (Aunt Jo's scrap-bag, vol. 3.) Alcott, L. M. Bost., 1874. 5—31.

Curate and the rector, The. N. Y., 1871. 6—39.

Curious myths of the middle ages. Illus. Baring-Gould, S. Lond., 1872. 3—19.

Curiosities of literature. Disraeli, I. Lond. and N. Y, 1859. 3 v. O—3.

Curse of Clifton, The. (Same as " Fallen pride.") Southworth, E. D. E. N. Phil., 1852. 6—37.

Curtis, George Ticknor. Life of Daniel Webster. N. Y., 1870. 2 v. 12—66.

Curtis, George William. Nile notes of a howadji. N. Y., 1856. 17—104.

—— Howadji in Syria. N. Y., 1867. 17—104.

—— Prue and I. N. Y., 1867. O—1.

—— The Potiphar papers. Illus. N. Y., 1869. O—1.

—— Lotus-eating : a summer book. Illus. N. Y., 1868. O—1.

—— Trumps: a novel. Illus. N. Y., 1870. O—1.

Curtis, Josiah. Analytical and sanitary observations on the census of Boston, May, 1855, with the report of the joint special committee. Bost., 1856. L.

Curzon, Robert. A visit to monasteries in the Levant. N. Y., 1849. 17—103.

Custer, *General* George A., A complete life of. Illus. Whittaker, F. N. Y., n. d. 40—224.

Cutter, William. The life of Israel Putnam, major-general in the army of the American revolution. Illus. N. Y., 1861. 11—64.

Cuvier, George Léopold Chrétien Frédéric Dagobert, *Baron*. Recueil des éloges historiques lus dans les séances publiques de l'Institut de France. Paris, 1861. 3 v. W.

—— Discours sur les révolutions du globe, avec des notes et un appendice. Paris, 1864. W.

—— et A. Brongniart. Essai sur la géographie minéralogique des environs de Paris. Paris, 1811. T.

—— et A. Brongniart. Description géologique des environs de Paris. Paris 1822. V.

Cyclopædia of the best thoughts of Charles Dickens, compiled and alphabetically arranged by F. G. de Fontaine, N. Y., 1873. 2—7.

*———, The standard library of political, constitutional, statistical, and forensic knowledge. Lond., 1848. 4 v. 18—108.

——— of drawing, (Appleton's.) W. E. Worthen, ed. N. Y., 1866. 15—87.

*———, British, of the arts and sciences. Illus. Partington, C. F. Lond., 1835. 2 v. 23—140.

*———, American annual, and register of important events. 1861-73. Appleton, D. 13 v. 23—136.

*———, The new American : a popular dictionary of general knowledge. G. Ripley and C. A. Dana, eds. N. Y., 1861-63. 16 v. 22—130.

*———, Penny. Lond., 1833-46. 29 v. 23—140 and 22—134.

*——— of the physical sciences. Illus. Nichol, J. P. Lond., 1860. 23—138.

*——— of commerce. Waterston, W. Lond., 1843. 21—128.

——— of wit and humor. Illus. Burton, W. E. N. Y., 1872. 2—7.

*——— of biography. Illus. Appleton, D. F. L. Hawks, ed. N. Y., 1856. 23—138.

*——— of commerce and commercial navigation. Homans, J. S. N. Y., 1858. 21—128.

———, Cottage, of history and biography. Illus. Pierce, E. M. Hartford, 1859. 23—138.

——— of commercial and business anecdotes. Illus. Kirkland, F. N. Y., 1864. 2 v. 2—7.

——— of English literature. Illus. Chambers, R. Phil., 1860. 2 v. 2—7.

——— of American literature. Illus. Duyckinck, E. A. N. Y., 1856. 2 v. 2—7.

——— of education, The. Kiddle, H., and A. J. Schem, eds. N. Y. and Lond., 1877. 1—1.

Daisy. "Elizabeth Wetherell." Phil., 1873. 2 v. in one. 7—42.

Daisy Burns: a tale. Kavanagh, J. N. Y., 1873. 7—41.

Daisy chain, The. Illus. Yonge, C. M. Lond. and N. Y., 1875. 5—30.

Dallas Galbraith. Davis, R. H. Phil., 1868. 6—35.

Daltons, The. Lever, C. J. Lond., n. d. 7—44.

Dana, Charles A. The household book of poetry. N. Y. and Lond., 1869. 16—94.

Dana, James D. Manual of geology; treating of the principles of the science, with special reference to American geological history. Illus. Phil., 1864. 15—91.

——— A system of mineralogy, comprising the most recent discoveries. Illus. N. Y. and Lond., 1850. 15—91.

——— Corals and coral islands. Illus. N. Y., 1872. 14—83.

Dana, Richard Henry, jr. Two years before the mast. A personal narrative. Bost., 1869. 17—102.

Danemark. (L'Univers.) Eyriès, J. B. Paris, 1846. D. R.

Dangerfield's rest ; or, before the storm : a novel of American life and manners. N. Y., 1864. P—2.

Dangerous game, A. Yates, E. Bost., 1874. 7—45.

Daniel Deronda. "George Eliot." N.Y., 1876. 2 v. 6—36.

Dante, Alighieri. The vision ; or hell, purgatory, and paradise. H. F. Cary, tr. Lond., 1819. 3 v. 16—95.

———, the divine comedy of. H.W. Longfellow, tr. Bost., 1871. 17—105.

Danvers papers, The. Yonge, C. M. Lond., 1867. 2—13.

Darby, William. *Universal geographical dictionary. Wash., 1843. 21—126.

Darlington, William. American weeds and useful plants. Illus. N. Y., 1859. T.

Darrell Markham. Braddon, M. E. N.Y., n. d. 5—29.

Darwin, Charles. Journal of researches into the natural history and geology of the countries visited during the voyage of H. M. S. Beagle round the world. N. Y., 1846. 2 v. 14—85.

——— on the origin of species by means of natural selection; or, the preservation of favored races in the struggle for life. N. Y., 1869. 14—81.

Darwin, Charles. The descent of man, and selection in relation to sex. Illus. N. Y., 1872. 2v. 14—81.

—— The expressions of the emotions in man and animals. Illus. N. Y., 1873. 14—81.

—— The movements and habits of climbing plants. Second edition revised. Illus. N. Y., 1876. 14—81.

—— Insectivorous plants. Illus. N.Y., 1875. 14—81.

Darwin, Erasmus. Zoonomia; or, the laws of organic life. Lond., 1801. 4 v. 14—83.

Darwiniana : essays and reviews pertaining to Darwinism. Gray, *Prof.* A. N. Y., 1876. 14—81.

Dash, *Countess, pseud.* See Saint Mars, *Vicomtesse de.*

* **Dates,** Dictionary of. Haydn, J. N. Y., 1872. 23—138.

——, The manual of. Townsend, G. H. Lond., 1862. 23—138.

Daubeny, Charles. A description of active and extinct volcanos, of earthquakes, and of thermal springs. Lond., 1848. 15—89.

D'Aubigne, J. H. Merle. History of the great reformation of the sixteenth century in Germany, Switzerland, etc. H. White, tr. Hartford, 1850-53. 5 v. in three. 32—196.

Daudet, Alphonse. Sidonie. (Fromont jeune et risler aîné.) Mary Neal Sherwood, tr. Bost., 1877. 3—18.

Daughter of an empress, The. Illus "Louise Mühlbach." N.Y., 1872. 4—21

—— of Bohemia, A. Illus. "Christian Reid." N. Y., 1874. 4—21.

—— of Heth, A. Black, W. N. Y., 1872 5—29.

D'Avenant, Charles, The political and commercial works of; collected and revised by *Sir* Charles Whitworth. Lond., 1771. 5 v. 25—151.

Davenport, Richard Alfred. The history of the bastile and of its principal captives. Illus. Lond. and N. Y., 1875. 40—223.

Davenport Dunn. Lever, C. J. Phil., n. d. 5—29.

D'Avezac, *M.* Îles de l'Afrique (L'Univers.) Paris, 1848. D. R.

David Copperfield. Illus. Dickens, C. N. Y., 1863. 2 v. 2 copies. 3—15 and 16.

David Elginbrod. MacDonald, G. Bost., n. d. 7—45.

Davidson, Lucretia Maria, Life of. (Library of American biography, vol. 7.) 11—65.

Davie, William Richardson, Life of. (Library of American biography, vol. 25.) 11—65.

Davies, *Mrs.* Christian, Life and adventures of. De Foe, D. Oxford, 1840. 27—163.

Davies, Theodore. Losing to win: a novel. N. Y., 1874. 5—31.

Davis, Matthew S. Memoirs of Aaron Burr, with miscellaneous selections from his correspondence. N. Y., 1835. 2 v. 13—75.

Davis, Rebecca Harding. Dallas Galbraith. Phil., 1868. 6—35.

—— Margaret Howth: a story of to-day. Bost., 1862. 41—223.

—— Waiting for the verdict. Illus. N. Y., 1863. 6—39.

Davis, William M. Nimrod of the sea; or, the American whaleman. Illus. N. Y., 1874. 7—41.

Davy, *Sir* Humphry. Consolations in travel; or, the last days of a philosopher. Lond., 1830. 27—164.

——, The collected works of; edited by his brother, John Davy. Lond., 1839-40. 9 v. 27—164.

Contents.

Vol. 1. Memoirs of the life of Sir Humphry Davy;
Vol. 2. Early miscellaneous papers; An introductory lecture, and outlines of lectures, on chemistry.
Vol. 3. Researches, chemical and philosophical.
Vol. 4. Elements of chemical philosophy.
Vol. 5. Bakerian lectures; and Miscellaneous papers.
Vol. 6. Miscellaneous papers; and Researches.
Vol. 7. Discourses delivered before the Royal Society; Elements of agricultural chemistry, part 1st.
Vol. 8. Elements of agricultural chemistry, part 2nd; and Miscellaneous lectures.
Vol. 9. Salmonia, or, days of fly-fishing; and Consolations in travel.

Dawson, George Mercer. Report on the geology and resources of the region in the vicinity of the forty-ninth parallel, from the Lake of the Woods to the Rocky Mountains, with lists of plants and animals collected, and notes on the fossils. Montreal, 1875. L.

Dawson, John William. The story of the earth and man. Illus. N. Y., 1874. 15—91.

Day, Lal Behari. Govinda Sámanta; or, the history of a Bengal Ráiyat. Lond., 1874. 3—16.

Day, Sherman. Historical collections of the State of Pennsylvania. Illus. Phil., 1843. 31—189.

Day, Thomas. The history of Sandford and Merton. Illus. Phil., 1869. 39.

Days of Bruce, The. Aguilar, G. N. Y., 1872. 2 v. 5—34.

Day's ride, A. Illus. Lever, C. J. N. Y., 1872. 5—29.

De Bow, James D. B. The industrial resources of the Southern and Western States. N. O., 1853. 3 v. 18—110.
—— The commercial review of the South and West. N. O., 1847-53. 14 v. D. R.

De Costa, B. F. Lake George: its scenes and characteristics, with glimpses of the olden times; to which is added some account of Ticonderoga, with a description of the route to Schroon Lake and the Adirondacks; with an appendix containing notes on Lake Champlain. Illus. N. Y., 1868. 17—102.
—— The Northmen in Maine; a critical examination of views expressed in connection with the subject, by Dr. J. H. Kohl, in vol. 1 of the new series of the Maine Historical Society; to which are added criticisms on other portions of the work, and a chapter on the discovery of Massachusetts Bay. Albany, 1870. 30—183.

De Foe, Daniel. History of the plague in London in 1665; and The consolidator. Oxford, 1840. 27—162.
—— Religious courtship; or, historical discourses on the necessity of marrying religious husbands and wives, and of employing only religious servants. Oxford, 1840. 27—163.
—— The memoirs of Captain George Carleton, and the life and adventures of Mrs. Christian Davies. Oxford, 1840. 27—163.

De Foe, Daniel. A system of magic or, a history of the black art. Oxford, 1840. 27—163.
—— The life and adventures of Duncan Campbell. Oxford, 1841. 27—163.
—— New voyage round the world. Oxford, 1840. 27—163.
—— The family instructor. Oxford, 1841. 2 v. 27—163.
—— The complete English tradesman. Oxford, 1841. 27—163.
——, The life of. Chalmers. Oxford, 1841. 27—163.
—— The life and adventures of Robinson Crusoe. Illustrated by J. D. Watson. London, 1863. 38.

De Forest, John William. European acquaintance; being sketches of people in Europe. N. Y., 1858. 17—103.
—— Miss Ravenel's conversion from secession to loyalty. N. Y., 1867. 4—25.
—— Kate Beaumont. Illus. Bost., 1872, 5—28.
—— History of the Indians of Connecticut, from the earliest known period to 1850. Illus. Hartford, 1853. 30—181.
—— Playing the mischief: a novel. N. Y., 1875. 41—230.

De Hass, Willis. History of the early settlement and Indian wars of Western Virginia. Illus. Wheeling, 1851. 31—188.

De Kalb County, Illinois, History of. Illus. Boies, H. L. Chicago, 1868. 31—186.

De la Beche, Sir Henry Thomas. See La Beche, Sir H. T. de.

De la Rame, Louisa. See La Rame, L. de.

De Lolme, Jean Louis. The rise and progress of the English constitution; with introduction and notes by A. J. Stephens. Lond., 1838. 2 v. 26—157.

De Medici, Lorenzo, The life of. Roscoe W. Phil., 1803. 3 v. 12—70.

De Mille, James. The cryptogram: a novel. Illus. N. Y., 1874. 6—35.
—— The American baron: a novel. Illus. N. Y., 1872. 6—35.
—— The Dodge Club; or, Italy in 1859. Illus. N. Y., 1870. 2—9.
—— A comedy of terrors. Bost., 1872. 6—35.

De Mille, James. Cord and creese
Illus. N. Y., 1873. 6—35.
—— An open question: a novel. Illus.
N. Y., 1873. 6—35.
—— The lady of the ice: a novel. Illus.
N. Y., 1872. 6—35.
—— The lily and the cross: a tale of
Acadia. Illus. Bost., 1875. 6—35.
—— The living link: a novel. Illustrated by W. L. Sheppard. N. Y., 1874.
6—35.
De Quincey, Thomas. Literary reminiscences; from the autobiography of
an English opium-eater. Bost., 1859. 2
v. 2—12.
—— Historical and critical essays. Bost.,
1859. 2 v. 2—12.
—— The Cæsars. Bost., 1858. 2—12.
—— Letters to a young man, and other
papers. Bost., 1861. 2—12.
—— The note-book of an English opium-eater. Bost., 1855. 2—12.
—— Confessions of an English opium-eater, and Suspiria de profundis. Bost.,
1862. 2—12.
—— Biographical essays. Bost., 1860.
2—12.
—— Memorials, and other papers. Bost.,
1856. 2 v. 2—12.
—— Narrative; and Miscellaneous papers. Bost., 1859. 2 v. 2—12.
—— Miscellaneous essays. Bost., 1860.
2—12.
—— Essays on philosophical writers and
other men of letters. Bost., 1860. 2 v.
2—12.
—— Theological essays, and other papers. Bost., 1854. 2 v. 2—12.
—— The logic of political economy, and
other papers. Bost., 1859. 2—12.
—— The avenger, a narrative; and other papers. Bost., 1859. 2—12.
—— Essays on the poets and other English writers. Bost., 1859. 2—12.
De Witt, Madame C. Guizot. Motherless; or, a Parisian family. Illus. Miss
Muloch, tr. N. Y., 1871. P—3.
—— A French country family. Illus.
Mrs. Muloch Craik, tr. N. Y., 1868.
3—20.
De Witt Clinton, Life of. Renwick, J.
N. Y., 1840. 13—79.
Dead alive, The. Illus. Collins, W. W.
Bost., 1874. 6—38.

Dead marquise, The. Kip, L. N. Y., 1873.
P—3.
—— secret, The. Collins, W. W. Phil.,
n. d. 5—28.
—— men's shoes: a novel. Braddon,
M. E. N. Y., 1876. 5—29.
—— to the world. Bauer, C. Bost.,
1875. 41—228.
Dead-sea fruit. Illus. Braddon, M. E.
N. Y., 1872. 5—29.
Dean, Amos. The history of civilization. Albany, 1868-69. 7 v. 36—215.
Deane, Milly. Marjory. Lond., 1872.
0—3.
Dean's English, The. Moon, G. W. Lond.,
1868. 27—160.
Dear lady Disdain: a novel. McCarthy,
J. N. Y., 1876. 6—35.
*Debates in Congress, Abridgment of
the, 1789-1856. Benton, T. H. N. Y.,
1856-58. 9 v. D. R.
—— on the federal constitution. Elliot,
J. Wash., 1836. 5 v. D. R.
Debenham's vow. Illus. Edwards, A. B.
N. Y., 1870. 6—38.
Debit and credit. Freytag, G. N.Y., 1871.
0—2.
Decameron, The. Boccaccio, G. Lond.,
1841. 1—4.
Decatur, Stephen, Life of. (Library of
American biography, vol. 21.) 11—65.
Deerslayer, The. Cooper, J. F. Phil.,
1841. 2 v. in one. 3—14.
Defences of Washington, A report on the.
Barnard, J. G. Wash., 1871. V.
Deirdrè. (No Name series.) Joyce, R. D.
Bost., 1876. 17—105.
Deism disarmed; or, a short answer to
Paine's "Age of Reason," on principles
self-evident, but seldom produced.
Pamphlet. Lond., 1794. E.
Delafield, Richard. Report on the art
of war in Europe, in 1854, 1855, and 1856.
Illus. Wash., 1860. Ex. doc. No. 59,
36th Congress, 1st session. 2 v. X.
Delamotte, F. Examples of modern
alphabets, plain and ornamental, including german, old english, saxon, italic,
perspective, greek, hebrew, court-hand,
engraving, tuscan, riban, gothic, rustic,
and arabesque; with several original designs, and an analysis of the old roman
and old english alphabets. Illus. Lond.,
1866. 19—113.

Delano, A. Life on the plains and among the diggings; being scenes and adventures of an overland journey to California; with particular incidents of the route, mistakes and sufferings of the emigrants; the Indian tribes; the present and the future of the Great West. Illus. Auburn, 1854. 17—101.

Democracy in America. Tocqueville, C. A. de. N. Y., 1862. 29—177.

Demosthenes, The orations of. T. Leland, tr. Lond., 1830. 2 v. 13—79.

Dendy, Walter Cooper. The philosophy of mystery. N. Y., 1847. 14—85.

Dene hollow: a novel. Wood, E. P. Phil., n. d. 41—230.

Denis, Ferdinand. Portugal. (L'Univers.) Paris, 1846. D. R.

Denis Donne. Thomas, A. N. Y., 1865. 5—28.

—— Duval. Illus. Thackeray, W. M. Lond., 1869. 5—32.

Denison, Mary A. Victor Norman, rector. Phil., 1873. O—2.

Denmark, Sweden, and Norway, History of. Dunham, S. A. Lond., 1839. 3 v. 36—220.

Depths of the sea, The. Illus. Thompson, C. W. N. Y. and Lond., 1873. 14—83.

Derby, George Horatio, (*John Phœnix.*) Phœnixiana; or, sketches and burlesques. N. Y., 1870. 3—19.

Dermot Mac Morrogh; or, the conquest of Ireland. Adams, J. Q. Columbus, 1834. 16—100.

Dervishes, The. Illus. J. P. Brown. Phil., 1868. 28—169.

Descartes, René, Œuvres morales philosophiques de. Paris, n. d. W.

Descent of man, The. Illus. Darwin, C. N. Y., 1872. 2 v. 14—81.

Descripcion de las Indias occidentales. Herrera, A. de. Mad., 1730. 4 v. D. R.

Descriptio uberior graminum et plantarum calamariarum Americæ septentrionalis indigenarum et circurum. Muhlenberg, H. Phil., 1817. D. R.

Description géologique des environs de Paris. Cuvier, G. L., et A. Brongniart. Paris, 1822. V.

Deserted wife, The. Southworth, E. D. E. N. Phil., 1855. 6—37.

Desperate remedies: a novel. Hardy, T. N. Y., 1874. 4—24.

Destiny; or, the chief's daughter. Ferrier, M. Lond. and N. Y., n. d. 4—22.

Details of an unpaid claim of France for 24,000,000 francs, guaranteed by the parole of Napoleon the third. Phil., 1869. D. R.

Detlef, Carl, *pseud.* See Bauer, C.

Devereux: a tale. Bulwer-Lytton, *Sir* E. Phil., 1867. 5—33.

Dialogues of Plato, The. Jowett, B. N. Y., 1872. 4 v. 26—155.

Diamond cut diamond. Trollope, T. A. N. Y., 1874. 7—43.

Diana Carew; or, for a woman's sake. Forrester, *Mrs.* Phil., 1876. 41—228.

Diario de las Córtes; 1820 y 1821. Mad., 1821. D. R.

Diary of Mrs. Kitty Trevylyan. Charles, E. N. Y., 1868. 2—11.

—— of a late physician. Warren, S. N. Y., 1871. 3 v. in one. 7—45.

—— of an ennuyée. Jameson, A. M. Bost., 1866. 2—13.

—— : the H—— family, and other tales. Bremer, F. Lond., 1853. P—1.

—— In Turkish and Greek waters. Howard, G. W. F. Bost., 1855. 17—102.

Diavola; or, nobody's daughter. Braddon, M. E. N. Y., n. d. 5—29.

Diaz del Castilio, Bernal. The true history of the conquest of Mexico, written in 1568. Lond., 1800. 32—191.

—— Mexico. J. I. Lockhart, tr. Lond., 1844. 2 v. 32—192.

—— * Diccionario de la lengua castellana por la Academia Española. Mad., 1832. V.

Dictionario razonado de legislacion y jurisprudencia. Escriche, *Don* J. Mad., 1847. 2 v. D. R.

—— Supplement. Mad., 1847. D. R.

—— de la lengua castellana. Diaz del Castillo, B. Mad., 1832. V.

Dickens, Charles, The life of. Illus. Forster, J. Phil., 1872. 3 v. 11—60.

——, Works of, Riverside edition. Illus. N. Y., 1868. 28 vols. 3—16.

Contents.

American notes; and Pictures from Italy. 2 copies.

Barnaby Rudge. 2 vols.

Bleak House. 2 vols.
Christmas books.
David Copperfield. 2 vols.
Dombey and Son. 2 vols.
Great expectations.
Hard times, and reprinted pieces.
Little Dorrit. 2 vols.
Martin Chuzzlewit. 2 vols.
Nicholas Nickleby. 2 vols.
Old curiosity shop, and reprinted pieces. 2
vols.
Oliver Twist.
Our mutual friend. 2 vols.
Pickwick papers. 2 vols.
Same. (Household edition.) Illus. N. Y., 1861·
4 vols. in 2.
Tale of two cities.
Uncommercial traveller.

———, Works of. Library edition. Illus.
Bost. and Lond., n. d. 30 v. 3—15.

Contents.
American notes.
Bleak House. 2 vols.
Barnaby Rudge. 2 vols.
Christmas books.
David Copperfield. 2 vols.
Dombey and Son. 2 vols.
Edwin Drood.
Great expectations.
Hard times.
History of England.
Little Dorrit. 2 vols.
Martin Chuzzlewit. 2 vols.
Nicholas Nickleby. 2 vols.
Old curiosity shop. 2 vols.
Oliver Twist.
Our mutual friend. 2 vols.
Pickwick papers. 2 vols.
Pictures from Italy.
Sketches by "Boz."
Tale of two cities.
Uncommercial traveller.

——— Same. Globe edition. Illustrated
by Darley and Gilbert. N. Y., 1874. 15
v. 3—15.

——— Our mutual friend. (Condensed
classics.) N. Y., 1876. 5—33.

——— Memoirs of Joseph Grimaldi; edited
by "Boz." Phil., 1838. 2 v. in 1. 3—15.

———, A cyclopædia of the best thoughts
of. Compiled and alphabetically arranged by F. G. de Fontaine. N. Y.,
1873. 2—7.

Dickens dictionary, The. Illus. Pierce,
G. A. Bost., 1872. 3—16.

Dickenson, Anna E. What answer?
Bost., 1869. 2—13.

Dick 's recitations and readings. N. Y.,
1876. 2 v. 40—221.

*Dictionary of the English language, An
American. Webster, N. Springfield,
Mass., 1872. 22—131.

*———, A new, of the English language.
Richardson, C. Phil., 1847. 2 v. 22—
131.

*——— of the English language, A. Wor-
cester, J. E. Bost., 1860. 22—131.

*——— of the Spanish and English lan-
guages. Neuman, H., and G. Barretti.
Bost., 1849. 23—137.

*———. A copious and critical English-
Latin lexicon. Riddle, J. E., and T. K.
Arnold. N. Y., 1849. 22—131.

*———, French and English pronouncing.
Spiers, A., and M. Surenne. N. Y., 1852·
23—138.

*——— Same. School edition, complete
in one volume. N. Y., 1875. 23—138.

*———, Royal: English and French, and
French and English. Paris, 1846-49.
2 v. 22—131.

*———. A Greek-English lexicon. Lid-
dell, H. G., and R. Scott. N. Y., 1848
23—137.

*———, An abridgment of Ainsworth's,
English and Latin. Morell, T. Phil.,
1859. 23—137.

*———, Anglo-Saxon and English. Bos-
worth, J. Lond., 1849. 23—137.

*——— of the German and English lan-
guages. Adler, G. J. Phil., 1849. 22—
131.

*——— of archaic and provincial words,
obsolete phrases, proverbs, and ancient
customs, from the fourteenth century.
Halliwell, J. O. Lond., 1847. 2 v. 23—
137.

*——— of Americanisms. Bartlett, J. R.,
Bost., 1860. 23—137.

——— of modern slang, cant, and vulgar
words, by a London antiquary. Lond.,
1860. 27—162.

——— of phase and fable. Brewer, E. C.
Lond., n. d. 16—96.

*——— of Latin quotations, proverbs·
maxims, and mottos; with a selection
of Greek quotations. Riley, H. T.
Lond., 1856. 16—96.

*——— of the Scottish language. Jamie-
son, J. Edin., 1867. 23—139.

*———, A critical, of English literature
and British and American authors·

Allibone, S. A. Phil., 1871. 3 v. 23—137.

———. Great truths by great authors: a dictionary of aids to reflection. Phil., 1856. 27—161.

*———, Comprehensive, of the Bible. Illus. Barnum, S. W. N. Y., 1871. 23—140.

*——— of the Holy Bible. Illus. Calmet, A. Charlestown, 1812. 5 v. 21—127.

*———, A classical: containing an account of the principal proper names mentioned in ancient authors, and intended to elucidate all the important points connected with the geography, history, biography, mythology, and fine arts of the Greeks and Romans; together with an account of coins, weights, and measures, with tabular values of the same. Anthon, C. N. Y., 1860. 22—132.

*———. Bibliotheca classica; or, a dictionary of all the principal names and terms relating to the ancients. Lempriere, J. Phil., 1856. 22—132.

*———, A classical and archæological, of the manners, customs, laws, institutions, arts, etc., of the celebrated nations of antiquity, and of the middle ages. Nuttall, P. A. Lond., 1840. 22—132.

*——— of Greek and Roman antiquities· Illus. Smith, W. Lond., 1848. 22—132.

*——— of Greek and Roman biography and mythology. Smith, W. Bost. and Lond., 1849. 3 v. 22—132.

*——— of biography and mythology, Universal pronouncing. Thomas, J. Phil., 1870. 2 v. 23—137.

*———, A general biographic. Blake, J. S. Bost., 1848. 23—138.

*———, Biographical; containing a brief account of the first settlers of New England. Elliot, J. Bost., 1809. 23—139.

*———, A general biographical. Gorton, J. Lond., 1833. 3 v. 23—139.

*———, A new general biographical. Rose, H. J. Lond., 1853. 12 v. 23—139.

——— of American biography. Drake, F. S. Bost., 1874. 23—137.

*———, A new American biographical. Rogers, T. J. Phil., 1829. 23—139.

*Dictionary, A biographical and critical, of painters, engravers, sculptors, and architects. Spooner, S. N. Y., 1853. 23—140.

*——— of dates relating to all ages and nations. Haydn, J. B. Vincent, ed. N. Y., 1872. 23—138.

*———, geographical, statistical, and historical, of the various countries, places, and principal natural objects in the world. McCulloch, J. R. N. Y., 1852. 2 v. 21—126.

*———, Universal geographical. Darby, W. Wash., 1843. 21—126.

*——— of the arts, sciences, and manufactures. Illus. Francis, G. W. Lond., 1846. 22—132.

*——— of arts, manufactures, and mines. Illus. Ure, A. N. Y., 1848. 22—133.

*———, Rudimentary, of terms used in civil and naval architecture, etc. Weale, J. Lond., 1849-50. 21—128.

*———, An architectural. Nicholson, P. Lond., 1819. 2 v. 21—125.

*———, The imperial, English, technological, and scientific, with supplement. Illus. Ogilvie, J. Lond., 1853. 3 v. 22—131.

*———, Universal technological; or, familiar explanations of the terms used in all arts and sciences. Crabb, G. Lond., 1823. 2 v. 21—126.

*——— of the U. S. Congress and the general government. Lanman, C. Hartford, 1868. 22—132.

——— of the United States Congress. Lanman, C. Phil., 1859. 22—132.

*———, Appleton's, of machines, mechanics, engine-work, and engineering. Illus. N. Y., 1861. 2 v. 21—125.

*———, American mechanical. Illus. Knight, E. H. N. Y., 1874-76. 3 v. 23—138. .

*———, Practical, theoretical, and historical, of commerce and commercial navigation. McCulloch, J. R. Phil., 1849. 2 v. 21—127.

——— of geology and mineralogy. Humble, W. Lond., 1843. 15—91.

*——— of all officers who have served in the army of the United States from 1789 to 1853. Gardner, C. K. N. Y., 1853. 23—133.

*Dictionary, A comprehensive medical. Thomas, J. Phil., 1874. 23—133.

——, The Dickens : a key to the characters and principal incidents in the tales of Charles Dickens. Illns. Pierce, G. A. Bost., 1872. 3—16.

*Dictionnaire de l'Académie française, avec complément. Paris, 1852. 3 v. X.

*—— de la conversation et de la lecture inventaire raisonné des notions générales les plus indispensable à tous, par une société de savants et de gens de lettres, sous la direction de M. W. Duckett. Paris, 1853. 16 v. L.

—— grand, Français-anglais et Anglais-français. Fleming et Tibbins. 2 v. Paris, 1846-49. 22—131.

—— encyclopédique de la France. Le Bas, P. (L'Univers.) Paris, 1840-45. 12 v. texte, et 3 v. planches. D. R.

*Digest of the laws of the corporation of the city of Washington. Burch, S. Wash., 1823. T.

Digested index of decisions of the supreme courts of Ohio, Indiana, and Illinois. Conover, J. F. Phil., 1834. T.

Dillon, Arthur. A winter in Iceland and Lapland. Lond., 1840. 2 v. 17—103.

Dillon, John B. A history of Indiana, from its earliest exploration by Europeans to the close of the territorial government, in 1816; comprehending a history of the discovery, settlement, and civil and military affairs of the territory of the U. S. northwest of the river Ohio, and a general view of the progress of public affairs in Indiana, from 1816 to 1856. Illus. Indianapolis, 1859. 31—186.

Dimitri Roudine: a novel. Turgenef, I. S. N. Y., 1873. 4—22.

Dionysius Halicarnassensis, The Roman antiquities of. E. Spelman, tr. Lond., 1758. 4 v. 34—203.

Discarded daughter, The. Southworth, E. D. E. N. Phil., 1852. 6—37.

Discovery of the Great West. Parkman, F. Bost., 1871. 28—166.

Discussions on philosophy, literature, and education. Hamilton, W. N. Y., 1868. 14—84.

Diseases of cattle in the United States; reports made to the Commissioner of Agriculture. Wash., 1869. D. R.

Disosway, E. T. South meadows: a tale of long ago. Phil., 1874. 3—15.

Disowned, The. Bulwer-Lytton, Sir E. Phil., 1869. 5—33.

Disraeli, Benjamin. Lothair. N. Y., 1871. 4—24.

—— Vivian Grey, and other tales. Lond. and N. Y., n. d. 4—24.

—— The young duke; and Coningsby. Lond. and N. Y., n. d. 4—24.

—— Henrietta Temple: a love story. Lond., 1871. 4—24.

—— Sybil; or, the two nations. Lond., 1871. 4—24.

—— Venetia. Lond., 1871. 4—24.

—— Tancred; or, the new crusade. Lond., 1871. 4—24.

—— Alroy; Ixion in heaven; The infernal marriage; and Popanilla. Lond., 1871. 4—24.

—— Contarini Fleming: a psychological romance; and The rise of Iskander. Lond., 1871. 4—24.

Disraeli, Isaac. The calamities and quarrels of authors; with some inquiry respecting their moral and literary characters. Lond. and N. Y., 1859. O—3.

—— Curiosities of literature. Lond. and N. Y., 1859. 3 v. O—3.

—— Commentaries on the life and reign of Charles the first, king of England. Lond., 1828-31. 5 v. 34—205.

—— The literary character, or, the history of men of genius, drawn from their own feelings and confessions; Literary miscellanies; and An inquiry into the character of James the first. Lond., 1859. 27—161.

Dissertations and discussions. Mill, J. S. Bost., 1868. 4 v. 28—167.

*District of Columbia, The statutes (revised) in force in the. 42d Congress, 3d session. 21—128.

Disturnell, John. Influence of climate in North and South America: showing the varied climatic influences operating in the equatorial, tropical, sub-tropical, temperate, cold, and frigid regions. N. Y., 1867. 15—92.

—— A gazetteer of the State of New York. Albany, 1843. 31—190.

Diversions of Purley, The. Tooke, J. H. Lond., 1840. Q—1.

Divine comedy of Dante Alighieri. H. W. Longfellow, tr. Bost., 1871. 17—105.
—— love and wisdom. Swedenborg, E. N. Y., 1872. 1—3.
—— providence. Swedenborg, E. N. Y., 1873. 1—3.

Dixon, William Hepworth. William Penn: an historical biography from new sources, with an extra chapter on the Macaulay charges. Phil., 1851. 11—63.

Doctor Antonio. Ruffini, G. N. Y., 1867. 6—40.
—— Johns. Mitchell, D. G. N. Y., 1866. 2 v. P—1.
—— Ox's experiment, and other stories. Verne, J. Bost., 1874. 5—31.
—— Syntax's three tours, Illus. Combe, W. Lond., n. d. 16—96.
—— Thorne. Trollope, A. N. Y., 1870. 7—43.
—— Basilius. Dumas, A. D. Lond. and N. Y., n. d. 12—57.
—— Bushwhacker, The sayings and doings of. Cozzens, F. S. N. Y., 1871. 28—169.

Doctor's wife, The. Braddon, M. E. N. Y., n. d. 5—29.

Dodd family abroad, The. Lever, C. J. Lond., n. d. 7—44.

Doddridge, Philip. Some remarkable passages in the life of Col. James Gardiner, who was slain at the battle of Preston Pans Sept. 21, 1745. Bost., 1792. 12—72.

Dodge, J. R., (Statistician U. S. Department of Agriculture.) Centennial album of agricultural statistics, including maps, charts, diagrams, illustrations of industrial colleges, and type specimens of breeds of farm animals. Wash., 1876. C.

Dodge, Mary Abigail, (Gail Hamilton.) Stumbling-blocks. Bost., 1868. E.
—— Woman's worth and worthlessness; the complement to "A new atmosphere." N. Y., 1872. 2—10.
—— A new atmosphere. Bost., 1865. P—3.
—— Child world. Illus. Bost., 1873. 2 v. 39.
—— Twelve miles from a lemon. N. Y., 1874. 19—114.
—— Nursery noonings. N. Y., 1875. 6—39.

Dodge, Mary Mapes. Rhymes and jingles. Illus. N. Y., 1875. 39.

Dodge, Richard Irving. The plains of the great west and their inhabitants; being a description of the plains, game, Indians, etc., of the Great North American Desert; with an introduction by W. Blackmore. Illus. N. Y., 1877. 10—57.

Dodge Club, The. Illus. De Mille, J. N. Y., 1870. 2—9.

Dodgson, Charles Lutwidge, (Lewis Carroll.) The hunting of the snark: an agony in eight fits. Illustrated by Henry Holiday. Lond., 1876. 17—105.

Doesticks. Illus. Thomson, M. N. Y., 1859. 2—11.

Doesticks, Q. K. Philander, pseud. See Thomson, M.

Doing and dreaming. "Edward Garrett." N. Y., 1875. 41—228.
—— his best. Illus. Trowbridge, J. T. Bost., 1873. 39.

Dollars and cents. "Elizabeth Warner." Phil., 1871. 7—43.

Dolores. Forrester, Mrs. Phil., 1875. 41—228.

Dombey and son. Illus. Dickens, C. N. Y., 1868. 2 v. 2 copies. 3—15 and 16.

Domestic management and expenditure, Things a lady would like to know concerning. Southgate, H. Lond., 1877. 20—122.

Dominican republic: report of the commission of inquiry to Santo Domingo. Wash., 1871. T.

Don Quixote de la Mancha. Illus. Cervantes-Saavedra, M. de. Lond., 1819. 4 v. 2—8.

Donne, John, Poetical works of; with a memoir. Bost., 1864. 16—19.

Doolittle, Justus. Social life of the Chinese; with some account of their religious, governmental, educational, and business customs and opinions, with special but not exclusive reference to Fuhchau. Illus. 2 v. in one. N. Y., 1876. 9—52.

Dora. Illus. Kavanagh, J. N. Y., 1873. 6—35.

Doran, John. Habits of men, with remnants of record touching the makers of both. N. Y., 1865. 19—114.

Doran, John. Knights and their days. N. Y., 1864. 19—114.

—— Table traits with something on them. N. Y., 1865. 19—114.

—— Monarchs retired from business. N. Y., 1865. 2 v. 11—60.

—— "Their majesties' servants;" Annals of the English stage, from Thomas Betterton to Edmund Kean;—actors—authors—audiences. N. Y., 1865. 2 v. 19—114.

—— Lives of the queens of England of the house of Hanover. N. Y., 1865. 2 v. 11—60.

Doric race, The history and antiquities of the. Müller, C. O. H. Truffnell and G. C. Lewis, trs. Oxford, 1830. 2 v. 35—209.

Dorothy Fox. Illus. Parr, L. Phil., 1873. 5—29.

Dorr, Julia C. R. Expiation. Phil., 1873. 0—1.

—— Sibyl Huntington: a novel. Phil., 1873. 5—30.

Double story, A. MacDonald, G. N. Y., n. d. 7—45.

Douglas, Amanda M. Santa Claus land. Illus. Bost., 1874. 39.

Douglas, Sir Howard. An essay on the principles and construction of military bridges, and the passage of rivers in military operations. Lond., 1832. T.

Dove in the eagle's nest, The. Yonge, C. M. N. Y., 1872. 5—30.

Dover, George J. W. A. Ellis, Lord. The life of Frederic the second, king of Prussia. Lond., 1832. 2 v. 12—71.

Dower house, The. Thomas, A. N. Y., 1868. 5—28.

Downing, Andrew Jackson. The architecture of country houses; including designs for cottages, farm-houses, and villas. Illus. N. Y., 1866. 15—90.

—— Cottage residences; or, a series of designs for rural cottages and villas, and their gardens and grounds. Illus. N. Y., 1853. 15—90.

Downing, Major Jack, pseud. See Smith, Seba.

Down in Tennessee. "Edmund Kirke." N. Y., 1865. 2—13.

Doyle, Richard. The foreign tour of Messrs. Brown, Jones, and Robinson; being a history of what they saw and

did in Belgium, Germany, Switzerland, and Italy. Illus. N. Y., 1871. 17—101.

Dragoon campaigns to the Rocky Mountains: a history of the regiment of United States dragoons, by a dragoon. N. Y., 1836. 2—13.

Drake, Francis S. * Dictionary of American biography, including men of the time; containing nearly ten thousand notices of persons of both sexes, of native and foreign birth, who have been remarkable, or prominently connected with the arts, sciences, literature, politics, or history, of the American continent; giving also the pronunciation of many of the foreign and peculiar American names, a key to the assumed names of writers, and a supplement. Bost., 1874. 23—137.

Drake, Joseph Rodman. The culprit fay: a poem. Illus. N. Y., 1871. 16—100.

Drake, Samuel Gardner. Biography and history of the Indians of North America, from its first discovery. Bost., 1851. 30—178.

—— Tragedies of the wilderness. Bost., 1841. 2—13.

Dramatic works of Goethe. Lond., 1870. 2—11.

—— works of J. Sheridan Knowles. Lond., n. d. 17—106.

Draper, John William. Thoughts on the future civil policy of America. N.Y., 1865. 26—155.

—— History of the intellectual development of Europe. N. Y., 1869. 28—165.

—— History of the conflict between religion and science. N. Y., 1875. 15—88.

—— History of the American civil war; containing the causes of the war, and the events preparatory to it. N.Y., 1868. 3 v. 30—179.

Drawing-room plays and parlor pantomimes. Collected by C. Scott. Lond., 1870. 2—12.

Drayton, John. View of South Carolina, as respects her natural and civil concerns. Charleston, 1802. 31—188.

Draytons and the Davenants, The. Charles, E. N. Y., n. d. 3—20.

Dream-life. Mitchell, D. G. N. Y., 1869. 3—19.

"Drifting about." Illus. Massett, S. N. Y., 1863. 2—10.

Drummer-boy, The. Illus. Trowbridge, J. T. Bost., 1867. 6—39.

Dryden, John, Poetical works of. Bost., 1864. 5 v. 16—99.

Contents.

Vol. 1. Life of Dryden, by the Rev. J. Mitford; Miscellaneous poems.
Vol. 2. Miscellaneous poems; Epistles; Elegies; Epitaphs.
Vol. 3. Songs, Odes, and A masque; Prologues and Epilogues; Translations from Theocritus, Lucretius, and Horace.
Vol. 4. Poems; Translations from Boccace; Translations from Ovid's Metamorphoses.
Vol. 5. Translations from Ovid's Epistles and Art of love; Translations from Juvenal, Persius, and Homer.

Du Chaillu, Paul Belloni. Explorations and adventures in Equatorial Africa. Illus. N. Y., 1862. 17—102.

—— A journey to Ashango-land, and further penetration into Equatorial Africa. Illus. N. Y., 1874. 40—225.

—— My Apingi kingdom; with life in the Great Sahara, and sketches of the chase of the ostrich, hyena, etc. Illus. N. Y., 1875. 10—57.

—— The country of the dwarfs. Illus. N. Y., 1875. 10—57.

Du Halde, P. The general history of China. Illus. Lond., 1741. 4 v. 36—216.

Dudevant, Amantine Lucile Aurore Dupin, (*George Sand.*) Consuelo: a novel. F. Robinson, tr. Phil., 1870. 7—41.

—— The countess of Rudolstadt: a sequel to "Consuelo." Phil., 1870. 7—41.

—— Fanchon, the cricket; or, la petite Fadette. Phil., 1871. 7—41.

—— The miller of Angibault: a novel. *Miss* Mary E. Dewey, tr. Bost., 1871. 7—41.

—— Mauprat: a novel. Virginia Vaughan, tr. Bost., 1870. 7—41.

—— Antonia: a novel. Virginia Vaughan, tr. Bost., 1870. 7—41.

—— Monsieur Sylvester: a novel. F. G. Shaw, tr. Bost., 1870. 7—41.

—— The snow man: a novel. Virginia Vaughan, tr. Bost., 1872. 7—41.

—— Cessarine Dietrich. E. Stanwood, tr. Bost., 1871. 41—230.

—— My sister Jeannie: a novel. S. R. Crocker, tr. Bost., 1874. 7—41.

Duer, William Alexander. The life of William Alexander, earl of Stirling;

with selections from his correspondence. N. Y., 1847. Q—2.

Duflot de Mofras, *M.* Exploration du territoire de l'Orégon, des Californies, et de la Mer Vermeille, pendant les années 1840–42. Illus. Paris, 1844. 2 v. W.

—— Atlas de l'exploration du territoire de l'Orégon, etc. Paris, 1844. U.

Dumas, Alexandre Davy. The count of Monte Cristo. N. Y., n. d. 5—31.

—— The Vicomte de Bragelonne. Lond. and N. Y., n. d. 5—31.·

—— Memoirs of a physician. Lond. and N. Y., n. d. 5—31.

—— Nanon; or, women's war. Lond. and N. Y., n. d., 5—31.

—— The two Dianas. Lond. and N. Y., n. d. 5—31.

—— The three musketeers. Lond. and N. Y., n. d. 5—31.

—— Cardinal Mazarin; or, twenty years after: sequel to "The three musketeers." Lond. and N. Y., n. d. 5—31.

—— Dr. Basilius. Lond. and N. Y., n. d. 5—31.

—— Chevalier D'Harmental; or, the conspirators. Lond. and N. Y., n. d. 5—31.

—— Ascanio. Lond. and N. Y., n. d. 5—31.

—— Chicot, the jester; or, the lady of Monsoreau. Lond. and N. Y., n. d. 5—31.

—— Taking the bastile; or, six years later. Lond. and N. Y., n. d. 5—31.

—— Life and adventures of. Fitzgerald, P. Lond., 1873. 2 v. 13—76.

—— Love and liberty: a thrilling narrative of the French revolution of 1792. Phil., 1874. 5—31.·

—— The conscript: an historical novel of the days of the first Napoleon. Phil., 1874. 5—31.

—— The countess of Charny; or, the fall of the French monarchy, being the "fourth series" of the "Memoirs of a physician." Phil., 1853. 3—20.

—— The chevalier; being the "sixth series" and end of the "Memoirs of a physician." Phil., 1864. 3—20.

—— Adventures of a marquis: a novel. Phil., 1864. 3—20.

Dumas, Alexandre Davy. Six years later; or, the taking of the bastile: being the "third series" of the "Memoirs of a physician." Phil., 1875. 3—20.

—— The count of Monte Cristo. Phil., 1869. 3—20.

—— Twenty years after: "second series" of "The three guardsmen." Phil., n. d. 3—20.

—— Bragelonne, the son of Athos: "third series" of "The three guardsmen." Phil., n. d. 3—20.

—— The queen's necklace; or, the secret history of the court of Louis XVI: being the "second series" of the "Memoirs of a physician." Phil., 1875. 3—20.

—— Memoirs of a physician; or, the secret history of the court of Louis XV. Phil., 1864. 3—20.

—— The countess of Monte Cristo: a companion to the "Count of Monte Cristo." Phil., 1871. 3—20.

—— The forty-five guardsmen: a novel. Phil., n. d. 3—20.

—— Edmond Dantes: a sequel to the "Count of Monte Cristo." Phil., 1849. 3—20.

—— The iron mask: "fourth series" of "The three guardsmen." Phil., 1875. 3—20.

—— Louise la Valliere: "fifth series" of "The three guardsmen." Phil., 1872. 3—20.

—— Andree de Taverney; or, the down-fall of the French monarchy: being the "fifth series" of "The Memoirs of a physician." Phil., 1875. 3—20.

—— The iron hand; or, the knight of Mauleon. Phil., n. d. 3—20.

—— The three guardsmen: a novel. Phil., n. d. 3—20.

—— The Mohicans of Paris: a novel. Phil., n. d. 3—20.

—— The horrors of Paris: sequel to "The Mohicans of Paris." Phil., n. d. 3—20

—— Isabel of Bavaria, queen of France: being the mysteries of the court of Charles VI. Phil., n. d. 3—20.

—— Annette; or, the lady of the pearls. Phil., n. d. 3—20.

—— The man with five wives. Phil., n. d. 3—20.

Dumas, Alexandre Davy. The count of Moret; or, Richelieu and his rivals. H. S. Williams, jr., tr. Phil., n. d. 3—20·

—— The Corsican brothers. Phil., n. d. 3—20.

—— The marriage verdict. Phil., n. d. 3—20.

—— Madame de Chamblay: a novel. Phil., n. d. 3—20.

—— The black tulip: a novel. Phil., n. d. 3—20.

—— Sketches in France. Phil., n. d. 3—20.

Dumas, Alexandre, jr. Camille; or, the camelia-lady: the only true, complete, and original translation, from which have been adapted for the stage the drama of "Camille," and the opera of "La Traviata." Phil., n. d. 5—34.

Dumont, Pierre Etienne Louis. Recollections of Mirabeau, and of the two first legislative assemblies of France. Lond., 1832. 12—67.

Duncan, P. Martin. The transformations (or metamorphoses) of insects. Illus. Phil., n. d. 14—83.

Dunham, Samuel Astley. History of the Germanic empire. (Lardner's cabinet cyclopædia.) Lond., 1834-35. 3 v. 36—219.

—— history of Denmark, Sweden, and Norway. Lond., 1839. 3 v. 36—220.

Dunlap, William. History of the New Netherlands, province of New York, to the adoption of the federal constitution. N. Y., 1839-40. 2 v. 31—190.

Dunlop, Robert Glasgow. Travels in Central America: a journal of nearly three years' residence in the country. Lond., 1847. 9—54.

Dunn, Henry. Guatimala; or, the United Provinces of Central America in 1827-28. N. Y., 1828. 36—217.

Dunn, Matthias. An historical, geological, and descriptive view of the coal trade of the north of England, Ireland, and Belgium. Newcastle-upon-Tyne, 1844. T.

—— A treatise on the winning and working of collieries. Illus. Newcastle-upon-Tyne, 1852. D. R.

Durbin, John Price. Observations in Europe; principally in France and Great

Britain. Illus. N. Y., 1855. 2 v. 17—104.

——— Observations in the East ; chiefly in Egypt, Palestine, Syria, and Asia Minor. Illus. N. Y., 1854. 2 v. 17—104.

Durnton Abbey: a novel. Trollope, T. A. N. Y., 1872. 7—43.

Dutchman's fireside, The. Paulding, J. K. N. Y., 1863. 2—8.

Dutch Republic, The rise of the. Motley, J. L. N. Y., 1856. 3 v. 36—218.

Duxbury, Massachusetts, A history of the town of. Winsor, J. Bost., 1849. 30—182.

Duyckinck, Evert A. * Portrait gallery of eminent men and women of Europe and America ; embracing history, statesmanship, naval and military life, philosophy, the drama, science, literature, and art ; with biographies. Illus. N. Y., n. d. 2 v. 26—153.

——— and George L. Cyclopædia of American literature. Illus. N. Y., 1856. 2 v. 2—7.

Dwellers in Five Sisters Court, The. Scudder, H. E. N. Y., 1876. 41—226.

Dwight, Benjamin W. Modern philology: its discoveries, history, and influence. N. Y., 1865. 14—81.

——— Same: second series. N. Y., 1869. 14—81.

Dwight, Theodore. History of the. Hartford convention; with a review of the policy of the United States Government which led to the war of 1812. N. Y., 1833. 29—177.

——— The Roman republic of 1849; with accounts of the inquisition, and the siege of Rome, and biographical sketches. N. Y., 1851. 35—213.

Dwight, Theodore, jr. The history of Connecticut, from the first settlement to the present time. N. Y., 1840. 30—181.

Dwight, Timothy, Life of. (Library of American biography, vol. 14.) 11—65.

Dwyer, John. The principles and practice of hydraulic engineering, applied to arterial and thorough drainage, the conveyance of water, and mill-power. Dub., 1852. 15—87.

Dyeing and calico-printing, A treatise on. Illus. N. Y., 1846. T.

Dyer, David. History of the Albany penitentiary. Albany, 1867. D. R.

Dymond, Jonathan. Essays on the principles of morality, and on the private and political rights and obligations of mankind. N. Y., 1844. 27—162.

——— An inquiry into the accordancy of war with the principles of Christianity, and an examination of the philosophical reasoning by which it is defended. Phil., n. d. 27—159.

Dynevor Terrace ; or, the clue of life. Yonge, C. M. Lond. and N. Y., 1870. 5—30.

E pluribus unum. Prince, L. B. N. Y., 1867. 26—155.

Eagle's nest, The. Ruskin, J. N.Y., 1875. 18—108.

Earle, John, D. D. Microcosmography; or, a piece of the world discovered, in essays and characters ; to which are added, notes and an appendix by Philip Bliss. L. L. Williams, ed. Albany, 1867. 19—116.

Earl's promise, The. Riddell, J. H. Leip., 1873. 2 v. in one. 41—226.

Early dawn, The. Charles, E. N. Y., n. d. 3—20.

——— Italian painters, Memoirs of the. Jameson, A. M. Bost., 1836. 27—162.

——— dramas and romances. Schiller, F. Lond., 1867. 2—11.

——— man in Europe. Illus. Rau, C. N. Y., 1876. 40—225.

——— voyages, travels, and discoveries of the English nation, Collection of. Hakluyt, R. Lond., 1809-12. 5 v. 8—47.

Earth, The. Illus. Reclus, E. N. Y., 1872. 14—83.

——— and man, The. Guyot, A. Bost., 1855. 14—83.

——— and man, The story of the. Illus. Dawson, J. W. N. Y., 1874. 15—91.

——— and sea. Illus. Figuier, L. Lond., 1870. 14—88.

Earthly paradise: a poem. Morris, W. Bost., 1868-71. 2 v. 17—105.

Earthquakes and volcanos. Illus. Ponton, M. Lond., 1870. 15—89.

East and West poems. Harte, F. Bret. Bost., 1871. 16—100.

East Lynne. Wood, E. P. N. Y., n. d. 5—29.

Eastern India, History, antiquities, etc., of. Martin, R. M. Lond., 1838. 3 v. 33—200.

—— Vermont, History of. Illus. Hall, B. H. N. Y., 1853. 30—183.

Eaton, William, Life of. (Library of American biography, vol. 9.) 11—65.

Ebb-tide, and other stories. Illus. "Christian Reid." N. Y., 1872. 5—28.

Ecce cœlum. Burr, E. F. Bost., 1872. E.

—— Deus. Parker, J. Bost., 1868. E.

—— homo. Seely, J. R. Bost., 1870. E.

Echoes of the foot-hills. Harte, F. Bret. Bost., 1875. 17—106.

Eckel, Lizzie St. John. Maria Monk's daughter: an autobiography. Illus. N. Y., 1874. 6—36.

Eckstein, George Frederick. A practical treatise on chimneys; with remarks on stoves, the consumption of smoke and coal, ventilation, etc. Lond., 1852. T.

Edelweiss. Auerbach, B. Bost., 1871. 7—46.

Edgeworth, Maria. Tales and novels. N. Y., 1860. 2 v. P—3.

Contents.
Vol. 1. Castle Rackrent; An essay on Irish bulls; An essay on the noble science of self-justification; Moral tales.
Vol. 4. Tales of fashionable life.

Edinburgh cabinet library. Illus. Edin., 1832-44. 38 v. 28—167 and 168.

Contents.
Vol. 1. Narrative of discovery and adventure in the polar seas and regions.
Vol. 2. Narrative of discovery and adventure in Africa.
Vol. 3. View of ancient and modern Egypt.
Vol. 4. Palestine; or, the Holy Land.
Vol. 5. Lives and voyages of Drake, Cavendish, and Dampier; Discoveries in the South Sea; History of the buccaneers.
Vols. 6, 7, and 8. Historical and descriptive account of British India.
Vol. 9. Historical view of the progress of discovery on the more northern coasts of America.
Vol. 10. The travels and researches of Alexander von Humboldt in America and Russia.
Vol. 11. Life of Sir Walter Raleigh, with sketches of Burleigh, Essex, Secretary Cecil, Sidney, and Spenser.
Vol. 12. Nubia and Abyssinia.
Vols. 13 and 14. History of Arabia, ancient and modern.
Vol. 15. Historical and descriptive account of Persia; with a description of Afghanistan and Beloochistan.
Vol. 16. Lives of eminent zoologists, from Aristotle to Linnæus.
Vol. 17. History and present condition of the Barbary States.
Vols. 18, 19, and 20. Historical and descriptive account of China.
Vol. 21. Historical account of the circumnavigation of the globe.
Vol. 22. Life of King Henry the eighth, with sketches of Wolsey, More, Erasmus, Cromwell, and Cranmer.
Vols. 23 and 24. Scandinavia, ancient and modern; a history of Denmark, Sweden, and Norway.
Vols. 25, 26, and 27. Historical and descriptive account of British America.
Vol. 28. Historical and descriptive account of Iceland, Greenland, and the Faroe Islands.
Vols. 29, 30, and 31. Italy and the Italian islands.
Vol. 32. Mesopotamia and Assyria.
Vol. 33. Polynesia; or, an historical account of the principal islands in the South Sea, including New Zealand.
Vol. 34. Voyages round the world; from the death of Captain Cook to the present time.
Vols. 35, 36, and 37. The United States of America.
Vol. 38. The travels of Marco Polo.

Edinburgh essays, by members of the university. Edin., 1857. 27—159.

—— review, The. 1856-60. 4 v. X.

Edmond Dantes: a sequel to "The count of Monte Cristo." Dumas, A. D. Phil., 1849. 3—20.

Edna Browning: a novel. Holmes, M. J. N. Y. and Lond., 1874. 7—42.

Education, The cyclopædia of. H. Kiddle and A. J. Schem, eds. N. Y. and Lond., 1877. 1—1.

Edwards, Amelia Blandford. The ordeal for wives: a novel. N. Y., 1872. 6—38.

—— In the days of my youth: a novel. Phil., 1874. 6—38.

—— Philip Earnscliffe; or, the morals of May Fair: a novel. N. Y., 1873. 6—39.

—— Half a million of money: a novel. N. Y., 1873. 6—38.

—— Debenham's vow. Illus. N. Y., 1870. 6—38.

—— The ladder of life: a heart-history. N. Y., 1875. 6—38.

—— Barbara's history: a novel. N. Y., 1875. 6—38.

—— My brother's wife: a life history. N. Y., 1875. 6—38.

—— Hand and glove: a novel. N. Y. 1875. 6—38.

Edwards, Amelia Blandford. Miss Carew: a novel. N. Y., 1875. 6—38.

Edwards, Annie. Estelle: a novel. N. Y., n. d. 3—15.

—— Leah: a woman of fashion. N. Y., n. d. 3—15.

—— A point of honor: a novel. N. Y., 1870. 6—39.

—— Archie Lovell: a novel. N. Y., n. d. 6—39.

—— Ought we to visit her? a novel. N. Y., n. d. 6—39.

—— Steven Lawrence, yeoman: a novel. Illus. N. Y., n. d. 6—39.

—— Susan Fielding: a novel. Illus. N. Y., n. d. 6—39.

—— Miss Forrester: a novel. N. Y., 1873. 6—39.

—— A vagabond heroine. N. Y., 1873. 7—46.

Edwards, Bryan. The history, civil and commercial, of the British colonies in the West Indies. Phil., 1806. 4 v. 32—191.

Edwards, Jonathan, Life of. (Library of American biography, vol. 8.) 11—65.

Edwards, Matilda Betham. Kitty. N. Y., 1870. 6—35.

——; The Sylvestres; or, the outcasts. Illus. Phil., 1872. 41—230.

Edwards, William H. A voyage up the river Amazon, including a residence at Pará. N. Y., 1847. 9—53.

Edwin Brothertoft. Winthrop, T. Bost., 1862. 4—24.

—— Drood. Illus. Dickens, C. Bost. and Lond., n. d. 3—15.

Eggleston, Edward. The end of the world: a love story. Illus. N. Y., 1872. 7—45.

—— The Hoosier schoolmaster. Illus. N. Y., 1871. 7—45.

—— The circuit rider: a tale of the heroic age. Illus. N. Y., 1874. 7—45.

Egypt, History of. Sharpe, S. Lond., 1846. 36—216.

——, Ancient, under the Pharaohs. Kenrick, J. Lond., 1850. 2 v. 36—216.

—— under the Ptolemies, History of. Sharpe, S. Lond., 1838. 36—216.

——, A pilgrimage to. Illus. Smith, J. V. C. Bost., 1852. 17—101.

—— Last letters from. Gordon, L. A. Lond., 1875. 9—53.

Egypt and Iceland in the year 1874. Taylor, J. B. N. Y., 1874. 40—222.

Égypte, Ancienne. (L'Univers.) Champollion-Figeac. Paris, 1839. D. R.

——, depuis la conquête des Arabes, jusqu'à la domination française. (L'Univers.) Marcel. Paris, 1848. D. R.

Egyptians, Manners and customs of the ancient. Illus. Wilkinson, Sir J. G. Lond., 1837-41. 1st and 2d series. 6 v. 36—216.

Eichendorff, Joseph von. Memoirs of a good-for-nothing. C. G. Leland, tr. N. Y., 1866. 6—36.

Eight cousins; or, the aunt-hill. Illus. Alcott, L. M. Bost., 1875. 5—31.

Eighteenth century, History of. Schlosser, F. C. D. Davison, tr. Lond., 1843-52. 8 v. 32—194.

Eighth commandment, The. Reade, C. Bost., 1860. 7—42.

Eirene; or, a woman's right. Amee, M. C. N. Y., 1871. 6—35.

El restaurador. Mad., 1823. W.

Elbow-room: a novel without a plot. Illus. "Max Adeler." Phil., 1876. 2—8.

Elder, William. The enchanted beauty, and other tales, essays, and sketches. Phil., 1859. 3—20.

Eldon, Lord Chancellor, The public and private life of. Twiss, H. Phil., 1844. 2 v. 11—59.

Eldorado; or, adventures in the path of empire. Taylor, J. B. N. Y., 1868. 17—103.

Eleanor's victory. Illus. Braddon, M. E. N. Y., 1870. 5—29.

Electoral votes for President and Vice-President of the United States, Proceedings and debates of Congress relating to counting the. Compiled and printed by order of the House of Representatives, Dec. 23, 1876. Wash., 1877. 18—108.

Elements of international law. Wheaton, H. Bost., 1855. 21—123.

—— of punctuation. Wilson, J. Bost., 1856. 14—85.

—— of morality, The. Whewell, W. N. Y., 1845. 2 v. E.

—— of drawing. Illus. Ruskin, J. N. Y., 1864. 26—158.

Eliana. Lamb, C. N. Y., 1870. 27—159.

Eliot, George, pseud. See Evans, Marian.

Eliot, George. The wit and wisdom of. Bost., 1873. 2—9.

Eliot, John. *A biographical dictionary, containing a brief account of the first settlers, and other eminent characters in New England. Bost., 1809. 23—139.

Eliot, Rev. John, Life of. (Library of American biography, vol. 5.) 11—65.

Eliot, Samuel. History of civil liberty; ancient Romans and early Christians. Bost., 1853. 2 v. 32—196.

Elizabeth, The age of. (Epochs of history.) Creighton, M. N. Y., 1876. 32—193.

Ellen Middleton : a tale. Fullerton, Lady G. Balt., n. d. 41—228.

Ellery, William, Life of. (Library of American biography, vol. 6.) 11—65.

Ellicott, Andrew, Journal of, when late commissioner on behalf of the United States for determining the boundary between the United States and the possessions of his Catholic Majesty in America. Phil., 1803. 9—51.

Elliot, Frances. Romance of old court life in France. Illus. N. Y., 1874. 5—28.

—— Diary of an idle woman in Italy. Lond., 1871. 2 v. in one. 9—53.

Elliot, Jonathan. The debates in the several state conventions on the adoption of the federal constitution ; with the journal of the federal convention, etc. Wash., 1836. 5 v. D. R.

Elsie Magoon ; or, the old still-house in the hollow. Gage, F. D. Phil., 1867. O—3.

—— Venner. Holmes, O. W. Bost., 1874. 2 v. in one. 4—23.

Elster's folly. Wood, E. P. Phil., n. d. 41—190.

Emerson, Ralph Waldo. Representative men ; seven lectures. Bost., 1861. 27—161.

——, The prose works of. Bost., 1870, 2 v. 27—161.

—— May-day, and other pieces. Bost., 1867. 17—106.

——, Poems of. Bost., 1865. 17—107.

—— The conduct of life. Bost., 1875. 40—222.

—— Letters and social aims. Bost., 1876. 19—116.

Emily Chester. Seemüller, A. M. C. Bost., 1870. P—2.

Eminent women of the age. Illus. Parton, J., Greeley, H., and others. Hartford, 1871. 13—74.

Emma : a novel. Austen, J. Lond., 1870. 4—27.

Emmons, Lieut. George F., U. S. N. * The navy register of the United States, from 1775 to 1853. Wash., 1853. 24—141.

Emory, William H. Report on the United States and Mexican boundary survey, made under the direction of the Secretary of the Interior. Illus. Wash., 1859. Ex. doc. No. 135, 34th Congress, 1st session. 3 v. X.

—— Views along the boundary between the United States and Mexico. Q—1.

Empress Catharine the second, Memoirs of the, written by herself ; with a preface by A. Herzen. N. Y., 1859. 13—76.

—— Josephine, The. Illus. " Louise Mühlbach." N. Y., 1867. 4—21.

—— Josephine, The life of the. Headley, P. C N. Y., 1856. 11—61.

Enchanted beauty, The. Elder, W. Phil., 1859. P—2.

*Encyolopædia Britannica ; or, dictionary of arts, sciences, and general literature ; with preliminary dissertations on the history of the sciences, etc. Edin., 1842. 21 v. 22—129 and 23—135.

*—— of civil engineering. Illus. Cresy, E. Lond., 1856. 22—133.

*—— Same. Lond., 1847. 2 v. 15—87.

*—— of useful arts ; comprising agriculture, horticulture, commerce, political economy, carpentry, fortification, and naval architecture. Lond., 1848. T.

*—— Americana. Phil., 1849. 14 v. 22—133.

*—— of the plants of Great Britain. Loudon, J. C. Lond., 1836. 15—90.

*—— of geography. Murray, H. Phil., 1845. 3 v. 21—126.

——, The political text-book, or. Cluskey, M. W. Wash., 1857. 18—108.

*——, Iconographic, of science, literature, and art. Illus. Heck, J. G. N. Y., 1851. 4 v. text, and 2 v. plates. Q—1.

——, Family ; or, compendium of useful knowledge. Illus. Goodrich, C. A. N. Y., 1860. 23—138.

Encyclopædia of architecture. Illus. Gwilt, J. Lond., 1842. 15—90.

—— of antiquities, and elements of archæology, classical and mediæval. Illus. Fosbroke, T. D. Lond., 1843. 2 v. 28—165.

——, Zell's popular. Illus. Colange, L. Phil., 1876. 2 v. 36—215.

End of the world, The. Illus. Eggleston, E. N. Y., 1872. 7—45.

England, A child's history of. Illus. Dickens,C. Bost. and Lond.,n.d. 3—15.

——, History of. Mackintosh, Sir J. Lond., 1853. 2 v. 33—199.

——, History of. Mahon, Lord. N. Y., 1849. 2 v. 34—207.

——, History of. (Lardner's cabinet cyclopædia.) Mackintosh, Sir J. Lond., 1830. 10 v. 34—207.

——, History of. Froude, J. A. N. Y., 1867-70. 12 v. 34—204.

——, History of. Hume, D. Lond., 1848. 6 v. 33—198.

——, History of. Smollett, T. Lond., 1848. 4 v. 33—198.

——, History of. Goldsmith, O. Lond., 1819. 4 v. 33—198.

——, A history of. Lingard, J. Paris, 1840. 8 v. 34—208.

——, History of. Macaulay, T. B. N.Y., 1849-56. 4 v. 34—204.

——, History of. Macaulay, Catharine. Lond., 1746. 2 v. 33—197.

——, History of, during the thirty years' peace, 1816-46. Martineau, Harriet. Lond., 1849-50. 2 v. 34—208.

——, Pictorial history of. Craik, G. L., and C. Macfarlane. N. Y., 1846-48. 4 v. 33—197.

——, History of the conquest of. Thierry, J. N. A. Lond., 1847. 2 v. 34—205.

——, History of the revolution of 1688 in. Mackintosh, Sir J. Phil., 1835. 34—205.

——, History of the commonwealth of. Godwin,W. Lond., 1824-28. 4 v. 33—198.

——, History of the rebellion and civil wars in, from 1641. Clarendon, Earl of. Oxford, 1717. 7 v. 34—208.

—— under the reigns of Edward the sixth and Mary. Tytler, P. F. Lond., 1839. 2 v. 34—207.

——. (Romance of history.) Illus. Neele, H. Lond., n. d. 2—8.

England, The comic history of. Illus. Beckett, G. A. a'. Lond., n. d. 2—9.

——, The constitutional history of. Hallam, H. N. Y., 1873. 2 v. 27—161.

——, The constitutional history of. Stubbs, Rev. W. Oxford, 1875. 2 v. 34—206.

—— and Italy, Stray studies from. Green, J. R. N. Y., 1876. 40—222.

—— and its people, First impressions of. Miller, H. Bost., 1868. 9—53.

——, Notes on. Taine, H. A. N. Y., 1872. 10—56.

——, The history of, from the year 1830 to 1874. Molesworth,W. N. Lond., 1874. 3 v. 34—207.

——, The history of the Norman conquest of. Freeman, E. A. Oxford and N. Y., 1873. 4 v. 34—207.

——, Chapters in the history of popular progress in. Routledge, J. Lond., 1876. 28—170.

England's reformation : a poem. Ward, T. Balt., n. d. 17—107.

English and Scottish ballads. Child, F. J. • ed. Bost., 1864. 8 v. 16—97.

—— constitution, The rise and progress of the. De Lolme, J. L. Lond., 1838. 2 v. 26—157.

—— governess at the Siamese court. Illus. Leonowens, A. H. Bost., 1873. 17—101.

—— grammar. Murray, L. York, Eng., 1816. 2 v. 22—132.

—— language, a hand-book of the. Latham, R. G. N. Y., 1866. 14—81.

—— language in its elements and forms. Fowler, W. C. N. Y., 1860. 22—132.

—— language, The origin and history of the. Marsh, G. P. N. Y., 1869. 14—81.

—— language, Lectures on the. First series. Marsh, G. P. N. Y., 1867. Q—2.

—— literature, Three centuries of. Yonge, C. D. N. Y., 1872. 28—169.

—— literature, History of. Taine, H. A. N. Y., 1871. 2 v. 26—154.

—— literature, Cyclopædia of. Illus. Chambers, R. Phil., 1860. 2 v. 2—7.

—— literature, A complete manual of. Shaw, T. B. N. Y., 1870. 28—170.

—— revolution, History of the. Guizot, F. P. G. Oxford, 1838. 2 v. 34—206.

—— humorists, The. Illus. Thackeray, W. M. Lond., 1869. 5—32.

English people, A short history of the. Green, J. R. N. Y., 1876. 34—207.
—— poets, The late. R. H. Stoddard, ed. N. Y., 1867. 17—106.
—— stage, The romance of the. Fitzgerald, P. Lond., 1874. 2 v. 2—8.
—— statesmen. Higginson, T. W. N. Y., 1875. 40—222.
Enigmas of life. Greg., W. R. Bost., 1874. 28—169.
Entick, John. The general history of the late war. Illus. Lond., 1763-64. 5 v. 34—208.
Boneguski; or, the Cherokee chief. A tale of past wars. By an American. Wash., 1839. 2 v. in one. P—2.
Epicurean: The, a romance. Moore, T. N. Y., 1875. 41—228.
Epigrams, Ancient and modern. Booth, J. Lond., 1863. 16—96.
Episodes in an obscure life. N. Y., 1871. 0—1.
Epochs of history: The French revolution and first empire: an historical sketch. Morris, W. O'C. N. Y., n. d. 35—213.
—— The fall of the Stuarts, and Western Europe from 1678 to 1697. Hale, Rev. E. N. Y., n. d. 32—193.
—— The age of Elizabeth. Creighton, M. N. Y., 1876. 32—193.
—— The first two Stuarts and the Puritan revolution, 1603-1660. Gardiner, S. R. Bost., 1876. 34—207.
—— The early Plantaganets. Stubbs, W. N. Y., n. d. 34—207.
—— The Greeks and the Persians. Rev. G. W. Cox, ed. N. Y., 1876. 35—209.
—— The Athenian empire. Rev. G. W. Cox, ed. N. Y., n. d. 35—209.
—— Roman history:—the early empire, from the assassination of Julius Cæsar to that of Domitian. Capes, W. W. N. Y., n. d. 35—312.
Equatorial Africa, Explorations and adventures in. Illus. Du Chaillu, P. B. N. Y., 1862. 17—102.
Erckmann, Emile and Alexandre Chatrian. The invasion of France in 1814; comprising the night march of the Russian army past Phalsburg. Illus. N. Y., 1871. 5—31.
—— Madame Thérèse; or, the volunteers of '92. Illus. N. Y., 1869. 5—31.

Erckmann, Emile and A. Chatrian. A miller's story of the war; or, the plébiscite. By one of the 7,500,000 who voted "yes." Illus. N.Y., 1872. 5—31.
—— The conscript; a story of the French war of 1813. Illus. N. Y., 1872. 5—31.
—— Waterloo; a sequel to "The conscript of 1813." Illus. N. Y., 1872. 5—31.
—— The blockade of Phalsburg; an episode of the end of the empire. Illus. N. Y., 1872. 5—31.
—— The Forest house, and Catherine's lovers. J. Simms, tr. Lond., 1871. 5—31.
—— Friend Fritz: a tale of the banks of the Lauter. N. Y., 1877. 5—31.
—— The outbreak of the great French revolution, related by a peasant of Lorraine. Mrs. C. Hoey, tr. Lond., 1871. 3 v. 41—227.
Ersilia. Poynter, Miss. N. Y., 1876. 41—228.
Ernest Linwood. Hentz, C. L. Phil., 1869. 4—25.
—— Maltravers. Bulwer-Lytton, Sir E. Phil., 1869. 5—33.
Escriche, Don Joaquin. Diccionario razonado de legislacion y jurisprudencia. Mad., 1847. 2 v. D. R.
—— Supplement. Mad., 1847. D. R.
Espagne. (L'Univers.) Lavallée, J., et A. Guéronlt. Paris, 1844. D. R.
——, depuis l'expulsion des Maures jusqu'à l'année 1847, par Lavallée, J.; Îles Baléares et Pithyuses, par Lacroix; Sardaigne, par Grégory; Corse, par Colonna. Paris, 1847. (L'Univers.) D. R.
Espy, James P. The philosophy of storms. Bost., 1841. 15—92.
Essay on war and its accordancy with the principles of Christianity. Dymond, J. Phil., n. d. 27—159.
—— on crimes and punishments, translated from the Italian; with a commentary attributed to M. de Voltaire. Lond., 1767. 27—161.
—— on moral command. Rolt, J. Lond., 1842. E.
Essays, Critical and miscellaneous, by T. B. Macaulay. (Modern British essayists.) Bost., 1856. 27—159.
—— in criticism. Arnold, M. Bost., 1869. 27—159.

Essays in literary criticism. Hutton, R. H. Phil., n. d. 40—222.

—— on the progress of nations. Seaman, E. C. N. Y., 1852. 18—109.

—— on philosophical writers and other men of letters. De Quincey, T. Bost., 1860. 2 v. 2—12.

—— on the poets, and other English writers. De Quincey,.T. Bost., 1859. 2—12.

—— on the principles of morality. Dymond, J. N. Y., 1844. 27—162.

——, Political, economical, and philosophical. Rumford, Count. Lond., 1797-1802. 3 v. 27—159.

——, Historical and biographical, political, social, literary, and scientific. Miller, H. Bost., 1866. 27—159.

—— written in the intervals of business. Helps, Sir A. Bost., 1872. 28—165.

Estelle Russell. N. Y., 1870. 5—28.

——: a novel. Edwards, A. N. Y., n. d. 3—15.

États-Unis, Histoire et description des voies de communication aux. Chevalier, M. Paris, 1840. 2 v. W.

Ethnography and philology of the Indian tribes of the Missouri Valley. Hayden, F. V. Phil., 1862. V.

Études sur les glaciers. Agassiz, L. Neuchâtel, 1840. Avec les planches. U.

Eugene Aram: a tale. Bulwer-Lytton, Sir E. Phil., 1867. 5—33.

Euripides, Works of. R. Potter, tr. Lond., 1832. 3 v. 17—107.

Contents.

Vol. 1. Biographical sketch of Euripides; The tragedies.

Vols. 2 and 3. Tragedies.

Europe, General history of civilization in. Guizot, F. P. G. N. Y., 1846. 4 v. 33—202.

——, History of. Alison, Sir A. N. Y., 1850. 8 v. 1st and 2d series. 32—192.

——, History of modern. Russell, W. N. Y., 1853. 3 v. 32—193.

——, Observations in. Illus. Durbin, J. P. N. Y., 1854. 2 v. 17—104.

——, View of the state of, during the middle ages. Hallam, H. Lond., 1846-48. 3 v. 26—156.

——, Hints for six months in. Latrobe, J. H. B. Phil., 1869. 8—50.

——, past and present. Ungewitter, F. H. N. Y. and Lond., 1850. 32—192.

European acquaintance. De Forest, J. W. N. Y., 1858. 17—103.

—— art, Wonders of. Illus. Viardot, L. N. Y., 1874. 28—169.

—— life and manners. Colman, H. Bost. and Lond., 1849. 2 v. 8—49.

—— morals, History of. Lecky, W, E. H. N. Y., 1875. 2 v. 32—195.

Eustace diamonds, The. Trollope, A. N. Y., 1872. 5—28.

Eutaw: a sequel to "The Forayers." Illus. Simms, W. G. N. Y., 1856. 41—229.

Evans, Augusta J. See Wilson, A. J.

Evans, Marian, (*George Eliot.*) See Lewes, M.

Evelina; or, the history of a young lady's introduction to the world. Burney, N. Y., 1873. 2 v. in one. 41—227. .

—— Same. Lond., 1791. 2 v. 7—46.

Everett, Edward. Orations and speech on various occasions. Bost., 1850-59. 3 v. 25—151.

Everett, William. On the Cam: lectures on the University of Cambridge in England. Cambridge, 1865. 28—166.

Ewbank, Thomas. A descriptive and historical account of hydraulic and other machines for raising water, ancient and modern. N. Y., 1850. 15—92.

Examination of Sir Wm. Hamilton's philosophy. Mill, J. S. Bost., 1866. 2 v. 14—84.

Excelsior: helps to progress in religion, science, and literature. Illus. N. Y., 1854. 2 v. 28—170.

Excursions. Thoreau, H. D. Bost., 1866. 17—104.

Exemplary novels of Cervantes-Saavedra, M. de. Lond., n. d. P—2.

Exotics: attempts to domesticate them. J. F. C. and L. C., trs. Bost., 1876. 17—106.

Expedition to St. Peter's River, Lake Winnepeck, and Lake of the Woods. Keating, W. H. Phil., 1824. 2 v. 8—48.

—— against Fort Du Quesne, in 1755, under Major-General Edward Braddock, The history of. Sargent, W. Phil., 1855. 30—179.

—— to the China seas and Japan, by Commodore M. C. Perry, U. S. N. Illus. Hawks, F. L. Wash., 1856. 3 v. 8—47.

Expiation. Dorr, J. C. R. Phil., 1873. 5—30.

Explorations in Texas, New Mexico, California, Sonora, and Chihuahua. Illus. Bartlett, J. R. N. Y., 1854. 2 v. 10—56.

—— and surveys to ascertain a route for a railroad from the Mississippi River to the Pacific Ocean, made under the direction of the Secretary of War in 1853. Illus. Wash., 1855. 13 v. D. R.

Exploring expedition, United States. Illus. Wilkes, C. N. Y., 1851. 5 v. 9—51.

—— expedition from Santa Fé, N. M., to the junction of the Grand and Green Rivers of the Great Colorado of the West, in 1859, with a geological report by Prof. J. S. Newberry. Illus. Wash., 1876. D. R.

—— tour beyond the Rocky Mountains, Journal of an. Parker, S. Auburn, 1846. 8—50.

Expressions of the emotions in man and animals. Illus. Darwin, C. N.Y., 1873. 14—81.

Extraordinary popular delusions, Memoirs of. Illus. Mackay, C. Lond., n. d. 19—116.

Eyriès, J. B. Danemark. (L'Univers.) Paris, 1846. D. R.

Fables, original and selected; with an introductory dissertation on the history of fable, comprising biographical notices of eminent fabulists, by G. Moir Bussey. Illus. N. Y., 1869. 19—115.

—— and tales of Pompeii and Herculaneum. Illus. Le Gros, W. B. Lond., 1835. 16—100.

—— of Æsop. Illus. G. T. Townsend, tr. Lond., 1871. 38.

—— for critics; or, better, a glance at a few of our literary progenies (Mrs. Malaprop's word) from the tub of Diogones; a vocal and musical medley: that is, a series of jokes by a wonderful quiz who accompanies himself with a rub-a-dub-dub, full of spirit and grace, on the top of the tub. Bost., 1849. 17—106.

Factory girl, The. Braddon, M. E. N.Y., n. d. 5—29.

Faerie queene, The. Spenser, E. Vols. 1-4. 16—99.

Fair France. Muloch, D. M. N. Y., 1871. O—3.

—— God, The. Wallace, L. Bost., 1873. O—1.

—— play. Southworth, E. D. E. N. Phil., 1868. 6—36.

—— puritan, The. Herbert, H. W. Phil., 1875. 41—228.

—— Saxon, A. McCarthy, J. N. Y. 1873. 7—41.

—— to see: a novel. Lockhart, L.W. M. N. Y., 1872. 6—35.

Fairfax; or, the master of Greenway Court. Cooke, J. E. N. Y., 1868. 4—26.

Fairfaxes of England and America, The. Neill, E. D. Albany, 1868. 40—224.

Fairfield, Francis Gerry. Ten years with spiritual mediums: an inquiry concerning the etiology of certain phenomena called spiritual. N. Y., 1875. 14—85.

Fairy book, The. Muloch, D. M. N. Y., 1872. 38.

—— tales, Holme Lee's. Illus. Lond. and N. Y., n. d. 38.

—— tales told again. Illustrated by G. Doré. Lond., Paris, and N. Y., n. d. 38.

Faith Unwin's ordeal. Craik, G. M. N. Y., 1867. 5—33.

Falconar, James, jr. The secret revealed of the authorship of Junius's letters. Lond., 1830. 19—117.

Falconer, William, Poetical works of; with a life, by the Rev. J. Mitford. Bost., 1863. 16—99.

Fallen pride; same as the " Curse of Clifton." Southworth, E. D. E. N. Phil., 1868. 6—37.

False colors. Thomas, A. N. Y., 1869. 5—28.

Familiar letters of John Adams and his wife, Abigail Adams, during the revolution. N. Y., 1876. 40—222.

* —— quotations. Bartlett, J. Bost., 1871. 16—96.

* —— quotations, An index to. Grocott, J. C. Liver., 1871. 16—96.

Family doom, The. Southworth, E. D. E. N. Phil., 1869. 6—36.

—— instructor, The. De Foe, D. Oxford, 1841. 2 v. 27—163.

—— secret, A. " Elzey Hay." Phil., 1876. 41—230.

Fanchon, the cricket. "George Sand." Phil., 1871. 7—41.

Far from the madding crowd. Hardy, T. N. Y., 1874. 5—30.

Faraday as a discoverer. Tyndall, J. N. Y., 1873. 11—64.

Farjeon, B. L. Blade-o'-grass. Illus. N. Y., 1872. 6—35.

—— London's heart: a novel. Illus. N. Y., 1873. 6—35.

—— Golden grain: a sequel to "Blade-o'-grass." Illus. N. Y., 1874. 6—35.

—— Bread and cheese and kisses. Illus. N. Y., 1874. 6—35.

—— Grif: a story of Australian life. N. Y., 1874. 6—35.

—— Joshua Marvel. N. Y., 1872. 6—35.

—— At the sign of the silver flagon: a novel. N. Y., 1875. 6—35.

—— Jessie Trim: a novel. N. Y., 1875. 6—35.

Farm ballads. Illus. Carleton, W. N. Y., 1873. 16—95.

—— legends. Illus. Carleton, W. N. Y., 1876. 16—95.

Farmer's vacation, A. Illus. Waring, G. E. Bost., 1876. 10—56.

Farnham, Eliza W. California, indoors and out; or, how we farm, wine, and live generally in the Golden State. N. Y., 1856. 17—102.

Farquharson, Martha, *pseud.* See Finley, M.

Fast friends. Illus. Trowbridge, J. T. Bost., 1875. 39.

—— life on the modern highway. Illus. Taylor, J. N. Y., 1874. 2—11.

Fatal marriage, The. Southworth, E. D. E. N. Phil., 1863. 6—37.

—— marriages, The. Cockton, H. Phil., n. d. 41—230.

—— passion, A. Bernard, C. de. N. Y. and Paris, 1874. 5—30.

Fated to be free: a novel. Ingelow, J. Bost., 1875. 41—228.

Father and daughter. Bremer, F. Phil., n. d. 1'—1.

Fathers and sons: a novel. Turgenef, I. S. N. Y., 1872. 4—28.

Faust: a tragedy. Goethe, J. H. von. Bost., 1860. 10—100.

Fawcett, Edgar. Purple and fine linen: a novel. N. Y. and Lond., 1873. 5—30.

Featherstonhaugh, George William. A canoe voyage up the Minnay Sotor. Illus. Lond., 1847. 2 v. 18—58.

* **Federal** government: its officers and their duties. Gillet, R. H. N. Y., 1872. 21—128.

—— government, History of the. Bradford, A. Bost., 1840. 29—176.

—— constitution, The writings of John Marshall upon the. Bost., 1839. 25—148.

Federalist on the new constitution; written in 1788 by Mr. Hamilton, Mr. Madison, and Mr. Jay, with an appendix containing the letters of "Pacificus" and "Helvidius" on the proclamation of neutrality of 1793. Hallowell, 1852. 28—165.

—— Same, with the Continentalist and other papers by Hamilton. J. C. Hamilton, ed. Phil., 1864. 28—165.

Felix Holt. "George Eliot." N. Y., 1866. 6—36.

Fellah, The. About, E. Lond., 1870. 6—40.

Fénelon, François de Salignac de la Mothe, Œuvres de, précédées d'études sur la vie, par M. Aimé Martin. Paris, 1865. 3 v. W.

—— Adventures of Telemachus, Dr. Hawkesworth, tr.; with a life of Fénelon by Lamartine; an essay on his genius and character by Villemain; and critical and bibliographical notices, etc., etc. O. W. Wight, ed. N. Y., 1872. 7—41.

Fenton's quest. Illus. Braddon, M. E. N. Y., 1871. 5—29.

Fenwick, Thomas. A treatise on subterraneous surveying, and the variation of the magnetic needle. Lond. 1822. T.

Ferdinand and Isabella, History of the reign of. Prescott, W. H. N. Y., 1851. 3 v. 12—69.

Ferdinand count Fathom, The adventures of. Smollett, T. Lond., 1872. 41—229.

Ferguson, Adam. History of the progress and termination of the Roman republic. Phil., 1841. 35—212.

Ferguson, James. Rude stone monuments in all countries; their ages and uses. Illus. Lond., 1872. 14—82.

Fern, Fanny, *pseud.* See Parton, Sara P. Fern leaves from Fanny's port-folio. Illus. Parton S. P. Auburn, 1853. 2—10.

Ferree, P. V. The heroes of the war for the Union and their achievements : a complete history of the great rebellion. First series. Cin., 1864. 24—143.

Ferrier, Mary. The inheritance. Lond. and N. Y., n. d. 4—22.

—— Marriage. Lond. and N. Y., n. d. 4—22.

—— Destiny ; or the chief's daughter. Lond. and N. Y., n. d. 4—22.

Fessenden, William Pitt, Memorial addresses on the life and character of; delivered in the Senate and House of Representatives, 41st Congress, 2d session, Dec. 14, 1869. Wash., 1870. T.

Feuchtwanger, Lewis. A treatise on gems, in reference to their practical and scientific value. N. Y., 1838. T.

Feuillet, Octave. The romance of a poor young man. N. Y., 1875. 41—228.

—— The story of Sibylle. M. H. T., tr. Bost., 1872. 41—230.

'Fictitious names, Handbook of. Hamst, O. Lond., 1868. 28—166.

Field, Henry Martyn, *D. D.* From the lakes of Killarney to the Golden Horn. N. Y., 1877. 10—57.

Field, *Mrs.* Henry M. Home sketches in France, and other papers. N. Y., 1875. 10—57.

Field, Kate. Pen photographs of Charles Dickens's readings : taken from life. Illus. Bost., 1871. 28—166.

—— Ten days in Spain. Illus. Bost., 1875. 17—104.

Field, Maunsell B. Memories of many men and of some women ; being personal recollections of emperors, kings, queens, princes, presidents, statesmen, authors, and artists at home and abroad, during the last thirty years. N. Y., 1874. 28—169.

Field of ice, The. Illus. Verne, J. Lond. and N. Y., 1875. 5—31.

Fields, James T. Yesterdays with authors. Bost., 1872. 2—11.

Fields, Thomas W. Pear-culture: a manual for the propagation, planting, cultivation, and management of the pear tree. Illus. N. Y., 1859. V.

Fielding, Henry, The miscellaneous works of. N. Y., 1861. 4 v. 5—34.

Contents.

Vols. 1 and 2. Tom Jones; or, the history of a foundling.
Vol. 3. Amelia.
Vol. 4. Adventures of Joseph Andrews; and History of the life of the late Mr. Jonathan Wild, the great.

Fielding; or, society, and other tales. Ward, R. P. Phil., 1837. 3 v. in one. O—3.

Fifine at the fair, and other poems. Browning, R. Bost., 1872. 16—96.

Fifty years in the magic circle. Illus. Blitz, A. Hartford, 1871. 2—8.

Fighting the air: a novel. Marryat, *Miss* F. Leip., 1875. 2 v. in one. 41—226.

Figuier, Louis. The vegetable world : being a history of plants, with their botanical descriptions and peculiar properties. Illus. Lond. and N. Y., n. d. 14—82. •

—— Reptiles and birds: a popular account of their various orders, with a description of the habits and economy of the most interesting. Illus. P. Gillmore, ed. N. Y., 1870. 14—82.

—— Mammalia : their various orders and habits popularly illustrated by typical species. Illus. N. Y., 1870. 14—82.

—— Primitive man. Illus. N. Y., 1871. 15—89.

—— The to-morrow of death ; or, the future life according to science. Illus. S. R. Crocker, tr. Bost., 1875. 15—89.

—— The insect world : being a popular account of the orders of insects ; with a description of the habits and economy of some of the most interesting species. Illus. N. Y., 1872. 14—83.

—— The world before the deluge. Illus. N. Y., 1869. 14—83.

—— The ocean world : being a description of the sea and its living inhabitants. Illus. Lond., n. d. 14—83.

—— The human race. Illus. N. Y., 1872. 15—89.

—— Earth and sea. Illus. W. H. D. Adams, tr. Lond., 1870. 14—83.

Findley, William. History of the insurrection in the four western counties of Pennsylvania, in the year 1794. Phil., 1796. 31—189.

Finley, Martha, (*Martha Furquharson.*) Old-fashioned boy. Phil., 1871. 7—16.

Fireside saints, Mr. Candle's breakfast talk, and other papers. Jerrold, D. Bost., 1873. O—1.

—— travels. Lowell, J. R. Bost., 1865. 28—165.

First families of the Sierras. "Joaquin Miller." Chicago, 1876. 41—223.

—— principles of a new philosophy. Spencer, H. N. Y., 1868. 14—84.

Fish and fishing. Illus. "Frank Forester." N. Y., 1859. 2—9.

Fisher, Frances C, (*Christian Reid.*) A daughter of Bohemia: a novel. Illus. N. Y., 1874. 4—21.

—— Nina's atonement, and other stories. Illus. N. Y., 1873. 5—28.

——Carmen's inheritance. Illus. Phil., 1873. 5—23. ·

—— Valerie Aylmer: a novel. N. Y., 1872. 5—28.

—— Morton house: a novel. Illus. N. Y., 1873. 5—28. ·

—— Mabel Lee: a novel. Illus. N. Y., 1872. 5—28.

—— Ebb-tide, and other stories. Illus. N. Y., 1872. 5—28.

—— Hearts and hands: a story in sixteen chapters. N. Y., 1875. 5—28.

—— A question of honor: a novel. N. Y., 1875. 4—26.

Fisher, Richard S. The book of the world: being an account of all republics, empires, kingdoms, and nations. N. Y:, 1850. Vol. 2. 2—7.

Fisher-maiden, The. Björnson, B. N. Y., 1874. 5—30.

Fishing in American waters. Illus. Scott, G. C. N. Y., 1873. 19—115.

Fiske, John. Myths and myth-makers: old tales and superstitions interpreted by comparative mythology. Bost., 1874. 28—165.

—— The unseen world, and other essays. Bost., 1876. 40—222.

Fitch, John, Life of. (Library of American biography, vol. 16.) 11—65.

Fitzgerald, Percy. The romance of the English stage. Lond., 1874. 2 v. 2—8.

—— Life and adventures of Alexander Dumas. Lond., 1873. 2 v. 13—76.

Fitzmaurice, *Lord* Edmond. Life of William, earl of Shelburne, afterward first marquis of Lansdowne; with extracts from his papers and correspondence. Lond., 1875-76. 3 v. 13—76.

Five nations of Canada, The history of. Colden, C. Lond., 1747. 29—177.

—— years in an English university. Bristed, C. A. N. Y., 1852. 2—12.

Flagellation and the flagellants: a history of the rod. Illus. Cooper, W. M. Lond., 1869. 2—10.

Flagg, William. A good investment: a story of the Upper Ohio. Illus. N. Y., 1872. 6—35.

Flagg, Wilson. The woods and byways of New England. Illus. Bost., 1872. 19—115.

Flammarion, Camille. The wonders of the heavens. (Illustrated library of wonders.) N. Y., 1874. 23—169.

Fleming and Tibbins. · Royal dictionary, English and French, and French and English. Paris, 1846-49. 2 v. 22—131.

Fletcher, *Miss* D. Kismet. (No Name series.) Bost., 1877. 41—226.

Fletcher, James. The history of Poland, from the earliest period. Lond., 1831. 36—217.

Fleurange. Craven, A. N. Y., 1873. 5—30. ·

Flint, Timothy. The history and geography of the Mississippi Valley, and the whole American continent. Cin., 1832. 2 v. in one. 29—176.

—— Recollections of the Mississippi Valley. Bost., 1826. 29—176.

Floating city, A. Illus. Verne, J. N. Y., 1874. 5—31.

Flora Australasica. Illus. Sweet, R. Lond., 1827-28. R—2.

Florence *of Worcester*, The chronicle of, with the two continuations: comprising annals of English history, from the departure of the Romans to the reign of Edward the first. T. Forester, tr. Lond., 1854. 33—201.

Florence, The makers of. Illus. Oliphant, M. O. W. Lond., 1876. 11—60.

Florentine history. Napier, H. E. Lond., 1846-47. 6 v. 35—212.

·—— history. Machiavel, N. Lond., 1674. 3o—212.

Florida, The territory of. Williams, J. L. N. Y., 1837. 31—185.

—— war, The origin, progress, and conclusion of the. Sprague, J. T. N. Y., 1848. 30—179.

Florine, princess of Burgundy. MacCabe, W. B. Balt., 1855. 6—39.

Flower, fruit, and thorn pieces. Richter, J. P. F. Bost., 1869. 2 v. 2—11.

Flowers of history. Roger de Wendover. Lond., 1849. 2 v. 33—201.

Fly leaves, by C. S. C. Calverly, C. S. N. Y., 1872. 17—10G.

Folle-Farine. "Ouida." Phil., 1871. 7–44.

Fontaine, Edward. How the world was peopled: ethnological lectures. N. Y., 1872. 15—89.

Fonvielle, Wilfrid de. Thunder and lightning. (Illustrated library of wonders.) T. L. Phipson, tr. and ed. N. Y., 1872. 28—169.

Foote, Andrew Hull. Africa and the American flag. Illus. N. Y., 1854. 9—54.

Foote, Henry S. Casket of reminiscences. Wash., 1874. 11—60.

Foote, William Henry. Sketches of Virginia, historical and biographical. Phil., 1850. 31—188.

—— Same. 2d series. Phil., 1855. 31—188.

Foot-prints of the Creator. Illus. Miller, H. Bost., 1869. 15—91.

For better or worse. Croly, J. C. Bost., 1875. 2—8.

—— ever and ever. Marryat, Miss F. Leip., 1866. 2 v. in one. 4—22.

—— her sake. Illus. Robinson, F. W. N. Y., 1869. 5—29.

—— lack of gold: a novel. Gibbon, C. N. Y., 1872. 5—28.

Forayers, The. Illus. Simms, W. G. N. Y., 1855. 41—229.

Forbes, Alexander. A history of Upper and Lower California, from their first discovery to the present time. Illus. Lond., 1839. 31—187.

Forbes, F. E. Five years in China, from 1842 to 1847: with an account of the occupation of the islands of Labuan and Borneo, by her majesty's forces. Illus. Lond., 1848. 8—49.

Forbes, Robert B. The voyage of the Jamestown on her errand of mercy. Bost., 1847. L.

Force and matter. Büchner, L. Lond., 1864. 14—81.

Forces of nature, The. Illus. Guillemin, A. N. Y., 1872. 14—80.

Forester, Frank, pseud. See Herbert, H. W.

Forest house, and Catherine's lovers. Erckmann, E., and A. Chatrian. Lond., 1871. 5—31.

—— tragedy, and other tales. "Grace Greenwood." Bost., 1856. P—2.

Foregone conclusion, A. Howells, W. D. Bost., 1875. 5—31.

Forlorn hope, The. Yates, E. Lond. and N. Y., n. d. 7—45.

Forms of water, The. Illus. Tyndall, J. N. Y., 1872. 14—83.

Forney, John W. Anecdotes of public men. N. Y., 1874. 11—60.

Forrest, Edwin, The life of. Rees, J. Phil., 1874. 11—60.

Forrester, Fanny, pseud. See Chubbuck, Emily.

Forrester, Mrs. Dolores. Phil., 1875. 41—228.

—— Diana Carew; or, for a woman's sake. Phil., 1876. 41—228.

Fors clavigera. Illus. Ruskin, J. N. Y., 1871. 2 v. 18—108.

Forster, John. The life of Charles Dickens. Phil., 1872. 3 v. 11—60.

Forsyth, William. Life of Marcus Tullius Cicero. Illus. N. Y., 1869. 2 v. 11—64.

—— The novels and novelists of the eighteenth century; in illustration of the manners and morals of the age N. Y., 1871. 11—64.

—— History of the captivity of Napoleon at St. Helena; from the letters and journals of the late Lieut. General Sir Hudson Lowe, and official documents not before made public. N. Y., 1853. 2 v. 11—61.

Fortune, (Little classics, vol. 12.) Bost., 1875. 5—33.

Fortune-seeker, The. Southworth, E. D. E. N. Phil., 1866. 6—37.

Fortunes of Glencore, The. Lever, C. J. N. Y., 1872. 5—29.

France, Statistique de la, publiée par le ministère de l'agriculture et du commerce. Paris, 1840-43. 2 v. D. R.

——. Statistique de l'industrie à Paris résultant de l'enquête faite par la chambre de commerce pour les années 1847-48. D. R.

Francis, George Henry. Orators of the age; comprising portraits, critical, biographical, and descriptive. N. Y., 1847. 13—79.

Francis, George W. The dictionary of the arts, sciences, and manufactures. Illus. Lond., 1846. 22—132.

Francis, John W. Old New York; or, reminiscences of the past sixty years; being an enlarged and revised edition of the anniversary discourse delivered before the N. Y. Historical Society, Nov. 17, 1857. N. Y., 1858. 31—190.

Francis the first, The court and reign of. Illus. Pardoe, J. Lond., 1849. 2 v. 12—70.

Frank Forester's fish and fishing of the United States and the British Provinces. Illus. Herbert, H. W. N. Y., 1850. 2—9.

—— Mildmay; or, the naval officer. Marryat, Capt. F. N. Y., 1857. 5—30.

—— Sinclair's wife, and other tales. Riddell, J. H. Lond., 1874. 3 v. 4—26.

Frankland, Sir Charles Henry; or, Boston in the colonial times. Nason, E. Albany, 1865. 40—224.

Franklin, Benjamin, The works of. Bost., 1840. 10 v. 25—150.

——, Life and times of. Parton, J. N. Y. and Lond., 1864. 2 v. 12—72.

Franklin, Sir John. Narrative of a journey to the shores of the Polar Sea, in the years 1819-22. Illus. Lond., 1823. 9—51.

Frazer, James B. An historical and descriptive account of Persia, from the earliest ages to the present time; including a description of Afghanistan and Beloochistan. Edin., 1834. 36—217.

Fred and Maria and me. Illus. Prentiss, E. N. Y., 1872. 39.

Frederic the second, king of Prussia, The life of. Dover, Lord. Lond., 1832. 2 v. 12—71.

—— the second, called Frederick the great, History of. Carlyle, T. N. Y., 1863-71. 6 v. 12—71.

Frederick the great, his court and times. Campbell, T. Lond., 1842-43. 4 v. 12—71.

—— the great and his family. Illus. "Louise Mühlbach." N. Y., 1871. 4—21.

—— the great and his court. Illus. "Louise Mühlbach." N. Y., 1871. 4—21.

Freedley, Edwin T. Opportunities for industry and the safe investment of capital; or, a thousand chances to make money. Phil., 1859. 28—166.

Freeman, Edward Augustus. The history of the Norman conquest of England; its causes and its results. Revised American edition. Oxford and N. Y., 1873. 4 v. 34—207.

—— Historical essays. 2d series. Lond. and N. Y., 1873. 40—222.

—— The history and conquests of the Saracens: six lectures delivered before the Edinburgh Philosophical Institution. Lond., 1876. 36—217.

—— General sketch of history; adapted for American students : new edition revised, with chronological table, maps, and index. N. Y., 1876. 40—221.

French, Benjamin Franklin. Historical collections of Louisiana. N.Y., 1846, and Phil., 1850. 1st and 2d vols. 31—187.

French country family, A. Illus. De Witt, C. G. Mrs. D. M. Craik, tr. N. Y., 1838. 3—20.

—— language, A theoretical and practical grammar of the. Levizac, J. P. V. L. de. Phil., 1861. 22—132.

—— revolution. Carlyle, T. N. Y., 1871. 2 v. 35—213.

—— revolution, History of the. Mignet, F. A. Lond., 1846. 35—213.

—— revolution, History of the. Lamartine, A. de. Lond., 1849. 35—213.

—— revolution, History of the. Michelet, J. C. Cocks, tr. Lond., 1847. 35—213.

—— revolution, History of the. Thiers, L. A. Lond., n. d. 35—214.

—— revolution, The outbreak of the great. Erckmann, E., and A. Chatrian. Lond., 1871. 3 v. 41—227.

—— revolution and first empire, The. (Epochs of history.) Morris, W. O'C. N. Y., n. d. 35—213.

Freneau, Philip. Poems relating to the American revolution, with an introductory memoir and notes by Evert A. Duyckinck. N. Y., 1865. 17—105.

Freytag, Gustav. Debit and credit; with a preface by C. C. J. Bunsen. N. Y., 1871. O—2.

—— The lost manuscript: a novel. *Mrs.* Malcolm, tr. N. Y., 1873. 6—38.

—— Ingo; the first novel of a series entitled, Our forefathers. *Mrs.* Malcolm, tr. N. Y., 1873. 6—38.

—— Ingraban; the second novel of a series entitled, Our forefathers. *Mrs.* Malcolm, tr. N. Y., 1873. 6—38.

Friedrich, Friedrich. The lost despatch. L. A. Williams, tr. Bost., 1871. 5—29.

Friend Fritz : a tale of the banks of the Lauter. Erckmann, E., and A. Chatrian. N. Y., 1877. 5—31.

Friends in council: a series of readings, and discourse thereon. Helps, *Sir* A. N. Y., 1869. 2 v. in one. 28—170.

Friendship of books and other lectures. Maurice, F. D. Lond., 1874. 28—169.

Friswell, J. Hain. The better self: essays for home life. Phil., 1875. 19—116.

Frithiof's saga. Tegnér, E. N. Y., 1871. 17—106.

Froissart, *Sir* John. Chronicles of England, France, Spain, and the adjoining countries, from the latter part of the reign of Edward II, to the coronation of Henry IV. T. Johnes, tr. 33—197.

From dawn to dark in Italy; a tale of the reformation in the sixteenth century. Illus. Lond., 1871. P—3.

—— fourteen to fourscore. Jewett, S. W. N. Y., 1871. P—3.

—— jest to earnest. Roe, *Rev.* E. P. N. Y., 1875. 6—38.

—— my youth up. Terhune, M. V. N. Y., 1875. 41—228.

—— the lakes of Killarney to the Golden Horn. Field, H. M., *D. D.* N. Y., 1877. 10—57.

—— the clouds to the mountains. Illus. Verne, J. Bost., 1874. 5—31.

—— the earth to the moon. Illus. Verne, J. N. Y., 1874. 5—31.

Frondes Agrestes. Ruskin, J. N. Y., 1875. 18—108.

Frost, John. Pioneer mothers of the west; or, daring and heroic deeds of American women ; comprising thrilling examples of courage, fortitude, devotedness, and self-sacrifice. Illus. Bost., 1875. 40—221.

—— Wild scenes of a hunter's life; or, the hunting and hunters of all nations, including Cumming's and Girard's adventures. Illus. Bost., 1875. 10—57.

Frost, Sarah Annie. Parlor acting charades, intended solely for performance in the drawing-room, and requiring no expensive scenery or properties to render them effective. N. Y., 1876. 41—226.

Frothingham, Octavius Brooks. Transcendentalism in New England : a history. N. Y., 1876. 40—224.

Froude, James Anthony. History of England, from the fall of Wolsey. N. Y., 1867-70. 12 v. 34—204.

——, Short studies on great subjects. N. Y., 1872-77. 3 v. O—2.

—— The English in Ireland in the eighteenth century. N. Y., 1873-74. 3 v. 34—205.

Frozen deep, The. Illus. Collins, W. W. Bost., 1875. 6—38.

Fruits of America, The. Illus. Hovey, C. M. Bost., 1851. Vol 1. V.

Fudge doings. " Ik Marvel." N. Y., 1855. 2 v. 2—11.

Fuller, Thomas. The history of the worthies of England ; with notes by P. A. Nuttall. Lond., 1840. 3 v. 13—75.

Fullerton, *Lady* Georgiana. A stormy life: a novel. Illus. N. Y., 1874. 5—28.

—— Mrs. Gerald's niece: a novel. N. Y., 1872. 5—28.

—— Too strange not to be true: a tale. Illus. N. Y., 1872. 5—28.

—— Reparation, and other tales. Balt., 1875. 41—228.

—— Ellen Middleton: a tale. Balt., n. d. 41—228.

—— Grantley manor: a tale. Balt., 1856. 41—228.

—— Rose Leblanc. N. Y., 1875. 41—228.

—— Lady-bird : a tale. Balt., 1868. 41—228.

Fulton, Robert, The life of. Colden, C. D. N. Y., 1817. 13—74.

Fulton, Robert, The life of. (Library of American biography, vol. 10.) 11—65. Fur country, The. Illus. Verne, J. Bost., 1874. 5—31.

Furber, George C. The twelve months' volunteer; or, journal of a private in the Tennessee regiment of cavalry in the campaign in Mexico, 1846-47, etc.; including a complete history of the war with Mexico. Illus. Cin., 1848. 30—180.

Future civil policy of America, Thoughts on the. Draper, J. W. N. Y., 1865. 26—155.

Gaboriau, Emile. Other people's money. Bost., 1875. 41—230.

Gabriel Vane. Loud, J. N.Y., 1856. P—3.

Gabrielle André. Baring-Gould, S. N. Y., 1871. 5—29.

Gael, Thoughts on the origin and descent of the. Grant, J. Edin., 1814. 34—204.

Gage, Francis Dana. Elsie Magoon; or, the old still-house in the hollow: a tale of the past. Phil., 1867. O—3.

Gale, George. Upper Mississippi; or, historical sketches of the mound-builders, the Indian tribes, and the progress of civilization in the Northwest; from A. D. 1600 to the present time. Illus. Chicago, 1867. 9—53.

Galibert, Léon, et Clément Pellé. Angleterre. (L'Univers.) Paris, 1842-44. 4 v. D. R.

Gallatin, Albert. The right of the United States of America to the northeastern boundary claimed by them, principally extracted from the statements laid before the king of the Netherlands. N. Y., 1840. L.

Gallop among American scenery, A. Silliman, A. E. N. Y., 1843. 8—50.

Galloway, Joseph, late speaker of the house of assembly of Pennsylvania, The examination of, before the house of commons. Lond., 1780. 34—203.

Gamboa, Francisco Xavier de. Commentaries on the mining ordinances of Spain. R. Heathfield, tr. Lond., 1830. 2 v. T.

Garcilaso de la Vega, the Inca. See La Vega, G. de.

Gardiner, Allen F. A visit to the Indians on the frontiers of Chili. Lond., 1841. 17—104.

Gardiner, James, Some remarkable passages in the life of. Doddridge, P. Bost., 1792. 12—72.

Gardiner, Margaret P., Countess of Blessington. A journal of conversations with Lord Byron; with a sketch of the life of the author. Bost., n. d. 27—161.

—— Blindpits: a story of Scottish life. N. Y., 1870. 7—41.

—— Quixstar: a novel. N. Y., 1873. 7—41.

Gardiner, Samuel Rawson. The thirty years' war, 1618-1648. (Epochs of history.) Lond., 1874. 36—215.

—— The first two Stuarts and the Puritan revolution: 1603-1660. (Epochs of history.) Bost., 1876. 34—207.

Gardner, Celia E. Tested; or, hope's fruition: a story of woman's constancy. N. Y. and Lond., 1874. 7—43.

Gardner, Charles K. *A dictionary of all officers who have served in the army of the United States, from 1789 to 1853. N. Y., 1853. 23—132.

Gareth and Lynette. Illus. Tennyson, A. Bost., 1872. 16—99.

Garneau, François Xavier. Histoire du Canada, depuis sa découverte. Quebec, 1852. 3 v. W.

Garrett, Edward, pseud. See Mayo, I. F.

Garrick, David, The private correspondence of, with the most celebrated persons of his time. Lond., 1831. 2 v. S.

Garstang Grange. T. A. Trollope. Phil., n. d. 7—43.

Gaskell, Elizabeth Cleghorn. Wives and daughters: a novel. Illus. N. Y., 1866. 6—35.

—— The life of Charlotte Brontë. N. Y., 1868. 2 v. in one. 13—76.

—— Ruth, and other tales. Illus. Lond., 1873. 41—228.

—— Right at last, and other tales. N. Y., 1860. 41—228.

—— The moorland cottage. N. Y., 1868. 41—227.

—— Cranford. N. Y., 1874. 41—227.

Gass, Patrick. A journal of the voyages and travels of a corps of discovery, under the command of Captains Lewis and

Clarke, from the mouth of the river Missouri to the Pacific ocean, during the years 1804-06. Phil., 1810. 9—50.

Gates ajar, The. Phelps, E. S. Bost., 1869. 6—40.

Gatling guns. Report of the board of officers appointed by special orders No. 108, A. G. O., May 31, 1873. Wash., 1874. T.

Gaudeamus! Humorous poems translated from the German of Joseph Victor Scheffel and others, by Charles G. Leland. Bost., 1872. 17—107.

Gay, John, Poetical works of; with a life of the author, by Dr. Johnson. Bost., 1864. 2 v. 16—97.

Gayarré, Charles E. A. History of Louisiana: the Spanish domination. N. Y., 1854. 31—187.

—— Louisiana: its colonial history and romance. N. Y., 1851-52. 2 v. 31—187.

*Gazetteer, The imperial; a general dictionary of geography. Blackie, W. G. Lond., 1855. 2 v. 21—124.

*——, Complete pronouncing; or, geographical dictionary of the world. Thomas and Baldwin, eds. Revised and enlarged. Phil., 1866. 21—124.

*——, a new and complete, of the United States. Baldwin, T., and J. Thomas. Phil., 1854. 21—124.

*——, A complete descriptive and statistical, of the United States of America. Haskel, D., and J. C. Smith. N. Y., 1850. 21—124.

Geier-Wally: a tale of the Tyrol. Hillern, A. von. N. Y., 1876. 5—33.

Geikie, James. The great ice age, and its relation to the antiquity of man. Illus. N. Y., 1874. 15—89.

Gell, Sir William. Pompeiana. Illus. Lond., 1832. 2 v. 17—102.

—— The topography of Rome and its vicinity. Lond., 1834. 2 v. 9—52.

—— and John P. Gandy. Pompeiana: the topography, edifices, and ornaments of Pompeii. Illus. Lond., 1821. 17—102.

Gemma. Trollope, T. A. Phil., n. d. 7—43.

Gems, A treatise on. Feuchtwanger, L. N. Y., 1838. T.

General history, ancient and modern, Elements of. Tytler, A. F. Concord, N. H., 1851. 32—193.

*—— history of the Turkes, The. Knolles, R. Lond., 1631. 34—203.

—— Lafayette, The life of. Headley, P. C. N. Y., 1859. 11—60.

Generalship; or, how I managed my husband: a tale. Roy, G. Cin., 1875. 3—19.

Genesis of the New England churches, The. Illus. Bacon, L. N. Y., 1874. 32—195.

—— of species, On the. Illus. Mivart, S. G. N. Y., 1871. 14—81.

Genial showman: reminiscences of Artemus Ward. Illus. Hingston, E. P. Lond., 1870. 11—60.

Gentle measures in the management and training of the young. Illus. Abbott, J. N. Y., 1872. 2—11.

Géodésie, Traité de. Puissant, L. Paris, 1842. 2 v. D. R.

Geoffrey Hamlyn, The recollections of. Kingsley, H. Bost., 1869. 7—43.

Geographia classica, with atlas. Butler, S. Phil., 1835. V.

Geographical and geological explorations and surveys west of the one-hundredth meridian. Illus. Wheeler, Lieut. G. M. Wash., 1875. Vols. 3 and 5. D. R.

—— Same; principally in Nevada and Arizona. Wash., 1872. D. R.

—— Same, in Utah, Nevada, and Arizona. D. R.

—— Same: report concerning the determination of the astronomical co-ordinates at Cheyenne and Colorado Springs. Wash., 1874. D. R.

—— Same: report on ornithology. Wash., 1874. D. R.

—— Same: progress report for 1872. Illus. Wash., 1874. D. R.

—— Same: catalogue of plants. Wash., 1874. D. R.

—— Same: Appendix FF of the annual report of the chief of engineers for 1874. Wash., 1874. D. R.

—— Same: report on invertebrate fossils. Wash., 1874. D. R.

—— Same: catalogue of vertebrata of the eocene of New Mexico. Wash., 1875. D. R.

Geographical and geological explorations and surveys west of the one-hundredth meridian: report upon a reconnaissance in Nevada, made in 1869. Wash., 1875. D. R.

—— Same: Appendix LL of the annual report of the chief of engineers for 1875. Illus. Wash., 1875. D. R.

—— Same: geological atlas. Wash., 1874. D. R.

——Same: topographical atlas. Wash., 1874. D. R.

Géographie minéralogique des environs de Paris, Essai sur la. Cuvier, G. L., et A. Brongniart. Paris, 1811. T.

Geological exploration of the fortieth parallel. Illus. King, C. Wash., 1870–76. Vols. 3, 5, and 6. D. R.

—— manual. La Beche, Sir H. T. de. Phil., 1832. 15—91.

—— observer, The. Illus. La Beche, Sir H. T. de. Phil., 1851. 15—91.

—— memoirs, A selection of. Illus. La Beche, Sir H. T. de. Lond., 1836. 15—91.

—— survey of Colorado and New Mexico. Hayden, F. V. Wash., 1869. L.

——survey of Wyoming. Illus. Hayden, F. V. Wash., 1871. L.

—— survey of Montana. Illus. Hayden, F. V. Wash., 1872. L.

—— Same. Illus. Hayden, F. V. Wash., 1873. L.

—— survey of Nebraska. Hayden, F. V. Wash., 1872. L.

—— survey of Canada: report of progress for the years 1853-56. Toronto, 1857. L.

——survey of Canada. Illus. Montreal. Lond., Paris, and N. Y., 1863. L.

—— survey of Wisconsin, Iowa, and Minnesota. Illus. Owen, D. D. Phil., 1852. 2 v. L.

—— report of the S. W. branch, Pacific R. R., in Missouri. Swallow, G. C. St. Louis, 1859. D. R.

—— survey of the State of Missouri, Reports on the; 1855-71. Illus. Jefferson City, 1873. L.

—— survey of Ohio: part 1st, Report of progress in 1869, by J. S. Newberry; part 2d, Report of progress in the second district, by E. B. Andrews; part 3d, Report on the geology of Montgomery

County, by Edward Orton. Illus. Columbus, 1871. L.

—— map of the State of New York. N. Y., 1842. L.

—— survey of Missouri: preliminary report on the iron ores and coal fields from the field work of 1872. Illus. N. Y., 1873. L.

—— survey of Indiana, First annual report of the, made during the year 1869. Indianapolis, 1869. L.

—— survey of the State of Iowa, Report of the. Illus. White, C. A. Des Moines, 1870. 2 v. L.

Géologie appliquée aux arts et à l'agriculture. Orbigny, C. D. d', et A. Gente. Paris, 1851. D. R.

Geology, The wonders of. Illus. Mantell, G. A. Lond., 1848. 2 v. 15—91.

——, The certainties of. Gibson, W. S. Lond., 1840. 15—91.

——, A new system of. Illus. Ure, A. Lond., 1829. 15—91.

——, Principles of. Illus. Lyell, Sir C. Phil., 1837. 2 v. 15—91.

——, Manual of. Illus. Dana, J. D. Phil., 1864. 15—91.

——, An introduction to. Richardson, G. F. Lond., 1851. 15—91.

——, An introduction to. Bakewell, R. New Haven, 1839. 15—91.

——, mineralogy, and theology. Illus. Buckland, W. Lond., 1837. 2 v. 15—91.

—— and mineralogy, Dictionary of. Humble, W. Lond., 1843. 15—91.

——, Lectures on. Van Rensselaer, J. N. Y., 1825. 15—91.

——, Popular. Miller, H. Bost., 1868. 15—91.

—— of Massachusetts. Hitchcock, E. Northampton, 1841. 2 v. L.

——of Tennessee. Safford, J. M. Nashville, 1869. L.

—— applied to the reclamation of land. Rooke, J. Lond, 1840. 15—91.

—— and terrestrial magnetism. Hopkins, E. Illus. Lond., 1865. 15—91.

—— and resources of the region in the vicinity of the forty-ninth parallel. Dawson, G. M. Montreal, 1875. L.

—— and topography of a portion of the Lake Superior land district, in the State of Michigan. Illus. Foster, J. W., and J. D. Whitney. Wash., 1850. D. R.

Geology, Illustrations of surface. (Smithsonian contributions to knowledge.) Phil., 1856. L.

Geologist's text-book. Ansted, D. T. Lond., 1845. T.

Geometry, Elements of. Playfair, J. N. Y., 1854. 15—88.

George the second, Memoirs of the reign of king. Walpole, H. Lond., 1847. 3 v. 34—206.

—— the third, History of the reign of. Hughes, T. S. Lond., 1835-36. 8 v. 34—206.

—— the third, History of the reign of. Bisset, R. Lond., 1803. 6 v. 34—206.

—— the third, Memoirs of the reign of king. Walpole, H. Lond., 1851. 4 v. 34—206.

—— Canterbury's will. Wood, E. P. Phil., n. d. 41—230.

Georgia, A history of. Stevens, W. B. N. Y., 1847. 1st vol. 31—187.

—— scenes, characters, and incidents. Illus. Longstreet, A. B. N. Y., 1854. 2—12.

Georgian era, The: memoirs of the most eminent persons who have flourished in Great Britain, from the accession of George the first to the demise of George the fourth. Lond., 1832-34. 4 v. 13—77.

Gerald Estcourt. Marryat, Miss F. Lond. and N. Y., n. d. 4—22.

—— Fitzgerald. Lever, C. J. N. Y., 1872. 5—29.

Gerda; or, the children of work. Schwartz, M. S. Phil., 1874. 6—38.

Germaine. About, E. Bost., 1860. 6—40.

German emperors, and their contemporaries. History of the. Illus. Peake, E. Phil., 1874. 36—219.

—— in America, The. Bogen, F. W. ron. N. Y., 1856. 27—164.

—— life and manners. Illus. Mayhew, H. Lond., 1865. 10—57.

—— political leaders. Tuttle, H. N.Y., 1876. 40—221.

—— tales. Auerbach, B. Bost., 1869. 2—13.

Germanic empire, History of the. (Lardner's cabinet cyclopædia.) Dunham, S. A. Lond., 1834-35. 3 v. 36—219.

Germany, History of. Menzel, W. Mrs. Geo. Horrocks, tr. Lond., 1848-49. 3 v. 36—219.

Germany, History of. Kohlrausch, J. D. Haas, tr. N. Y., 1853. 36—218.

Gerry, Elbridge, The life of. Austin, J. Bost., 1828. 2 v. 12—68.

Gerstäcker, Frederick. How a bri de was won; or, a chase across the pamp-as. Illus. Francis Jordan, tr. N. Y., 1872. 5—29.

Gesner, Abraham. New Brunswick; with notes for emigrants. Illus. Lond., 1847. 8—49.

Get thee behind me, Satan! Logan, O. N. Y., 1872. 41—228.

Getting on in the world; or, hints on success in life. Mathews, W. Chicago, 1876. 40—223.

Giannone, Pietro. The civil history of the kingdom of Naples. J. Ogilvie, tr. Lond., 1729-31. 2 v. 34—203.

Giant hunting. Cranch, C. P. Illus. Bost., 1860. 38.

Giants and dwarfs. Wood, E. J. Lond. 1868. 2—8.

Gibbes, Robert W. Documentary history of the American revolution. Columbia, S. C., 1853, and N. Y., 1857. 3 v. 31—188.

Gibbs, George. Memoirs of the administrations of Washington and John Adams; edited from the papers of Oliver Walcott. N. Y., 1846. 2 v. 25—149.

Gibbon, Charles. For lack of gold : a novel. N. Y., 1872. 5—28.

Gibbon, Edward. History of the decline and fall of the Roman empire; with notes by the Rev. H. H. Milman. N. Y., 1850. 4 v. 35—211.

Gibson, William Sidney. The certainties of geology. Lond., 1840. 15—91.

Giddings, Joshua Reed. History of the rebellion; its authors and causes. N. Y., 1864. 30—179.

Gieseler, Johann Carl Ludwig. Text-book of ecclesiastical history. F. Cunningham, tr. Phil., 1836. 3 v. 32—196.

Gift, Theodore, pseud. Pretty Miss Bellew: a tale of home life. N. Y., 1876. 41—228.

Gil Blas. Le Sage, A. R. Lond., 1809. v. 2—9.

Gilbart, James William. A practical treatise on banking, with a view of American banking systems, and statistics to 1860, by J. Smith Homans: to which is added "Money;" a lecture by H. C. Carey. Phil., 1860. 15—88.

Gilbert, John, J. D. Watson, and H. Weir. Household tales and fairy stories: a collection of the most popular favorites. Illus. Lond. and N. Y., 1872. 38.

Gilbert Gurney. Hook, T. E. Phil., 1836. 2 v. in one. P—2.

Gilded age, The. Illus. Clemens, S. L., and C. D. Warner. Hartford, 1874. 2—9.

Gilder, Richard Watson. The new day: a poem in songs and sonnets. Illus. N. Y., 1876. 17—106.

Gill, Thomas. The technical repository: containing practical information on subjects connected with discoveries and improvements in the useful arts. Illus. Lond., 1822-27. 11 v. 18—110.

—— Same. 2d series. Lond., 1827-30. 6 v. 18—109.

Gillespie, William Mitchell. A manual of the principles and practice of road-making. N. Y., 1853. T.

Gillet, Ransom H. The federal government: its officers, and their duties. N. Y., 1872. 21—128.

Gillies, John. History of ancient Greece, its colonies and conquests. Lond., 1820. Parts 1 and 2. 8 v. 35—210.

—— Aristotle's Ethics and Politics, comprising his practical philosophy, translated from the Greek; illustrated by introductions and notes; the critical history of his life; and a new analysis of his speculative works. Lond., 1813. 2 v. 28—170.

Gillmore, Parker. Prairie and forest: a description of the game of North America, with personal adventures in their pursuit. Illus. N. Y., 1874. 2—9.

Gilmore, James Roberts, (*Edmund Kirke.*) Among the pines; or,'South in secession time. N. Y., 1862. 2—10.

—— My southern friends. N. Y., 1863. 0—1.

—— Down in Tennessee and back by way of Richmond. N. Y., 1865. 2—13.

Gipsey's prophecy, The. Southworth, E. D. E. N. Phil., 1861. 6—36.

Girls of Feversham, The. Marryat, *Miss* F. Lond. and N. Y., n. d. 4—22.

Girl's romance, A. Robinson, F. W. N. Y., 1872. 5—29.

6 I

Girondists, History of the. Lamartine, A. de. N. Y., 1854. 2 v. 35—213.

Gladstone, William Ewart. Rome and the newest fashions in religion; three tracts;—the vatican decrees; vaticanism; speeches of the pope. N. Y., 1875. 40—225.

—— Homeric synchronism: an inquiry into the time and place of Homer. N. Y., 1876. 40—222.

Glass-making, Wonders of. Illus. Sauzay, A. N. Y., 1872. 28—169.

Glaucus; or, the wonders of the shore. Illus. Kingsley, C. Lond., 1873. 14—83.

Gleanings from the harvest-fields of literature, science, and art. Bombaugh, C. C. Balt., 1860. 2—10

Gleig, George Robert. Memoirs of the life of the Right Honorable Warren Hastings, first governor-general of Bengal. Lond., 1841. 3 v. 12—67.

—— Campaigns of the British army at Washington and New Orleans in the years 1814-15. Lond., 1847. 30—179.

Glossary of terms used in Grecian, Roman, Italian, and Gothic architecture. Illus. Turner, T. H. Oxford, 1850. 3 v. 15—90.

Godman, John D. American natural history, and the rambles of a naturalist; with a biographical sketch of the author. Illus. Phil., 1846. 2 v. in one. 14—83.

God-man; or, search and manifestation. Townsend, L. T. Bost., 1872. E.

Godolphin. Bulwer-Lytton, *Sir* E. Phil., 1869. 5—33.

Godwin, William. Mandeville: a tale of the seventeenth century in England. Edin., 1817. 3 v. P—2.

—— Adventures of Caleb Williams. N. Y., 1870. P—2.

—— History of the commonwealth of England, from its commencement to the restoration of Charles the second. Lond., 1824-28. 4 v. 33—198.

Goethe, Johann Wolfgang von. Wilhelm Meister's apprenticeship. R. D. Boylan, tr. Lond., 1870. 6—40.

—— Dramatic works: containing Faust, Iphigenia in Tauris, Torquato Tasso, and Egmont, Anna Swanwick, tr.; and Goetz von Berlichingen with the iron hand, *Sir* Walter Scott, tr. Lond., 1870. 2—11.

—— Novels and tales; containing Elective affinities, The sorrows of Werther, German emigrants, The good women, and A nouvelette. Lond., 1871. 2—11.

——, the autobiography of; truth and poetry from my own life. J. Oxenford, and *Rev.* A. J. W. Morrison, trs. Lond. 1868—71. 2 v. 12—72.

—— Correspondence with a child. Bost., 1868. 2—12.

—— Faust: a tragedy. C. T. Brooks, tr. Bost., 1869. 16—100.

—— Hermann and Dorothea. Ellen Frothingham, tr. Bost., 1870. 16—100.

——, Poems and ballads of. W. E. Aytoun and T. Martin, trs. N. Y., 1871. 17—106.

Goethe and Schiller: an historical romance. Illus. "Louise Mühlbach." N. Y., 1873. 4—21.

Gold and name. Schwartz, M. S. Bost., 1872. 5—28.

—— diggings, Sixteen months at the. Woods, D. B. N. Y., 1851. 9—50.

—— Elsie. "E. Marlitt." Phil., 1876. 7—42.

—— mines, Six months in the. Buffum, E. G. Phil., 1850. 17—101.

Golden grain: a sequel to "Blade-o'-grass." Illus. Farjeon, B. L. N. Y., 1874. 6—35.

—— legion, The. Longfellow, H. W. Bost., 1859. 16—95.

—— lion of Grandpère, The. Illus. Trollope, A. N. Y., 1872. 5—28.

Gold-foil, hammered from popular proverbs. Holland, J. G. N. Y., 1872. 3—18.

Goldsmith, Oliver. History of England, from the earliest times, to the death of George the second. Lond., 1819. 4 v. 33—198.

—— History of Greece, from the earliest state, to the death of Alexander the great. Lond., 1823. 2 v. 35—209.

—— History of Rome, from the foundation of the city of Rome to the destruction of the Western empire. Edin., 1812. 2 v. 35—211.

——, works of, with his life, by Waller. Lond. and N. Y., n. d. 2—7.

——, Life of, by Irving. N. Y., 1853. 3—19.

Goldsmith, Oliver. The Vicar of Wakefield; with a memoir by the *Rev.* R. A. Willmott. Lond., n. d. 5—33.

Good fight, A. Illus. Reade, C. N. Y., 1871. 7—42.

—— investment, A. Flagg, W. N. Y., 1872. 6—35.

"—— luck!" "E. Werner." Bost., 1874. 4—21.

—— match, A. Perrier, A. N. Y., 1873. 6—38.

"**Good-bye**, sweetheart!" Broughton, R. N. Y., 1872. 4—23.

Goodrich, Charles A. The family encyclopædia; or, compendium of useful knowledge. Illus. New edition by J. R. Bigelow, *M. D.* N. Y., 1860. 23—138.

Gordian knot, The. Brooks, C. S. N. Y., 1868. 5—28.

Gordon, Lucy Austin, *Lady Duff*. Last letters from Egypt ; to which are added letters from the Cape; with a memoir by her daughter, *Mrs.* Ross. Lond., 1875. 9—53.

Gordon, Thomas F. The history of New Jersey, from its discovery by Europeans, to the adoption of the federal constitution. Trenton, 1834. 31—189.

Gorton, John. *A general biographical dictionary. Lond., 1838. 3 v. 23—139.

Gorton. Samuel, Life of. (Library of American biography, vol. 15.) 11—65.

Gosse, Philip Henry. Life in its lower, intermediate, and higher forms; or, manifestations of the divine wisdom in the natural history of animals. Illus. N. Y., 1857. 14—85.

Gough, John B., Autobiography and personal recollections of; with twenty-six years' experience as a public speaker. Illus. Springfield, *Mass.*, 1870. 11—59.

Gould, Jeanie T. Marjory's quest. Illus. Bost., 1872. 4—26.

Govinda Sámanta. Day, L. B. Lond., 1874. 3—16.

Grace Lee. Kavanagh, J. N. Y., 1872. 7—41.

Graham, Catharine, (formerly Macaulay, Catharine.) History of England. Lond., 1746. 2 v. 33—197.

Graham, John A. Memoirs of John Horne Tooke; together with his valuable speeches and writings: also containing proofs identifying him as the author of the celebrated letters of Junius. N. Y., 1828. 19—117.

Grahame, James. The history of the United States of North America, from the plantation of the British colonies till their assumption of national independence. Phil., 1850. 2 v. 29—176.

—— an inquiry into the principle of population, etc. Edin., 1816. 14—84.

*Grammar of ornament. Jones, O. Lond., n.d. 14—80.

—— of the language of the Lenni Lenape, or, Delaware Indians. Zeisberger, D. Phil., 1827. L.

Grant, James. Thoughts on the origin and descent of the Gael; with an account of the Picts, Caledonians, and Scots; and observations relative to the authenticity of the poems of Ossian. Edin., 1814. 34—204.

Grant as a soldier and statesman. Illus. Howland, E. Lond., 1868. 11—60.

——, Ulysses S., Military history of. Badeau, A. N. Y., 1868. Vol. 1. 11—59.

—— and his campaigns. Illus. Coppée, H. N. Y., 1866. 11—59.

Grantley manor: a tale. Fullerton, *Lady* G. Balt., 1856. 41—228.

Granville De Vigne. "Onida." Phil., 1871. 7—44.

Gray, Asa. Manual of botany of the Northern United States, including Virginia, Kentucky, and all east of the Mississippi. Illus. N. Y., 1867. 15—90.

—— Darwiniana: essays and reviews pertaining to Darwinism. N. Y., 1876. 14—81.

Gray, John. Lectures on the nature and use of money. Edin., 1848. 15—92.

Gray, Robertson. Brave hearts: a novel. Illus. N. Y., 1873. 7—42.

Graydon, Alexander. Memoirs of his own time; with reminiscences of the men and events of the revolution. J. S. Littell, ed. Phil., 1846. 29—176.

Great Britain, History of. Miller, J. R. Lond., 1829. 34—206.

—— Britain, The history of progress in. Illus. Philp, R. K. Lond., 1859. 33—198.

—— Britain, Public works of. Illus. J. W. Simms, ed. Lond., 1846. V.

Great Britain. An impartial collection of the great affairs of state. Nalson, J. Lond., 1682. 2 v. 34—203.

—— expectations. Illus. Dickens, C. N. Y., 1868. 2 copies. 3—15 and 16.

—— ice age, The. Illus. Geikie, J. N. Y., 1874. 15—89.

—— lady: a romance. Illus. Van Dewall, M. Phil., 1874. 5—28.

—— rebellion, The. Headley, J. T. Hartford, 1867. 2 v. in one. 30—180.

—— reformation of the sixteenth century, The history of the. D'Aubigne, J. H. M. Hartford, 1850-53. 5 v. in three. 32—196.

—— truths by great authors: a dictionary of aids to reflection. Phil., 1856. 27—161.

Grecian and roman geography, An introduction to the study of. Long, G., and R. Dunglison. Charlottesville, *Va.*, 1829. 15—87.

Greece, History of. Grote, G. N, Y., 1853. 12 v. 35—211.

——, History of. Goldsmith, O. Lond., 1823. 2 v. 35—209.

——, History of. Mitford, W. Lond., 1838. 8 v. 35—210.

——, History of. Thirlwall, C. N. Y., 1848-51. 2 v. 35—209.

——, Ancient. Heeren, A. H. L. Lond., 1847. 35—209.

——, History of the manners and customs of ancient. St. John, J. A. Lond., n. d. 3 v. in one. 35—209.

——, History of ancient. Gillies, J. Lond., 1820. Parts 1 and 2. 8 v. 35—210.

—— and Russia, Travels in. Taylor, J. B. N. Y., 1870. 17—103.

——, Rambles and studies in. Illus. Mahaffy, J. P. Lond., 1876. 9—53.

*Greek and Roman biography and mythology, A dictionary of. Smith, W. Bost. and Lond., 1849. 3 v. 22—132.

—— and Roman antiquities, A dictionary of. Illus. Smith, W. Lond., 1848. 22—132.

*Greek-English lexicon. Liddell, H. G., and R. Scott. N. Y., 1848. 23—137.

Greeks and the Persians, The. (Epochs of History.) N. Y., 1876. 35—209.

—— of to-day, The. Tuckerman, C. K. N. Y., 1872. 17—103.

Greeley, Horace. The American conflict: a history of the great rebellion in the United States of America, 1860-64. Illus. N. Y., 1865-67. 2 v. 30—178.'

—— Recollections of a busy life; including reminiscences of American politics and politicians. Illus. N. Y., 1868. 11—60.

——, The life of. Ingersoll. Illus. Chicago, 1873. 11—59.

Green, John Rich. A short history of the English people. N. Y., 1876. 34—207.

—— Stray studies from England and Italy. N. Y., 1876. 40—222.

Green, Thomas J. Journal of the Texian expedition against Mier, subsequent imprisonment of the author, his sufferings, and final escape. Illus. N. Y., 1845. 8—49.

Green gate, The: a romance. Wichert, E. Phil., 1875. 41—229.

—— Mountain boys, The. Thompson, D. P. Bost., 1871. 2 v. in one. O—1.

Greene, Nathaniel, Memoirs of the life and campaigns of. Caldwell, C. Phil., 1819. 12—70.

——, Life of. (Library of American biography, v. 20.) 11—65.

Greenhow, Robert. The history of Oregon and California, and the other territories on the northwest coast of North America, from their discovery to the present day. Bost., 1847. 31—187.

Greenough, Sarah D. In extremis: a novelette. Bost., 1872. O—3.

Greenwood, Grace, *pseud.* See Lippincott, *Mrs.* S. J.

Greenwood, James. Legends of savage life. Illus. N. Y. and Lond., n. d. 39.

—— The seven curses of London. Bost., 1869. 19—114.

—— Low-life deeps: an account of the strange fish to be found there. Illustrated by A. Concanen. Lond., 1876. 2—12.

Greg, Thomas. A system for managing heavy and wet lands without summer fallows. Lond., 1841. V.

Greg, William Rathbone. Enigmas of life. Bost., 1874. 28—169.

—— Rocks ahead; or, the warnings of Cassandra. Bost., 1875. 40—222.

Gregg, Josiah. Commerce of the prairies; or, the journal of a Santa Fé trader. Illus. N. Y., 1864. 2 v. 2—13.

Gregory, John. A complete course of civil engineering. Lond., n. d. 15—97.

Gregory, Olinthus. A treatise of mechanics, theoretical, practical, and descriptive. Lond., 1826. 3 v.; 2 of text, and 1 of plates. 15—89.

—— Mathematics for practical men. 3d edition, revised and enlarged, by Henry Law. Lond., 1848. Q—1.

Grenville, George Nugent Temple, *Lord.* Some memorials of John Hampden, his party and his times. Illus. Lond., 1832. 2 v. 13—75.

Grenville papers, The. Smith, W. J. Lond., 1852-53. 4 v. T.

Greville, Charles Cavendish Fulke. A journal of the reigns of king George the fourth, and king William the fourth. Henry Reeve, ed. N. Y., 1875. 2 v. 34—207.

—— Same, (Bric-a-brac series, vol. 5.) N. Y., 1875. 11—61.

Grey, *Mrs.* E. C. Cousin Harry. Phil., n. d. O—2.

Grierson, James. Saint Andrews as it was and as it is; being the third edition of Dr. Grierson's delineations. Illus. St. Andrews, 1838. 33—202.

Grif: a story of Australian life. Farjeon, B. L. N. Y., 1874. 6—35.

Griffin, Frederick. Junius discovered. Bost., 1854. 19—117.

Griffin, John Joseph. A system of crystallography, with its application to mineralogy. Glasgow, 1841. 15—91.

—— A practical treatise on the use of the blow-pipe. Glasgow, 1827. 15—92.

Griffith Gaunt. Reade, C. Bost., 1871. 2 copies. 7—42.

Griffith, Thomas W. Sketches of the early history of Maryland. Balt., 1821. 31—189.

Grigg, John. Southern and Western songster: being a choice collection of the most fashionable songs. Phil., 1858. 16—100.

Grimm, Herman. Life of Michael Angelo. Fanny E. Bunnett, tr. Bost., 1869. 2 v. 12—69.

Guy Mannering. Scott, Sir W. Bost., 1868. 3—17.
—— Rivers: a tale of Georgia. Illus. Simms, W. G. N. Y., 1855. 41—229.

Guyot, Arnold. The earth and man: lectures on comparative physical geography, in its relation to the history of mankind. C. C. Felton, tr. Bost., 1855. 14—83.

Gwilt, Joseph. *An encyclopædia of architecture, historical, theoretical, and practical. Illus. Lond., 1842. 15—90.

Habberton, John. Helen's babies. Bost., 1876. 2 copies. 41—227.
—— The Barton experiment. N. Y., 1877. 41—227.

Habersham, Alexander W. My last cruise; or, where we went and what we saw; being an account of visits to the Malay and Loo Choo islands, the coasts of China, Formosa, Japan, Kamtschatka, Siberia, and the mouth of the Amoor River. Illus. Phil., 1857. 17—101.

Habitations of man in all ages, The. Illus. Viollet-le-Duc, E. E. Bost., 1876. 14—80.

Habits of men. Doran, J. N. Y., 1865. 19—114.

Hadermann, Jeanette R. Against the world. Bost., 1873. 4—22.

Hadley, James. Introduction to Roman law; in twelve academical lectures. N. Y., 1874. 19—114.

Haeckel, Ernst Heinrich. The history of creation; or, the development of the earth and its inhabitants by the action of natural causes: a popular exposition of the doctrine of evolution in general, and of that of Darwin, Goethe, and Lamarck in particular. Illus. N. Y. 1876. 2 v. 40—223.

Hague, James D. Mining industry; with geological contributions by Clarence King. Illus. Wash., 1870-71 Vols. 3 and 5. D. R.

Hakluyt, Richard. Collection of the early voyages, travels, and discoveries of the English nation. Lond., 1809-12. 5 v. 8—47.

Hale, Edward Everett. His level best, and other stories. Bost., 1873. 5—34.
—— Sybaris, and other homes. Bost., 1869. 27—162.
—— The Ingham papers: some memorials of the life of Capt. Frederic Ingham, U. S. N., sometime pastor of the first Sandemanian church in Naguadavick, and major general by brevet in the patriot service in Italy. Bost., 1869. 5—34.
—— If, yes, and perhaps: four possibilities and six exaggerations, with some bits of fact. Bost., 1874. 5—34.
—— Workingmen's homes: essays and stories. Bost., 1874. 27—162.
—— Ten times one is ten: the possible reformation, a story in nine chapters, by Col. Frederic Ingham. Bost., 1872. 5—34.
—— How to do it. Bost., 1872. 27—162.
—— Christmas eve and Christmas day: ten Christmas stories. Bost., 1874. 5—34.
—— Ups and downs: an every-day novel. Bost., 1873. 5—34.
—— Our new crusade: a temperance story. Bost., 1875. 5—34.
—— The fall of the Stuarts, and Western Europe, from 1678 to 1697. (Epochs of history.) N. Y., n. d. 32—193.
—— Philip Nolan's friends: a story of the change of western empire. N. Y., 1877. 41—227.

Half a million of money: a novel. Edwards, A. B. N. Y., 1873. 6—38.

Half-hours with the stars. Proctor, R. A. Lond., 1871. 14—80.
—— with the best authors. Knight, C. Lond., 1866. 4 v. 2—10.
—— with the best letter-writers and autobiographers. Knight, C. Lond. and N. Y., n. d. 2 v. 2—10.

Haliburton, Thomas Chandler. The clock-maker; or, the sayings and doings of Samuel Slick, of Slickville. Phil., 1838. 2—13.
—— The attaché; or, Sam Slick in England. N. Y., n. d. 3—20.

Halkett, John. Historical notes respecting the Indians of North America; with remarks on the attempts to convert and civilize them. Lond., 1825. 30—178.

Hall, Benjamin H. History of eastern Vermon^ ^ ^ts earliest settlement to the close of the eighteenth century; with a biographical chapter and appendixes. Illus. N. Y., 1858. 30—183.

Hall, James. Notes on the western States. Phil., 1838. 29—177..

Hall, Louisa Jane. Joanna of Sicily, queen of Naples and countess of Provence. Lond., 1824. 2 v. 13—74.

Hall, Anna Maria. Sketches of Irish character. Illus. Lond., n. d. 2—10.

Hall, William W. How to live long; or, health maxims, physical, mental, and moral. N. Y., 1875. 40—222.

Hallam, Henry. View of the state of Europe during the middle ages. Lond., 1846-48. 3 v. 26—156.

—— The constitutional history of England, from the accession of Henry the seventh, to the death of George the second. N. Y., 1873. 2 v. 27—161.

—— Introduction to the literature of Europe, in the fifteenth, sixteenth, and seventeenth centuries. Lond., 1847. 3 v. 27—161.

Halleck, Fitz-Greene, The poetical writings of, with extracts from those of Joseph Rodman Drake. James Grant Wilson, ed. N. Y., 1873. 17—105.

——, The life and letters of. Wilson, J. G. N. Y., 1869. 12—66.

Halliwell, James Orchard. *A dictionary of archaic and provincial words, obsolete phrases, proverbs, and ancient customs, from the fourteenth century. Lond., 1847. 2 v. 23—137.

Hamerton, Philip Gilbert. Chapters on animals. Illus. Bost., 1874. 39.

—— The unknown river. Illus. Bost., 1872. 28—165.

—— A painter's camp, in England, in Scotland, in France. Bost., 1873. 17—103.

—— Thoughts about art. Bost., 1874. 28—165.

—— The intellectual life. Bost., 1873. 28—166.

—— The sylvan year: leaves from the note-book of Raoul Du Bois. Bost., 1876. 40—222.

—— Round my house : notes of a rural life in France, in peace and war. Bost., 1876. 40—222.

Hamerton, Philip Gilbert. Wenderholme : a story of Lancashire and Yorkshire. Bost., 1876. 41—227.

Hamilton, Alexander, The works of; published by order of the Joint Library Committee of Congress. J. C. Hamilton ed. N. Y., 1851. 7 v. 25—148.

——, Jay, and Madison. The Federalist on the new constitution, written in 1788, with an appendix, containing the letters of " Pacificus " and " Helvidius " on the proclamation of neutrality of 1793; also the original articles of confederation, and the constitution of the United States. Hallowell, 1852. 28—165.

—— Same, with the Continentalist and other papers by Hamilton. J. C. Hamilton, ed. Phil., 1864. 28—165.

Hamilton, Lady Anne. Secret history of the court of England, from the accession of George the third to the death of George the fourth; including the mysterious death of the princess Charlotte. Lond., 1832. 2 v. in one. 33—200.

Hamilton, Gail, *pseud*. See Dodge, M. Abigail.

Hamilton, Sir William, *Prof*. Lectures on metaphysics. H. L. Mansel and J. Veitch, eds. Bost., 1869. 15—88.

—— Discussions on philosophy and literature, education, and university reform. N. Y., 1868. 14—84.

—— Lectures on logic. *Rev*. H. L. Mansel and J. Veitch, *M. A.*, eds. Bost., 1867. 14—82.

Hammer and anvil. Spielhagen, F. N.Y., 1870. 6—36.

Hammond, Samuel H., and L. W. Mansfield. Country margins and rambles of a journalist. N. Y., 1855. 17—104.

Hammond, William Alexander, *M. D.* Spiritualism and allied causes and conditions of nervous derangement. Illus. N. Y., 1876. 14—84.

Hampden, John, Some memorials of. Illus. Nugent, *Lord*. Lond., 1832. 2 v. 13—75.

Hamst, Olphar. *Hand-book of fictitious names ; being a guide to authors chiefly in the lighter literature of the nineteenth century, who have written under assumed names; and to literary forgers, impostors, plagiarists, and imitators. Lond., 186?. 23—166.

Hand and glove: a novel. Edwards, A. B. N. Y., 1875. 6—38.

—— of Ethelberta, The. Hardy, T. N. Y., 1876. 4—24.

Handy Andy: a tale of Irish life. Lover, S. Lond., n. d. 2 copies. 7—45.

Hanging of the crane, The. Illus. Longfellow, H. W. Bost., 1875. 17—105.

Hannah. Muloch, D. M. N. Y., 1872. 4—83.

—— Thurston. Taylor, J. B. N. Y., 1868. 5—34.

Hans Breitmann's ballads. Leland, C. G. Phil., 1871. 16—95.

Hansard, George Agar. The book of archery; being the complete history and practice of the art, ancient and modern ; with an account of the existing toxophilite societies. Illus. Lond., 1841. 2—9.

Hansard, T. C. The art of printing; its history and practice, from the days of John Gutenberg. Edin., 1851. 14—80.

Happy thoughts. Burnand, F. C. Bost., 1872. 2—13.

Happy-thought Hall. Illus. Burnand, F. C. Bost., 1872. 2—13.

Harbour bar The: a tale of Scottish life. N. Y., 1875. 41—227.

Hard cash. Illus. Reade, C. N. Y., 1873. 5—28.

—— times. Illus. Dickens, C. N. Y., 1868. 2 copies. 3—15 and 16.

Hardwick, Charles. Christ and other masters : an historical inquiry into some of the chief parallelisms and contrasts between Christianity and the religious systems of the ancient world, with special reference to prevailing difficulties and objections. F. Procter, ed. Lond., 1874. E.

Hardy, Thomas. Desperate remedies: a novel. N. Y., 1874. 4—24.

—— Under the greenwood tree: a rural painting of the Dutch school. N. Y., 1874. 5—30.

—— A pair of blue eyes : a novel. N. Y., 1874. 5—30.

—— Far from the madding crowd. N. Y., 1874. 5—30.

Hardy, Thomas. The hand of Ethelberta : a comedy in chapters. N. Y., 1876. 4—24.

Hare, Augustus J. C. Days near Rome. Illus. Phil., 1875. 2 v. in one. 17—102.

—— Memorials of a quiet life ; with an introduction by F. D. Huntington. N. Y., n. d. 2 v. 41—229.

Hargrave, Francis. Jurisconsult exercitations. Lond., 1813. Vol. 3. D. R.

Harland, Marion, *pseud.* See Terhune, M. V.

Harold. Bulwer-Lytton, *Sir* E. N. Y., 1869. 5—33.

—— a drama. Tennyson, A. Bost., 1877. 17—106.

Harris, John. The pre-Adamite earth : contributions to theological science. Bost., 1856. 14—81.

Harris, Miriam Coles. Rutledge. N. Y., 1875. 41—228.

—— Richard Vandermarck : a novel. N. Y., 1871. 41—228.

Harris, Thaddeus Mason. The journal of a tour into the territory northwest of the Allegheny mountains in 1803. Bost., 1805. 10—58.

—— Biographical memorials of James Oglethorpe, founder of the colony of Georgia. Bost., 1841. 11—62.

Harris, Thaddeus William. A treatise on some of the insects of New England which are injurious to vegetation. Cambridge, 1842. 14—83.

Harrison, Gabriel. The life and writings of John Howard Payne, the author of " Home, Sweet Home," the tragedy of Brutus, and other dramatic works. Albany, 1875. 11—59.

Harry Heathcote of Gangoil, and Lady Anna. Trollope, A. N. Y., 1874. 5—28.

—— Lorrequer. Lever, C. J. Phil., n. d. 5—20.

Harsha, David A. Lives of Rev. James Hervey and Rev. George Whitefield. Albany, 1866. 13—76.

Hart, John. A practical treatise on the construction of oblique arches. Illus. Lond., 1839. T.

Harte, Francis Bret. The luck of Roaring Camp, and other sketches. Bost., 1871. 3—19.

Harte, Francis Bret. East and west poems. Bost., 1871. 16—100.

—— Mrs. Skagg's husbands, and other sketches. Bost., 1873. 3—19.

——, The poetical works of. Illus. Bost., 1875. 17—106.

—— Condensed novels. Illus. Bost., 1873. 3—19.

—— Echoes of the foot-hills. Bost., 1875. 17—106.

—— Tales of the Argonauts, and other sketches. Bost., 1875. 3—19.

Harte, Walter. The history of the life of Gustavus Adolphus, king of Sweden, sirnamed the great. Lond., 1759. 2 v. 13—73.

Hartford convention, Otis's letters in defence of the. Bost., 1824. 29—177.

—— convention, History of the. Dwight, T. N. Y., 1833. 29—177.

Hartmann, Moritz. The last days of a king: a historical romance. M. E. Niles, tr. Phil., 1867. 4—24.

Hartwig, George. The subterranean world. Illus. N. Y., 1871. 14—83.

—— The aerial world: a popular account of the phenomena and life of the atmosphere. Illus. N. Y., 1875. 40—225.

Harvard university, The history of. Quincy, J. Cambridge, 1840. 2 v. 29—175.

Harveys. The. Kingsley, H. Berlin and Phil., 1872. 7—43.

Haskel, Daniel, and J. C. Smith. *A complete descriptive and statistical gazetteer of the United States of America. N. Y., 1850. 21—124.

Haskoll, W. Davis. The assistant engineer's railway guide in boring. Illus. Lond., 1846. T.

Hassaurek, Friedrich. Four years among Spanish Americans. N. Y., 1868. 17—104.

Hasselt, A. van. Belgique et Hollande. (L'Univers.) Paris, 1844. D. R.

Hastings, Warren, Memoirs of the life of. Gleig, G. R. Lond., 1841. 3 v. 12—67.

Hauff, Wilhelm. Arabian days' entertainments. Illus. H. P. Curtis, tr. Bost., 1871. 6—38.

Haunted homestead, The. Southworth, E. D. E. N. Phil., 1860. 6—37.

—— hearts. Cummins, M. S. Bost., 1869. 6—38.

Haunted tower, The. Wood, E. P. Phil., n. d. 41—230.

Haupt, Herman. General theory of bridge construction; containing demonstrations of the principles of the art, and their application to practice. N. Y., 1851. 15—87.

Hawaiian islands, The. Illus. Anderson, R. Boston, 1864. 17—101.

Hawkins, John H. W., Life of. Compiled by his son, Rev. William George Hawkins. Bost., 1863. Q—2.

Hawks, Francis L. Narrative of an expedition to the China seas and Japan, in the years 1852-54, by Commodore M. C. Perry, U. S. N. Illus. Wash., 1856. 3 v. 8—47.

Hawthorne, Julian. Bressant: a novel. N. Y., 1873. 3—14.

—— Saxon studies. Bost., 1876. 10—57.

—— Idolatry: a romance. Bost., 1874. 41—229.

Hawthorne, Nathaniel. True stories from history and biography. Bost., 1866. 3—18.

—— Passages from the American note-books. Bost., 1868. 2 v. 3—18.

—— The house of seven gables. Bost., 1868. 3—18.

—— The scarlet letter: a romance. Illus. Bost., 1875. 3—18.

—— Our old home; a series of English sketches. Bost., 1868. 3—18.

—— Mosses from an old manse. Bost., 1868. 2 v. 3—18.

—— Tanglewood tales; a second wonder-book. Illus. Bost., 1868. 3—18.

—— Twice-told tales. Bost., 1868. 2 v. 3—18.

—— The marble faun; or, the romance of Monte Beni. Bost., 1868. 2 v. 3—18.

—— The snow-image, and other twice-told tales. Bost., 1868. 3—18.

—— Septimius Felton; or, the elixir of life. Bost., 1872. 3—18.

—— The Blithedale romance. Bost., 1852. 3—18.

—— A study of. Lathrop, G. P. Bost., 1876. 40—221.

Hay, Elzey, pseud. See Andrews, F.

Hay, John. Pike County ballads, and other pieces. Bost., 1873. 17—106.

Hay, John. Castilian days. Bost., 1872. 17—102.

——, and Clara F. Guernsey, Margaret Hosmer, Harriet Prescott Spofford, Lucy H. Hooper, etc. Not pretty but precious, and other short stories. Illus. Phil., 1874. 5—28.

Hay, Mary Cecil. Old Myddleton's money : a novel. N. Y., 1875. 41—230.

Hayden, Ferdinand Vandever. * Sunpictures of Rocky Mountain scenery, with a description of the geographical and geological features, and some account of the resources of the Great West. N. Y., 1870. 9—51.

—— Preliminary field report of the United States geological survey of Colorado and New Mexico. Wash., 1869. L.

—— Preliminary report of the United States geological survey of Wyoming, and portions of contiguous territories. Wash., 1871. L.

—— Preliminary report of the United States geological survey of Montana, and portions of adjacent territories. Wash., 1872. L.

—— Sixth annual report of the United States geological survey of the territories, embracing portions of Montana, Idaho, Wyoming, and Utah ; being a report of progress of the explorations for the year 1872. Wash., 1873. L.

—— Annual report of the United States geological and geographical survey of the territories, embracing Colorado : a report of progress of the explorations for the year 1873. Wash., 1874. L.

—— Annual report of the United States geological and geographical survey of the territories, embracing Colorado and parts of adjacent territories : a report of progress of the exploration for the year 1874. Wash., 1876. L.

—— Birds of the Northwest : a handbook of the ornithology of the region drained by the Missouri river and its tributaries. Cones, E. Miscellaneous publications, No. 3. Wash., 1874. L.

—— Final report of the United States geological survey of Nebraska, and portions of the adjacent territories. Wash., 1872. L.

Hayden, Ferdinand Vandever. Contributions to the ethnography and philology of the Indian tribes of the Missouri valley. Phil., 1862. V.

Haydn, Joseph. * Dictionary of dates relating to all ages and nations, for universal reference. B. Vincent, ed. N. Y., 1872. 23—138.

Haydon, Benjamin Robert, Life, letters, and table talk of. Illus. (Sans Souci series.) N. Y., 1876. 40—221.

Hayes, Isaac Israel. The open polar sea : a narrative of a voyage of discovery toward the north pole. Illus. N. Y., 1869. 17—103.

—— An arctic boat journey, in the autumn of 1854. Illus. Bost., 1871. 9—53.

—— Cast away in the cold : an old man's story of a young man's adventures, as related by Capt. John Hardy,·mariner. Illus. Bost., 1872. 39.

Hayes, Rutherford B., Sketch of the life and character of. Howells, W. D. N. Y., 1876. 40—222.

Hayward, John. A gazetteer of Massachusetts, containing descriptions of all the counties, towns, and districts in the commonwealth ; also, of its principal mountains, rivers, capes, bays, harbors, islands, and fashionable resorts ; to which are added statistical accounts of its agriculture, commerce, ·and manufactures ; with a great variety of other useful information. Illus. Bost., 1849. 30—182.

—— A gazetteer of New Hampshire, containing descriptions of all the counties, towns, and districts in the State ; also of its principal mountains, rivers, waterfalls, harbors, islands, and fashionable resorts ; to which are added statistical accounts of its agriculture, commerce, and manufactures ; with a great variety of useful information. Illus. Bost., 1849. 30—183.

Hazard, Samuel. The register of Pennsylvania ; devoted to the preservation of facts and documents, and every other kind of useful information respecting the State. Phil., 1828–35. 8 v. X.

—— United States commercial and statistical register ; from July, 1839, to Jan., 1842. Phil., 1840–41. 5 v. 18—108.

Hazel-Blossoms. Whittier, J. G. Bost., 1875. 17—106.

Hazen, William Babcock. The school and the army in Germany and France; with a diary of siege life at Versailles. N. Y., 1872. 2—8.

Hazlitt, William. The life of Napoleon Buonaparte. Lond., 1852. 4 v. 11—61.

"He cometh not, she said:" a novel. Thomas, A. N. Y., 1875. 5—28.

—— knew he was right. Illus. Trollope, A. N. Y., 1870. 5—28.

—— would be a gentleman. Lover, S. Lond., n. d. 7—45.

Head of the family, The. Muloch, D. M. N. Y., 1873. 5—28.

Headley, Joel Tyler. The great rebellion. Hartford, 1863. 2 v. in one. 30—180.

—— Washington and his generals. N. Y., 1875. 2 v. in one. Q—2.

Headley, Phineas Camp. The life of the empress Josephine, first wife of Napoleon. N. Y., 1856. 11—61.

—— The life of General Lafayette. N. Y., 1850. 11—60.

—— The island of fire; or, a thousand years of the old Northmen's home:— 874-1874. Illus. Bost., 1875. 36—215.

Headship of Christ, The. Miller, H. Bost., 1868. 27—161.

Headsman. Illus. Cooper, J. F. N. Y., 1864. 3—14.

Health and education. Kingsley, C. N. Y., 1874. Q—2.

—— trip to the tropics. Willis, N. P. N. Y., 1853. 17—102.

Healy, Mary. A summer's romance. Bost., 1872. P—3.

Heart of Mid-Lothian. Scott, Sir W. Bost., 1869. 3—17.

Hearts and hands. "Christian Reid." N. Y., 1875. 5—28.

Heartsease; or, the brother's wife. Illus Yonge, C. M. N. Y., 1875. 5—30.

Heat as a mode of motion. Illus. Tyndall, J. N. Y., 1869. 15—88.

——, The phenomena and laws of. Illus. Cazin, A. N. Y., 1874. 28—169.

Heaven and hell. Swedenborg, E. Rev. S. Noble, tr. N. Y., 1872. 1—4.

——, The expanse of. Proctor, R. A. N. Y., 1874. 14—82.

Heavens, The. Illus. Guillemin, A. N. Y., 1872. 3—14.

——, The wonders of the. Illus. Flammarion, C. N. Y., 1874. 28—169.

——, The mechanism of the. Illus. Olmstead, D. Lond., 1850, 14—85.

Heck, J. G. * Iconographic encyclopædia of science, literature, and art. Illus. S. F. Baird., ed. and tr., N. Y., 1851. 4 v., text; 2 v., plates. Q—1.

Hedged in. Phelps, E. S. Bost., 1870. 6—40.

Hedley, John. A practical treatise on the working and ventilation of coalmines; with suggestions for improvements in mining. Lond., 1851. T.

Heeren, Arnold, H. L. A manual of ancient history, particularly with regard to the constitutions, the commerce, and the colonies of the states of antiquity. Lond., 1847. 32—193.

—— Ancient Greece; with three historical treatises. Geo. Bancroft, tr. Lond., 1847. 35—209.

—— Historical researches into the politics, intercourse, and trade of the principal nations of antiquity. Lond., 1846. 2 v. 33—201.

—— Historical researches into the politics, intercourse, and trade of the Carthagenians, Ethiopeans, and Egyptians. Lond., 1850. 33—201.

Heidenmauer, The. Illus. Cooper, J. F. N. Y., 1867. 3—14.

Heine, Heinrich. Book of songs. C. G. Leland, tr. N. Y., 1874. 17—106.

——, Pearls from. Illus. Phil., 1865. N.

——, Scintillations from the prose works of. S. A. Stern, tr. N. Y., 1873. 4—22.

—— prose miscellanies from. S. L. Fleishman, tr. Phil., 1876. 41—227.

Heir of Redclyffe, The. Yonge, C. M. N. Y., 1871. 2 v. 5—30.

—— to Ashley, The. Wood, E. P. N.Y., n. d. 5—29.

Held in bondage; or, Granville De Vigne: a tale of the day. "Ouida." Leip., 1873. 2 v. in one. 41—226.

Helen's babies. Habberton, J. 2 copies. Bost., 1876. 41—227.

Helps, Sir Arthur. Friends in council: a series of readings and discourse thereon. N. Y., 1869. 2 v. in one. 28—170.

Helps, Sir Arthur. Realmah. Lond., 1869. 3—18.

—— Casimir Maremma. Bost., 1871. 0—1.

—— Essays written in the intervals of business; to which is added an essay on organization in daily life. Bost., 1872. 28—165.

—— Brevia: short essays and aphorisms. Bost., 1871. 28—165.

—— Conversations on war and general culture. Bost., 1871. 28—165.

—— Companions of my solitude. Bost., 1870. 28—165.

—— Social pressure. Bost., 1875. 19—115.

Hemans, Felicia, Poetical works of; with a memoir by Mrs. L. H. Sigourney. Illus. Bost., 1864. 16—94.

Henderson, James. A history of the Brazil. Illus. Lond., 1821. 35—209.

Henrietta Temple. Disraeli, B. Lond., 1871. 4—24.

Henry, Caleb Sprague. About men and things: papers from my study table drawer. N. Y., 1873. 19—114.

Henry, John Joseph. An accurate and interesting account of the hardships and sufferings of that band of heroes who traversed the wilderness, in the campaign against Quebec, in 1775. Lancaster, 1812. 30—179.

Henry Dunbar. Illus. Braddon, M. E. N. Y., n. d. 5—20.

—— Esmond, The history of. Illus. Thackeray, W. M. Lond., 1869. 5—32.

—— of Monmouth. Tyler, J. E. Lond., 1838. 2 v. 12—67.

—— the eighth and his court. Illus. "Louise Mühlbach." N. Y., 1871. 4—21.

Henry, Patrick, Life of. (Library of American biography, vol. 11.) 11—65.

——, Sketches of the life and character of. Wirt, W. N. Y., 1860. 13—76.

Hentz, Caroline Lee. Ernest Linwood; or, the inner life of the author. Phil., 1869. 4—25.

Her dearest foe: a novel. Alexander, Mrs. N. Y., 1876. 7—44.

—— face was her fortune: a novel. Robinson, F. W. N. Y., 1875. 5—29.

—— good name: a novel. Bouveire, J. F. Lond., 1875. 3 v. in one. 6—40.

—— lord and master. Marryat, Miss F. Lond. and N. Y., n. d. 4—22.

Her majesty the queen: a novel. Cooke, J. E. Phil., 1873. 4—26.

Herbert, George, Poetical works of; with a memoir of the author, by the Rev. R. A. Willmot. Bost., 1864. 16—97.

Herbert, Henry William, (Frank Forrester.) Fish and fishing of the United States and British provinces of North America. Illus. N. Y., 1859. 2—9.

—— Wager of battle: a tale of Saxon slavery in Sherwood Forest. N. Y., 1855. P—3.

—— The cavaliers of England; or, the times of the revolutions of 1642 and 1688. N. Y., 1852. 27—161.

—— The captains of the old world, as compared with the great modern strategists. N. Y., 1852. 13—76.

—— The fair Puritan: an historical romance of the days of witchcraft. Phil., 1875. 41—228.

Here and hereafter; or, the two altars. Athern, A. Bost. and Lond., 1858. 4—26.

Hereward, the last of the English. Kingsley, C. Bost., 1866. 7—43.

Heriot, George. Travels through the Canadas; with a comparative view of the manners and customs of several of the Indian nations of North and South America. Lond., 1807. 8—47.

Hermann Agha. Palgrave, W. G. N. Y., 1872. 7—46.

—— and Dorothea. Goethe, J. W. von. Bost., 1870. 16—100.

Hermit in Philadelphia, The, by Peter Atall. Waln, R. Phil., 1821. 2—12.

Hermits, The. Illus. Kingsley, C. Lond., n. d. 11—60.

Hernando Cortés, the conqueror of Mexico, Dispatches of, addressed to the emperor Charles the fifth. G. Folsom, tr. N. Y. and Lond., 1843. 32—192.

Hero, A; and other tales. Muloch, D. M. N. Y., 1872. 4—23.

—— Carthew. Parr, L. N. Y., 1873. 4—25.

—— of the pen, A. "E.Werner." Bost., 1875. 41—230.

Herodotus, An analysis and summary of. Wheeler, J. T. Lond., 1852. 35—210.

Herodotus, An analysis and summary of. Rev. W. Beloe, tr. Lond., 1830. 3 v. 13—79.

Heroes, The. Illus. Kingsley, C. Lond., 1468. 38.

—— of Asgard. Illus. Keary, A. Lond., 1871. 38.

—— of the war for the Union, The. Ferree, P. V. Cin., 1864. 24—143.

Heroism. (Little classics, vol. 11.) Bost., 1875. 5—33.

Herrera, Antonio de. Descripcion de las Indias occidentales. Mad., 1730. , 4 v. D. R.

—— *Novus orbis sive descriptio Indiæ Occidentalis. Amstelodami, 1622. D. R.

Herrick, Robert. Hesperides; or, the works, both humane and divine, of. Bost., 1856. 2 v. 16—97.

Hertz, Henrik. King René's daughter: a Danish lyrical drama. T. Martin, tr. N. Y., n. d. 17—106.

Hervey, James. Meditations and contemplations. Phil., n. d. 28—170.

——, Life of. Harsha, D. A. Albany, 1866. 13—76.

Hesiod, Poetical works of. C. A. Elton, tr. Lond., 1832. 17—107.

Hesperides. Herrick, R. Bost., 1856. 2 v. 16—97.

Hesperus. Richter, J. P. F. Bost., 1865. 2 v. 7—41.

Hester Howard's temptation: a soul's story. Warfield, C. A. Phil., 1875. 7—41.

Hickey, William. The constitution of the United States of America. Phil., 1854. 21—125.

Hidden chains. Marryat, Miss F. Lond., 1876. 3 v. 4—22.

—— life, and other poems, A. Mac-Donald, G. N. Y., 1872. 17—106.

Hide and seek. Collins, W. W. Phil., n. d. 5—28.

Higginson, Thomas Wentworth. Oldport days. Illus. Bost., 1873. 19—115.

—— Army life in a black regiment. Bost., 1870. 19—115.

—— Malbone: an Oldport romance. Bost, 1871. P—2.

—— Out-door papers. Bost., 1871. 19—115.

—— Atlantic essays. Bost., 1871. 19—115.

Higginson, Thomas Wentworth. English statesmen. N. Y., 1875. 40—222.

High mills, The. Illus. Saunders, K. Phil., 1872. 5—28.

Higham, Mary R. Cloverly. N. Y., 1875. 41—226.

Highlands and the Highland clans, A history of the. Illus. Browne, J. Glas., 1838. 4 v. 34—203.

Hildreth, Richard. The history of the United States of America, from the adoption of the American constitution to the end of the sixteenth Congress. N. Y., 1851-60. 3 v. 29—174.

—— History of the United States, from the discovery of the continent to the organization of government under the federal constitution. N. Y., 1849-60. 3 v. 29—174.

—— Japan as it was and is. Bost., 1855. 17—104.

Hildreth, Samuel Prescott. Biographical and historical memoirs of the early pioneer settlers of Ohio; with narratives of incidents and occurrences in 1775; with a biographical notice of the author, by R. J. Meigs. Cin., 1852. 13—73.

—— Pioneer history; being an account of the first examinations of the Ohio valley and the early settlement of the Northwest territory. Cin., 1848. 29—176.

Hill, A. F. Secrets of the sanctum: an inside view of an editor's life. Phil., 1875. 40—222.

Hill, Britton A. Liberty and law under federative government. Phil., 1874. 27—161.

Hill, Octavia. Homes of the London poor. Lond., 1875. 19—116.

Hill, Thomas. The true order of studies. N. Y., 1876. 19—116.

Hillern, Wilhelmine von. By his own might: a romance. Phil., 1872. 6—38.

—— Only a girl; or, a physician for the soul: a romance. Mrs. A. L. Wister, tr. Phil., 1872. 6—38.

—— A twofold life. M. S., tr. Phil., 1873. 6—38.

—— Geier-Wally: a tale of the Tyrol. N. Y., 1876. 5—33.

Hills of the Shatemuc, The. "Elizabeth Wetherell." Phil., 1873. 7—42.

Hillyars and the Burtons, The. Kingsley, H. Bost., 1866. 7—43.

Hind, Henry Youle. Narrative of, the Canadian Red River exploring expedition of 1857; and of the Assinniboine and Saskatchewan exploring expedition of 1858. Illus. Lond., 1860. 2 v. 8—48.

Hincs, Gustavus. Oregon and its institutions; comprising a full history of the Willamette University, the first established on the Pacific coast. Illus. N, Y., 1868. 31—181.

Hingston, Edward P. The genial showman; being reminiscences of the life of Artemus Ward. Illus. Lond., 1870. 11—60.

Hinton, John Howard: History of the United States of America, from the earliest period to the present time. Illus. n. d. 6 v. 29—175.

Hirell: a novel. Saunders, J. N. Y., 1870. 5—29.

His level best. Hale, E. E. Bost., 1873. 5—34.

—— natural life: a novel. Clarke, M. C. N. Y., 1876. 41—230.

—— two wives. Ames, M. C. N. Y., 1676. 41—229.

Histoire ancienne. Millot, C. F. Paris, 1819. 3 v. D. R.

—— moderne. Millot, C. F. Paris, 1819. 4 v. D. R.

—— des Antilles, et des colonies Françaises, Espagnoles, Auglaises, Danoises, et Suédoises, Regnault ; suite des États-Unis, Regnault et Labaume ; Possessions Anglaises dans l'Amérique du Nord, La Croix ; Les Californies, etc., Denis. (L'Univers.) Paris, 1849. D. R.

Historical and dramatic works. Schiller, F. Lond., 1871. 2 v. 36—218.

—— and critical essays. De Quincey, T. Bost., 1859. 2 v. 2—12.

—— dramas. Schiller, F. Lond., 1870. 2—11.

—— essays. Mahon, Lord. Lond., 1861. Q—2.

—— essays. Thierry, J. N. A. Phil., 1845. 27—150.

—— essays. Freeman, E. A. Lond. and N. Y., 1873. 40—222.

—— gleanings, A legacy of. Illus. Bonney, C. V. R. Albany, 1875. 2 v. 40 — 224.

—— memoirs of my own time. Wraxall, Sir N. W. Lond., 1815. 2 v. 36—220.

Historical research respecting the opinions of the founders of the republic on negroes as slaves, as citizens, and as soldiers. Livermore, G. Bost., 1863. T.

—— researches among the Carthagenians, Ethiopians, and Egyptians. Heeren, A. H. L. Lond., 1850. 33—201.

—— researches into antiquity. Heeren, A. H. L. Lond., 1846. 2 v. 33—201.

—— view of the literature of the south of Europe. Sismondi, J. C. L. de. Lond., 1850. 2 v. 28—170.

—— atlas. Labberton, R. H. Phil., 1872. 33—197.

—— questions. Labberton, R. H. Phil., 1872. 33—197.

History and chronology, The every-day book of. Munsell, J. N. Y., 1858. 32—192.

—— and antiquities of every town in Massachusetts, Historical collections of the. Illus. Barber, J. W. Worcester, 1844. 30—183.

—— General sketch of. Freeman, E. A. N. Y., 1876. 40—221.

—— , philosophically illustrated. Miller, G. Lond., 1849. 4 v. 33—199.

—— of the captivity of Napoleon at St. Helena. Forsyth, W. N. Y., 1853. 2 v. 11—61.

—— of ten years, 1830-40. Blanc, L. Lond., 1844-45. 2 v. 35—213.

—— of the hen fever. Illus. Burnham, G. P. Bost., 1855. 2—10.

—— of prince Perrypets. Illus. Knatchbull-Hugessen, L. Lond., 1872. 39.

—— of the processes of manufacture and uses of printing, gas-light, pottery, glass, and iron. Illus. (From the Encyclopædia Britannica.) N. Y., 1864. 14—85.

—— of a mouthful of bread, The. Macé, J. N. Y., 1874. 15—88.

—— , Outlines of. Labberton. R. H. Phil., 1872. 33—197.

Hitchcock, Edward. Geology of Massachusetts. Northampton, 1841. 2 v. L.

—— Illustrations of surface geology. (Smithsonian contributions to knowledge.) Phil., 1856. L.

Hitherto: a story of yesterdays. Whitney, A. D. T. Bost. 1869. 7—44.

Hoadly, Charles J. The public records of the colony of Connecticut. Hartford, 1868–73. 3 v. 30—181.

Hoefer, Ferdinand. Afrique australe, orientale, et centrale, et l'empire de Maroc. (L'Univers.) Paris, 1848. D. R.

Höfer, Edmund. The old countess: a novel. Phil., 1870. 3—16.

Hoffman, David. Chronicles selected from the originals of Cartaphilus, the Wandering Jew; embracing a period of nearly nineteen centuries. Lond., 1853. 2 v. 26—156.

Hogarth, William. * The complete works of; in a series of one hundred and fifty superb engravings on steel from the original pictures; with an introductory essay by James Hannay, and descriptive letter-press by the *Rev.* J. Trusler and E. F. Roberts. Lond. and N.Y., n. d. N.

Hohensteins, The. Spielhagen, F. N. Y., 1870. 6—36.

Holbeach, Henry. Shoemakers' village. Lond., 1871. 2 v. in one. P—3.

Holden with the cords. Jay, W. M. L. N. Y., 1874. 6—33.

Holland, Josiah Gilbert. Kathrina: her life and mine, in a poem. N. Y., 1869. 16—96.

—— Bitter sweet: a poem. N. Y., 1868. 16—96.

—— Plain talks on familiar subjects: a series of popular lectures. N. Y., 1872. 3—18.

—— Lessons in life: a series of familiar essays by Timothy Titcomb. N. Y., 1872. 3—18.

—— Gold-foil, hammered from popular proverbs, by Timothy Titcomb. N. Y., 1872. 3—18.

—— Letters to the Joneses. Timothy Titcomb. N. Y., 1872. 3—18.

—— Miss Gilbert's career: an American story. N. Y., 1872. 3—18.

—— The bay-path: a tale of New England colonial life. N. Y., 1872. 3—18.

—— The marble prophecy, and other poems. N. Y., 1872. 16—96.

—— The mistress of the manse. N. Y., 1874. 17—105.

—— Arthur Bonnicastle: an American novel. Illustrated by Mary A. Hallock. N. Y., 1874. 3—18.

Holland, Josiah Gilbert. Sevenoaks: a story-of to-day. Illus. N.Y., 1875. 3—18.

Holland, Saba Smith, *Lady.* A memoir of the Rev. Sydney Smith; with a selection from his letters, edited by *Mrs.* Austin. N. Y., 1855. 2 v. 11—64.

Holland, William M. The life and political opinions of Martin Van Buren. Hartford, 1835. 11—64.

Hollister, H. Contributions to the history of the Lackawanna valley. N. Y., 1857. 31—189.

Holmes, Abiel. Annals of America, from the discovery by Columbus, in the year 1492, to the year 1826. Cambridge, 1829. 2 v. 29—176.

Holmes, Edward. The life of Mozart, including his correspondence. N. Y., 1845. 11—64.

Holmes, Mary J. Marian Grey; or, the heiress of Redstone Hall. N. Y. and Lond., 1871. P—1.

—— West Lawn and the rector of St. Mark's. N. Y. and Lond., 1874. 7—42.

—— Edna Browning; or, the Leighton homestead: a novel. N. Y. and Lond., 1874. 7—42.

Holmes, Oliver Wendell. The autocrat of the breakfast-table; every man his own Boswell. Bost., 1865. 2—13.

—— The professor at the breakfast-table. 2—10.

—— The poet at the breakfast-table. Bost., 1872. 2—11.

—— Astrea: the balance of illusions; a poem delivered before the Phi-Beta-Kappa Society of Yale College, Aug. 14, 1850. Bost., n. d. 16—100.

—— Border-lines of knowledge in some provinces of medical science: an introductory lecture. Bost., 1862. 15—89.

—— Songs in many keys. Bost., 1864. 17—106.

—— The poems of. Bost., 1872. 17—106.

—— Mechanism in thought and morals: an address delivered before the Phi-Beta-Kappa Society of Harvard University, June 29, 1870, with notes and afterthoughts. Bost., 1871. 27—162.

—— Elsie Venner: a romance of destiny. Bost., 1874. 2 v. in one. 4—23.

—— The guardian angel. Bost., 1872. 4—23.

Holmes, Oliver Wendell. Soundings from the Atlantic. Bost., 1872. 2—10.

Holst, H. *von.* The constitutional and political history of the United States; 1750 to 1833: State sovereignty and slavery. J. J. Lalor and A. B. Mason, trs. Chicago, 1876. 40—224.

Holstein, H. L. V. Ducoudray. Memoirs of Simon Bolivar, president liberator of the republic of Colombia, and his principal generals. Bost., 1829. 12—68.

Holton, Isaac F. New Granada: twenty months in the Andes. Illus. N. Y., 1857. 9—51.

Holy Bible, The. Oxford, 1856. E.
—— land, In the. Illus. Thompson, A. Lond., 1874. 17—101.
—— war, The. Illus. Bunyan, J. N. Y., 1866. 28—167.

Holyoake, George Jacob. The history of co-operation in England: its literature and its advocates: the pioneer period, 1812 to 1844. Phil., 1875. Vol. 1. 18—108.

Homans, J. Smith, and J. S. Homans, jr. *A cyclopædia of commerce and commercial navigation. N. Y., 1858. 21—128.

Home, The. Bremer, F. Phil., n. d. P—1.
—— fairy tales. Illus. Macé, J. N. Y., 1870. 38.
—— influence. Aguilar, G. N. Y., 1872. 5—34.
—— of Washington; or, Mount Vernon and its associations. Illus. Lossing, B. J. N. Y., 1870. 26—155.
—— ; or, life in Sweden, and Strife and peace. Bremer, F. Lond., 1853. P—1.
—— as found: sequel to "Homeward bound." Illus. Cooper, J. F. N. Y., 1870. 3—14.
—— scenes and heart studies. Aguilar, G. N. Y., 1870. 5—34.
—— sketches in France, and other papers. Field, *Mrs.* H. M. N. Y., 1875. 10—57.

Homer. The Odyssey;.with the Hymns, Epigrams, and Battle of the frogs and mice, literally translated. T. A. Buckley. N. Y., n. d. 27—163.
——, The Odyssey of, translated into English blank verse by William Cullen Bryant. Bost., 1873. 2 v. 17—106.

Homer, Works of. A. Pope, tr. Lond., 1833. 3 v. 17—107.
—— Iliad; reduced into English blank verse, by the *earl of Derby.* N. Y., 1869. 2 v. 16—96.

Homeric synchronism. Gladstone, W. E. N. Y., 1876. 40—222.

Homes for the people. Illus. Wheeler, G. N. Y., 1868. 15—90.
—— of American statesmen. Illus. Hartford and Lond., 1855. 2—9.
—— of the London poor. Hill, O. Lond., 1875. 19—116.
—— without hands: a description of the habitations of animals. Illus. Wood, J. G. N. Y., 1874. 15—90.

Homeward bound. Illus. Cooper, J. F. N. Y., 1865. 3—14.

Honduras, Explorations and adventures in. Illus. Wells, W. V. N. Y., 1857. 9—51.

Hood, Thomas, The prose works of. E. Sargent, ed. N. Y., 1865. 3 v. P—2.
——, Complete poetical works of. N. Y., 1869. 3 v. 16—96.
—— Tylney Hall. N. Y., 1873. 6—36.

Hook, Theodore Edward. Gilbert Gurney. Phil., 1836. 2 v. in one. P—2.

Hooke, Nathaniel. Roman history, from the building of Rome to the ruin of the commonwealth. Lond., 1830. 6 v. 35—212.

Hookham, Mary Ann. The life and times of Margaret of Anjou, queen of England and France; and of her father René " the good," king of Sicily, Naples, and Jerusalem; with memoirs of the houses of Anjou. Illus. Lond., 1872. 2 v. 13—76.

Hoosier schoolmaster, The. Illus. Eggleston, E. N. Y., 1871. 7—45.

Hope deferred. Pollard, E. F. N.Y., 1872. 5—28.

Hopes and fears; or, scenes from the life of a spinster. Yonge, C. M. N. Y., 1873. 5—30.

Hopkins, Evan. Geology and terrestrial magnetism. Illus. Lond., 1865. 15—91.

Hopkins, Livingston. A comic history of the United States. Illus. N. Y., 1876. 41—227.

Hopkins, Mark. The law of love, and love as a law; or, moral science, theoretical and practical. N. Y., 1869. E.
—— Strength and beauty : discussions for young men. N. Y., 1874. E.

Horace Templeton. Lever, C. J. Phil., n. d. 5—29.

Horæ lyricæ. Watts, I. Bost., 1864. 16—97.

Horatius Flaccus, Quintus, (Horace,) Works of, P. Francis, tr.; with the various odes translated by Ben Jonson, Cowley, Milton, Dryden, Pope, Addison, Swift, Bentley, Chatterton, Wakefield, Porson, and Byron. Lond., 1831. 2 v. 17—107.

Horne, Thomas Hartwell. An introduction to the study of bibliography; to which is prefixed a memoir on the public libraries of the antients. Illus. Lond., 1814. 2 v. 28—170.

Horrors of Paris, The: sequel to "Mohicans of Paris." Dumas, A. D. ., n. d. 3—20

Horry, P , and M. L. Weems. The life of Gen. Francis Marion, a celebrated partisan officer of the revolutionary war, against the British and tories in South Carolina and Georgia. Illus. Phil., 1860. 13—76.

Horse-shoe Robinson. Kennedy, J. P. N. Y., 1872. 6—39.

Hospital sketches. Illus. Alcott, L. M. Bost., 1872. 5—31.

Hostages to fortune: a novel. Illus. Braddon, M. E. N. Y., 1875. 5—29.

Hough, Franklin B. A history of St. Lawrence and Franklin counties, New York, from the earliest period to the present time. Illus. Albany, 1853. 31—190.
—— A history of Lewis county, in the State of New York, from the beginning of its settlement to the present time. Illus. Albany, 1860. 31—190.
—— A history of Jefferson county, in the State of New York, from the earliest period to the present time. Illus. Albany, 1854. 31—190.

Hours of exercise in the Alps. Illus. Tyndall, J. N. Y., 1873. 15—89.

House of Russell, Historical memoirs of the. Illus. Wiffin, J. H. Lond., 1833. 2 v. 33—200.

House of Austria, History of. Coxe, W. Lond., 1847. 3 v. 36—218.
—— of Israel, The. Illus. "Elizabeth Wetherell." N. Y., 1872. 7—42.
—— of seven gables. Hawthorne, N. Bost., 1868. 3—18.
—— in town, The: a sequel to "Opportunities." "Elizabeth Wetherell." N.Y., 1872. 7—42.

Household of Bouverie. Warfield, C. A. N. Y., 1860. 2 v. 7—41.
—— tales and fairy stories. Illus. Gilbert, J., and others. Lond. and N. Y., 1872. 38.

Houses of Lancaster and York, with the conquest and loss of France. (Epochs of history.) Gairdner, J. N. Y., 1875. 36—215.

Houstoun, Mrs. M. C. Texas and the gulf of Mexico ; or, yachting in the new world. Illus. Lond., 1844. 2 v. 17—104.

Hovey, C. M. The fruits of America ; containing richly-colored figures, and full descriptions of all the choicest varieties cultivated in the United States. Bost., 1851. Vol. 1. V.

How a bride was won. Illus. Gerstäcker, F. N. Y., 1872. 5—29.
—— he won her: a sequel to "Fair play." Southworth, E. D. E. N. Phil., 1869. 6—36.
—— I found Livingstone. Illus. Stanley, H. M. N. Y., 1872. 10—56.
—— Liza loved the king. "George Eliot." Bost., 1869. 16—100.
—— the world was peopled. Fontaine, E. N. Y., 1872. 15—89.
—— to do it. Hale, E. E. Bost., 1872. 27—162.
—— to lay out a garden. Illus. Kemp, E. N. Y., 1860. 15—90.
—— to live long. Hall, W. W. N. Y., 1875. 40—222.

Howadji in Syria. Curtis, G. W. N. Y., 1867. 17—104.

Howard, Blanche Willis. One summer. 2 copies. Bost., 1875. 5—33.

Howard, George William Frederick, earl of Carlisle. Diary in Turkish and Greek waters. Illus. C. C. Felton, ed. Bost., 1855. 17—102.

Howe, Henry. Historical collections of Ohio; containing a collection of the most

7 I

interesting facts, traditions, biographical sketches, anecdotes, etc., relating to its general and local history; with descriptions of its counties, principal towns, and villages. Illus. Cin., 1847. 31—185.

Howells, W. D. Venetian life. N. Y., 1867. 17—104.

—— Italian journeys. N. Y., 1867. 17—104.

—— Poems. Bost., 1873. 17—107.

—— Their wedding journey. Illus. Bost., 1874. 2—8.

—— Suburban sketches. Illus. Bost., 1872. 2—8.

—— A chance acquaintance. Bost., 1873. 5—34.

—— A foregone conclusion. Bost., 1875. 5—31.

—— Sketch of the life and character of Rutherford B. Hayes: also a biographical sketch of William A. Wheeler, with portraits. N. Y., 1876. 40—222.

Howison, Robert R. A history of Virginia, from its discovery and settlement by Europeans, to the present time. Phil., 1846-48. 2 v. 31—188.

Howland, Edward. Grant as a soldier and statesman : being a succinct history of his military and civil career. Illus. Lond., 1868. 11—60.

Howland, Marie. Papa's own girl : a novel. N. Y., 1874. 7—41.

Huc, Evariste Régis. A journey through the Chinese empire. N. Y., 1855. 2 v. 9—54.

Hudibras, and other poems. Butler, S. Lond., 1835. 2 v. 17—107.

Hudson, Charles. History of the town of Lexington, Middlesex County, Massachusetts, from its first settlement to 1868, with a genealogical register of Lexington families. Illus. Bost., 1868. 30—182.

Hudson, Frederic. Journalism in the United States, from 1690 to 1872. N. Y., 1873. 36—215.

Hudson, Henry, Life of. (Library of American biography, vol. 10.) 11—65.

Huggins, William. On the results of spectrum analysis applied to the heavenly bodies: a discourse delivered at Nottingham, before the British Associa-

tion, Aug. 24, 1866. Illus. Lond., 1866. 14—82.

Hughes, Thomas. The practice of making and repairing roads ; of constructing foot-paths, fences, and drains. Lond., 1838. T.

Hughes, Hon. Thomas. School-days at Rugby, by an old boy. Illus. Bost., 1869. 2—11.

—— Tom Brown at Oxford : a sequel to "School-days at Rugby." Bost., 1869 2 v. 2—11.

—— The scouring of the white horse; or, the long vacation ramble of a London clerk. Illus. Lond., 1859. O—3.

Hughes, Thomas Smart. History of the reign of George the third. Lond., 1835-36. 8 v. 34—206.

Hughes, William. An atlas of classical geography, constructed by William Hughes and edited by George Long; with a sketch of classical geography, and other additions. N. Y., 1856. 19—113.

Hugo, Victor. The man who laughs. Wm. Young, tr. N. Y., 1869. 4—21.

—— Les misérables : a novel. N. Y., 1869. 2 v. in one. 6—35.

—— Napoleon, the little. Lond., 1852. 11—61.

—— Ninety-three. F. L. Benedict, tr. N. Y., 1874. 7—41.

Huguenot family, The. Tytler, S. N. Y., 1868. P—2.

Huguenots in France after the revocation of the edict of Nantes. Smiles, S. N. Y., 1874. 35—213.

Hulda; or, the deliverer: a romance. Lewald, F. Phil., 1874. 7—43.

Human intellect, The. Porter, N. N. Y., 1869. 15—92.

—— race, The. Illus. Figuier, L. N.Y., 1872. 15—89.

—— race, here and hereafter, The hopes of the. Cobbe, F. P. N. Y., 1876. 40—222.

Humble, William. Dictionary of geology and mineralogy. Lond., 1843. 15—91.

Humboldt, Friedrich Heinrich Alexander von. Personal narrative of travels to the equinoctial regions of America, during the years 1799-1804. Thomasina Ross, tr. Lond., 1852. 3 v. 8—50.

Humboldt, Friedrich Heinrich Alexander *von*. Letters of, to Varnhagen von Ense; from 1827 to 1858. F. Kapp, tr. N. Y., 1860. 27—162.

—— Cosmos : a sketch of a physical description of the universe. E. C. Otté, tr. Lond., 1849-52. 4 v. 14—82.

—— Essai politique sur le royaume de la Nouvelle-Espagne. Paris, 1811. 2 v. U ; and atlas, X.

—— Atlas géographique et physique du royaume de la Nouvelle-Espagne. Paris, 1812. X. Texte, U.

—— Asie centrale : recherches sur les chaînes de montagnes et la climatologie comparée. Paris, 1843. 3 v. W.

—— Recueil d'observations astronomiques, d'opérations trigonométriques, et de mesures barométriques, faites pendant le cours d'un voyage aux régions équinoxiales du nouveau continent, depuis 1799 jusqu'en 1803. Paris, 1810. 2 v. D. R.

Hume, David. History of England from the invasion of Julius Cæsar to the revolution in 1688. Lond., 1848. 6 v. 33—198.

Humors of Falconbridge, The. Illus. Kelley, J. F. Phil., 1856. 2—8.

Humphreys, Henry Noel. *A history of the art of printing, from its invention to its wide-spread development in the middle of the sixteenth century ; preceded by a short account of the origin of the alphabet, and of the successive methods of recording events before the invention of printing. Illus. Lond., 1868. 14—80.

Humphry Clinker, The expedition of. Smollett, T. Lond., 1872. 41—229.

Hunt, Charles Havens. Life of Edward Livingston. N. Y., 1864. 11—60.

Hunt, Helen Maria. See Jackson, H. M.

Hunt, Richard M. Designs for the gateways of the southern entrances to the Central Park. Illus. N. Y., 1866. V.

Hunter, John D. Memoirs of a captivity among the Indians of North America, from childhood to the age of nineteen ; with anecdotes descriptive of their manners and customs. Lond., 1823. 10—58.

Hutchinson, Anne, Life of. (Library of American biography, vol. 16.) 11—65.

Hutchinson, Thomas. The history of the colony of Massachusetts Bay, from the first settlement thereof, in 1628, until its incorporation with the colony of Plymouth, province of Maine, 1691. Bost., 1764. 3 v. 30—182.

Hutton, Charles. Tracts on mathematical and philosophical subjects. Lond., 1812. 3 v. Q—1.

Hutton, Richard Holt. Essays in literary criticism : Goethe and his influence ; Nathaniel Hawthorne ; Arthur Hugh Clough ; Wordsworth and his genius ; George Eliot ; Matthew Arnold. Phil., n. d. 40—222.

Huxley, Thomas Henry. On the origin of species ; or, the causes of the phenomena of organic nature : a course of six lectures to workingmen. N. Y., 1872. 14—81.

——, and William Jay Youmans. The elements of physiology and hygiene. Illus. N. Y., 1866. 15—88.

Hyde, John, *jr.* Mormonism : its leaders and designs. N. Y., 1857, 27—162.

Hydraulic and other machines. Ewbank, T. N. Y., 1850. 15—92.

—— engineering, The principles and practice of. Dwyer, J. Dub., 1852. 15—87.

Hydraulics, A treatise on. Aubuisson de Voisins, J. F. D. Bost., 1852. 15—92.

——, Tracts on. Illus. T. Tredgold, ed. Lond., 1836. T.

Hypatia. Kingsley, C. Bost., 1870. 7—43.

Hyperion. Longfellow, H. W. Bost., 1865. 6—36.

I go a-fishing. Prime, W. C. N. Y., 1874. 8—49.

Iceland, A journey to ; and travels in Sweden and Norway. Pfeiffer, I. N. Y., 1852. 17—101.

—— and Lapland, A winter in. Dillon, A. Lond., 1840. 2 v. 17—103.

*Iconographic encyclopædia of science, literature, and art. Plates. Heck, J. G. N. Y., 1851. 2 v. Text, 4 v. 14—80.

Ida May. Langdon, M. Bost., 1854. P—1.

Ingelow, Jean. Stories told to a child. 1st and 2d series. Illus. Bost., 1866. 2 v. 39.

—— Mopsa, the fairy. Illus. Bost., 1871. 38.

—— Poor Matt; or, the clouded intellect. Bost., 1869. 39.

—— Off the Skelligs: a novel. Bost., 1872. 6—38.

—— Poems. Bost., 1869. 2 v. 16—99.

—— Fated to be free: a novel. Bost., 1875. 41—228.

Ingersoll, Charles Jared. History of the second war between the United States of America and Great Britain. Phil., 1852. Vol. 1. 31—186.

Ingersoll, Lurton Dunham. Iowa and the rebellion: a history of the troops furnished by the State to the armies of the Union. Phil., 1866. 31—186.

—— The life of Horace Greeley, founder of the New York Tribune, with extended notices of many of his contemporary statesmen and journalists. Illus. Chicago, 1873. 11—59.

Ingham papers, The. Hale, E. E. Bost., 1869. 5—34.

Ingo, first of "Our forefather" series. Freytag, G. N. Y., 1873. 6—38.

Ingoldsby, Thomas, *pseud*. See Barham, R. H.

Ingoldsby legends, The. Illus. Barham, R. H. N. Y., 1872. 17—105.

Ingraban, second of "Our forefather" series. Freytag, G. N. Y., 1873. 6—38.

Ingraham, Joseph Holt. The throne of David. Illus. Phil., 1860. 4—25.

—— The pillar of fire; or, Israel in bondage. Phil., 1860. 4—25.

—— The prince of the house of David; or, three years in the holy city. Phil., 1860. 4—25.

Ingraham, William. See Kip, W. I.

Initials, The. Tautphœus, J. M. Phil., n. d. 6—36.

Inman, Thomas. Ancient faiths embodied in ancient names; or, an attempt to trace the religious belief, sacred rites and holy emblems of certain nations by an interpretation of the names given to children by priestly authority, or assumed by prophets, kings and hierarchs. Illus. N. Y. and Lond., 1869-74. 2 v. 39—195.

Innocents abroad, The. Illus. "Mark Twain." Hartford, 1871. 2—9.

Inquisition, History of the. Illus. Rule, W. H. Lond., 1874. 2 v. 32—192.

Insect world, The. Illus. Figuier, L. N. Y., 1872. 14—83.

Insectivorous plants. Illus. Darwin, C. N. Y., 1875. 14—81.

Insects at home. Illus. Wood, J. G. Phil., 1873. 19—116.

—— of New England, A treatise on some of the. Harris, T. W. Cambridge, 1842. 14—83.

Institutes of ecclesiastical history. Mosheim, J. L. *von*. N. Y., 1851. 3 v. 32—196.

Insurrection in the four western counties of Pennsylvania, History of the. Findley, W. Phil., 1796. 31—189.

—— in the western parts of Pennsylvania, Incidents of the. Brackenridge, H. H. Phil., 1795. 31—189.

Intellectual development of Europe, History of the. Draper, J. W. N. Y., 1869. 28—165.

—— life, The. Hamerton, P. G. Bost., 1873. 25—165.

Intelligence, On. Taine, H. A. N. Y., 1872. 28—165.

—— of animals, The. Illus. Menault, E. N. Y., 1872. 28—169.

Interest tables. Oates, G. N. Y., 1851. Q—1.

International monthly magazine of literature, science and art. 1850-52. Illus. N. Y. 5 v. 20—120.

Introduction to the literature of Europe. Hallam, H. Lond., 1847. 3 v. 27—161.

Invasion of France in 1814. Illus. Erckmann, E., and A. Chatrian. N. Y., 1871. 5—31.

Inventions, discoveries, and origins, A history of. Beckmann, J. Lond., 1846. 2 v. 19—117.

Iowa and the rebellion. Ingersoll, L. D. Phil., 1866. 31—186.

——, Report of the geological survey of the State of. Illus. White, C. A. Des Moines, 1870. 2 v. L.

Ireland, History of. Leland, T. Dub., 1773. 3 v. 34—205.

——, The history of. Moore, T. Phil., 1835. 2 v. 34—205.

Ireland before and after the union with Great Britian. Martin, R. M. Lond., 1848. 34—205.

——, The English in. Froude, J. A. N. Y. 1873-74. 3 v. 34—205.

Irish sketch-book. Illus. Thackeray, W. M. Lond., 1870. 5—32.

Iron cousin, The. Clarke, M. C. N. Y., 1875. 41—228.

—— hand, The. Dumas, A. D. Phil., n. d. 3—20.

—— mask, The. Dumas, A. D. Phil., 1875. 3—20.

Iroquois, Notes on the. Schoolcraft, H. R. Albany, 1847. 30—178.

Irritation and insanity, A work on. Broussais, F. J. V. T. Cooper, tr. Lond., 1833. 15—92.

Irving, John T. Indian sketches, taken during an expedition to the Pawnee tribes. Phil., 1835. 2 v. 17—104.

Irving, Pierre M. The life and letters of Washington Irving. N. Y., 1862. 4 v. 12—69.

Irving, Washington. The Alhambra. N. Y., 1853. 3—19.

—— History of New York, by Diedrich Knickerbocker. N. Y., 1851. 3—19.

—— Bracebridge Hall; or the humorists: a medley, by Geoffrey Crayon, gent. N. Y., 1853. 3—19.

—— Mahomet and his successors. N. Y., 1853. 2 v. 3—19.

—— The adventures of Captain Bonneville, U. S. A., in the Rocky Mountains and the Far West. N. Y., and Lond., 1850. 3—19.

—— Astoria; or, anecdotes of an enterprise beyond the Rocky Mountains. N. Y. and Lond., 1852. 3—19.

—— The life and voyages of Christopher Columbus; to which are added those of his companions. Author's revised edition. N. Y., 1849. 3 v. 12—69.

—— Tales of a traveller. N. Y., 1867. 3—19.

—— Wolfert's roost and other papers, now first collected. N. Y., 1855. 3—19.

—— Conquest of Granada. N. Y., 1851. 3—19.

—— Oliver Goldsmith. N. Y., 1853. 3—19.

—— Life of George Washington. N. Y., 1855-59. 5 v. 13—74.

Irving, Washington. Life and letters of; by his nephew, P. M. Irving. N. Y., 1862-64. 12—69.

—— The sketch-book of Geoffrey Crayon, gent. Phil., 1871. 3—19.

—— Same. Author's revised edition. N. Y., 1864. 3—19.

Is it true? Muloch, D. M. N. Y., 1872. 39.

Isabel of Bavaria, queen of France. Dumas, A. D. Phil., n. d. 3—20.

——, the young wife and the old love. Jeaffreson, J. C. N. Y., 1857. 7—41.

Isabella Orsini. Guerrazzi, F. D. L Monti, tr. N. Y., 1859. 0—3.

Ishmael; or, in the depths. Southworth, E. D. E. N. Phil., 1876. 6—36.

Island of fire; or, a thousand years of the old Northmen's home. Illus. Headley, P. C. Bost., 1875. 36—215.

Isles of Shoals, Among the. Illus. Thaxter, C. Bost., 1873. 17—102.

Israel Mort, overman. Illus. Saunders, J. Phil., 1872. P—1.

Isthmus of Panama. Griswold, C. D. N. Y., 1852. 17—101.

—— Same. Illus. Otis, F. N. N. Y., 1867. 17—102.

It is never too late to mend. Reade, C. N. Y., 1873. 5—28.

—— is the fashion. Auer, A. son. Phil., 1872. 5—34.

Italia, Istoria d'. Guicciardini, F. Lond., 1821. W.

Italian art, Wonders of. Illus. Viardot, L. N. Y., 1874. 28—160.

—— girl, The. Washburn, K. S. Bost., 1874. 41—227.

—— journeys. Howells, W. D. N. Y., 1867. 17—104.

—— pictures, drawn with pen and pencil. Illus. Lond. and N. Y., n. d. 28—165.

—— republics, History of the. Sismondi, J. C. L. de. Phil., 1832. 35—212.

—— tragedy, Historical memoir on. Illus. Walker, J. C. Lond., 1799. 25—152.

Italie ancienne. (L'Univers.) Duruy, Filon, Lacroix, et Yanoski. Paris, 1850-51. 2 v. D. R.

Italy, Diary of an idle woman in. Elliot, F. Lond., 1871. 2 v. in one. 9—53.

Italy, from dawn to dark in: a tale of the reformation in the sixteenth century. Illus. Lond., 1871. P—3.

——. (Romance of history.) Illus. Macfarlane, C. Lond., n. d. 2—8.

——. Florence and Venice. Taine, H. A. N. Y., 1869. 17—103.

——. Rome and Naples. Taine, H. A. N. Y., 1874. 10—56.

Ivanhoe. Scott, Sir W. Bost., 1869. 3—17.

—— Same. (Condensed classics.) N. Y., 1876. 5—33.

Jack Hazard and his fortunes. Illus. Trowbridge, J. T. Bost., 1873. 39.

—— Hinton. Lever, C. J. Phil., n. d. 5—29.

—— Tier. Illus. Cooper, J. F. N. Y., 1873. 3—14.

Jackson, Andrew, Life of. Parton, J. Bost., 1870. 3 v. 40—224.

Jackson, Helen, (formerly Helen Maria Hunt.) Mercy Philbrick's choice. (No Name series.) Bost., 1876. 41—226.

—— Bits of travel. Illus. Bost., 1874. 40—221.

—— Bits of talk about home matters. Bost., 1873. 19—114.

Jacob Faithful. Marryat, Capt. F. N. Y., 1857. 5—30.

Jacob, Giles. *The law dictionary; explaining the rise, progress, and present state of the English law. Lond., 1809. 2 v. 21—123.

Jacobites, Memoirs of the. Thomson, K. B. Lond., 1845. 3 v. 11—62.

Jahn, Johann. Biblical archæology. T. C. Upham, tr. N. Y., 1849. 23—140.

Jamaica, Annals of. Bridges, G. W. Lond., 1828. 2 v. 33—200.

James, George Payne Rainsford. The life and times of Louis the fourteenth. Lond., 1851. 2 v. 12—72.

James, Henry, jr. A passionate pilgrim, and other tales. Bost., 1875. 41—228.

—— Roderick Hudson. Bost., 1876. 41—228.

—— The American. Bost., 1877. 41—228.

James the first, The court and times of. Birch, T. Lond., 1849. 2 v. 34—205.

—— the first, Secret history of the court of. Osborne, F. Edin., 1811. 2 v. 12—67.

Jameson, Anna Murphy. Legends of the madonna, as represented in the fine arts. Bost., 1866. 27—162.

—— Sacred and legendary art. Bost. 1866. 2 v. 27—162.

—— Characteristics of women, moral, poetical, and historical. Bost., 1866. 2—13.

—— The diary of an ennuyée. Bost., 1866. 2—13.

—— Studies, stories, and memoirs. Bost., 1866. 2—13.

—— Legends of the monastic orders, as represented in the fine arts. Bost., 1866. 27—162.

—— sketches of art, literature, and character. Bost., 1866. 2—13.

—— Memoirs of the loves of the poets; biographical sketches of women celebrated in ancient and modern poetry. Bost., 1866. 27—162.

—— Memoirs of early Italian painters. Bost., 1866. 27—162.

—— A commonplace book of thoughts, memories, and fancies, original and selected. N. Y., 1855. 2—13.

Jamieson, Alexander. Mechanics of fluids for practical men, comprising hydrostatics. Illus. Lond., 1837. 15—92.

—— Mechanics for practical men; treatises on the composition and resolution of forces, the centre of gravity, and the mechanical powers. Illus. Lond., 1845. 15—89.

Jamieson, John. Dictionary of the Scottish language; in which the words are explained in their different senses, authorized by the names of the writers by whom they are used; or the titles of the works in which they occur, and derived from their originals. Abridged by Dr. Johnston. A new edition, revised and enlarged by J. Longmuir. Edin., 1867. 23—139.

Jane Eyre. "Currer Bell." N. Y., n. d. 2 copies. 7—45.

Janet's home. Keary, A. Lond., 1866. P—3.

Janet's love and service. Robertson, M. M. N. Y., n. d. 6—39.

Jamney, Samuel M. The life of William Penn; with selections from his correspondence and autobiography. Phil., 1852. 11—63.

Japan and the Japanese in the nineteenth century, from recent Dutch travels, especially the narrative of von Siebold. Lond., 1852. 10—57.

—— and around the world. Illus. Spalding, J. W. N. Y., 1855. 10—57.

—— as it was and is. Hildreth, R. Bost., 1855. 17—104.

—— in our day. Illus. J. B. Taylor, ed. N. Y., 1874. 17—101.

Japhet in search of a father. Marryat, Capt. F. N. Y., 1857. 5—30.

Jaques, John. The history of Junius and his works; and a review of the controversy respecting the identity of Junius, etc. Lond., 1843. 19—117.

Jay, John, The life of: by his son, Wm. Jay. N. Y., 1833. 2 v. 13—73.

Jay, W. M. L. Holden with the cords. N. Y., 1874. 6—38.

Jay, William. The life of John Jay; with selections from his correspondence, and miscellaneous papers. N. Y., 1833. 2 v. 13—73.

Jeaffreson, John Cordy. Isabel, the young wife and the old love. N. Y., 1857. 7—41.

—— Olive Blake's good work: a novel. N. Y., 1871. 7—41.

—— Lottie darling: a novel. N. Y., 1874. 7—41.

—— Live it down: a story of the light lands. N. Y., 1873. 7—41.

—— Not dead yet: a novel. N. Y., 1864. 7—41.

—— Brides and bridals. Lond., 1872. 2 v. 3—20.

Jefferson, Thomas. Notes on the State of Virginia; with an appendix, relative to the murder of Logan's family. Trenton, 1803. 31—188.

——, The writings of: published by order of the joint committee of Congress on the library, from the original manuscripts. H. A. Washington, ed. Wash., 1853-54. 9 v. 25—147.

——, The life of. Randall, H. S. N. Y., 1868. 3 v. 12—66.

Jefferson, Thomas, The life of. Tucker, G. Phil., 1837. 2 v. 12—66.

——, Memoir, correspondence, and miscellanies from the papers of. T. Jefferson Randolph, ed. Charlottesville, 1829. 4 v. 12—66.

——, Life of. Parton, J. Bost., 1874. 40—224.

——, The private life of. Pierson, H. W. N. Y., 1862. 24—142.

Jefferson county, N. Y., A history of. Illus. Hough, F. B. Albany, 1854. 31—190.

Jeffrey, Francis. Contributions to the Edinburgh review. (Modern British essayists.) Bost., 1854. 27—159.

Jenkin, Mrs. C. "Who breaks—pays." N. Y., 1873. 6—38.

—— Madame de Beaupré. N. Y., 1869. 7—46.

—— Skirmishing. N. Y., 1870. 6—38.

—— A Psyche of to-day. N. Y., 1874. 6—38.

—— Within an ace. N. Y., 1875. 6—38.

—— Jupiter's daughters: a novel. N. Y., 1874. 6—38.

Jenkins, Edward. Little Hodge. N. Y., 1873. 3—19.

Jenny Lind in America. Rosenberg, C. G. N. Y., 1851. 8—50.

Jerrold, Douglas, Works of; with an introductory memoir by his son, W. Blanchard Jerrold. Lond., n. d. 5 v. 0—1.

Contents.

Vol. 1. St. Giles and St. James; Punch's letters to his son.

Vol. 2. The story of a feather; Cakes and ale.

Vol. 3. Mrs. Caudle's curtain-lectures; Men of character; Punch's complete letter-writer.

Vol. 4. A man made of money; Sketches of the English; The chronicles of Clovernook; The sick giant and the doctor dwarf.

Vol. 5. Life of Douglas Jerrold.

—— Fireside saints, Mr. Caudle's break-fast talk, and other papers, now first collected. Bost., 1873. 0—1.

Jerrold, William Blanchard. The best of all good company;—Charles Dickens, W. M. Thackeray, Walter Scott, and Douglas Jerrold. Illus. Bost., 1874. 28—169.

Jerusalem delivered: an heroic poem. Tasso, T. Lond., 1802. 2 v. 16—95.

Jerusalem, Recovery of; a narrative of exploration and discovery in the city and the Holy Land, by Capts. Wilson and Warren, R. E.; with an introduction by Arthur Penrhyn Stanley. W. Morrison, ed. Illus. N. Y., 1873. 8—48.

Jessamine: a novel. "Marion Harland." N. Y. and Lond., 1874. 7—44.

Jesse, John Heneage. Memoirs of the court of England during the reign of the Stuarts; including the protectorate. Phil., 1840. 4 v. 34—205.

——— The pretenders and their adherents: memoirs of the chevalier prince Charles Edward and their adherents. Lond., 1846. 2 v. 12—67.

Jessie Trim. Farjeon, B. L. N. Y., 1875. 6—35.

Jesuits, History of the. Steinmetz, A. Lond., 1848. 3 v. 32—195.

——— in North America. Parkman, F. Bost., 1872. 28—166.

Jesus Christ, Life of. Neander, A. J. W. N. Y., 1858. 13—78.

——— Same. Taylor, J. N. Y., 1859. 2 v. 13—78.

Jewett, Susan W. From fourteen to fourscore, N. Y., 1871. 6—38.

Jewish coinage, History of. Illus. Madden, F. W. Lond., 1864. 15—88.

——— church, Lectures on the history of the. Stanley, A. P. N.Y., 1877. 32—196.

Jewitt, Lewellyn, and S. C. Hall. The stately homes of England. Illus. Phil., n. d. 40—225.

Jews, The history of the. Milman, H. H. Lond., 1829. 3 v. 36—217.

Joanna of Sicily, queen of Naples, and countess of Provence; with correlative details of the literature and manners of Italy and Provence in the thirteenth and fourteenth centuries. L. J. Hall. Lond., 1824. 2 v. 13—74.

Jocelyn's mistake. Spender, Mrs. J. K. Bost., 1875. 41—230.

Johannes Olaf: a novel. Wille, E. de. Bost., 1873. P—2.

John, Eugenie, (E. Marlitt.) The little moorland princess. Mrs. A. L. Wister, tr. Phil., 1872. 7—42.

——— Gold Elsie. Mrs. A. L. Wister, tr. Phil., 1871. 7—42.

——— Countess Gisela. Mrs. A. L. Wister, tr. Phil., 1872. 7—42.

John, Eugenie, (E. Marlitt.) The old mamselle's secret. Mrs. A. L. Wister, tr. Phil., 1874. 7—42.

——— The second wife: a romance. Mrs. A. L. Wister, tr. Phil., 1874. 7—42.

——— Over yonder: a novelette. Phil., 1873. 7—42.

——— Magdalena; and The lonely ones, by Paul Heyse. Phil., 1870. 7—42.

——— at the councillors; or, a nameless history. Mrs. A. L. Wister, tr. Phil., 1876. 7—42.

John Brent. Winthrop, T. Bost., 1862. 4—24.

——— de Lancaster: a novel. Cumberland, R. N. Y., 1809. 2 v. P—3.

——— Dorrien: a novel. Kavanagh, J. N. Y., 1875. 7—41.

——— Godfrey's fortunes. Taylor, J. B. N. Y., 1868. 5—34.

——— Halifax, gentleman. Illus. Muloch, D. M. N. Y., 1872. 4—23.

——— Milton and his times: an historical novel. Illus. Ring, M. N. Y., 1868. 5—29.

——— of Barneveld, The life and death of. Illus. Motley, J. L. N. Y., 1874. 2 v. 11—59.

——— Marchmont's legacy. Braddon, M. E. N. Y., 1863. 5—29.

——— Thompson, blockhead, and other stories. Parr, L. C. Phil., n. d. 4—25.

——— Worthington's name: a novel. Benedict, F. L. N. Y., 1874. 5—23.

Johns, Richard. The calendar of victory; being a record of British valour and conquest, by sea and land, on every day in the year. Lond., 1855. 21—128.

Johnson, Andrew, Impeachment and trial of. Wash., 1868. 3 v. 29—177.

———, Speeches of, while president of the United States, with a biographical introduction. Moore, F. Bost., 1865. 26—157.

——— Life and speeches of. Foster, L. N. Y., 1866. 11—64.

Johnson, Anna C. Peasant life in Germany. N. Y., 1858. 17—101.

Johnson, Samuel, The works of; with Murphy's essay. Rev. Robert Lynham, ed. Lond., 1825. 6 v. 26—154.

Contents.

Vol. 1. Essay on the life and genius of Dr. Johnson; part first of the "Rambler."

Vol. 2. Part second of the "Rambler," and the "Idler."

Vol. 3. Adventures and lives of the English poets.

Vol. 4. Lives of the English poets, and Lives of eminent persons.

Vol. 5. Philological, political, and miscellaneous tracts; and Reviews and criticisms.

Vol. 6. Journey to the western islands and Scotland; History of Rasselas, prince of Abyssinia; Tales of imagination; Poems; Poemata; Letters; Prayers and meditations; Sermons.

——, The life of. Boswell, J. Lond., 1811. 5 v. 13—78.

Johnson, T. and J. W. Law catalogue. Phil., 1850. 2 v. L.

Johnson, Virginia W. A sack of gold: a novel. N. Y., 1875. 6—35.

Johnson, Walter R. A report to the Navy Department of the United States, on American coals applicable to steam navigation, and to other purposes. Wash., 1844. T.

Johnson, Sir William, The life and times of. Stone, W. L. Albany, 1865. 2 v. 11—59.

Johnston, Alexander Keith. The physical atlas: a series of maps and illustrations of the geographical distribution of natural phenomena. Lond., 1849. R.

Johnston, James F. W. Notes on North America; agricultural, economical, and social. Bost. and Edin., 1851. 2 v. 29—175.

Johnston, Joseph Eggleston. Narrative of military operations, directed, during the late war between the States. Illus. N. Y., 1874. 30—180.

Johonnot, James. School-houses. Illus. N. Y., 1871. 19—117.

Jones, Charles C. Historical sketch of Tomo-chi-chi, Mico of the Yamacraws. Albany, 1868. 30—178.

Jones, John B. A rebel war clerk's diary at the Confederate States capital. Phil., 1866. 2 v. 30—181.

Jones, John Paul, Life and character of. Sherburne, J. H. N. Y., 1851. 12—66.

——, Paul, Mémoires de. M. André, tr. Paris, 1798. W.

——, Paul, The life of. Mackenzie, A. S. N. Y., 1846. 2 v. 12—66.

Jones, M. The black prince: a book for boys. Illus. Lond. and N. Y., n. d. 38.

Jones, Owen. "The grammar of ornament; illustrated by examples from

various styles of ornament. Lond., n. d. 14—80.

Jones, Sir William. An essay on the law of bailments. Lond., 1833. T.

——, Memoirs of. Teignmouth, Lord. Lond., 1806. 2 v. 12—70.

Jorrocks' jaunts and jollities, by John Jorrocks. Surtees, R. S. Phil., 1838. 2 v. in one. 2—10.

Jorrocks, John, pseud. See Surtees, R. S.

Joseph Andrews, Adventures of; and the life of Jonathan Wild. Fielding, H. N. Y., 1861. 5—34.

—— and his friend. Taylor, J. B. N. Y. and Lond., 1870. 5—34.

—— Grimaldi, Memoirs of. Dickens, C. Phil., 1838. 2 v. in one. 3—15.

—— Noirel's revenge. Cherbuliez, V. N. Y., 1872. 7—46.

—— the Jew: the story of an old house. N. Y., 1874. 5—28.

—— the second and his court. Illus. "Louise Mühlbach." N. Y., 1875. 4—21.

Josephus, Flavius, The works of. W. Whiston, tr. Edin., 1865. 36—217.

Joshua Marvel. Farjeon, B. L. N. Y., 1872. 6—35.

Journal of Andrew Ellicott. Phil., 1803. 9—51.

—— of a naturalist. Darwin, C. N. Y., 1846. 2 v. 14—85.

—— of conversations with Lord Byron, by the Countess of Blessington. Bost., n. d. 27—161.

—— of Claude Blanchard, Commissary of the French auxiliary army sent to the United States during the American revolution. Albany, 1876. 40—224.

Journalism in the United States, from 1690 to 1872. Hudson, F. N. Y., 1873. 36—215.

* **Journals** of Congress from 1774 to '85. 6 v. D. R.

Journey round the world, Narrative of a. Simpson, Sir G. 2 v. Lond, 1847. 9—51.

—— round my room, A. Maistre, X. de. N. Y., 1871. 28—169.

—— to the north pole, A. Illus. Verne, J. Lond. and N. Y., 1875. 5—31.

—— to the center of the earth, A. Illus. Verne, J. Bost., n. d. 5—31.

Joutel, M. A journal of the last voyage performed by Mons. de la Sale to the

Gulf of Mexico, to find the mouth of the Mississippi River. Lond., 1714. 9—53.

Joyce, Robert Dwyer. Deirdrè. (No Name series.) Bost., 1876. 17—105.

Judd, Sylvester. Margaret: a tale of the real and the ideal, blight and bloom. Bost., 1871. 6—38.

Judicial ,puzzles gathered from the state trials. Paget, J. San Fran., 1876. 40—221.

Judson, Emily C., (*Fanny Forrester.*) Alderbrook: a collection of village sketches, poems, etc. Bost., 1856. 2—10.

Judson, L. Carroll. A biography of the signers of the declaration of independence; and of Washington and Patrick Henry. Phil., 1839. 12—86.

Jukes, Joseph Beete. Excursions in and about Newfoundland during the years 1839-40. Lond., 1842. 2 v. 9—53.

Julius Cæsar, History of. Napoleon the third. N. Y., 1865-67. 3 v. 35—213.

Jullian, Pierre L. P. de. Memoirs of Joseph Fouché, duke of Otranto, minister of general police of France. Bost., 1825. 11—64.

June, Jennie, *pseud.* See Croly, Jennie C.

Junius, including letters by the same writer under other signatures, and his confidential correspondence with Mr. Wilkes and Mr. H. S. Woodfall. Lond., 1812. 3 v. 19—117.

—— discovered. Griffin, F. Bost., 1854. 19—117.

——, The authorship of the letters of, elucidated; including a memoir of Lieut. Col. Isaac Barré, M. P. Britton, J. Lond., 1848. 19—117.

——, An inquiry concerning the author of the letters of. Lond., 1814. 19—117.

——. The secret revealed of the authorship of Junius's letters. Falconar, J. Lond., 1830. 19—117.

——, Letters on, addressed to John Pickering, esq., showing that the author of that celebrated work was Earl Temple. Newhall, I. Bost., 1831. 19—117.

——, Memoirs of John Horne Tooke; containing proofs identifying him as the author of the celebrated letters of. Graham, J. A. N. Y., 1828. 19—117.

——, Arguments and facts demonstrating that the letters of, were written by

John Lewis De Lolme, LL. D. Busby, T. Lond., 1816. 19—117.

—— unmasked; or, Lord George Sackville proved to be Junius. Manning, J. B. Bost., 1828. 19—117.

——. The claims of Sir Philip Francis, K. B., to the authorship of Junius's letters disproved; with some inquiry into the claims of the late Charles Lloyd, esq., etc. Barker, E. H. Lond., 1828. 19—117.

——, The history of, and his works; and a review of the controversy respecting the identity of Junius, etc. Jaques, J. Lond., 1843. 19—117.

——. "A letter to an honourable brigadier-general, commander-in-chief of his majesty's forces in Canada," ascribed to Junius; to which is added "A refutation of the letter, etc., by an officer." Reprinted from a rare tract in the British Museum. N. W. Simons, ed. Lond., 1841. 19—117.

Jupiter's daughters: a novel. Jenkin, C. N. Y., 1874. 6—38.

Jurisconsult exercitations. Hargrave, F. Lond., 1813. Vol. 3. D. R.

Justin Harley: a romance of old Virginia. Illus. Cooke, J. E. Phil., 1874. 4—25

Kalevala, Selections from the; with an introduction and analysis of the poem. John A. Porter, tr. N. Y., 1869. 17—106.

Kaloolah; or, journeyings to the Djébel Kumri: an autobiography of Jonathan Romer. Mayo, W. S. N. Y., 1854. 17—103.

Kames, Henry Home, *Lord.* Elements of criticism, with analyses and translations of ancient and foreign illustrations A. Mills, ed. N. Y., 1866. 14—83.

—— Sketches of the history of man Edin., 1778. 3 v. 15—89.

Kane, Elisha Kent. Arctic explorations the second Grinnell expedition in search of Sir John Franklin, 1853-55. Illus. Phil., 1857. 2 v. 9—52.

—— The United States Grinnell expedition in search of Sir John Franklin: a personal narrative. Illus. N. Y., 1854. 9—52.

and the sayings and doings of sundry of the towns-people; interspersed with sketches of the most remarkable and distinguished characters of that place and its vicinity, by Solomon Second-thoughts, schoolmaster, from original MSS. indited by him, and now made public at the request and under the patronage of the great new-light democratic central committee of Quodlibet. Phil., 1860. 6—39.

—— Rob of the bowl: a legend of St. Inigoe's. Phil., 1861. 6—39.

—— Mr. Ambrose's letters on the rebellion. N. Y., 1865. 26—155.

Kennedy, William. Texas: the rise, progress, and prospects of the republic of Texas. Lond., 1841. 2 v. 31—187.

Kenneth, my king: a novel. Brock, S. A. N. Y. and Lond., 1873. 6—38.

Kenrick, John. Ancient Egypt under the Pharaohs. Lond., 1850. 2 v. 36—216.

Kent, James. Commentaries on American law. N. Y., 1848. 21—128.

Kentucky, The history of. Marshall, H. Frankfort, 1824. 2 v. 31—186.

——, Historical sketches of. Illus. Collins, L. Maysville, *Ky.*, 1850. 31—186.

——, A history of the commonwealth of. Butler, M. Louisville, 1834. 31—186.

Khiva, A ride to. Burnaby, F. N. Y., 1877. 10—57.

Kidder, Daniel P. Sketches of a residence and travels in Brazil. Illus. Phil., 1845. 2 v. 10—58.

Kidder, Frederic. History of the Boston massacre, March 5, 1770; consisting of the narrative of the town, the trial of the soldiers, and a historical introduction containing unpublished documents of John Adams, and explanatory notes. Albany, 1870. 30—182.

Kiddle, Henry, and Alexander J. Schem, *editors.* The cyclopædia of education: a dictionary of information for teachers, school officers, parents, and others. N. Y. and Lond., 1877. 1—1.

Kilmeny. Black, W. N. Y., 1870. 5—29.

Kimball, Richard B. Was he successful? a novel. N. Y. and Leipsic, 1864. 0—3.

King, Charles. A memoir of the construction, cost, and capacity of the Cro-

ton aqueduct; with an account of the civic celebration of the 14th of October, 1842, on occasion of the completion of the great work. N. Y., 1843. D. R.

King, Clarence. Mountaineering in the Sierra Nevada. Bost., 1872. 17—104.

—— United States geological exploration of the fortieth parallel. Wash., 1870-71. Vols. 3 and 5. D. R.

King, Thomas. The modern style of cabinet-work exemplified. Illus. Lond., 1862. V.

King and the commonwealth: a history of Charles I and the rebellion. Cordery, B. M., and J. S. Phillpotts. Phil., 1876. 34—206.

—— of the mountains, The. About, E. Bost., 1861. 6—40.

—— Arthur: a poem. Bulwer-Lytton, *Sir* E. N. Y., 1871. 17—105.

—— René's daughter: a Danish lyrical drama. Hertz, H. N. Y., n. d. 17—106.

—— George the fourth and king William the fourth, A journal of the reigns of. Greville, C. C. F. N. Y., 1875. 2 v. 34—207.

Kinglake, Alexander William. Invasion of the Crimea: its origin, and an account of its progress, down to the death of Lord Raglan. N. Y., 1868-75. 5 v. 33—198.

Kingman, Bradford. History of North Bridgewater, Plymouth County, Massachusetts, from its first settlement to the present time, with family registers. Illus. Bost., 1866. 30—182.

King's own, The. Marryat, *Capt.* F. N. Y., 1857. 5—30.

Kingsborough, Edward King, *viscount.* Antiquities of Mexico, comprising fac-similes of ancient Mexican paintings and hieroglyphics; with the monuments of New Spain, by M. Dupaix. Lond., 1830-48. 9 v. U.

Kingsley, Charles. Westward ho! or, the voyages and adventures of Sir Amyas Leigh, kn't. Lond. and N. Y., 1871. 7—43.

—— Two years ago. Bost., 1866. 7—43.

—— Hypatia; or, new foes with an old face. Bost., 1870. 7—43.

—— Hereward, the last of the English. Bost., 1866. 7—43.

Knight, Charles. Half-hours with the best authors. Lond., 1866. 4 v. 2—10.
—— Half-hours with the best letter-writers and autobiographers; forming a collection of memoirs and anecdotes of eminent persons. Lond. and N. Y., n. d. 2 v. 2—10.
—— Cyclopædia of London, 1851. Illus. 27—160.
—— Passages from the life of. N. Y., 1874. 12—66.

Knight, Cornelia, and Thomas Raikes. Personal reminiscences by. (Bric-a-brac series.) Illus. N. Y., 1875. 19—114.

Knight, Edward H. American mechanical dictionary; being a description of tools, instruments, machines, processes, and engineering; history of inventions; general technological vocabulary, and digest of mechanical appliances in science and the arts. Illus. N.Y., 1874-76. 3 v. 23—138.

Knight, Richard Payne. The symbolical language of ancient art and mythology : an inquiry. A new edition, with introduction, additions, notes translated into English, and a new and complete index by Alexander Wilder. N. Y., 1876. 40—225.

Knight of Gwynne, The. Lever, C. J. Lond., n. d. 7—44.

Knights hospitallers, History of the. Vertot D'Aubeuf, R. A. de. Edin., 1757. 5 v. 30—184.
—— and their days. Doran, J. N. Y., 1864. 19—114.

Knolles, Richard. * General historie of the Turkes, from the first beginning of that nation to the rising of the Othoman familie, with all the notable expeditions of the Christian princes against them; with the lives and conquests of the Othoman kings and emperours. Lond., 1631. 34—203.

Knowles, James Sheridan, The dramatic works of. Lond., n. d. 17—106.

Knox, John, The life of. McCrie, T. Edin., 1813. 2 v. 40—223.

Kohlrausch, Friedrich. History of Germany, from the earliest period. J. D. Haas, tr. N. Y., 1853. 36—218.

Koran, commonly called the Alcoran of Mohammed; translated into English immediately from the original Arabic,

with explanatory notes taken from the most approved commentators; to which is prefixed a preliminary discourse, by George Sale; and a memoir of the translator. Phil., 1874. 19—116.

Krafft, J. Ch. Recueil d'architecture civile, avec les planches. Paris, 1829. V.
—— Traité sur l'art de la charpente. Paris, 1840. 2 v. V.
—— Maisons de Paris, et de ses environs, avec planches. Paris, 1849. U.

La Beche, Sir Henry Thomas de. A geological manual Phil., 1832. 15—91.
—— A selection of geological memoirs contained in the "Annales des mines," by Brongniart, Humboldt, von Buch, and others. Illus. Lond., 1836. 15—91.
—— The geological observer. Illus. Phil., 1851. 15—91.

La Bruyère, J. de. The characters of Theophrastus; illustrated by physiognomical sketches. Lond., 1831. 27—162.

La Hodde, Lucien de. The cradle of rebellions: a history of the secret societies of France. N. Y., 1864. 34—214.

La Motte-Fouqué, Friedrich, baron de. Undine, and other tales; containing The two captains, Aslauga's knight, and Sintram and his companions. Illus. N. Y., 1871. 38.

La Rame, Louise de, (Ouida.) Idalia : a novel. Phil., 1870. 2 copies. 7—44.
—— Chandos : a novel. Phil., 1871. 7—44.
—— Tricotrin : the story of a waif and stray. Phil., 1871. 7—44.
—— Beatrice Boville, and other stories. Phil., 1868. 7—44.
—— Puck. Phil., 1870. 7—44.
—— Folle-Farine. Phil., 1871. 7—44.
—— Randolph Gordon, and other stories. Phil., 1867. 7—44.
—— Cecil Castlemaine's gage; Lady Marabout's troubles; and other stories. Phil., 1867. 7—44.
—— Granville De Vigne; or, held in bondage: a tale of the day. Phil., 1871. 7—44.
—— Under two flags : a novel. Phil., 1867. 2 copies. 7—44.

La Rame, Louise de, (*Ouida.*) Strathmore; or, wrought by his own hand : a life romance. Phil., 1871. 7—44.

—— Pascarel : only a story by "Ouida." Phil., 1873. 7—44.

—— In a winter city : a story of the day. Phil., 1876. 7—44.

—— Two little wooden shoes : a sketch by "Ouida." Tauchnitz edition. Leipzig, 1874. 41—226.

—— Held in bondage ; or, Granville De Vigne : a tale of the day. Tauchnitz edition. Leipzig, 1873. 2 v. in one. 41—226.

—— A leaf in the storm ; A dog of Flanders ; and other stories by "Ouida ;" with a preface written by the author for this edition. Tauchnitz edition. Leipzig, 1872. 41—226.

—— Signa : a story. Tauchnitz edition. Leipzig, 1875. 41—226.

—— Ariadne : the story of a dream. Phil., 1877. 7—44.

La Rochefoucauld, François, *duc de,* Moral reflections, sentences, and maxims of ; and of Stanislaus, king of Poland. N. Y., 1853. W.

—— Constitutions des treize États-Unis de l'Amérique. Phil. et Paris, 1783. W.

La Rochefoucauld-Liancourt, François Alexandre Frédéric, *duc de.* Voyage dans les États-Unis d'Amérique, fait eu 1795-97. Paris. 8 v. W.

La Salle, Robert, *cavalier de,* Life of. (Library of American biography, vol. 11.) 11—65.

La Syrie, la Terre-Sainte, l'Asie Mineure, etc. Illustrées : une série de vues dessinées d'après nature par W. H. Bartlett, et Wm. Purser : les explications des gravures par John Carne. Lond. et Paris, 1836. 9—55.

Labberton, Robert H. Outlines of history, with original tables, chronological, genealogical, and literary. Phil., 1872. 33—297.

—— Historical questions logically arranged and divided : the companion book to "Outlines of history." Phil., 1872. 33—197.

—— An historical atlas, containing a chronological series of one hundred maps at successive periods, from the dawn of

history to the present day. Phil., 1872. 33—197.

Labor in Europe and America. Young, E. Wash., 1875. X.

Lackawanna valley, Contributions to the history of the. Hollister, H. N. Y., 1857. 31—189.

Lacroix, Paul. Manners, customs, and dress, during the middle ages, and during the renaissance period. Illus. N. Y., 1874. 28—165.

Lacy diamonds, The. N. Y., 1875. 41—230.

Ladder of life, The. Edwards, A. B. N.Y., 1875. 6—38.

Lady Audley's secret. Braddon, M. E. N. Y., n. d. 5—29.

Lady-bird : a tale. Fullerton, *Lady* G. Balt., 1868. 41—228.

Lady Byron vindicated. Stowe, H. B. Bost., 1870. 2—9.

—— Hester. Yonge, C. M. Lond., 1874. 5—30.

—— Judith. Illus. McCarthy, J. N. Y., 1871. 6—35.

—— Lisle, The. Braddon, M. E. N. Y., n. d. 5—29.

—— Susan. Austen, J. Lond., 1872. 4—27.

—— of La Garaye, The. Norton, C. E. S. Lond., 1871. 16—100.

—— of Lyons ; or, love and pride : a play. Bulwer-Lytton, *Sir* E. Leipsic, 1849. 17—105.

—— of the lake, The. Scott, *Sir* W. N. Y., 1873. 17—105.

—— of the isle, The. Southworth, E. D. E. N. Phil., 1859. 6—37.

—— of the ice, The. Illus. De Mille, J. N. Y., 1872. 6—35.

Lafayette, *Marquis de.* Life of. Headley, P. C. N. Y., 1859. 11—60.

Lafever, Minard. The beauties of modern architecture. Illus. N. Y.,1849. T.

Lahontan, N., *le baron de.* Mémoires de l'Amérique septentrionale. 1715. W.

Lake George. Illus. De Costa, B. F. N. Y., 1868. 17—102.

Lakes and rivers between Lake Huron and the river Ottawa, Plans of various, to accompany the geological reports for 1853-56. Toronto, 1857. X.

Lamartine, Alphonse Marie Louis de. History of the French revolution of 1848. Lond., 1849. 35—213.

—— Memoirs of celebrated characters. N. Y., 1854. 2 v. 13—76.

—— History of the Girondists; or, personal memoirs of the patriots of the French revolution. H. T. Ryde, tr. N. Y., 1854. 2 v. 35—213.

—— Twenty-five years of my life, and memoirs of my mother. *Lady* Herbert, tr. Lond., 1872. 2 v. 11—62.

Lamb, Charles, The works of; including his most interesting letters. *Sir* Thomas Noon Talfourd, ed. N. Y., 1867. 27—159.

—— Eliana; being the hitherto uncollected writings of Charles Lamb. N. Y., 1870. 27—159.

Lamb, Hazlitt, and others, Personal recollections of. (Bric-a-brac series.) Illus. N. Y., 1875. 11—61.

Lamon, Ward H. The life of Abraham Lincoln, from his birth to his inauguration as president. Illus. Bost., 1872. 12—66.

Lampadius, W. A. Life of Felix Mendelssohn-Bartholdy. W. L. Gage, tr. N. Y., 1866. 11—64.

Lamplighter, The. Cummins, M. S. Bost., 1870. 6—38.

Lances of Lynwood, The. Illus. Yonge, C. M. Lond., 1868. 39.

Land at last. Yates, E. Lond. and N. Y., n. d. 7—45.

—— of Thor, The. Illus. Browne, J. R. N. Y., 1867. 17—104.

—— of the white elephant, The. Illus. Vincent, F. N. Y., 1874. 17—101.

Landor, Walter Savage. Imaginary conversations. Bost., 1876-77. 4 v. 20—122.

Contents.

1st series: Classical dialogues, Greek and Roman.

2d series: Dialogues of sovereigns and statesmen.

3rd series: Dialogues of literary men.

4th series: Dialogues of literary men continued, Dialogues of famous women, and Miscellaneous dialogues.

Lands of the Saracen. Taylor, J. B. N. Y., 1869. 17—103.

Langdon, Mary, *pseud.* See Pike, M. H.

L'Angleterre et de l'Amérique, Affaires de. Anvers, 1776. 16 v. D. R.

8 I

Language, Lectures on the English. Marsh, G. P. N. Y., 1867. 14—81.

——, Lectures on the science of. Müller, M. N. Y., 1868. 14—81.

—— Same. 2d series. N. Y., 1868. 14—81.

Lanman, Charles. Red-book of Michigan; a civil, military, and biographical history. Det., 1871. 31—186.

—— *Dictionary of the United States congress; containing biographical sketches of its members, from the foundation of the government. Phil., 1859. 22—132.

—— *Dictionary of the United States congress and the general government: fifth edition, brought down to include the fortieth congress. Hartford, 1868. 22—132.

—— * Biographical annals of the civil government of the United States, during its first century, from original and official sources. Wash., 1876. 22—132.

Lanoye, Ferdinand Tugnot de. Rameses the great; or, Egypt 3300 years ago. (Illustrated library of wonders.) N. Y., 1872. 28—169.

Laporte, Laurent. Sailing on the Nile. Virginia Vaughn, tr. Bost., 1872. 17—103.

Larcom, Lucy. An idyl of work. Bost., 1875. 17—106.

Lardner, Dionysius. Popular lectures on science and art. Illus. N. Y., 1850. Vol. 2. T.

L'art de vérifier les dates. Warden, D. B. Paris, 1826-44. 10 v. D. R.

Larwood, Jacob, *pseud.* See Sadler, L. R.

Las Cases, Emmanuel Dieudonné Marin, Joseph, *comte de.* Memoirs of the life, exile, and conversations of the emperor Napoleon. Illus. N. Y., 1855. 4 v. 11—61.

Last chronicle of Barset. Illus. Trollope, A. N. Y., 1867. 5—28.

—— days of a king: a historical romance. Hartmann, M. Phil., 1867. 4—24.

—— days of Pompeii. Bulwer-Lytton, *Sir* E. Phil., 1869. 5—33.

—— journals of David Livingstone in Central Africa. Illus. N. Y., 1875. 17—101.

Le Gros, W. B. Fables and tales suggested by the frescoes of Pompeii and Herculaneum. Illus. Lond., 1835. 16—100.

Le Sage, Alain René, Œuvres de, précédée d'une notice biographique et littéraire par M. Prosper Poitevin. Illus. Paris, 1857. W.
—— The adventures of Gil Blas of Santillane. B. H. Malkin, tr. Lond., 1809. 4 v. 2—9.

Leaf in the storm: a dog of Flanders; and other stories. "Ouida." Leipzig, 1872. 41—226.

Leah: a woman of fashion. Edwards, A. N. Y., n. d. 3—15.

Leaves from Margaret Smith's journal. Whittier, J. G. Bost., 1849. 27—162.
—— from my log-book. Grummett, F. Phil., 1835. 8—50.

Lecky, William Edward Hartpole. History of European morals from Augustus to Charlemagne. N. Y., 1869. 2 v. 32—195.
—— History of the rise and influence of the spirit of rationalism in Europe. N. Y., 1870. 2 v. 27—161.

Leçons françaises de littérature et de morale. Noël et De la Place. Bruxelles, 1852. W.

Lectures delivered at Broadmead chapel, Bristol, by the late John Foster. Lond., 1855. 2 v. 28—170.
—— on the history of France. Stephen, Sir J. N. Y., 1852. 35—214.
—— on the history of Christian dogmas. Neander, A. J. W. Lond., 1858. 2 v. 32—195.
—— on the English language. Marsh, G. P. N. Y., 1867. Q—2.
—— to young men. Beecher, H. W. N. Y., 1851. E.

Ledyard, John, Life of. (Library of American biography, vol. 24.) 11—65.

Lee, Arthur, LL. D., The life of. Lee, R. H. Bost., 1829. 2 v. 11—59.

Lee, Charles, Life of. (Library of American biography, vol. 18.) 11—65.

Lee, Henry. Memoirs of the war in the southern department of the United States: a new edition, with corrections left by the author, and with notes and

additions by H. Lee, the author of the "Campaign of '81." Wash., 1827. 30—181.

Lee, Holme, *pseud.* See Parr, H.

Lee, Richard H. Memoir of the life of Richard Henry Lee, and his correspondence with the most distinguished men in America and Europe, illustrative of their characters, and of the events of the American revolution. Phil., 1825. 2 v. 12—68.
—— Life of Arthur Lee, LL. D. Bost., 1829. 2 v. 11—59.

Lee, Richard Henry, Memoir of the life of. Lee, R. H. Phil., 1825. 2 v. 12—68.

Lee, T. J. A collection of tables and formulæ useful in surveying, geodesy, and practical astronomy; including elements for the projection of maps. Wash., 1853. 15—87.

Lefèbre, M. Wonders of architecture. (Illustrated library of wonders.) N. Y., 1875. 28—169.

Legal and political hermeneutics. Lieber, F. Bost., 1839. 15—88.

Legaré, Hugh Swinton, Writings of: prefaced by a memoir of his life, edited by his sister. Charleston, 1846. 2 v. 28—170.

Legend of Jubal, and other poems. "George Eliot." Bost., 1874. 17—106.

Legends of the Madonna. Jameson, A. M. Bost., 1866. 27—162.
—— of Number Nip. Illus. Lemon, M. Lond., 1864. 39.
—— of savage life. Illus. Greenwood, J. N. Y. and Lond., n. d. 39.
—— of the patriarchs and prophets. Baring-Gould, S. N. Y., 1872. 27—161.
—— of the monastic orders. Jameson, A. M. Bost., 1866. 27—162.

Legge, James. The life and teachings of Confucius, with explanatory notes. Phil., 1874. 13—76.

Leighton, Alexander. Curious storied traditions of Scottish life. Edin., 1860. 41—227.

Leighton court. Kingsley, H. Bost., 1866. 7—43.

Leila, or the siege of Granada ; Calderon, the courtier; and The pilgrims of the Rhine. Bulwer-Lytton, Sir E. Phil., 1868. 5—33.

Leisler, Jacob, Life of. (Library of American biography, vol. 13.) 11—65.

Leisure-day rhymes. Saxe, J. G. Bost., 1875. 17—105.

Leithart, John. Practical observations on the mechanical structure, mode of formation, the repletion, or filling up, and the intersection and relative age of mineral veins. Illus. Lond., 1838. 15—91.

Leland, Charles Godfrey. Hans Breitmann's ballads. Phil., 1871. 16—95.

—— Pidgin-English sing-song; or, songs and stories in the China-English dialect, with a vocabulary. Phil., 1876. 17—106.

Leland, Thomas. History of Ireland, from the invasion of Henry the second. Dub., 1773. 3 v. 34—205.

Lemon, Mark. Legends of Number Nip. Illus. Lond., 1864. 39.

Lempriere, John. * Bibliotheca classica; or, a dictionary of all the principal names and terms relating to the ancients. Phil., 1856. 22—132.

Lenzen, Marie. Not in their set; or, in different circles of society. M. S., tr. Bost., 1874. 6—37.

Leo the tenth, The life and pontificate of. Roscoe, W. Lond., 1846. 2 v. 11—65.

Leon, Edwin de. Askaros Kassis, the Copt: a romance of modern Egypt. Phil., 1870. 7—44.

Leonora Casaloni. Trollope, T. A. Phil., n. d. 7—43.

Leonowens, Anna Harriette. The romance of the harem. Illus. Bost., 1873. 17—101.

—— The English governess at the Siamese court: being recollections of six years in the royal palace at Bangkok. Illus. Bost., 1873. 17—101.

Les misérables. Hugo, V. N. Y., 1869. 2 v. in one. 6—35.

—— Same: authorized copyright, English translation. Sixth edition, revised. Lond., n. d. 6—35.

Leslie, Frank. * Pictorial history of the American civil war. E. G. Squier, ed. N. Y., 1862. Vol. 1. V.

Lessing, Gotthold Ephraim. Nathan the wise: a dramatic poem; preceded by a brief account of the poet and his works, and followed by Kuno Fischer's essay on the poem. Ellen Frothingham, tr. · N. Y., 1873. 17—106.

Lessons in life. Holland, J. G. N. Y., 1872. 3—18.

—— from nature, as manifested in mind and matter. Mivart, S. G. N. Y., 1876. 40—222.

Letters and social aims. Emerson, R. W. Bost., 1876. 19—116.

—— from the East. Bryant, W. C. N. Y., 1869. 17—104.

—— of a traveller. Bryant, W. C. N. Y., 1870. 17—104.

—— written by the earl of Chesterfield to his son. Phil., 1868. P—2.

—— to a young man. De Quincey, T. Bost., 1861. 2—12.

—— to the Joneses, by "Timothy Titcomb." N. Y., 1872. 3—18.

—— to various persons. Thoreau, H. D. Bost., 1865. 19—115.

—— to the President on the foreign and domestic policy of the Union. Carey, H. C. Phil. and Lond., 1858. L.

—— of Major Jack Downing. Smith, S. N. Y., 1834. 2—13.

—— (select) of Major Jack Downing. Smith, S. Phil., 1834. 2—13.

Levana. Richter, J. P. F. Bost., 1866. P—1.

Levant, In the. Warner, C. D. Bost., 1877. 10—56.

Lever, Charles James. The Dodd family abroad. Lond., n. d. 7—44.

—— The Daltons; or, three roads in life. Lond., n. d. 7—44.

—— The confessions of Con Cregan, the Irish Gil Blas. Lond. and N. Y., n. d. 7—44.

—— Maurice Tiernay, the soldier of fortune. Lond., n. d. 7—44.

—— Barrington. Lond., n. d. 7—44.

—— Jack Hinton, the guardsman. Phil., n. d. 5—29.

—— The knight of Gwynne: a tale of the time of the Union. Lond., n. d. 7—44.

—— Tom Burke, "of Ours:" a novel. Phil., n. d. 5—29.

—— Charles O'Malley, the Irish dragoon. Phil., n. d. 5—29.

—— The Bramleighs of Bishop's Folly: a novel. N. Y., 1871. 5—29.

Lever, Charles James. Gerald Fitzgerald, "the Chevalier." N. Y., 1872. 5—29.

———— That boy of Norcott's. Illus. N. Y., 1869. 5—29.

———— The fortunes of Glencore: a novel. N. Y.,1872. 5—29.

———— Davenport Dunn: a novel. Phil., n. d. 5—29.

———— Arthur O'Leary: a novel. Phil., n. d. 5—29.

———— A day's ride: a life's romance. Illus. N. Y.,1872. 5—29.

———— Sir Brook Fossbrooke: a novel. N. Y., 1872. 5—29.

———— The Martins of Cro' Martin. N. Y., 1869. 5—29.

———— Roland Cashel. Illus. N. Y., n. d. 5—29.

———— One of them. N. Y., 1872. 5—29.

———— Luttrell of Arran. N. Y., 1867. 5—29.

———— Sir Jasper Carew, knt.: his life and experiences. N. Y., 1872. 5—29.

———— Tony Butler. N.Y.,1872. 5—29.

———— Harry Lorrequer: his confessions and experiences. Phil., n. d. 5—29.

———— Kate O'Donoghue: a novel. Phil., n. d. 5—29.

———— Horace Templeton: a novel. Phil., n. d. 5—29.

Levizac, J. P. V. L. de. A theoretical and practical grammar of the French language. A. Bolmar, ed. Phil., 1861. 22—132.

Lewald, Fanny. Hulda; or, the deliverer: a romance. Mrs. A. L. Wister, tr. Phil.,1874. 7—43.

Lewes, George Henry. The biographical history of philosophy, from its origin in Greece, down to the present day. N. Y., 1857. 2 v. 14—84.

———— Three sisters and three fortunes; or, Rose, Blanche, and Violet. N.Y., n.d. 5—28.

———— On actors and the art of acting. Leipzig, 1875. 40—221.

Lewes, Marian Evans, (*George Eliot.*) Romola. N. Y., 1876. 6—36.

———— Silas Marner; and scenes of clerical life. Bost., 1869. 6—36.

———— Felix Holt, the radical. N. Y., 1866. 6—36.

———— The mill on the floss. N. Y., 1876. 6—36.

Lewes, Marian Evans, (*George Eliot.*) Adam Bede. N. Y., 1874. 6—36.

———— How Lisa loved the king. Bost., 1869. 16—100.

———— The Spanish Gypsy: a poem. Bost., 1868. 16—99.

———— Middlemarch; a study of provincial life. N. Y., 1873. 2 v. 6—36.

———— Scenes of clerical life. Illus. N. Y., 1874. 6—36.

———— The legend of Jubal and other poems, by George Eliot. Bost., 1874. 17—106.

———— Wit and wisdom of George Eliot. Bost., 1873. 2—9.

———— Daniel Deronda. N. Y., 1876. 2 v. 6—36.

Lewis, Meriwether, and William Clarke. Travels to the source of the Missouri River and across the American continent to the Pacific Ocean, in the years 1804-06. Lond., 1815. 3 v. 10—58.

Lewis, Tayler. "The light by which we see light;" or, nature and the scriptures: a course of lectures delivered before the Theological seminary and Rutgers college. N. Y., 1875. E.

Lewis the fourteenth, The age of. Voltaire, F. A. Lond., 1752. 2 v. 12—72.

———— county, N. Y., A history of. Illus. Hough, F. B. Albany, 1860. 31—190.

Lexington, History of the town of. Illus. Hudson, C. Bost., 1868. 30—182.

Liberia as I found it in 1858. Cowan, A. M. Frankfort, 1858. 17—101.

Liberty, History of;—ancient Romans and early Christians. Eliot, S. Bost., 1853. 2 v. 32—196.

———— and law under a federative government. Hill, B. A. Phil., 1874. 27—161.

———— and slavery, An essay on. Bledsoe, A. T. Phil., 1856. 27—161.

* **Library** of Congress, Catalogue of the. 1861-74. 8 v. 1—4.

*———— of the Department of State of the United States, Catalogue of the. 1825. D. R.

———— notes. Russell, A. P. N. Y., 1875. 40—222.

Liddell, Henry George, and Robert Scott. *A Greek-English lexicon, based on the German work of Francis Passow. N. Y., 1848. 23—137.

Lieber, Francis. The stranger in America; or, letters to a gentleman in Germany. Phil., 1835. 26—155.
—— On civil liberty and self-government. Phil., 1853. 2 v. 19—115.
—— Legal and political hermeneutics; or, principles of interpretation and construction in law and politics. Bost.,1839. 15—88.
—— Manual of political ethics, designed chiefly for the use of colleges and students at law. T. D. Woolsey, ed. Phil., 1875. 2 v. 18—108.
Liebig, Justus von. Complete works on chemistry. Phil., n. d. 15—87.
Life. (Little classics, vol. 4.) Bost., 1875. 5—33.
—— and death of Jason : a poem. Morris, W. Bost., 1871. 17—106.
—— drama, and other poems. Smith, A. Bost., 1859. 16—100.
—— for a life, A. Muloch, D. M. N. Y., 1874. 4—23.
—— in Danbury. Illus. Bailey, J. M. Bost., 1874. 2—11.
—— in its lower, intermediate, and higher forms. Illus. Gosse, P. H. N. Y., 1857. 14—85.
—— in Normandy ; sketches of French fishing, farming, cooking, natural history, and politics, drawn from nature. Illus. Edin., 1863. 2 v. 17—101.
—— on the plains and among the diggings. Illus. Delano, A. Auburn, 1854. 17—101.
—— ; its nature, varieties, and phenomena. Grindon, L. H. Phil., 1867. 14—81.
—— and sayings of Mrs. Partington. Illus. Shillaber, B. P. N. Y., 1854. 2—8.
Life's assize, A. Riddel, J. H. Lond.,1871. 3 v. 4—26.
Light and electricity. Tyndall, J. N. Y., 1871. 15—89.
—— science for leisure hours. Proctor, R. A. N. Y., 1871. 14—82.
Lights and shadows of Scottish life. Wilson, J. Phil., 1871. 2—13.
Lily and the cross, The. Illus. De Mille, J. Bost., 1875. 6—35.
Limes, calcareous cements, mortars, etc., Observations on. Illus. Pasley, Sir C. W. Lond., 1847. T.

Limits of religious thought examined. Mansel, H. L. Bost., 1868. E.
Lincoln, Abraham, The life of. Illus. Lamon, W. H. Bost., 1872. 12—66.
—— Same. Illus. Barrett, J. H. Cin., 1865. 12—66.
——, Benjamin, Life of. (Library of American biography, vol. 23.) 11—65.
Lindisfarn Chase: a novel. Trollope, T. A. N. Y.,1874. 7—43.
Lingard, John. A history of England, from the first invasion by the Romans. Paris, 1840. 8 v. 34—208.
Linley Rochford: a novel. McCarthy, J. N. Y., 1874. 6—35.
Linton, Eliza Lynn. The atonement of Leam Dundas. Illus. Phil., 1876. 41—230.
Lionel Lincoln. Illus. Cooper, J. F. N. Y., 1864. 3—14.
* **Lippincott's** complete pronouncing gazetteer. Revised and enlarged. Phil., 1866. 21—124.
—— magazine of literature, science, and education. Illus. 1868-72. Phil. 10 v. 20—119 and 120.
Lippincott, Sara Jane, (*Grace Greenwood.*) A forest tragedy, and other tales. Bost., 1856. P—2.
—— New life in new lands: notes of travel by Grace Greenwood. N. Y., 1873. 9—53.
—— Bonnie Scotland: tales of her history, heroes, and poets, by Grace Greenwood. Illus. Bost., 1872. P—3.
L'isthme de Panama. Chevalier, M. Paris, 1844. D. R.
Literary character of men of genius. Disraeli, I. Lond., 1859. 27—161.
—— criticism, Essays in. Hutton, R. H. Phil., n. d. 40—222.
—— reminiscences. De Quincey, T. Bost., 1859. 2 v. 2—12.
Literature of the age of Elizabeth. Whipple, E. P. Bost., 1869. 28—166.
——, The might and mirth of. Macbeth, J. W. V. N. Y., 1875. 40—224.
Little barefoot, The. Illus. Auerbach, B. Bost., 1867. 7—46.
—— classics. Rossiter Johnson, ed. Bost., 1874. 6 v. 5—33.

Contents.

Vol. 1. Exile: Ethan Brand; The swans of Lir; A night in a workhouse; The outcasts of

Poker Flat; The man without a country; Flight of a Tartar tribe.

Vol. 2. Intellect: The house and the brain; D'outre mort; The fall of the house of Usher; Chops, the dwarf; Wakefield; Murder considered as one of the fine arts; The captain's story.

Vol. 3. Tragedy: The murders in the rue Morgue; The Lauson tragedy; The iron shroud; The bell-tower; The Kathayan slave; The story of La Roche; The vision of sudden death.

Vol. 4. Life: Rab and his friends; A romance of real life; The luck of Roaring-Camp; Jerry Jarvis's wig; Beauty and the beast; David Swan; Dreamthorp; A bachelor's revery; The grammar of life; My châteaux; Dream children; The man in the reservoir; Westminster abbey; The puritans; Gettysburgh.

Vol. 5. Laughter: A Christmas carol; The haunted crust; A dissertation upon roast pig; The total depravity of inanimate things; The skeleton in the closet; Sandy Wood's sepulchre; A visit to the Asylum for Aged and Decayed Punsters; Mr. Tibbot O'Leary, the curious; Neal Malone.

Vol. 6. Love: Love and skates ; The maid of Malines; The story of Ruth; The rise of Iskander.

Vol. 7. Iris; The Rosicrucian; The south breaker ; The snow-storm; The king of the peak.

Vol. 8. Mystery: The ghost; The four-fifteen express; The signal-man; The haunted ships; A raft that no man made; The invisible princess; The advocate's wedding-day; The birth-mark.

Vol. 9. Comedy: Barney O'Reirdon, the navigator; Haddad-Ben-Ahab, the traveller; Bluebeard's ghost; The pic-nic party; Father Tom and the Pope; Johnny Darbeyshire; The gridiron; The box-tunnel.

Vol. 10. Childhood: A dog of Flanders; The king of the golden river; The lady of Shalott; Marjorie Fleming; Little Jakey; The lost child; Goody Gracious and the forget-me-not; A faded leaf of history; A child's dream of a star.

Vol. 11. Heroism: Little Briggs and I; Ray; Three November days; The forty-seven Rônins; A chance child; A leaf in the storm.

Vol. 12. Fortune: The gold bug; The fairy finder; Murad, the unlucky; The children of the public; The rival dreamers; The three-fold destiny.

Little Dorrit. Illus. Dickens, C. N. Y., 1868. 2 v. 2 copies. 3—15 and 16.

—— duke, The. Illus. Yonge, C. M. Lond., 1869. 38.

—— foxes, by "Christopher Crowfield." Stowe, H. B. Bost., 1873. 39.

—— Hodge. Jenkins, E. N. Y., 1873. 3—19.

Little men. Alcott, L. M. Bost., 1871. 5—31.

—— moorland princess, The. "E. Marlitt." Phil., 1875. 7—42.

—— pussy willow. Illus. Stowe, H. B. Bost., 1870. 39.

—— savage, The. Illus. Marryat, Capt. F. Lond. and N. Y., n. d. 5—30.

—— Sunshine's holiday. Illus. Muloch, D. M. N. Y., 1871. 39.

—— Wanderlin, and other fairy tales. Keary, A. Lond., 1865. 38.

—— women. Alcott, L. M. Bost., 1873. 2 v. 5—31.

Live it down: a novel. Jeaffreson, J. C. N. Y., 1873. 7—41.

Livermore, George. An historical research respecting the opinions of the founders of the republic on negroes as slaves, as citizens, and as soldiers. Bost., 1863. T.

Lives of men of letters and science who flourished in the time of George the third. Illus. Brougham, H. Lond., 1845. 11—63.

Living link, The. Illus. De Mille, .J. N. Y., 1874. 6—35.

Livingston, Edward, Life of. Hunt, C. H. N. Y., 1864. 11—60.

Livingston, John. Portraits of eminent Americans now living; including President Pierce and his cabinet. N. Y., Lond., and Paris, 1854. 12—68.

Livingston, William, A memoir of the life of. Sedgwick, T. N. Y., 1833. 12—70.

Livingstone, David. Missionary travels and researches in South Africa; including a sketch of sixteen years' residence in the interior. Illus. N. Y., 1858. 17—102.

—— Last journals in Central Africa, from 1865 to his death; continued by a narrative of his last moments and sufferings, obtained from his faithful servants Chuma and Susi, by Horace Waller. Illus. N. Y., 1875. 17—101.

Livius, Titus. The history of Rome. George Baker, tr. Phil., 1840. 2 v. 35—212.

—— Same. Lond., 1833. 7 v. 13—79.

Lisa: a Russian novel. Turgenef, I. S. N. Y., 1872. 4—22.

Lloyd, William Watkins. The age of Pericles: a history of the politics and arts of Greece, from the Persian to the Peloponnesian war. Lond., 1875. 2 v. 40—225.

Lobley, J. Logan. Mount Vesuvius: a descriptive, historical, and geological account of the volcano, with a notice of the recent eruption. Loud., 1868. 15—89.

Locke, John, The philosophical works of; with an essay and notes by J. A. St. John. Lond., 1867. 2 v. 14—84.

Lockhart, John Gibson. Ancient Spanish ballads, historical and romantic : a new and revised edition, with a biographical notice. Bost., 1861. 17—105.

—— The life of Sir Walter Scott, bart., abridged from the larger work. Edin., 1871. 11—64.

Lockhart, Lawrence W. M. Fair to see : a novel. N. Y., 1872. 6—35.

Loftie, W. J. A century of Bibles; or, the authorized version from 1611 to 1711, to which is added Wm. Kilburne's tract on dangerous errors in the late printed Bibles, 1659, with lists of Bibles in the British museum, Bodleian, Stuttgart, and other libraries. Lond., 1812. 15—88.

Logan, James. The Scottish Gaël; or, Celtic manners, as preserved among the Highlanders ; being an historical and descriptive account of the inhabitants, antiquities, and national peculiarities of Scotland ; more particularly of the northern, or Gaëlic parts of the country, where the singular habits of the aboriginal Celts are most tenaciously retained. Illus. Lond., 1831. 2 v. 34—204.

Logan, Olive. See Sikes, *Mrs.* W.

Logic, A system of. Mill, J. S. N. Y., 1869. 14—81.

——, Lectures on. Hamilton, *Sir* W. Bost., 1867. 14—82.

—— of political economy, The. De Quincey, T. Bost., 1859. 2—12.

Loménie, Louis L. de. Beaumarchais and his times: sketches of French society in the eighteenth century, from unpublished documents. H. S. Edwards, tr. N. Y., 1857. 11—64.

London. Illus. C. Knight, ed. Lond., 1851. 6 v. 33—198.

*——— art journal, 1867-68. 2 v. 26—153.

London, Cyclopædia of. Illus. Knight, C. Lond., 1851. 27—160.

——, exhibited in 1851. Illus. Weale, J. Lond., n. d. 27—160.

——, Illustrations of the public buildings of. Illus. Pugin, A., and J. Britton. Lond., 1838. 2 v. 15—87.

—— quarterly review, The. 1854-59. 6 v. X.

—— social life, Impressions of. Nadal, E. S. N. Y., 1875. 19—116.

London's heart: a novel. Farjeon, B. L. Illus. N. Y., 1873. 6—35.

Long, George, and Robley Dunglison. An introduction to the study of Grecian and Roman geography. Charlottesville, *Va.*, 1829. 15—87.

Long Island, The history of. Illus. Thompson, B. F. N. Y., 1843. 2 v. 31—189.

Longfellow, Henry Wadsworth. Outre-mer: a pilgrimage beyond the sea. Bost., 1865. 17—103.

—— Kavanagh : a tale. Bost., 1859. 6—36.

—— Hyperion : a romance. Bost., 1865. 6—36.

—— Three books of song. Bost., 1872. 16—95.

—— The golden legend. Bost., 1859. 16—95.

—— The New England tragedies. Bost., 1868. 17—106.

—— Aftermath. Bost., 1874. 17—106.

—— The masque of Pandora, and other poems. Bost., 1876. 17—106.

—— The hanging of the crane. Illus. Bost., 1875. 17—105.

—— Poems, revised edition. Bost., 1866. 4 v. 16—95.

Contents.

Vol. 1. Voices of the night; Ballads and other poems ; Poems on slavery ; The Spanish student.

Vol. 2. The belfry of Bruges, and other poems ; Evangeline ; The seaside and the fireside.

Vol. 3. The golden legend ; The courtship of Miles Standish ; Birds of passage.

Vol. 4. The song of Hiawatha ; Tales of a wayside inn ; Birds of passage.

Longinus, Dionysius. Quem nova versione donavit, notis illustravit. Z. Pierce. 1724. D. R.

Longstreet, Augustus B. Georgia scenes, characters, incidents, etc., in the

Knight, Charles. Half-hours with the best authors. Lond., 1866. 4 v. 2—10.
—— Half-hours with the best letter-writers and autobiographers; forming a collection of memoirs and anecdotes of eminent persons. Lond. and N. Y., n. d. 2 v. 2—10.
—— Cyclopædia of London, 1851. Illus. 27—160.
—— Passages from the life of. N. Y., 1874. 12—66.
Knight, Cornelia, and Thomas Raikes. Personal reminiscences by. (Bric-a-brac series.) Illus. N. Y., 1875. 19—114.
Knight, Edward H. American mechanical dictionary; being a description of tools, instruments, machines, processes, and engineering; history of inventions; general technological vocabulary, and digest of mechanical appliances in science and the arts. Illus. N. Y., 1874-76. 3 v. 23—138.
Knight, Richard Payne. The symbolical language of ancient art and mythology : an inquiry. A new edition, with introduction, additions, notes translated into English, and a new and complete index by Alexander Wilder. N. Y., 1876. 40—225.
Knight of Gwynne, The. Lever, C. J. Lond., n. d. 7—44.
Knights hospitallers, History of the. Vertot D'Aubeuf, R. A. de. Edin., 1757. 5 v. 30—184.
—— and their days. Doran, J. N. Y., 1864. 19—114.
Knolles, Richard. * General historie of the Turkes, from the first beginning of that nation to the rising of the Othoman familie, with all the notable expeditions of the Christian princes against them; with the lives and conquests of the Othoman kings and emperours. Lond., 1631. 34—203.
Knowles, James Sheridan, The dramatic works of. Lond., n. d. 17—106.
Knox, John, The life of. McCrie, T. Edin., 1813. 2 v. 40—223.
Kohlrausch, Friedrich. History of Germany, from the earliest period. J. D. Haas, tr. N. Y., 1853. 36—218.
Koran, commonly called the Alcoran of Mohammed; translated into English immediately from the original Arabic,

with explanatory notes taken from the most approved commentators; to which is prefixed a preliminary discourse, by George Sale; and a memoir of the translator. Phil., 1874. 19—116.
Krafft, J. Ch. Recueil d'architecture civile, avec les planches. Paris, 1829. V.
—— Traité sur l'art de la charpente. Paris, 1840. 2 v. V.
—— Maisons de Paris, et de ses environs, avec planches. Paris, 1849. U.

La Beche, Sir Henry Thomas de. A geological manual. Phil., 1832. 15—91.
—— A selection of geological memoirs contained in the "Annales des mines," by Brougniart, Humboldt, von Buch, and others. Illus. Lond., 1836. 15—91.
—— The geological observer. Illus. Phil., 1851. 15—91.
La Bruyère, J. de. The characters of Theophrastus; illustrated by physiognomical sketches. Lond., 1831. 27—162.
La Hodde, Lucien de. The cradle of rebellions : a history of the secret societies of France. N. Y., 1864. 34—214.
La Motte-Fouqué, Friedrich, baron de. Undine, and other tales; containing The two captains, Aslauga's knight, and Sintram and his companions. Illus. N. Y., 1871. 38.
La Rame, Louise de, (Ouida.) Idalia: a novel. Phil., 1870. 2 copies. 7—44.
—— Chandos : a novel. Phil., 1871. 7—44.
—— Tricotrin : the story of a waif and stray. Phil., 1871. 7—44.
—— Beatrice Boville, and other stories. Phil., 1868. 7—44.
—— Puck. Phil., 1870. 7—44.
—— Folle-Farine. Phil., 1871. 7—44.
—— Randolph Gordon, and other stories. Phil., 1867. 7—44.
—— Cecil Castlemaine's gage; Lady Marabout's troubles; and other stories. Phil., 1867. 7—44.
—— Granville De Vigne; or, held in bondage : a tale of the day. Phil., 1871. 7—44.
—— Under two flags : a novel. Phil., 1867. 2 copies. 7—44.

Macaulay, Thomas Babington, The life and letters of. Trevelyan, G. O. N. Y., 1876. 2 v. 11—59.

Macbeth, John Walker Vilant. The might and mirth of literature: a treatise on figurative language, in which upwards of six hundred writers are referred to and two hundred and twenty figures illustrated; embracing a complete survey, on an entirely new plan, of English and American literature; interspersed with historical notices of the progress of the language, with anecdotes of many of the authors, and with· discussions of the fundamental principles of criticism and of the weapons of oratory. N. Y., 1875. 40—224.

McCabe, James D. The illustrated history of the centennial exhibition, held in commemoration of the one hundredth anniversary of American independence; with a full description of the great buildings and all the objects of interest exhibited in them; embracing, also, a concise history of the origin and success of the exhibition, and biographies of the leading members of the centennial commission, to which is added a complete description of the city of Philadelphia. Phil., 1876, 40—225.

MacCabe, William Bernard. Florine, princess of Burgundy; a tale of the first crusaders. Balt., 1855. P—3.

McCarthy, Justin. Lady Judith: a tale of two continents. Illus. N. Y., 1871. 6—35.

—— a fair Saxon: a novel. N. Y., 1873. 7—41.

—— Linley Rochford: a novel. N. Y., 1874. 6—35.

—— Paul Massie: a romance. N. Y., n. d. 7—41.

—— Dear lady Disdain: a novel. N. Y., 1876. 6—35.

McClure, A. K. Three thousand miles through the Rocky Mountains. Illus. Phil., 1869. 17—102.

McCrie, Thomas. The life of John Knox: containing illustrations of the history of the reformation in Scotland; with biographical notices of the principal reformers, and sketches of the progress of literature in Scotland, during a great part of the sixteenth century; to

which is subjoined an appendix, consisting of letters and other papers, hitherto unpublished. Edin., 1813. 2 v. 40— 223.

McCullagh, W. Torrens. The industrial history of free nations, considered in relation to their domestic institutions and external policy. Lond., 1846. 2 v. 36—215.

McCulloch, John R. *A dictionary, geographical, statistical, and historical, of the various countries, places, and principal natural objects in the world. N. Y., 1852. 2 v. 21—126.

—— *A dictionary, practical, theoretical, and historical, of commerce and commercial navigation. H. Vethake, ed. Phil., 1849. 2 v. 21—127.

—— A statistical account of the British empire. Lond., 1837. 2 v. 18—109.

—— The principles of political economy; with a sketch of the rise and progress of the science. Edin., 1825. 15— 88.

M'Culloh, James H., jr. Researches on America; being an attempt to settle some points relative to the aborigines of America. Balt., 1817. 30—178.

McCulloh, R. S. Reports from the secretary of the treasury, of scientific investigations in relation to sugar and hydrometers. Wash., 1848. 8.

Macdonald, Duncan George Forbes. British Columbia and Vancouver's island; comprising a description of these dependencies; their physical character, climate, capabilities, population, trade, natural-history, geology, ethnology, gold-fields, and future prospects; also an account of the manners and customs of the native Indians. Lond., 1862. 33— 200.

Macdonald, George. Wilfrid Cumbermede: an autobiographical story. Illus. N. Y., 1872. 7—45.

—— The princess and the goblin. Illus. N. Y., 1871. 7—45.

—— The vicar's daughter: an autobiographical story; sequel to "Annals of a quiet neighbourhood," and the "Seaboard parish." Illus. Bost., 1872. 7— 45.

—— Annals of a quiet neighbourhood. Illus. N. Y., 1874. 7—45.

MacDonald, George. The seaboard parish: a sequel to the "Annals of a quiet neighbourhood." Illus. N. Y., 1873. 7—45.

—— Within and without. N. Y., 1872. 17—106.

—— A hidden life, and other poems. N. Y., 1872. 17—106.

—— Ranald Bannerman's boyhood. Illus. Phil., 1874. 39.

—— Alec Forbes of Howglen: a novel. N. Y., 1874. 6—35.

—— Malcolm: a romance. Phil., 1875. 6—35.

—— A double story. N. Y., n. d. 7—45.

—— St. George and St. Michael: a novel. Illus. N. Y., n. d. 7—45.

—— Guild court: a London story. N. Y., 1868. 6—35.

—— Robert Falconer. Lond., n. d. 7—45.

—— Thomas Wingfold, curate. N. Y., 1876. 7—45.

—— David Elginbrod. Bost., n. d. 7—45.

Macé, Jean. Home fairy tales. Illus. Mary L. Booth, tr. N. Y., 1870. 33.

—— The servants of the stomach. N. Y., 1868. 15—88.

—— The history of a mouthful of bread, and its effect on the organization of men and animals. Mrs. A. Gatty, tr. N. Y., 1874. 15—88.

Macfarlane, Charles. Romance of history; Italy. Illus. Lond., n. d. 2—8.

Macfarlane, James. The coal-regions of America; their topography, geology, and development, with a colored geographical map of Pennsylvania, a railroad map of all the coal-regions, and numerous other maps and illustrations. N. Y., 1873. V.

MacGahan, J. A. Campaigning on the Oxus, and the fall of Khiva. Illus. N. Y., 1874. 17—101.

McGilchrist, John. Richard Cobden, the apostle of free trade; his political career and public services: a biography. N. Y., 1865. 13—79.

Macgregor, John. The progress of America, from the discovery by Columbus to the year 1846. Lond., 1847. 2 v. 8.

—— Commercial statistics: a digest of the productive resources, commercial legislation, customs tariffs, navigation, port and quarantine laws and charges, shipping, imports and exports, and the moneys, weights, and measures of all nations; including all the British commercial treaties with foreign states. Lond., 1850. 5 v. R—1.

—— A thousand miles in the Rob Roy canoe, on rivers and lakes of Europe. Illus. Bost., 1871. 17—101.

—— The Rob Roy on the Baltic: a canoe cruise through Norway, Sweden, Denmark, Schleswig-Holstein, the North Sea, and the Baltic. Illus. Bost., n. d. 17—101.

—— The Rob Roy on the Jordan, Nile, Red Sea, and Gennesareth: a canoe cruise in Palestine and Egypt, and the waters of Damascus. Illus. N. Y., 1870. 17—101.

McGregor, John. British America. Edin., 1833. 2 v. 33—200.

Machiavelli, Niccolo. *The Florentine history. Lond., 1674. 35—212.

Mackay, Alexander. The western world; or, travels in the United States in 1846-47. Phil., 1849. 2 v. 8—50.

Mackay, Charles. Memoirs of extraordinary popular delusions and the madness of crowds. Illus. Lond., n. d. 19—116.

McKenney, Thomas L. Memoirs, official and personal; with sketches of travel among the northern and southern Indians. Illus. N. Y., 1846. 2 v. in one. 30—178.

—— and James Hall. History of the Indian tribes of North America, with biographical sketches and anecdotes of the principal chiefs. Illus. Phil., 1848-50. 3 v. 30—178.

—— *Same. Phil., 1836. 3 v. V.

Mackenzie, Alexander. Voyages from Montreal, on the river St. Lawrence, through the continent of North America, to the Frozen and Pacific oceans, in the years 1789-93. Lond., 1801. 10—55.

Mackenzie, Alexander Slidell. The life of Commodore Oliver Hazard Perry. N. Y., 1843. 2 v. 13—78.

—— The life of Paul Jones. N. Y., 1846. 2 v. 12—66.

Mackenzie, Alexander Slidell. Life of Stephen Decatur. (Library of American biography, vol. 2L.) 11—65.

Mackintosh, Sir James. History of England. (Lardner's cabinet cyclopædia.) Lond., 1830. 10 v. 34—207.

—— History of the revolutions in England in 1688, comprising a view of the reign of James second, from his accession to the enterprise of the prince of Orange. Phil., 1835. 34—205.

—— History of England, from the earliest times, to the final establishment of the reformation. Lond., 1853. 2 v. 33—199.

——, The miscellaneous works of. (Modern British essayists.) Bost., 1854. 27—159.

McLain, Mary Webster. Wedding garments; or, Bessie Morris's diary. N. Y., 1875. P—1.

McLaurin, John, Sermons and essays of. J. Gillies, ed. Phil., 1811. E.

Macleod, Alexander. Talking to the children. N. Y., 1872. 38.

Macleod, Norman. Character sketches. Illus. N. Y., n. d. P—3.

Macmillan, Hugh. First forms of vegetation. Illus. Lond., 1874. 14—85.

Macomb, Capt. J. N. Report on the exploring expedition from Santa Fé, N. M., to the junction of the Grand and Green rivers of the great Colorado of the west, in 1859; with a geological report by Prof. J. S. Newberry. Illus. Wash., 1876. D. R.

McPherson, Edward. The political history of the United States of America during the great rebellion, from Nov. 6, 1860, to July 4, 1864. Wash., 1864. 30—178.

—— Same. 2d ed. 1865. 30—178.

—— Same during the period of reconstruction, from April 15, 1865, to July 15, 1870. Wash., 1871. 30—180.

—— A hand-book of politics for 1872 and 1874, being a record of important political action, national and state. Wash., 1872-74. 2 v. 18—108.

—— Hand-book of politics for 1876: being a record of important political action, national and state, from July 15, 1874, to July 15, 1876. Wash., 1876. 18—108.

Macquoid, Katharine S. Patty. Lond. and N. Y., 1871. P—3.

—— My story: a novel. Illus. N. Y., 1875. 6—35.

Macready, William Charles. Reminiscences and selections from his diaries and letters. Sir F. Pollock, ed. N. Y., 1875. 12—71.

Macy, Obed. The history of Nantucket; being a compendious account of the first settlement of the island by the English, together with the rise and progress of the whale fishery. Bost., 1835. 33—201.

Mad Dumaresq: a novel. Marryat, Miss F. Leipzig, 1873. 2 v. in one. 4—22.

—— Monkton, and other stories. Collins, W. W. Phil., n, d. 5—28.

Madame de Beaupré. Jenkin, C. N. Y., 1869. 7—46.

—— de Chamblay: a novel. Dumas, A. D. Phil., n. d. 3—20.

—— de Staël: an historical novel. Bülte, A. N. Y., 1869. 6—39.

—— Thérèse. Illus. Erckmann, E., and A. Chatrian. N. Y., 1869. 5—31.

Madcap violet: a novel. Black, W. N. Y., 1877. 4—26.

Madden, Frederic W. History of Jewish coinage, and of money in the Old and New Testaments. Illus. Lond., 1864. 15—88.

Madeleine. Kavanagh, J. N. Y., 1852. 7—41.

Mademoiselle Fifty Millions. "Countess Dash." A. De V. Chaudron, tr. N. Y., 1869. 5—28.

Madison, James, Selections from the private correspondence of, from 1813 to 1836: published exclusively for private distribution. Wash., 1859. 25—150.

——, History of the life and times of. Rives, W. C. Bost., 1859. Vol. 1. 11—59.

——, Letters and other writings of; published by order of Congress. Phil., 1865. 4 v. 25—150.

Magdalena. John E. Phil., 1870. 7—42.

Magnalia Christi Americani; or, the ecclesiastical history of New England. Mather, C. Hartford, 1853. 2 v. 32—196.

Mahaffy, John Pendleton. Rambles and studies in Greece. Illus. Lond., 1876. 9—53.

Mantell, Gideon Algernon. Petrifactions and their teachings; or, a handbook to the gallery of the British museum. Illus. Lond., 1851. 15—91.

—— The medals of creation; or, first lessons in geology and in the study of organic remains. Lond., 1844. 2 v. 14—85.

—— A pictorial atlas of fossil remains: illustrations selected from Parkinson's "Organic remains of a former world," and Artis's "Antediluvian phytology." Lond., 1850. 14—80.

Manual of public libraries, institutions, and societies in the United States and British provinces. Rhees, W. J. Phil., 1859. V.

*—— of dates, The: a dictionary of reference to all the most important events in the history of mankind. Townsend, G. H. Lond., 1862. 23—138.

Manufactures of iron. Illus. Overman, F. Phil., 1851. T.

——, The philosophy of. Ure, A. Lond., 1835. T.

Maps of the District of Columbia and city of Washington; and plats of the squares and lots of the city. Wash., 1852. 26—153.

—— accompanying the report of the Commissioner of the General Land Office, 1866, part 2. X.

Marble faun, The. Hawthorne, N. Bost., 1868. 2 v. 3—18.

—— prophecy, and other poems. Holland, J. G. N. Y., 1872. 16—96.

Marcoy, Paul. *Travels in South America, from the Pacific ocean to the Atlantic ocean. Illus. 2 v. N. Y., 1875. N.

Marcy, Randolph B. Border reminiscences. Illus. N. Y., 1872. 2—12.

—— Exploration of the Red River of Louisiana, in the year 1852. Illus. Wash., 1853. D. R.

Margaret: a tale. Judd, S. Bost., 1871. 6—38.

—— and her bridesmaids. Stretton, J. C. Bost., 1864. 6—38.

—— Howth. Davis, R. H. Bost., 1862. 41—228.

—— Moncrieffe, the first love of Aaron Burr: a romance of the revolution. Burdett, C. N. Y., 1860. 3—19.

Margaret of Anjou, The life and times of. Illus. Hookham, M. A. Lond., 1872. 2 v. 13—76.

Maria Monk's daughter. Illus. Eckel, L. S. J. N. Y., 1874. 6—36.

Marian Grey; or, the heiress of Redstone Hall. Holmes, M. J. N. Y. and Lond., 1871. P—1.

Marie Antoinette, The life of. Yonge, C. D. Lond., 1876. 2 v. 40—223.

—— and her son. Illus. "Louise Mühlbach." N. Y., 1872. 4—21.

Marietta. Trollope, T. A. Phil., n. d. 7—43.

Marion, Fulgence. Wonderful balloon ascents; or, the conquest of the skies. Illus. N. Y., 1870. P—2.

—— The wonders of optics. (Illustrated library of wonders.) C. W. Quin, tr. and ed. N. Y., 1872. 28—169.

—— The wonders of vegetation. (Illustrated library of wonders.) Schele De Vere, ed. N. Y., 1874. 28—169.

Marion, Francis, Life of. Illus. Horry, P. and M. L. Weems. Phil., 1860. 13—76.

Marjorie Daw, and other people. Aldrich, T. B. Bost., 1873. 39.

Marjorie's quest. Illus. Gould, J. T. Bost., 1872. 4—26.

Marjory. Milly Deane. Lond., 1872. O—3.

Marlborough, *Duke of,* Memoirs of the. Coxe, W. Lond., 1847-48. 3 v. 11—61.

——, John, *duke of,* Military life of. Alison, *Sir* A. N. Y., 1848. 11—61.

Marlborough, Sarah Churchill, *duchess of.* Private correspondence, illustrative of the court and times of Queen Anne; and select correspondence of her husband, John, duke of Marlborough. Lond., 1838. 2 v. 11—61.

——, Memoirs of, and of the court of Queen Anne. *Mrs.* Thomson. Lond., 1839. 2 v. 11—61.

Marlitt, E., *pseud.* See John, E.

Marmion. Scott, *Sir* W. N. Y., 1871. 17—105.

Maroon, The. Simms, W. G. Phil., 1855. 6—39.

Marquis and merchant: a novel. Collins, M. N. Y., 1871. 5—28.

Marriage. Ferrier, M. Lond. and N. Y., n. d. 4—22.

and the sayings and doings of sundry of the towns-people; interspersed with sketches of the most remarkable and distinguished characters of that place and its vicinity, by Solomon Second-thoughts, schoolmaster, from original MSS. indited by him, and now made public at the request and under the patronage of the great new-light democratic central committee of Quodlibet. Phil., 1860. 6—39.

—— Rob of the bowl: a legend of St. Inigoe's. Phil., 1861. 6—39.

—— Mr. Ambrose's letters on the rebellion. N. Y., 1865. 26—155.

Kennedy, William. Texas: the rise, progress, and prospects of the republic of Texas. Lond., 1841. 2 v. 31—187.

Kenneth, my king: a novel. Brock, S. A. N. Y. and Lond., 1873. 6—38.

Kenrick, John. Ancient Egypt under the Pharaohs. Lond., 1850. 2 v. 36—216.

Kent, James. Commentaries on American law. N. Y., 1848. 21—128.

Kentucky, The history of. Marshall, H. Frankfort, 1824. 2 v. 31—186.

——, Historical sketches of. Illus. Collins, L. Maysville, *Ky.*, 1850. 31—186.

——, A history of the commonwealth of. Butler, M. Louisville, 1834. 31—186.

Khiva, A ride to. Burnaby, F. N. Y., 1877. 10—57.

Kidder, Daniel P. Sketches of a residence and travels in Brazil. Illus. Phil., 1845. 2 v. 10—58.

Kidder, Frederic. History of the Boston massacre, March 5, 1770; consisting of the narrative of the town, the trial of the soldiers, and a historical introduction containing unpublished documents of John Adams, and explanatory notes. Albany, 1870. 30—182.

Kiddle, Henry, and Alexander J. Schem, *editors*. The cyclopædia of education: a dictionary of information for teachers, school officers, parents, and others. N. Y. and Lond., 1877. 1—1.

Kilmeny. Black, W. N. Y., 1870. 5—29.

Kimball, Richard B. Was he successful? a novel. N. Y. and Leipsic, 1864. O—3.

King, Charles. A memoir of the construction, cost, and capacity of the Cro-

ton aqueduct; with an account of the civic celebration of the 14th of October, 1842, on occasion of the completion of the great work. N. Y., 1843. D. R.

King, Clarence. Mountaineering in the Sierra Nevada. Bost., 1872. 17—104.

—— United States geological exploration of the fortieth parallel. Wash., 1870-71. Vols. 3 and 5. D. R.

King, Thomas. The modern style of cabinet-work exemplified. Illus. Lond., 1862. V.

King and the commonwealth: a history of Charles I and the rebellion. Cordery, B. M., and J. S. Phillpotts. Phil., 1876. 34—206.

—— of the mountains, The. About, E. Bost., 1861. 6—40.

—— Arthur: a poem. Bulwer-Lytton, *Sir* E. N. Y., 1871. 17—105.

—— René's daughter: a Danish lyrical drama. Hertz, H. N. Y., n. d. 17—106.

—— George the fourth and king William the fourth, A journal of the reigns of. Greville, C. C. F. N. Y., 1875. 2 v. 34—207.

Kinglake, Alexander William. Invasion of the Crimea: its origin, and an account of its progress, down to the death of Lord Raglan. N. Y., 1868-75. 5 v. 33—198.

Kingman, Bradford. History of North Bridgewater, Plymouth County, Massachusetts, from its first settlement to the present time, with family registers. Illus. Bost., 1866. 30—182.

King's own, The. Marryat, *Capt.* F. N. Y., 1857. 5—30.

Kingsborough, Edward King, *viscount*. Antiquities of Mexico, comprising fac-similes of ancient Mexican paintings and hieroglyphics; with the monuments of New Spain, by M. Dupaix. Lond., 1830-48. 9 v. U.

Kingsley, Charles. Westward ho! or, the voyages and adventures of Sir Amyas Leigh, kn't. Lond. and N. Y., 1871. 7—43.

—— Two years ago. Bost., 1866. 7—43.

—— Hypatia; or, new foes with an old face. Bost., 1870. 7—43.

—— Hereward, the last of the English. Bost., 1866. 7—43.

Kingsley, Charles. Sir Walter Raleigh and his time; with other papers. Bost., 1859. 13—77.

—— The water-babies: a fairy tale for a land-baby. Bost., 1869. 38.

—— The heroes; or, Greek fairy tales for • my children. Illus. Lond., 1868. 38.

—— Poems; including the Saint's tragedy, Andromeda, songs, ballads, etc. Lond. and N. Y., 1872. 16—99.

—— Alton Locke, tailor and poet: an autobiography. N. Y., n. d. 7—43.

—— Health and education. N. Y., 1874. 19—114.

—— Glaucus; or, the wonders of the shore. Illus. Lond., 1873. 14—83.

—— The hermits. Illus. Lond., n. d. 11—60.

—— Plays and Puritans, and other historical essays. Lond., 1873. 28—166.

—— Prose idylls, new and old. Lond., 1874. 28—166.

—— At last: a Christmas in the West Indies. Illus. Lond., 1874. 17—102.

—— Phaethon; or, loose thoughts for loose thinkers. Cambridge, 1859. 28—166.

—— His letters and memories of his life, edited by his wife. Abridged from the London edition. N. Y., 1877. 11—64.

Kingsley, Henry. Stretton: a novel. Illus. N. Y., 1869. 6—35.

—— Ravenshoe. Lond., 1864. 7—43.

—— Austin Elliot. Bost., 1863. 7—43.

—— The recollections of Geoffrey Hamlyn. Bost., 1869. 7—43.

—— The Hillyars and the Burtons: a story of two families. Bost., 1866. 7—43.

—— Leighton court: a country-house story. Bost., 1866. 7—43.

—— Silcote of Silcotes. Lond., 1869. 7—43.

—— Tales of old travel. Illus. Lond. and N. Y., 1869. 2—10.

—— The lost child. Illus. Lond. and N. Y., 1871. 6—35.

—— The Harveys. Berlin and Phil., 1872. 7—43.

—— Old Margaret: a novel. Berlin and Phil., 1872. 7—43.

—— The boy in gray. Illus. Lond., 1871. 39.

Kip, Leonard. The dead marquise: a romance. N. Y., 1873. P—3.

Kip, William Ingraham. The early Jesuit missions in North America; compiled and translated from the letters of the French Jesuits, with notes. Albany, 1873. 29—177.

Inheritance, The. Ferrier, M. Lond. and N. Y., n. d. 4—22.

Kirby, Mary and Elizabeth. The world at home; or, pictures and scenes from far-off lands. Illus. Lond. and N. Y., 1872. 38.

Kirke, Edmund, pseud. See Gilmore, J. R.

Kirkland, Frazar. The pictorial book of anecdotes and incidents of the war of the rebellion, civil, military, naval, and domestic. Hartford, 1866. 2—7.

—— Clyclopædia of commercial and business anecdotes. Illus. N. Y., 1864. 2 v. 2—7.

Kirkland, Samuel, Life of. (Library of American biography, v. 25.) 11—65 —

Kismet. (No Name series.) Fletcher. D. Bost., 1877. 41—226.

Kissing the rod. Yates, E. Lond. and N. Y., n. d. 7—45.

Kitty. Edwards, M. B. N. Y., 1870. 6—35.

Klaczko, Julian. Two chancellors: prince Gortchakoff and prince Bismarck. F. P. Ward, tr. N. Y., 1876. 40—222.

Knatchbull - Hugessen, Edward Hugessen. Puss-cat mew, and other stories for my children. Illus. N. Y., 1871. 38.

—— Crackers for Christmas. Illus. N. Y., 1872. 39.

—— Moonshine: fairy stories. Illus. Lond., 1874. 39.

—— Tales at tea-time: fairy stories. Illus. Lond., 1872. 39.

—— Whispers from Fairy land. Illus. N. Y., 1875. 39.

—— River legends; or, father Thames and father Rhine. Illustrated by Doré. Lond., 1875. 39.

Knatchbull - Hugessen, Louisa. The history of prince Perrypets: a fairy tale. Illus. Lond., 1872. 39.

Knickerbocker's history of New York. Irving, W. N. Y., 1851. 3—19.

Knight, Charles. Half-hours with the best authors. Lond., 1866. 4 v. 2—10.

—— Half-hours with the best letter-writers and autobiographers; forming a collection of memoirs and anecdotes of eminent persons. Lond. and N. Y., n. d. 2 v. 2—10.

—— Cyclopædia of London, 1851. Illus. 27—160.

—— Passages from the life of. N. Y., 1874. 12—66.

Knight, Cornelia, and Thomas Raikes. Personal reminiscences by. (Bric-a-brac series.) Illus. N. Y., 1875. 19—114.

Knight, Edward H. American mechanical dictionary; being a description of tools, instruments, machines, processes, and engineering; history of inventions; general technological vocabulary, and digest of mechanical appliances in science and the arts. Illus. N. Y., 1874-76. 3 v. 23—138.

Knight, Richard Payne. The symbolical language of ancient art and mythology : an inquiry. A new edition, with introduction, additions, notes translated into English, and a new and complete index by Alexander Wilder. N. Y., 1876. 40—225.

Knight of Gwynne, The. Lever, C. J. Lond., n. d. 7—44.

Knights hospitallers, History of the. Vertot D'Aubeuf, R. A. de. Edin., 1757. 5 v. 30—184.

—— and their days. Doran, J. N. Y., 1864. 19—114.

Knolles, Richard. * General historie of the Turkes, from the first beginning of that nation to the rising of the Othoman familie, with all the notable expeditions of the Christian princes against them; with the lives and conquests of the Othoman kings and emperours. Lond., 1631. 34—203.

Knowles, James Sheridan, The dramatic works of. Lond., n. d. 17—106.

Knox, John, The life of. McCrie, T. Edin., 1813. 2 v. 40—223.

Kohlrausch, Friedrich. History of Germany, from the earliest period. J. D. Haas, tr. N. Y., 1853. 36—218.

Koran, commonly called the Alcoran of Mohammed; translated into English immediately from the original Arabic, with explanatory notes taken from the most approved commentators; to which is prefixed a preliminary discourse, by George Sale; and a memoir of the translator. Phil., 1874. 19—116.

Krafft, J. Ch. Recueil d'architecture civile, avec les planches. Paris, 1829. V.

—— Traité sur l'art de la charpente. Paris, 1840. 2 v. V.

—— Maisons de Paris, et de ses environs, avec planches. Paris, 1849. U.

La Beche, Sir Henry Thomas de. A geological manual. Phil., 1832. 15—91.

—— A selection of geological memoirs contained in the "Annales des mines," by Brongniart, Humboldt, von Buch, and others. Illus. Lond., 1836. 15—91.

—— The geological observer. Illus. Phil., 1851. 15—91.

La Bruyère, J. de. The characters of Theophrastus; illustrated by physiognomical sketches. Lond., 1831. 27—162.

La Hodde, Lucien de. The cradle of rebellions: a history of the secret societies of France. N. Y., 1864. 34—214.

La Motte-Fouqué, Friedrich, baron de. Undine, and other tales; containing The two captains, Aslauga's knight, and Sintram and his companions. Illus. N. Y., 1871. 38.

La Rame, Louise de, (Ouida.) Idalia: a novel. Phil., 1870. 2 copies. 7—44.

—— Chandos: a novel. Phil., 1871. 7—44.

—— Tricotrin: the story of a waif and stray. Phil., 1871. 7—44.

—— Beatrice Boville, and other stories. Phil., 1868. 7—44.

—— Puck. Phil., 1870. 7—44.

—— Folle-Farine. Phil., 1871. 7—44.

—— Randolph Gordon, and other stories. Phil., 1867. 7—44.

—— Cecil Castlemaine's gage; Lady Marabout's troubles; and other stories. Phil., 1867. 7—44.

—— Granville De Vigne; or, held in bondage: a tale of the day. Phil., 1871. 7—44.

—— Under two flags: a novel. Phil., 1867. 2 copies. 7—44.

Mendelssohn - Bartholdy, Felix, Letters of: from Italy and Switzerland. *Lady* Wallace, tr. N. Y., 1869. 27—162.

—— Same, from 1833 to 1847. P. and C. Mendelssohn-Bartholdy, eds. *Lady* Wallace, tr. N. Y., 1868. 27—162.

——, Life of. Lampadius, W. A. N. Y., 1866. 11—64.

Menzel, Wolfgang. The history of Germany, from the earliest period. *Mrs.* G. Horrocks, tr. Lond., 1848-49. 3 v. 36—219.

Mercedes of Castile. Illus. Cooper, J. F. N. Y., 1864. 3—14.

Merchant of Berlin, The. Illus. "Louise Mühlbach." N. Y., 1872. 4—21.

—— vessels, navy, and revenue-marine service of the United States, A list of. Wash., 1875. X.

Mercy Philbrick's choice. (No Name series.) Jackson, H. Bost., 1876. 41—226.

Meridiana. Illus. Verne, J. N. Y., 1874. 5—31.

Merrivale, Charles. History of the Romans under the empire. Lond., 1850. 3 v. 35—211.

—— A general history of Rome, from the foundation of the city to the fall of Augustulus, B. C. 753–A. D. 476. N. Y., 1875. 35—212.

Metallic wealth of the United States. Illus. Whitney, J. D. Phil., 1854. T.

Metaphysics, Lectures on. Hamilton, *Sir* W. Bost., 1869. 15—88.

Metastasio, Pietro Bonaventura, Dramas and other poems of. J. Hoole, tr. Lond., 1800. 3 v. 16—95.

Metcalfe, Samuel L. Caloric: its mechanical, chemical, and vital agencies in the phenomena of nature. Phil., 1859. 2 v. 15—88.

Methodist pulpit, south, The. Illus. Smithson, W. T. Wash., 1859. 32—195.

Metropolis improvement, First report of the select committee on. Lond., 1840. 13 v. D. R.

Metropolitan Sanitary Commission. Lond., 1847. D. R.

Meunier, Victor Amédée. Adventures on the great hunting grounds of the world. (Illustrated library of wonders.) N. Y., 1873. 28—169.

Mexican war, The. Mansfield, E. D. N. Y., 1851. 30—179.

Mexico. Diaz, B. J. I. Lockhart, tr. Lond., 1844. 2 v. 32—192.

—— and its religion. Illus. Wilson, R. A. N. Y., 1855. 17—104.

—— as it was and as it is. Illus. Mayer, B. N. Y., 1844. 9—52.

——, History of the conquest of. Prescott, W. H. N. Y., 1841. 3 v. 2 copies. 32—191.

——, History of. Clavigero, F. S. Lond., 1787. 2 v. 32—191.

——, History of. Mill, N. Lond., 1824. 32—191.

—— in 1827. Ward, *Sir* H. G. Lond., 1828. 2 v. 32—191.

——, Notes on. Poinsett, J. R. Lond., 1825. 32—191.

——, Recollections of. Thompson, W. N. Y. and Lond., 1846. 8—49.

——, The rambler in. Latrobe, C. J. N. Y., 1836. 32—192.

——, True history of the conquest of. Diaz, B. Lond., 1800. 32—191.

——, Six months' residence and travels in. Illus. Bullock, W. Lond., 1824. 9—52.

——. The despatches of Hernando Cortes. G. Folsom, tr. N. Y. and Lond., 1843. 32—192.

Michael Strogoff, the courier of the Czar. Illus. Verne, J. N. Y., 1877. 5—31.

Michaux, François André. Travels to the westward of the Allegheny mountains, in the States of Ohio, Kentucky, Tennessee, and return through the upper Carolinas. B. Lambert, tr. Lond., 1805. 10—58.

Michelet, Jules. History of France. N. Y., 1847. 2 v. 35—214.

—— History of the French revolution. C. Cocks, tr. Lond., 1847. 35—213.

—— France before Europe. Bost., 1871. 35—213.

Micheline: a tale. Illus. Bersier, *Mme.* N. Y., 1876. 41—228.

Michigan, Fourth annual report of the secretary of the State Board of Agriculture of. Lansing, 1865. D. R.

——, Red-book of. Lanman, C. Det., 1871. 31—186.

Microcosmography; or, a piece of the world discovered. Earle, J. Albany, 1867. 19—116.

Middlemarch. "George Eliot." N. Y., 1873. 2 v. 6—36.

Mignet, François Auguste Alexis. History of the French revolution, from 1789 to 1814. Lond., 1846. 35—213.

Mildred Arkell. Wood, E. P. Phil., 1865. 41—229.

Miles Wallingford: sequel to "Afloat and ashore." Illus. Cooper, J. F. N. Y., 1870. 3—14.

Military Academy, Register of the officers and graduates of the United States. Cullum, G. W. N. Y., 1850. R—2.

——— bridges. Douglas, Sir H. Lond., 1832. T.

——— commission to Europe, in 1855 and 1856. Report of Major Alfred Mordecai, of the ordnance department. Wash., 1860. X.

——— laws of the United States. Callan, J. F. Balt., 1858. 18—109.

——— life of John, duke of Marlborough. Alison, Sir A. N. Y., 1848. 11—61.

——— posts and stations, Outline description of, in the year 1871. War Department, Quartermaster-general's office. Wash., 1872. V.

Mill, James, and Horace Hayman Wilson. The history of British India. Lond., 1848. 9 v. 33—200.

Mill, John Stuart. The subjection of women. N. Y., 1870. 3—19.

——— Dissertations and discussions, political, philosophical, and historical. Bost., 1868. 4 v. 23—167.

——— A system of logic, ratiocinative and inductive; being a connected view of the principles of evidence and methods of scientific investigation. N. Y., 1869. 14—81.

——— An examination of Sir William Hamilton's philosophy, and of the principal philosophical questions discussed in his writings. Bost., 1866. 2 v. 14—84.

——— The positive philosophy of Auguste Comte. Bost., 1866. 14—84.

Mill, Nicholas. History of Mexico, from the Spanish conquest. Lond., 1824. 32—191.

Mill on the Floss, The. "George Eliot." N. Y., 1876. 6—36.

Miller, Cincinnatus Hiner, (Joaquin Miller.) Songs of the sun-lands. Bost., 1873. 17—106.

——— Songs of the Sierras. Bost., 1874. 17—106.

——— The ship in the desert. Bost., 1875. 17—105.

——— First fam'lies of the Sierras. Chicago, 1876. 41—228.

——— The one fair woman. N. Y., 1876. 3 v. in one. 41—228.

Miller, George. History philosophically illustrated, from the fall of the Roman empire to the French revolution. Lond., 1849. 4 v. 33—202.

Miller, Hugh. First impressions of England and its people. Bost., 1868. 9—33.

——— The cruise of the Betsey; or, a summer ramble among the fossiliferous deposits of the Hebrides. Bost., 1867. 10—58.

——— The headship of Christ and the rights of the Christian people. Bost., 1868. 27—161.

——— Tales and sketches. Bost., 1868. 3—18.

——— My schools and schoolmasters; or, the story of my education. Bost., 1869. 2—11.

——— Essays, historical, biographical, political, social, literary, and scientific. Peter Bayne, ed. Bost., 1866. 27—159.

——— The old red sandstone; or, new walks in an old field; with a series of geological papers read before the Royal Physical Society of Edinburgh. Illus. Bost., 1858. 15—91.

——— Foot-prints of the Creator; or, the asterolepis of Stromness; with a memoir of the author, by Louis Agassiz. Illus. Bost., 1869. 15—91.

——— Popular geology: a series of lectures, with descriptive sketches from a geologist's portfolio, and an introductory résumé of the progress of geological science within the last two years, by Mrs. Miller. Bost., 1863. 15—91.

——— The testimony of the rocks; or, geology in its bearings on the two theologies, natural and revealed. Bost., 1869. 15—91.

Miller, Hugh, The life and letters of. Bayne, P. Bost., 1871. 2 v. 13—76.
—— , The life and times of. Brown, T. N. N. Y., 1859. Q—2.

Miller, Lydia, (Mrs. Hugh Miller.) Cats and dogs; or, notes and anecdotes of two great families of the animal kingdom. Illus. Lond. and N. Y., 1872. 38.

Miller, J. R. History of Great Britain, from the death of George the second to the coronation of George the fourth. (Continuation of Hume and Smollett.) Lond., 1829. 34—206.

Miller, R. Kalley. The romance of astronomy. Lond., 1875. 14—83.

Miller, Stephen F. The bench and bar of Georgia: memoirs and sketches, with an appendix containing a court-roll from 1790 to 1857. Phil., 1858. 2 v. 2—9.

Miller, William Allen. Elements of chemistry, theoretical and practical. Part 1st, Chemical physics. Illus. N. Y., 1864. 15—87.

Miller of Angibault, The. "George Sand." Bost., 1871. 7—41.

Miller's story of the war, A. Illus. Erckmann, E., and A. Chatrian. N. Y., 1872. 5—31.

Millingen, John G. The passions; or, mind and matter illustrated by considerations on hereditary insanity. Lond., 1848. 14—81.

Milly Darrell, and other tales. Braddon, M. E. Lond., 1873. 3 v. 41—227.

Millot, Claude François-Xavier. Histoire ancienne. Paris, 1819. 3 v. D. R.
—— Histoire moderne. Paris, 1819. 4 v. D. R.
—— Histoire d'Angleterre. Paris, 1820. 2 v. D. R.
—— Histoire de France. Paris, 1820. 3 v. D. R.

Milman, Henry Hart. The history of the Jews. Lond., 1829. 3 v. 36—217.
—— History of Latin Christianity, including that of the popes to the pontificate of Nicolas the fifth. N. Y., 1870. 8 v. 32—196.

Mills, Robert. Statistics of South Carolina. Charleston, 1826. 31—188.

Milton, John, The prose works of, with a preface by J. A. St. John. Lond., 1853. 5 v. 28—170.

Milton, John, The poetical works of, with a life by the Rev. J. Mitford. Bost., 1853. 3 v. 16—98.

Miner, Charles. History of Wyoming, in a series of letters from Charles Miner to his son, Wm. Penn Miner, esq. Phil., 1845. 31—189.

Mineral resources of the United States. Sutro, A. Balt., 1868. D. R.
—— veins, Practical observations on. Illus. Leithart, J. Lond., 1838. 15—91.
—— waters of the United States and Canada. Illus. Moorman, J. J. Balt., 1867. 19—117.

Mineralogy, A system of. Illus. Dana, J. D. N. Y. and Lond., 1850. 15—91.
—— , An elementary introduction to. Illus. Phillips, W. Lond., 1837. 15—91.
—— , Practical. Illus. Chapman, E. J. Lond. and Paris, 1843. 15—91.

Mines, Traité de l'exploitation des. Combes, C. Paris, 1844-45. 3 v. with atlas. D. R.

Mining industry. Hague, J. D. Vol. 3 of the U. S. geological exploration of the fortieth parallel. Wash., 1870. D. R.
—— ordinances of Spain, Commentaries on the. Gamboa, F. X. de. Lond., 1830. 2 v. T.

Minisink region, A history of the. Stickney, C. E. Middletown, N. Y., 1867. 31—189.

Minister's wooing, The. Stowe, H. B. Bost., 1872. 6—35.

Minnesota and Dakotah. Andrews, C. C. Wash., 1857. 8—50.
—— and its resources; with camp-fire sketches. Illus. Bond, J. W. Chicago, 1856. 31—187.
—— , The history of. Neill, E. D. Phil., 1858. 31—187.

Minnie Hermon. Brown, T. W. N. Y., 1855. P—3.

Minot, George Richards. Continuation of the history of the province of Massachusetts Bay, from the year 1748 to 1765. Bost., 1798-1803. 2 v. in one. 30—183.

Mirabeau, Honoré Gabriel Riquetti, comte de, Memoirs of, biographical, literary, and political, by himself, his father, his uncle, and his adopted child. Lond., 1836. 4 v. 12—67.
—— , A life history of. Phil., 1848. 12—67.

Mirabeau, Honoré Gabriel Riquetti, comte de, Recollections of. Dumont, E. Lond., 1832. 12—67.

Mirèio: a Provençal poem. Mistral, F. Bost., 1874. 17—106.

Miscellaneous essays. De Quincey, T. Bost., 1860. 2—12.

—— essays by Archibald Alison. (Modern British essayists.) Bost., 1854. 27—159.

—— papers of John Smeaton. Illus. Lond., 1814. T.

Miscellanies, old and new. Smith, J. C., D. D. N. Y., 1876. 40—222.

—— upon various subjects. Aubrey, J. Lond., 1857. 27—162.

Miss Angel: a novel. Illus. Thackeray, A. I. N. Y., 1875. 4—21.

—— Carew: a novel. Edwards, A. B. N. Y., 1875. 6—33.

—— Dorothy's charge: a novel. Benedict, F. L. N. Y., 1874. 5—28.

—— Gilbert's career. Holland, J. G. N. Y., 1872. 3—18.

—— Forrester: a novel. Edwards, A. N. Y., 1873. 6—39.

—— Hitchcock's wedding dress. N. Y., 1876. 41—227.

—— Mackenzie. Trollope, A. Lond., n. d. 7—43.

—— Molly. Butt, B. M. N. Y., 1876. 41—227.

—— Moore: a tale for girls. Illus. Craik, G. M. N. Y., 1874. 39.

—— Ravenel's conversion from secession to loyalty. De Forest, J. W. N. Y., 1867. 4—25.

—— or Mrs. ? and other stories. Collins, W. W. Phil., n. d. 5—28.

—— Van Kortland: a novel. Benedict, F. L. N. Y., 1874. 5—28.

Missing bride, The. Southworth, E. D. E. N. Phil., 1855. 6—37.

Mission, The; or, scenes in Africa. Illus. Marryat, Capt. F. N. Y., n. d. 5—30.

Mississippi valley, Discovery and exploration of the. Shea, J. G. N. Y., 1852. 29—176.

—— valley, The history and geography of the. Flint, T. Cin., 1832. 2 v. in one. 29—176.

—— valley, Recollections of the. Flint, T. Bost., 1826. 29—176.

Missouri, A gazetteer of the state of. Wetmore, A. St. Louis, 1837. 31—186.

Missouri, Gazetteer of. Illus. Campbell, R. A. St. Louis, 1875. 31—186.

Mr. Midshipman Easy. Marryat, Capt. F. N. Y., 1857. 5—30.

—— Smith; — a part of his life. Walford, L. B. N. Y., 1875. 41—228.

—— Sponge's sporting tour. Illus. Surtees, R. S. N. Y., 1856. 2—8.

—— Vaughan's heir. Benedict, F. L. N. Y., 1875. 6—35.

—— Wynyard's ward : a novel. "Holme Lee." N. Y., 1367. 4—24.

Mrs. Gerald's niece : a novel. Fullerton, Lady G. N.Y., 1872. 5—28.

—— Halliburton's troubles: a novel. Wood, E. P. N. Y., n. d. 5—29.

—— Mainwaring's journal. Marshall, E. N. Y., 1876. 41—228.

—— Partington, Life and sayings of. Illus. Shillaber, B. P. N. Y., 1854. 2—8.

—— Skagg's husbands, and other sketches. Harte, F. B. Bost., 1873. 3—19.

Mistral, Frédéric. Mirèio: a Provençal poem. Harriet W. Preston, tr. Bost., 1874. 17—106.

Mistress and maid. Muloch, D. M. N. Y., 1872. 4—23.

—— of the manse, The. Holland, J. G. N. Y., 1874. 17—105.

Mitchel, Ormsby McKnight. The astronomy of the Bible. N. Y., 1868. 14—82.

—— Popular astronomy : a concise elementary treatise on the sun, planets, satellites, and comets. Illus. N. Y. 1867. 14—82.

—— The planetary and stellar worlds : a popular exposition of the great discoveries and theories of modern astronomy, in a series of ten lectures. N. Y., 1869. 14—82.

Mitchell, Donald Grant, (Ik Marvel.) Reveries of a bachelor; or, a book of the heart. N. Y., 1871. 3—20.

—— Dream-life: a fable of the seasons. N. Y., 1869. 3—19.

—— Dr. Johns: a narrative of certain events in the life of an orthodox minister of Connecticut. N. Y., 1866. 2 v. P—1.

—— Fudge doings: being Tony Fudge's record of the same. Ik Marvel. N. Y., 1855. 2 v. 2—11.

Mitchell, John. Manual of practical assaying, intended for the use of metallurgists, captains of mines, and assayers in general. Lond., 1846. T.

Mitchell, Samuel Augustus. * New general atlas, containing maps of the various countries of the world, plans of cities, etc., embraced in seventy-nine quarto maps. Phil., 1874. R.

Mitford, Mary Russell. Our village: sketches of rural character and scenery. Lond., 1870. 2 v. 2—11.

Mitford, William. History of Greece. Lond., 1838. 8 v. 35—210.

Mivart, St. George. On the genesis of species. Illus. N. Y., 1871. 14—81.

—— Man and apes: an exposition of structural resemblances and differences bearing upon questions of affinity and origin. Illus. N. Y., 1874. 14—81.

—— Lessons from nature, as manifested in mind and matter. N. Y., 1876. 40—222.

Modern alphabets, Examples of. Illus. Delamotte, F. Lond., 1866. 19—113.

—— British Plutarch. Taylor, W. C. N. Y., 1846. 11—63.

—— Greece. Illus. Baird, H. M. N. Y., 1865. 17—101.

—— history, Lectures on. Smyth, W. Bost., 1851. 32—193.

—— history, A course of lectures on. Schlegel, F. Lond., 1849. 32—193.

—— history, Introductory lectures on. Arnold, T. N. Y., 1847. 32—193.

—— painters. Illus. Ruskin, J. N. Y., 1864. 5 v. 26—158.

—— persecution; or, insane asylums unveiled, and married woman's liabilities. Illus. Packard, E. P. W. Hartford, 1874. 2 v. 28—169.

—— philology. Dwight, B. W. N. Y., 1865. 14—81.

—— Same. 2d series. N. Y., 1869. 14—81.

—— philosophy, Course of the history of. Cousin, V. N. Y., 1866. 2 v. 14—84.

—— skepticism: a course of lectures delivered at the request of the Christian Evidence Society. N. Y., 1871. E.

—— style of cabinet-work exemplified. Illus. King, T. Lond, 1862. . V.

Mohammed Ali and his house. Illus. "Louise Mühlbach." N. Y., 1872. 4—21.

Mohammedanism and its sects, The history of. Taylor, W. C. Lond., 1834. 27—162.

Mohicans of Paris, The. Dumas, A. D. Phil., n. d. 3—20.

Molecular physics in the domain of radiant heat, Contributions to. Illus. Tyndall, J. N. Y., 1873. 15—88.

Molesworth, William Nassau. The history of England from the year 1830 to 1874. Lond., 1874. 3 v. 34—207.

Molière, Jean Baptiste Poquelin de, Œuvres complètes de, avec des notes de tous les commentateurs. Paris, 1866. W.

Molina, Don J. Ignatius. History of Chili, geographical, natural, and civil. Middletown, Conn., 1808. 2 v. 36—216.

Mommsen, Theodor. The history of Rome. Rev. W. P. Dickson, tr. N. Y., 1871-72. 4 v. 35—211.

Monarch of Mincing Lane, The. Illus. Black, W. N. Y., 1871. 5—29.

Monarchs retired from business. Doran, J. N. Y., 1865. 2 v. 11—60.

Monasteries in the Levant, A visit to. Curzon, R. N. Y., 1849. 17—103.

Monastery, The. Scott, Sir W. Bost., 1869. 3—17.

Monette, John W. History of the discovery and settlement of the valley of the Mississippi. N. Y., 1848. 2 v. 29—176.

Monikins, The. Illus. Cooper, J. F. N. Y., 1873. 3—14.

Monsieur Sylvestre: a novel. "George Sand." Bost., 1870. 7—41.

Monstrelet, Enguerrand de, Chronicles of;—containing an account of the cruel civil wars between the houses of Orleans and Burgundy; of the possession of Paris and Normandy by the English; their expulsion thence; and of other memorable events that happened in the kingdom of France, as well as in other countries. A history of fair example to the French, beginning at the year MCCCC, where that of Sir John Froissart finishes, and ending at the year MCCCCLXVII, and continued by others to the year MDXVI. Illus. F. Johnes, tr. Lond., 1849. 2 v. 33—197.

Montague, Lady Mary Wortley, Letters of; written during her travels in Europe, Asia, and Africa. Lond., 1785. 27—162.

Montaigne, Michel Equem de. Essais de, avec des notes de tous les commentateurs. Paris, 1859. W.

——, The essays of: from the French edition of Peter Coste. Lond., 1811. 3 v. 27—160.

Montana Territory, Report of a reconnaissance in. Illus. Ludlow, W. Wash.. 1876. D. R.

Montesquieu, Charles de Secondat, baron de. Roman empire: reflections on its rise and fall. Edin., 1775. 35—213.

—— The spirit of the laws. T. Nugent, tr. Dub., 1792. 2 v. 26—157.

——, Œuvres complètes de. Paris, 1866. W.

Montgomery, James. Poetical works of; with a memoir of the author. Bost., 1860. 5 v. 16—95.

Contents.

Vol. 1. Wanderer of Switzerland; West Indies; Prison amusements; Miscellaneous poems.
Vol. 2. The world before the flood; Thoughts on wheels; The climbing boy's soliloquies; Songs of Zion; Miscellaneous poems.
Vol. 3. Greenland; Narratives; Translations from Dante; Miscellaneous poems.
Vol. 4. The Pelican Islands; Sacred and scriptural subjects; Miscellanies; Appendix.
Vol. 5. Original hymns; Posthumous poems.

Montgomery, James. A practical detail of the cotton manufacture of the United States of America, compared with that of Great Britain. Glasgow, 1840. T.

Montgomery, Richard, Life of. (Library of American biography, vol. 1.) 11—55.

Monthly mirror: reflecting men and manners; 1792 to 1810. Illus. Lond. 26 v. Q.

Moods. Alcott, L. M. Bost..1864. 5—31.

Moon, George Washington. The dean's English: a criticism on the dean of Canterbury's essays on the queen's English. Lond., 1868. 27—160.

Moon, The. Illus. Proctor, R. A. N. Y., 1873. 14—82.

——, Wonders of the. Illus. Guillemin, A. N. Y., 1873. 2—169.

Moonshine: fairy stories. Illus. Knatchbull-Hugessen. E. H. Lond.. 1874. 39.

Moonstone, The. Illus. Collins, W. W. N. Y., 1869. 6—38.

Moore, Mrs. Bloomfield. On dangerous ground; or, Agatha's friendship: a romance of American society. Phil., 1876. 41—228.

Moore, Frank. Diary of the American revolution, from newspapers and original documents. Illus. N. Y., 1860. 2 v. 30—179.

—— *Rebellion record : a diary of American events. Illus. N. Y., 1861-63. 12 v. 30—180

—— Speeches of Andrew Johnson, president of the United States; with a biographical introduction. Bost., 1865. 26—157.

—— Anecdotes, poetry, and incidents of the war: north and south. 1860—65. Illus. N. Y., 1866. 2—7.

Moore, George. The power of the soul over the body. considered in relation to health and morals. N. Y., 1854. E.

—— On the use of the body in relation to the mind. N. Y., 1849. E.

Moore, H. N. Life and services of General Anthony Wayne. Illus. Phil., 1845. 13—79.

Moore, Rachel Wilson. Journal kept during a tour to the West Indies and South America, in 1863-64, with notes from the diary of her husband; together with his memoir, by Geo. Truman, M. D. Phil., 1867. 8—49.

Moore, Thomas. The history of Ireland. Phil., 1835. Vol. 1. 34—205.

—— Same, from the earliest kings of that realm. down to its latest chief. Phil., 1846. Vol. 2. 34—205.

——, The poetical works of. Phil.. 1869. 16—93.

—— The epicurean: a romance. N. Y., 1875. 41—228.

—— The letters and journals of Lord Byron, with notices of his life. Illus. N. Y., 1875. 40—22.

—— and Jerdan, Personal reminiscences by. (Bric-a-brac series.) Illus. N. Y., 1875. 19—114.

—— The poetical works of, as corrected by himself in 1843. Illus. N. Y. 1851. 2 v. 16—94.

Moore, Thomas. Memoirs of the life of the Right Hon. Richard Brinsley Sheridan. N. Y., 1853. 2 v. 13—78.
—— Travels of an Irish gentleman in search of a religion. Balt., n. d. E.
Moorland, cottage, The. Gaskell, E. C. N. Y., 1868. 41—227.

Moorman, John J. The mineral waters of the United States and Canada; with general directions for reaching mineral springs. Illus. Balt., 1867. 19—117.

Mopsa, The fairy. Illus. Ingelow, J. Bost., 1871. 38.

Moral reflections, sentences, and maxims of Francis, duc de la Rochefoucauld, and of Stanislaus, king of Poland. N. Y., 1853. E.

Moralistes français. Paris, 1869. W.

Morals of Abou Ben Adhem, The. D. R. Locke, ed. Bost., 1875. 2—9.

More, Hannah. Cœlebs in search of a wife. Phil., 1866. O—3.

More happy thoughts. Burnand, F. C. Bost., 1871. 2—13.

Morell, Thomas. *An abridgment of Ainsworth's dictionary, English and Latin. Phil., 1859. 23—137.

Morgan, R. W. Christianity and modern infidelity: their relative intellectual claims compared. N. Y., 1859. E.

Moriad; or, the end of the Jewish state. Ben Asaph. Nashville, 1857. 16—100.

Morley, Henry. The life of Bernard Palissy of Saintes. Bost., 1853. 2 v. 12—72.

Morley, Susan. Aileen Ferrers: a novel. N. Y., 1875. 6—35.
—— Throstlethwaite. Phil., 1876. 41—229.

Mormonism : its leaders and designs. Hyde, J. N. Y., 1857. 27—162.

Morning glories. Illus. Alcott, L. M. N. Y., 1871. 5—31.

Morris, Benjamin Franklin. Christian life and character of the civil institutions of the U. S. developed in the official and historical annals of the republic. Phil., 1864. T.

Morris, Gouverneur, The life of. Sparks, J. Bost., 1832. 3 v. 11—60.

Morris, Thomas. The life of; edited by his son, B. F. Morris. Cin., 1856. Q—2.

Morris, William. The earthly paradise: a poem. Bost., 1868–71. 2 v. 17—105.
—— The life and death of Jason: a poem. Bost., 1871. 17—106.
—— The lovers of Gudrun: a poem. Bost., 1870. 17—106.
—— Love is enough; or, the freeing of Pharamond: a morality. Bost., 1873. 17—106.
—— The Æneids of Virgil done into English verse. Bost., 1876. 17—105.

Morris, William O'Connor. The French revolution and first empire; an historical sketch; with an appendix upon the bibliography of the subject, and a course of study by Hon. A. D. White. N. Y., n. d. 35—213.

Mortars and cements, A treatise on. Vicat, L. J. Lond., 1837. T.

Morton house: a novel. Illus. "Christian Reid." N. Y., 1873. 5—28.

Morton, Samuel George. Crania Americana; or, a comparative view of the skulls of various aboriginal nations of North and South America; with an essay on the varieties of the human species. Illus. Phil. and Lond., 1839. V.

Moschus, Poetical works of. F. Fawkes, tr. Lond., 1832. 17—107.

Mose Evans. Baker, W. M. N. Y., 1874. 7—43.

Mosheim, John Lawrence von. Institutes of ecclesiastical history, ancient and modern. J. Murdock, tr. N. Y., 1851. 3 v. 32—196.

Moslih-Eddin, S. B. A., pseud. See Peard, F. M.

Mosses from an old manse. Hawthorne, N. Bost., 1868. 2 v. 3—18.

Mother-in-law, The. Southworth, E. D. E. N. Phil., 1860. 6—37.

Motherless. Illus. De Witt, C. G. N. Y., 1871. P—3.

Mother's recompense, The: sequel to "Home influence." Aguilar, G. N. Y., 1872. 5—34.
—— trials, A. Ponsonby, E. N. Y., 1860. P—1.

Motley, John Lothrop. The rise of the Dutch republic. N. Y., 1856. 3 v. 36—218.
—— History of the United Netherlands, from the death of William the silent to

the twelve years' truce, 1609. N. Y., 1868. 4 v. 36—218.

—— The life and death of John of Barneveld, advocate of Holland ; with a view of the primary causes and movements of the thirty years' war. Illus. N. Y., 1874. 2 v. 11—59.

Moulton, Louise Chandler. Some women's hearts. Bost., 1874. 5—34.

—— Bed-time stories. Illus. Bost., 1874. 39.

Mount Vesuvius. Lobley, J. L. Lond., 1868. 15—89.

Mountains and mole-hills. Illus. Marryat, F. N. Y., 1855. 17—104.

Mowatt, Anna Cora Ritchie. See Ritchie, A. C. M.

Mozart, Johann Chrysostom Wolfgang Amadeus, Letters of : 1769 to 1791. Translated from the collection of Ludwig Nohl, by *Lady* Wallace. N. Y., 1866. 2 v. 26—158.

——, The life of. Holmes, E. N. Y., 1845. 11—64.

Mozley, J. B., *D. D.* Ruling ideas in early ages, and their relation to old testament faith : lectures delivered to graduates of the University of Oxford. N. Y., 1877. 18—108.

—— Sermons preached before the University of Oxford, and on various occasions. N. Y., 1876. 18—108.

Mühlbach, Louise, *pseud.* See Mundt, C. M.

Muhlenberg, Henry. Descriptio uberior graminum et plantarum calamariarum Americæ septentrionalis indigenarum et circurum. Phil., 1817. D. R.

Mulford, E. The nation : the foundations of civil order and political life in the United States. N. Y., 1875. 40—224.

Müller, Carl Otfried. The history and antiquities of the Doric race. H. Truffnell and G. C. Lewis, trs. Oxford, 1830. 2 v. 35—209.

Muller, Christine, *pseud.* See Walrée, E. C. W. *van.*

Müller, Friedrich Max. Lectures on the science of language ; delivered in 1861. N. Y., 1868. 14—81.

—— Same. 2d series. N. Y., 1863. 14—81.

Muller, John. Principles of physics and meteorology. Illus. Phil., 1848. 15—92.

Müller, John *von.* Universal history. Bost., 1837. 4 v. 32—193.

Mundt, Clara Müller, (*Louise Mühlbach.*) The story of a millionaire. N. Y., 1872. 7—41.

—— Mohammed Ali and his house : an historical romance. Illus. N. Y., 1872. 4—21.

—— Henry the eighth and his court. Illus. N. Y., 1871. 4—21.

—— Andreas Hofer. Illus. F. Jordan, tr. N. Y., 1868. 4—21.

—— Napoleon and Blucher. Illus. F. Jordan, tr. N. Y., 1867. 4—21.

—— Napoleon and the queen of Prussia : an historical novel. Illus. F. Jordan, tr. N. Y., 1868. 4—21.

—— Joseph the second and his court. Illus. Adelaide De V. Chaudron, tr. N. Y., 1868. 4—21.

—— The empress Josephine. Illus. *Rev.* W. Binet, tr. N. Y., 1867. 4—21.

—— Marie Antoinette and her son. Illus. *Rev.* W. L. Gage, tr. N. Y., 1872. 4—21.

—— Queen Hortense. Illus. C. Coleman, tr. N. Y., 1871. 4—21.

—— Frederick the great and his family. Illus. *Mrs.* C. Coleman and daughters, trs. N. Y., 1871. 4—21.

—— Frederick the great and his court. Illus. *Mrs.* C. Coleman and daughters, trs. N. Y., 1871. 4—21.

—— Prince Eugene and his times. Illus. Adelaide De V. Chaudron, tr. N. Y., 1874. 4—21.

—— Louisa of Prussia and her times. Illus. F. Jordan, tr. N.Y., 1867. 4—21.

—— The daughter of an empress. Illus. N. Greene, tr. N. Y., 1872. 4—21.

—— Old Fritz and the new era. Illus. Peter Langley, tr. N. Y., 1868. 4—21.

—— The merchant of Berlin : an historical novel. Illus. A. Coffin, tr. N. Y., 1872. 4—21.

—— Berlin and Sans-Souci ; or, Frederick the great and his friends : an historical novel. Illus. *Mrs.* C. Coleman and daughters, trs. N. Y., 1873. 4—21.

—— Two life-paths : a romance. N. Greene, tr. N. Y., 1869. 4—21.

My story: a novel. Illus. Macqnoid, K. S. N. Y., 1875. 6—35.
—— wife and I. Illus. Stowe, H. B. N. Y., 1872. 6—35.
—— winter on the Nile among the mummies and Moslems. Illus. Warner, C. D. Hartford, 1876. 10—56.
—— young Alcides. Yonge, C. M. N. Y., 1876. 5—30.
Mysteries of Paris. Illus. " Eugene Sue." Lond., 1845, 3 v. 4—21.
Mysterious island, The : the modern Robinson Crusoe. Illus. Verne, J. W. H. G. Kingston, tr. N. Y., 1876. 5—31.
Mystery : (Little classics, vol. 8.) Bost., 1875. 5—33.
——, The. Wood, E. P. Phil., n. d. 41—230.
—— of Dark Hollow, The. Southworth, E. D. E. N. Phil., 1875. 6—37.
Mythology, Manual of. Illus. Murray, A. S. N. Y., 1874. 19—144.
——, Zoological. Gubernatis, A. de. N. Y., 1872. 2 v. 14—82.
Myths and myth-makers. Fiske, J. Bost., 1874. 28—165.

Nabathæan agriculture, An essay on the age and antiquity of the book of the. Renan, E. Lond., 1862. V.
Nadal, Ehrman Syme. Impressions of London social life ; with other papers suggested by an English residence. N. Y., 1875. 19—116.
Nalson, John. An impartial collection of the great affairs of state from the beginning of the Scottish rebellion, in the year MDCXXXIX, to the murther of King Charles I, wherein the first occasions and the whole series of the late troubles in England, Scotland, and Ireland are faithfully represented ; taken from authentick records, and methodically digested. Lond., 1682. 2 v. 34—203.
Names of men, nations, and places, History of. Salverte, A. J. E. B. Lond., 1864. 2 v. 26—156.
Nancy : a novel. Broughton, R. N. Y., 1874. 5—29.
Nanon ; or, women's war. Dumas, A. D. Lond. and N. Y., n. d. 5—31.

Nantucket, History of. Macy, O. Bost., 1835. 33—201.
Napheys, George H. The transmission of life : counsels on the nature and hygiene of the masculine function. Phil., 1874. 1—4.
—— The physical life of woman : advice to the maiden, wife, and mother. Phil., 1874. 1—4.
Napier, Henry Edward. Florentine history, from the earliest authentic records, to the accession of Ferdinand the third, grand duke of Tuscany. Lond., 1846-47. 6 v. 35—212.
Napier, Sir William Francis Patrick. History of the war in the peninsula, and in the south of France. Phil., 1842. 4 v. 33—199.
Naples, The civil history of the kingdom of. Giannone, P. Lond., 1729-31. 2 v. 34—203.
Napoleon and Blucher. Illus. " Louise Mühlbach." N. Y., 1867. 4—21.
—— and the queen of Prussia. Illus. " Louise Mühlbach." N. Y., 1868. 4—21.
——, his court and family, Memoirs of. Illus. Abrantès, L. P. J., duchesse d'. N. Y., 1854. 2 v. 11—61.
—— Bonaparte, Memoirs of. Illus. Bourrienne, L. A. F. de. Edin., n. d. 2 v. 11—61.
—— Buonaparte, The life of. Hazlitt, W. Lond., 1852. 4 v. 11—61.
——, Memoirs of the life, exile, and conversations of the emperor. Illus. Las Cases, E. D. M. J. N. Y., 1855. 4 v. 11—61.
——, History of the captivity of. Forsyth, W. N. Y., 1853. 2 v. 11—61.
—— the little. Hugo, V. Lond., 1852. 11—61.
Narrative. De Quincey, T. Bost., 1859. 2 v. 2—12.
—— of military operations, directed during the late war between the states. Illus. Johnston, J. E. N. Y., 1874. 30—180.
—— of my captivity among the Sioux Indians. Illus. Kelly, F. Hartford, 1873. 17—104.
Nason, Elias. 'Sir Charles Henry Frankland, bart. ; or, Boston in the colonial times. Albany, 1865. 40—224.

Nathalie: a tale. Kavanagh, J. N. Y., 1872. 7—41.

Nathan the wise: a dramatic poem. Lessing, G. E. N. Y., 1873. 17—106.

National education in Europe. Barnard, H. Hartford, 1854. L.

Natural history. Illus. Tenney, S. N.Y., 1866. 14—82.

—— history of man, The. Illus. Prichard, J. C. Lond. and Paris, 1848. 15—89.

—— history, Elements of. Illus. Ruschenberger, W. S. W. Phil., 1860. 2 v. 14—85.

—— history of the United States of America, Contributions to the. Illus. Agassiz, L. Bost., 1857-60. 3 v. V.

Naturalist's library. Sir Wm. Jardine, ed. Illus. Edin., 1840-62. 40 v. 14—86.

Contents.

Vol. 1. Ornithology: Birds of Great Britain and Ireland, part 1, with A memoir of Sir Robert Sibbald.

Vol. 2. Birds of Great Britain and Ireland, and A memoir of William Smellie.

Vol. 3. Same, with A memoir of John Walker, D. D.

Vol. 4. Same, with A memoir of Alexander Wilson.

Vol. 5. Nectarinadæ, or sun-birds; and Memoir of Francis Willoughby, F. R. S.

Vol. 6. Humming-birds, and Memoir and anecdotes of Carl Linnæus.

Vol. 7. Same, and Memoir of Thomas Pennant.

Vol. 8. Game birds, and Memoir of Sir Thos. Stamford Raffles.

Vol. 9. Pigeons, by Prideaux John Selby, and Memoir of Caius Plinius Secundus.

Vol. 10. Parrots, by Prideaux John Selby, and Memoir of Thomas Bewick.

Vol. 11. Birds of Western Africa, by W. Swainson; and A memoir of James Bruce.

Vol. 12. Same, and A memoir of Francis le Vaillant.

Vol. 13. Fly-catchers, by W. Swainson, and A memoir of Baron Albert von Haller.

Vol. 14. Gallinaceous birds, and A memoir of Aristotle.

Vol. 15. Mammalia: Introduction by Lt.-Col. Charles Hamilton Smith; with A memoir of Dru Drury.

Vol. 16. Lions and tigers, and A memoir of Cuvier.

Vol. 17. British quadrupeds, by W. Macgillivray, and A memoir of Ulysses Aldrovandi.

Vol. 18. Dogs, by Lt.-Col. C. H. Smith, and A memoir of Peter Simon Pallas.

Vol. 19. Same, and A memoir of Don Felix d'Azara.

Vol. 20. Horses, by Lt.-Col. C. H. Smith, and A memoir of Conrad Gesner.

Vol. 21. Deer, antelopes, camels, etc., and A memoir of Peter Camper.

Vol. 22. Goats, sheep, oxen, etc., and A memoir of John Hunter.

Vol. 23. Thick-skinned quadrupeds, and A memoir of Sir Hans Sloane.

Vol. 24. Marsupialia; or, pouched animals, by G. R. Waterhouse, and A memoir of John Barclay, M. D.

Vol. 25. Amphibious carnivora, by R. Hamilton, and A memoir of François Peron.

Vol. 26. Whales, etc., by R. Hamilton, and A memoir of Le Comte de Lacépède.

Vol. 27. Monkeys, and A memoir of George Louis le Clerc Buffon.

Vol. 28. Entomology: Introduction by James Duncan, and Memoirs of John Swammerdam and Charles de Geer.

Vol. 29. British butterflies, by James Duncan, and A memoir of Abraham Gottlob Werner.

Vol. 30. British moths, sphinxes, etc., by J. Duncan, and A memoir of Maria Sibilla Merian.

Vol. 31. Foreign butterflies, by J. Duncan, and A memoir of Jean Baptiste Pierre Antoine de Monet, chevalier de Lamarck.

Vol. 32. Exotic moths, by J. Duncan, and A memoir of Pierre-André Latreille.

Vol. 33. Beetles, by J. Duncan, and A memoir of John Ray.

Vol. 34. Bees, and A memoir of Francis Huber.

Vol. 35. Ichthyology, by J. S. Bushnan, and A memoir of Hippolito Salivani.

Vol. 36. British fishes, by R. Hamilton, and A memoir of Wm. Rondelet.

Vol. 37. Same, and A memoir of Frederick Henry Alexander von Humboldt.

Vol. 38. Fishes of the perch family, and A memoir of Joseph Banks.

Vol. 39. Fishes of British Guiana, by R. H. Schomburgk, and A memoir of the author.

Vol. 40. Same, and A memoir of John Lewis Burckhardt.

Nature and the supernatural. Bushnell, H. N. Y., 1859. 15—92.

—— and use of money, Lectures on the. Gray, J. Edin., 1848. 15—92.

—— and the scriptures. Lewis, T. N. Y., 1875. E.

Naval academy, Historical sketch of the U. S. Soley, *Prof.* J. R. Wash., 1876. R—2.

—— history of England, Early. Southey, R. Phil., 1835. 33—199.

—— history of Great Britain. Campbell, J. Lond., 1813. 8 v. 33—199.

—— history of the United States. Clark, T. Phil., 1814. 2 v. 30—179.

Naval observatory, Instruments and publications of the U. S. Illus. Wash., 1876. D. R.

—— tactics, A manual of. Ward, J. H. N. Y., 1859. 18—109.

Navarrete, *Don* Martin Fernandez de. Coleccion de los viages y descubrimientos. Mad., 1825-37. 5 v. W.

Navy of the United States of America, History of. Cooper, J. F. Lond., 1839. 2 v. 30—179.

——, The history of the. Illus. Boynton, C. B. N. Y., 1867-68. 2 v. 30—179.

* —— register of the United States, from 1775 to 1853; with a brief history of each vessel's service and fate as appears upon record; to which is added a list of private armed vessels, fitted out under the American flag, previous and subsequent to the revolutionary war, with their services and fate, etc. Emmons, *Lieut.* G. F., *U. S. N.* Wash., 1853. 24—141.

* ——, Regulations for the government of the U. S. Wash., 1870. R—2.

Neal, Daniel. The history of the Puritans; or, protestant non-conformists, from the reformation to 1688. Bath, *Eng.*, 1793-97. 5 v. 32—195.

Neander, August Johann Wilhelm. The life of Jesus Christ in its historical connexion and historical development. *J.* M'Clintock and C. E. Blumenthal, trs. N. Y., 1858. 13—78.

—— Lectures on the history of Christian dogmas. *Dr.* J. L. Jacobi, ed.; J. E. Ryland, tr. Lond., 1858. 2 v. 32—195.

Near to nature's heart. Roe, *Rev.* E. P. N. Y., n. d. 6—38.

Nebraska in 1857. Woolworth, J. M. Omaha, 1857. 31—187.

Neele, Henry. (Romance of history.) England. Illus. Lond., n. d. 2—8.

Neighbors, The. Bremer, F. Phil., n. d. P—1.

Neighbor's wives. Trowbridge, J. T. Bost., 1867. 6—39.

Neighbours, and other tales. Bremer, F. Lond., 1870. P—1.

Neill, Edward Duffield. The history of Minnesota, from the earliest French explorations to the present time. Phil., 1858. 31—187.

Neill, Edward Duffield. The Fairfaxes of England and America in the 17th and 18th centuries, including letters from and to Hon. William Fairfax, president of the council of Virginia, and his sons, Rev. George William Fairfax, and Rev. Bryan, eighth Lord Fairfax, the neighbours and friends of George Washington. Albany, 1868. 40—224.

Nelly Brooke. Marryat, *Miss* F. Lond. and N. Y., n. d. 4—22.

Nero: an historical play. Story, W. W. Lond. and N. Y., 1875. 17—105.

Netherlands, History of the revolt of the. Schiller, F. Lond., 1847. 2 v. 36—218.

—— Same. 2—11.

Neuman, H., and G. Barretti. * Dictionary of the Spanish and English languages. Bost., 1849. 2 v. 23—137.

Nevada, Mineral resources of; letter from the acting Secretary of the Interior to Congress, Jan'y 5, 1863. D. R.

Never again. Illus. Mayo, W. S. N. Y., 1873. 6—39.

New atmosphere, A. "Gail Hamilton." Bost., 1865. P—3.

—— Bedford, The history of. Ricketson, D. New Bedford, 1858. 30—182.

—— Brunswick, with notes for emigrants. Illus. Gesner, A. Lond., 1847. 8—49.

—— concordance to the Holy Scriptures. Butterworth, J. Bost., 1858. E.

—— day, The: a poem in songs and sonnets. Illus. Gilder, R. W. N. Y., 1876. 17—106.

—— England, History of. Palfrey, J. G. Bost., 1865. 3 v. 29—176.

—— England legends. Illus. Spofford, H. P. Bost., 1871. 2—8.

—— England tale, A. Sedgwick, C. M. N. Y., 1852. 6—39.

—— England tragedies, The. Longfellow, H. W. Bost., 1868. 17—106.

—— Granada: twenty months in the Andes. Illus. Holton, I. F. N. Y., 1857. 9—51.

—— Hampshire Historical Society, Collections of the. Concord, 1824-37. 5 v. 30—183.

—— Hampshire, The history of. Barstow, G. Concord, 1842. 30—183.

—— Hampshire, A gazetteer of. Illus. Hayward, J. Bost., 1849. 30—183.

New history of Sandford and Merton, The. Illus. Burnand, F. C. Bost., 1872. 39.

—— Jersey, Historical collections of the State of. Barber, J. W., and H. Howe. Newark, 1844. 31—189.

—— Jersey, The history of. Gordon, T. F. Trenton, 1834. 31—189.

—— Jersey, Official register of the officers and men of, in the revolutionary war. Stryker, W. S. Trenton, 1872. X.

—— life in new lands. Lippincott, S. J. N. Y., 1873. 9—53.

—— Magdalen, The. Illus. Collins, W. W. N. Y., 1874. 6—38.

—— Netherland; or, New York under the Dutch, History of. O'Callaghan, E. B. N. Y., 1846-49. 2 v. 31—190.

—— Netherlands, province of New York, History of. Dunlap, W. N. Y., 1839-40. 2 v. 31—190.

—— pantheon; or, historical dictionary of the gods, demi-gods, heroes, and fabulous personages of antiquity. Illus. Bell, J. Lond., 1790. 2 v. 23—137.

—— priest in Conception bay, The story of the. Illus. Lowell, R. T. S. N. Y., 1873. 2 v. in one. P—1.

—— Timon: a poetical romance. Bulwer-Lytton, Sir E. Leipzig, 1849. 17—105.

—— Timothy, The. Baker, W. M. N. Y., 1870. 7—43.

—— voyage round the world. De Foe, D. Oxford, 1840. 27—163.

—— world compared with the old, The. Illus. Townsend, G. A. Hartford, 1870. 17—102.

Newcomes, The. Illus. Thackeray, W. M. Lond., 1869. 2 v. 2 copies. 5—31 and 32.

Newfoundland, Excursions in and about. Jukes, J. B. Lond., 1842. 2 v. 9—53.

Newhall, Isaac. Letters on Junius, addressed to John Pickering, esq.; showing that the author of that celebrated work was Earl Temple. Bost., 1831. 19—117.

Newspaper directory, American; containing lists of all the newspapers and periodicals published in the United States and Canada. Rowell, G. P. N. Y., 1872 and 1875. 2 v. 23—135.

Newton Forster. Marryat, Capt. F. N. Y., 1857. 5—30.

Newton, John, The works of, with a memoir of his life, by the Rev. Richard Cecil. N. Y., 1860. 25—148.

Newtown, The annals of. Riker, J. N. Y., 1852. 31—189.

New-Year's bargain, The. Illus. Coolidge, S. Bost., 1874. 38.

New York, A gazetteer of the state of. Disturnell, J. Albany, 1843. 31—190.

——, Census of the state of, 1865. Albany, 1867. D. R.

—— city and state in the olden time, Annals and occurrences of. Watson, J. F. Phil., 1846. 31—190.

—— Croton aqueduct, Description of the. Illus. Schramke, T. N. Y. and Berlin, 1846. D. R.

—— Geological map of the state of. N. Y., 1842. L.

——, Historical collections of the state of. Illus. Barber, J. W. N. Y., 1851. 31—190.

—— Historical Society, Proceedings of the. N. Y., 1844-50. 7 v. 31—190.

—— Historical Society, Collections of the. N. Y., 1811-29. 5 v. 31—190.

—— Same. 2d series. N. Y., 1841-49. 2 v. 31—190.

—— State Agricultural Society, Transactions of the. Illus. Albany, 1850. D. R.

——, The natural history of. Illus. N. Y., 1843. 19 v. S.

Contents.

Zoology. James E. De Kay. 5 vols.
Botany. John Torrey. 2 vols.
Mineralogy. Lewis C. Beck. 1 vol.
Geology. William W. Mather, Ebenezer Emmons, Lardner Vanuxem, and James Hall. 4 vols.
Palæontology. James Hall. 2 vols.
Agriculture. Ebenezer Emmons. 5 vols.

New York, Old. Francis, J. W. N. Y., 1858. 31—190.

——, past, present, and future. Illus. Belden, E. P. N. Y., 1850. 31—190.

Nicaragua and the interoceanic canal. Illus. Squier, E. G. N. Y., 1852. Vol. 2. 10—56.

——, The war in. Walker, W. Mobile, 1860. 36—217.

Nichol, John Pringle. *A cyclopædia of the physical sciences; comprising acoustics, astronomy, dynamics, electricity, heat, hydrodynamics, magnetism, philosophy of mathematics, meteorology, optics, pneumatics, statics, etc. Illus. Lond., 1860. 23—138.

Nicholas Nickleby. Illus. Dickens, C. N. Y., 1868. 2 v. 2 copies. 3—15 and 16.

Nicholson, Peter. *An architectural dictionary, containing a correct nomenclature and derivation of the terms employed by architects, builders, and workmen. Lond., 1819. 2 v. 21—125.

—— Principles of architecture ; comprising fundamental rules of the art, with their application to practice ; also rules for shadows, and for the five orders. Illus. Sixth edition, by Joseph Gwilt. Lond., 1848. T.

—— A practical treatise on the art of masonry and stone-cutting. Illus. Lond., 1835. T.

—— A new and improved practical builder and workman's companion. Illus. Lond., n. d. 3 v. T.

—— Carpentry : being a comprehensive guide-book for carpentry and joining. Illus. Lond., 1852. 2 v. T.

Nick of the woods ; or, the Jibbenainosay. Bird, R. M. N. Y., n. d. 3—16.

Niebuhr, Barthold Georg. Lectures on ancient history, from the earliest times to the taking of Alexandria. Phil., 1852. 3 v. 32—193.

Night and morning. Bulwer-Lytton, *Sir* E. Phil., 1868. 5—33.

Nile, The land of the. Illus. Adams, W. H. D. Lond. and N. Y., 1871. 9—53.

—— notes of a howadji. Curtis, G. W. N. Y., 1856. 17—104.

—— tributaries of Abyssinia, The. Illus. Baker, *Sir* S. W. Phil., 1871. 17—101.

Niles, Hezekiah. Principles and acts of the revolution in America ; or, an attempt to collect and preserve some of the speeches, orations, and proceedings, with sketches and remarks on men and things. Balt., 1822. 25—152.

—— Weekly register, containing political, historical, geographical, scientifical, astronomical, statistical, and biographical documents, essays, and facts, with a record of the events of the times, from

Sept., 1811, to July, 1849. Balt. and Phil. 76 v. D. R.

Nimrod of the sea; or, the American whaleman. Illus. Davis, W. M. N. Y., 1874. 7—41.

Nina Gordon. Stowe, H. B. Bost., 1871. 6—35.

Nina's atonement, and other stories. Illus. "Christian Reid." N. Y., 1873. 5—28.

Nine little goslings. Illus. Coolidge, S. Bost., 1875. 38.

Ninety-three. Hugo, V. F. L. Benedict, tr. N. Y., 1874. 7—41.

Nineveh and its remains. Layard, A. H N. Y., 1850. 2 v. 9—52.

No alternative : a novel. Thomas, A. Phil., n. d. 5——31.

—— intentions. Marryat, *Miss* F. Leip., 1874. 2 v. in one. 4—22.

—— man's friend. Robinson, F. W. N. Y., 1867. 5—29.

—— name. Illus. Collins, W. W. N.Y. 1872. 6—38.

"**No Name**" series. Deirdrè. Joyce, R. D. Bost., 1876. 17—105.

—— Mercy Philbrick's choice. Jackson, H. Bost., 1876. 41—226.

—— Kismet. Fletcher, D. Bost., 1877. 41—226.

Noble life, A. Muloch, D. M. N. Y., 1871. 4—23.

—— lord, A : sequel to "The lost heir of Linlithgow." Southworth, E. D. E. N. Phil., 1872. 6—36.

Noblesse oblige. N. Y., 1876. 41—227.

Noctes ambrosianæ. Wilson, J., and others. N. Y., n. d. 5 v. 2—9.

Noel, *Lady* Augusta. Owen Gwynne's great work. N. Y., 1875. 41—228.

Nordhoff, Charles. Northern California, Oregon, and the Sandwich Islands. Illus. N. Y., 1874. 17—101.

—— California for health, pleasure and residence : a book for travellers and settlers. Illus. N. Y., 1874. 17—101.

—— Politics for young Americans. N.Y., 1875. 19—114.

Normandy, Life in. Illus. Edin., 1863. 2 v. 17—101.

Norse mythology. Anderson, R. B. Chicago, 1876. 40—224.

Norseman's pilgrimage, A. Boyesen, H. H. N. Y., 1875. 41—227.

Norsemen in the west, The. Illus. Ballantyne, R. M. Lond. and N. Y., 1872. 6—38.

North America. Trollope, A. N. Y., 1863. 17—104.

—— America, Historical account of discoveries and travels in. Murray, II. Lond., 1829. 2 v. 10—58.

—— America, Notes on. Johnston, J. F. W. Bost. and Edin., 1851. 2 v. 29—175.

—— America, The early Jesuit missions in. Ingraham, Kip, W. Albany, 1873. 29—177.

—— American Indians, Sketches of the history, manners, and customs of the. Buchanau, J. Lond., 1824. 30—178.

—— American Indians, Illustrations of the manners, customs, and condition of the. Illus. Catlin, G. Lond., 1841. 2 v. 30—178.

—— and South America, Influence of climate in. Disturnell, J. N. Y., 1867. 15—92.

—— Bridgewater, History of. Illus. Kingman, B. Bost., 1866. 30—182.

—— British Review, The. 1855–59. 3 v. X.

—— Carolina, Historical sketches of. Illus. Wheeler, J. H. Phil., 1851. 2 v. in one. 31—188.

—— Carolina, The history of. Martin, F. X. N. O., 1829. 2 v. 31—188.

—— pole, Narrative of an attempt to reach the. Illus. Parry, W. E. Lond., 1828. 8—47.

—— star and the southern cross, The. Weppner, M. Lond., 1876. 2 v. 40—222.

North, Christopher, *pseud.* See Wilson, John.

Northanger Abbey: a novel. Austen, J. Lond., 1870. 4—27.

North-eastern boundary, The right of the United States of America to the. Gallatin, A. N. Y., 1840. L.

Northern California, Oregon, and the Sandwich Islands. Illus. Nordhoff, C. N. Y., 1874. 17—101.

—— travel. Taylor, J. B. N. Y., 1869. 17—103.

North-west coast, The. Illus. Swan, J. G. N. Y., 1857. R—2.

——, Travels in the. Illus. Schoolcraft, H. R. Albany, 1821. 9—52.

North-west passage, Narrative of a second voyage in search of a. Illus. Ross, *Sir* J. Lond., 1835. 2 v. V.

—— passage, Journal of a voyage for the discovery of a. Illus. Parry, W. E. Lond., 1821. 8—47.

—— passage, Journal of a second voyage for the discovery of a. Illus. Parry. W. E. Lond., 1824. 8—47.

—— passage, Journal of a third voyage for the discovery of a. Illus. Parry, W. E. Lond., 1826. 8—47.

North-western territory, Notes on the early settlement of the. Burnet, J. Cin., 1847. 29—177.

Norton, Caroline Elizabeth Sarah. Lost and saved. Phil., 1864. 6—39.

—— Old Sir Douglas. Phil. and Lond., 1867. O—1.

—— The lady of La Garaye. Lond., 1871. 16—100.

—— Stuart of Dunleath: a story of the present time. N. Y., 1867. 5—28.

Norwood; or, village life in New England. Illus. Beecher, H. W. N. Y., 1874. 7—42.

Not dead yet: a novel. Jeaffreson, J. C. N. Y., 1864. 7—41.

—— in their set. Lenzen, M. Bost., 1874. 6—37.

—— pretty but precious, and other short stories. Illus. Hay, J., and others. Phil., 1874. 5—28.

—— wisely but too well. Broughton, R. N. Y., 1871. 6—35.

Notary's nose, The. About, E. N. Y., 1874. 41—226.

Note-book of an English opium-eater. De Quincey, T. Bost., 1855. 2—12.

Noted names of fiction, Dictionary of the. Wheeler, W. A. Bost., 1872. 28—165.

Nothing new: tales. Muloch, D. M. N. Y., 1870. 5—28.

Nott, Josiah Clark, and George R. Gliddon. Indigenous races of the earth; or, new chapters of ethnological inquiry, contributed by A. Maury, F. Pulszky, and J. A. Meigs, *M. D.* Illus. Phil., 1857. 14—80.

—— Types of mankind; or, ethnological researches based upon the ancient monuments, paintings, sculptures, and crania of races; and upon their natural, geographical, philological, and biblical history; illustrated by selections from the inedited papers of Samuel George Morton, *M. D.*, and by contributions from *Prof.* L. Agassiz, W. Usher, *M. D.*, and *Prof.* H. S. Patterson. Illus. Phil., 1854. 14—80.

Nouveau voyage dans l'Amérique septentrionale. Robin. Phil. et Paris, 1782. W.

Nouvelle Espagne. Humboldt, F. H. A. *von.* Paris, 1811. 2 v. U. Atlas, X.

Novels and novelists of the eighteenth century. Forsyth, W. N. Y., 1871. 11—64.

—— and tales. Goethe, J. W. *von.* Lond., 1871. 2—11.

Now and then. Warren, S. N. Y., 1848. 7—45.

Nugent, George Nugent Temple Grenville, *lord.* See Grenville, G. N. T.

Nursery noonings. "Gail Hamilton." N. Y., 1875. 6—39.

Nuttall, P. Austin. *A classical and archæological dictionary of the manners, customs, laws, institutions, arts., etc., of the celebrated nations of antiquity, and of the middle ages. Lond.,1840. 22—132.

Oak openings. Illus. Cooper, J. F. N. Y., 1864. 3—14.

Oates, George. Interest tables at seven per cent. on any sum from one to ten thousand dollars, from one day to one year. N. Y., 1851. Q—1.

Oblique arches, Construction of. Illus. Hart, J. Lond., 1839. T.

—— bridges, An essay on. Buck, G. W. Lond., 1839. T.

Observations in the east. Illus. Durbin, J. P. N. Y., 1854. 2 v. 17—104.

—— on the historical work of the late Right Hon. Charles James Fox. Rose, G. Lond., 1809. T.

—— on the popular antiquities of Great Britain. Brand, J. Lond., 1853-55. 3 v. 27—163.

O'Callaghan, Edmund B. History of New Netherland; or, New York under the Dutch. N. Y., 1846-49. 2 v. 31—190.

Occult sciences, The. Salverte, A. J. E. B. N. Y., n. d. 2 v. 14—85.

Occupations of a retired life, The. Illus. "Edward Garrett." N. Y., n. d. 3—15.

Ocean, The. Illus. Reclus, E. N. Y., 1873. 14—83.

—— world, The. Illus. Figuier, L. Lond., n, d. 14—83.

Ockley, Simon. The history of the Saracens; comprising the lives of Mohammed and his successors, to the death of Abdalmelik, the eleventh caliph, with an account of their most remarkable battles, sieges, and revolts. Lond.,1847. 36—217.

Odd couple, An. Oliphant, M. O. W. Phil., n. d. 41—228.

Odyssey, The. Homer. N.Y.,n. d. 27—163.

—— Same, translated by Cowper. Vol. 13, Cowper's works. 16—100.

—— Same, translated by Pope. Lond., 1833. 3 v. 16—95.

—— Same, translated into English blank verse by W. C. Bryant. Bost., 1873. 2 v. 17—106.

Off the Skelligs: a novel. Ingelow, J. Bost., 1872. 6—38.

*Official register of the United States, 1816-75. 28 v. 24—145 and 146.

Ogilvie, John. *The imperial dictionary, English; technological and scientific, with supplement. Illus. Lond., 1853. 3 v. 22—131.

Ogilvies, The. Muloch, D. M. N. Y., 1871. 4—23.

Oglethorpe, James, Life of. (Library of American biography, vol. 12.) 11—65.

——, Biographical memorials of. Harris, T. M. Bost., 1841. 11—62.

Ohio, Biographical and historical memoirs of the early pioneer settlers of. Hildreth, S. P. Cin., 1852. 13—73.

——, Centennial history of Licking county. Smucker, I. Newark, 1876. 29—176.

——, Geological survey of. Columbus, 1871. L.

——, Historical collections of. Illus. Howe, H. Cin., 1847. 31—185.

—— valley, A pioneer history of the. Hildreth, S. P. Cin., 1848. 29—176.

O'Keefe, Kelly, and Taylor, Personal reminiscences by. (Bric-a-brac series.) Illus. N. Y., 1875. 11—61.

One fair woman. "Joaquin Miller." N. Y., 1876. 3 v. in one. 41—228.

—— of them. Lever, C. J. N. Y., 1872. 5—29.

—— summer. Howard, B. W. Bost., 1875. Two copies. 5—33.

O'Neall, John Belton. Biographical sketches of the bench and bar of South Carolina. Charleston, 1859. 2 v. 2—9.

Onis, D. Luis de. Memoria sobre las negociaciones entre España y los Estados-Unidos de América, que dieron motivo al tratado de 1819. Mad., 1820. D. R.

Only a clod. Braddon, M. E. N. Y., n. d. 5—29.

—— a fiddler. Andersen, H. C. N. Y., 1871. 6—39.

—— a girl. Hillern, W. von. Phil., 1872. 6—38.

—— herself. Thomas, A. N. Y., 1870. 5—28.

Open polar sea, The. Illus. Hayes, I. I. N. Y., 1869. 17—103.

—— question : a novel. Illus. De Mille, J. N. Y., 1873. 6—35.

Opening a chestnut burr. Roe, Rev. E. P. N. Y., n. d. 6—38.

Opportunities : a sequel to "What she could." Illus. "Elizabeth Wetherell." N. Y., 1871. 7—42.

—— for industry, and the safe investment of capital. Freedley, E. T. Phil., 1859. 28—166.

Opportunity: a novel. Seemüller, A. M. C. Bost., 1871. 2 copies. P—2.

Optics, The wonders of. Illus. Marion, F. N. Y., 1872. 28—169.

Oration on the tragedy of the 5th of March, 1770. Warren, J. Bost., 1775. 27—160.

Orators of the age. Francis, G. H. N. Y., 1847. 13—79.

Orbigny, Charles Dessalines d', et A. Gente. Géologie appliquée aux arts et à l'agriculture, comprenant l'ensemble des révolutions du globe. Paris, 1851. D. R.

Ordeal for wives, The. Edwards, A. B. N. Y., 1872. 6—38.

Oregon and California in 1848. Illus. Thornton, J. Q. N. Y., 1849. 2 v. 9—53.

—— and California, The history of. Greenhow, R. Bost., 1847. 31—187.

Oregon and Eldorado. Bulfinch, T. Bost., 1866. 31—187.

—— and its institutions. Illus. Hines, G. N. Y., 1868. 31—187.

—— territory, The. Twiss, T. N. Y., 1846. 31—187.

—— trail, The. Parkman, F. Bost., 1872. 28—166.

O'Reilly, John Boyle. Songs from the southern seas, and other poems. Bost., 1873. 17—106.

Organic remains of a former world. Illus. Parkinson, J. Lond., 1833. Vols. 1 and 3. 14—80.

Origin of civilization, The. Illus. Lubbock, Sir J. N. Y., 1870. 14—81.

—— of representative government in Europe, History of the. Guizot, F. P. G. Lond., 1852. 33—202.

—— of species, On the. Darwin, C. N. Y., 1869. 14—81.

—— of species, On the. Huxley, T. H. N. Y., 1872. 14—81.

Original fables. Illus. Prosser, Mrs. Lond., n. d. 38.

* —— lists of persons of quality; emigrants, religious exiles, political rebels, serving men sold for a term of years, apprentices, children stolen, maidens pressed, and others who went from Great Britain to the American plantations, 1600-1700 ; with their ages, the localities where they formerly lived in the mother country, the names of the ships in which they embarked, and other interesting particulars : from MSS. preserved in the state paper department of her majesty's public record office, England. J. Camden Hotten, ed. N. Y., 1874. 19—115.

Orlando Furioso. Ariosto, L. Lond., 1799. 5 v. 16—95.

Orleans, Louis Philippe, d'; compte de Paris. History of the civil war in America. L. F. Tasistro, tr. Henry Coppée, ed. Phil., 1875-76. Vols. 1 and 2. 30—181.

Orley farm. Illus. Trollope, A. N. Y., 1871. 5—28.

Orton, James. The Andes and the Amazon ; or, across the continent of South America. Illus. N. Y., 1872. 17—102.

Osborne, Francis. Secret history of the

court of James the first. Edin., 1811. 2 v. 12—67.

Ossian, Poems of. J. Macpherson, tr. N. Y., 1810. 2 v. 16—100.

Ossoli, Margaret Sarah Fuller, *marchioness d'.* Woman in the nineteenth century, and kindred papers relating to the sphere, condition, and duties of woman. A. B. Fuller, ed. With an introduction by Horace Greeley. Bost., 1855. 2—8.

Oswald, Cray. Wood, E. P. Phil., n. d. 41—230.

Otis, F. N. Isthmus of Panama. History of the Panama railroad, and of the Pacific Mail Steamship Company; together with a traveller's guide and business man's hand-book for the Panama railroad, and the lines of steamships connecting it with Europe, the United States, the North and South Atlantic and Pacific coasts, China, Australia, and Japan. Illus. N. Y., 1867. 17—102.

Otis, Harrison Gray. Letters in defence of the Hartford convention, and the people of Massachusetts. Bost., 1824. 29—177.

Otis, James, Life of. (Library of American biography, vol. 12.) 11—65.

—— Same. Tudor, W. Bost., 1823. 12—70.

Other girls, The. Illus. Whitney, A. D. T. Bost., 1873. 7—44.

—— people's money. Gaboriau, E. Bost., 1875. 41—230.

—— worlds than ours. Illus. Proctor, R. A. N. Y., 1871. 14—82.

Ottoman and Spanish empires. Ranke, L. Phil., 1845. 36—217.

Ought we to visit her? a novel. Edwards, A. N. Y., n. d. 6—39.

Ouida, *pseud.* See La Rame, Louise de.

Our flag:—origin and progress of the flag of the United States of America. Illus. Preble, G. H. Albany, 1872. 29—176.

—— mutual friend. Illus. Dickens, C. N. Y., 1868. 2 v. 2 copies. 3—15 and 16.

—— Same. (Condensed classics.) N. Y. 1876. 5—33.

—— new crusade: a temperance story. Hale, E. E. Bost., 1875. 5—34.

—— new way round the world. Illus. Coffin, C. C. Bost., 1869. 17—101.

Our old home. Hawthorne, N. Bost., 1868. 3—18..

—— village. Mitford, M. R. Lond., 1870. 2 v. 2—11.

Out of town. Burnand, F. C. Lond., 1870. 2—13.

—— of the hurly-burly; or, life in an odd corner. Illus. "Max Adeler." Phil., 1874. 2—8.

Outcast, The. Reade, W. W. Lond., 1875. 3—17.

Out-door papers. Higginson, T. W. Bost., 1871. 19—115.

Out-doors at Idlewild. Willis, N. P. N. Y., 1855. P—2.

Outre-mer: a pilgrimage beyond the sea. Longfellow, H. W. Bost., 1865. 17—103.

Over yonder: a novelette. John, E. Phil., 1873. 7—42.

Overman, Frederick. The manufacture of iron, in all its various branches; with an essay on the manufacture of steel. Illus. Phil., 1851. T.

Owen, David Dale. Report of a geological survey of Wisconsin, Iowa, and Minnesota, and, incidentally, of a portion of Nebraska territory. Illus. Phil., 1852. 2 v. L.

Owen, Meredith, *pseud.* See Lytton, R. B.

Owen, Robert Dale. Beyond the breakers: a story of the present day. Illus. Phil., 1874. 5—28.

Owen Gwynne's great work. Noel, *Lady* A. N. Y., 1875. 41—228.

Oxford essays, contributed by members of the university. Lond., 1857. 27—159.

P's and **Q's**; or, the question of putting upon. Illus. Yonge, C. M. Lond., 1872. 39. ´

Pacha of many tales, The. Marryat, *Capt.* F. N. Y., 1857. 5—30.

Pacific states of North America, The native races of the. Bancroft, H. H. N. Y., 1874. Vol. 1. 19—115.

Packard, *Mrs.* E. P. W. Modern persecution; or, insane asylums unveiled, and married woman's liabilities, as demonstrated by the action of the Illinois legislature. Illus. Hartford, 1874. 2 v. 28—169.

Paget, John. Judicial puzzles gathered from the state trials. San Fran., 1876. 40—221.

Paine, Thomas, The works of. Phil., 1797. 2 v. 28—170.

Painter's camp, A. Hamerton, P. G. Bost., 1873. 17—103.

Pair of blue eyes, A. Hardy, T. N. Y., 1874. 5—30.

Palestine. (L'Univers.) Munk. Paris, 1845. D. R.

——, A pilgrimage to. Illus. Smith, J. V. C. Bost., 1853. 17—101.

Palfrey, John Gorham. History of New England during the Stuart dynasty. Bost., 1865. 3 v. 29—176.

Palfrey, William, Life of. (Library of American biography, vol. 17.) 11—65.

Palgrave, Sir Francis. History of the Anglo-Saxons. Illus. Lond., 1867. 36—219.

Palgrave, Francis Turner. The children's treasury of English song. N. Y., 1875. 17—106.

Palgrave, William Gifford. Hermann Agha: an eastern narrative. N. Y., 1872. 7—46.

Palissy, Bernard, The life of. Morley, H. Bost., 1853. 2 v. 12—72.

Palmetto-leaves. Illus. Stowe, H. B. Bost., 1873. 17—102.

Palou, Francisco. Relacion historica de la vida y apostolicas Tareas, del venerable Padre Fray Junipero Serra. México, 1787. D. R.

Paludan-Müller, Frederick. The fountain of youth. Illus. H. W. Freeland, tr. Phil., 1867. P—1.

Pampas and Andes, The. Bishop, N. H. Bost., 1869. 17—102.

Papacy and the civil power, The. Thompson, R. W. N. Y., 1876. 18—108.

Papa's own girl: a novel. Howland, M. N. Y., 1874. 7—41.

Paraguay, Histoire du. Amsterdam, 1780. 3 v. W.

——, Letters on. Robertson, J. P. and W. P. Lond., 1839. 3 v. 36—216.

Pardoe, Julia. The court and reign of Francis the first, king of France. Illus. Lond., 1849. 2 v. 12—70.

—— Reginald Lyle. N. Y., 1854. O—3.

Paris, John Ayrton. Philosophy in sport made science in earnest; being an at-

tempt to illustrate the first principles of natural philosophy by the aid of the popular toys and sports of youth. Illus. Phil., 1847. 38.

Paris sketch-book, The. Illus. Thackeray, W. M. Lond., 1869. 5—32.

Paris universal exposition, Report of the U. S. commissioners to the. Published under the direction of the Secretary of State. W. P. Blake, ed. Wash. 1870. 6 v. 19—113.

Contents.

Vol. 1. Introduction, with selections from the correspondence of [Commissioner-General N. M. Beckwith, and others; General survey of the exposition, with a report on the character and condition of the United States section; Report on the fine arts, Frank Leslie; The fine arts, applied to the useful arts; Extract from the report of the international committee on weights, measures, and coins. Bibliography of the exposition of 1867; General alphabetical index.

Vol. 2. The production of iron and steel in its economic and social relations, Abram S. Hewitt; Report upon the precious metals, William P. Blake; The progress and condition of several departments of industrial chemistry, J. Lawrence Smith.

Vol. 3. Machinery and processes of the industrial arts and apparatus of the exact sciences, Frederick A. P. Barnard.

Vol. 4. Examination of the telegraphic apparatus, and the processes in telegraphy, Samuel F. B. Morse; Steam-engineering, as illustrated by the exposition, Wm. S. Auchincloss; Engineering and public works, Wm. P. Blake; Béton-Coignet: its fabrication and uses, L. F. Beckwith; Asphalt and bitumen as applied in construction, A. Beckwith; Buildings, building-materials, and methods of building, James H. Bowen; Mining and mechanical preparation of ores, H. F. Q. D'Aligny and Messrs. Huet, Geyler, and Lepainteur.

Vol. 5. Quantities of cereals produced in different countries compared, S. B. Ruggles; The quality and characteristics of the cereal products exhibited, G. S. Hazzard; Report on the preparation of food, W. E. Johnston; The manufacture of beet-root sugar and alcohol; The manufacture of pressed and agglomerated coal; Photographs and photographic apparatus; Outline of the history of the Atlantic cables, H. F. Q. D'Aligny; Culture and products of the vine, and the production of wine in California, Messrs. Wilder, Thompson, Flagg, and Barry; School-houses, and the means of promoting popular education, J. R. Freese; Munitions of war exhibited at the exposition, C. B. Norton and W. J. Valentine; Instruments and apparatus of medicine, surgery, hygiene, etc., T. W. Evans;

Report on musical instruments, Paran Stevens.
Vol. 6. Wool and manufactures of wool, E. R. Mudge and J. L. Hayes; Report on cotton, E. R. Mudge and B. F. Nourse; Silk and silk manufactures, E. C. Cowdin; Clothing and woven fabrics, Paran Stevens; Report on education, J. W. Hoyt; List of the reports.

Parish churches. Illus. Brandon, R. and J. Arthur. Lond., 1848. 40—225.

Parisiana, The. Illus. Bulwer-Lytton, *Sir* E. N. Y., 1874. 2 v. in one. 5—31.

Parker, Joseph. Ecce Deus: essays on the life and doctrines of Jesus Christ, with controversial notes on "Ecce homo." Bost., 1868. E.

Parker, Samuel. Journal of an exploring tour beyond the Rocky Mountains. Auburn, 1846. 8—50.

Parkinson, James. Organic remains of a former world. Illus. Lond., 1833. Vols. 1 and 3. 14—80.

Parkman, Francis. The California and Oregon trail: being sketches of prairie and Rocky Mountain life. Bost., 1872. 28—166.

—— The discovery of the great west. Bost., 1871. 28—166.

—— France and England in North America: a series of historical narratives. Bost., 1871. 28—166.

—— The Jesuits in North America, in the seventeenth century. Bost., 1872. 28—166.

—— The conspiracy of Pontiac, and the Indian war, after the conquest of Canada. Bost., 1870. 2 v. 28—166.

—— The old régime in Canada. Bost., 1874. 28—166.

Parkwater; or, told in the twilight. Wood, E. P. Phil., n. d. 41—230.

Parlor acting charades. Frost, S. A. N. Y., 1876. 41—226.

Parnell, *Sir* Henry. A treatise on roads: illustrated by the practice of Telford. Lond., 1838. T.

Parnell, Thomas, Poetical works of; with a life, by Oliver Goldsmith. Bost., 1864. 16—97.

Parr, Harriet, (*Holme Lee.*) Fairy tales. Illus. Lond., and N. Y., n. d. 33.

—— Sylvan Holt's daughter. N. Y., 1860. 4—24.

—— Kathie Brande: a fireside history of a quiet life. N. Y., 1857. 4—24.

Parr, Harriet, (*Holme Lee.*) Annis Warleigh's fortunes: a novel. N. Y., 1867. 4—24.

—— Mr. Wynyard's ward: a novel. N. Y., 1867. 4—24.

Parr, Louisa. Hero Carthew; or, the Prescotts of Pamphillon: a novel. N. Y., 1873. 4—25.

—— John Thompson, and other stories. Phil., n. d. 4—25.

—— Dorothy Fox. Illus. Phil., 1873. 5—29.

Parrot, Friedrich. Journey to Ararat. W. D. Cooley, tr. Illus. N. Y., 1846. 10—57.

Parry, William Edward. Journal of a voyage for the discovery of a north-west passage from the Atlantic to the Pacific, performed in the years 1819-20. Illus. Lond., 1821. 8—47.

—— Journal of a second voyage for the discovery of a north-west passage, in the years 1821-23. Illus. Lond., 1824. 8—47.

—— Journal of a third voyage for the discovery of a north-west passage. Illus. Lond., 1826. 8—47.

—— Narrative of an attempt to reach the north pole, in the year 1827. Illus. Lond., 1828. 8—47.

Partington, Charles F. *The British cyclopædia of the arts and sciences. Illus. Lond., 1835. 2 v. 23—140.

Partisan, The: a romance of the revolution. Illus. Simms, W. G. N. Y., n. d. 41—229.

—— leader, The. Tucker, B. N. Y., 1861. 26—157.

Parton, James. Life and times of Benjamin Franklin. N. Y. and Lond., 1864. 2 v. 12—72.

—— The humorous poetry of the English language, from Chaucer to Saxe. Bost., 1870. 16—95.

——, Greeley, and others. Eminent women of the age; being narratives of the lives and deeds of the most prominent women of the present generation. Illus. Hartford, 1871. 13—74.

—— The life and times of Aaron Burr, lieutenant-colonel in the army of the revolution, United States senator, vice-president of the United States, etc. Bost., 1872. 2 v. 40—224.

Parton, James.` Life of Thomas Jefferson, third president of the United States. Bost., 1874. 40—224.

—— Life of Andrew Jackson. Bost., 1870. 3 v. 40—224.

Parton, Sara Payson, (*Fanny Fern.*) Rose Clark. ` N. Y., 1856. O—3.

—— Fern leaves from Fanny's portfolio. Illus. Auburn, 1853. 2—10.

—— Caper-sauce: a volume of chit-chat about men, women, and things, by "Fanny Fern." N. Y., 1872. 2—8.

Pascal, Blaise, The thoughts, letters, and opuscules of. O. W. Wight, tr. N. Y., 1869. 2—11.

——, The provincial letters of; with his life. *Rev.* T. M'Crie, tr.; O` W. Wight, ed. N. Y., 1866. P—2.

Pascarel. "Ouida." Phil., 1873. 7—44.

Paschal, George W. The constitution of the United States, defined and carefully annotated. Wash., 1868. 21—125.

Pasley, *Sir* Charles William. Observations on limes, calcareous cements, mortars, stuccos, and concrete. Illus. Lond., 1847. T.

Passionate pilgrim, A. James, H. Bost., 1875. 41—228.

Passions; or, mind and matter illustrated by considerations on hereditary insanity. Millingen, J. G. Lond., 1848. 14—81.

Past and present. Carlyle, T. Lond., 1843. 28—169.

Pathfinder, The. Illus. Cooper, J. F. N. Y., 1864. 3—14.

Patmore, Coventry. The victories of love. Lond., 1863. 16—100.

Patty. Macquoid, K. S. Lond. and N. Y., 1871. P—3.

Paul and Virginia. Illus. St. Pierre, J. H. B. de. N. Y., 1873. 7—42.

—— Clifford. Bulwer-Lytton, *Sir* E. Phil., 1868. 5—33.

—— Fane. Willis, N. P. N. Y., 1857. O—3.

—— Massie: a romance. McCarthy, J. N. Y., n. d. 7—41. ·

Paulding, James K., Literary life of; compiled by his son, W. I. Paulding. N. Y., 1867. 13—76.

—— A book of vagaries; comprising the new mirror for travellers, and other

whim-whams. W. I. Paulding, ed. N. Y., 1868. 2—10.

—— Tales of the good woman, by a doubtful gentleman. W. I. Paulding, ed. N. Y., 1867. 2—8.

—— The Dutchman's fireside: a tale. W. I. Paulding, ed. N. Y., 1868. 2—8.

—— The Bulls and the Jonathans; comprising John Bull and Brother Jonathan, and John Bull in America. W. I. Paulding, ed. N. Y., 1867. 2—8.

Pausanias, the Spartan. Bulwer-Lytton, *Sir* E. Leipzig, 1876. 5—33.

Payne, John Howard, The life and writings of. Harrison, G. Albany, 1875. 11—59.

—— The tragedy of Brutus; or, the fall of Tarquin; with original cast of characters in 1833. Albany, 1875. 16—100.

Peake, Elizabeth. History of the German emperors and their contemporaries. Illus. Phil., 1874. 36—219.

Pear-culture. Illus. Fields, T. W. N. Y., 1859. V.

Peard, Frances M., (*S. B. A. Moslih-Eddin.*) The rose garden. Bost., 1872. 7—46.

—— Unawares. Bost., 1872. 7—46.

Pearl of Orr's island, The. Stowe, H. B. Bost., 1869. 6—35.

Pearls from Heine. Illus. Phil., 1865. N.

Peasant life in Germany. Johnson, A. C. N. Y., 1858. 17—101.

Peculiar. Sargent, E. N. Y., 1864. 6—38.

* **Peerage** and baronetage of the British empire, Dictionary of the. Burke, J. B. Lond., 1853. 11—59.

Peg Woffington, and other tales. Reade, C. Bost., 1869. 7—42.

Pelham; or, adventures of a gentleman. Bulwer-Lytton, *Sir* E. Phil., 1867. 5—33.

Peloponnesian war, History of. Thucydides. Phil., 1840. 35—209.

Pen photographs of Charles Dickens's readings. Illus. Field, K. Bost., 1871. 28—166.

Pendennis, The history of. Illus. Thackeray, W. M. Lond., 1868. 2 v. 5—32.

Peninsular war, History of. Napier, *Sir* W. F. P. Phil., 1842. 4 v. 33—199.

—— Same. Southey, R. Lond., 1828. 4 v. 33—199.

Penn, William. The life of. Janney, S.
M. Phil., 1852. 11—63.
—— The life of. (Library of American
biography, vol. 22.) 11—65.
——, Memoirs of the public and private
life of. Clarkson, T. Lond. and Phil.,
1849. 11—63.
——, an historical biography of. Dixon,
W. H. Phil., 1851. 11—63.
Pennsylvania, Historical collections of
the State of. Illus. Day, S. Phil.,
1843. 31—189.
——, Memoirs of the Historical Society
of. Phil., 1826-50. 4 v. 31—189.
• —— volunteers, History of. Bates, S.
P. Harrisburgh, 1869-71. 5 v. X.
——, The history of. Proud, R. Phil.,
1797-98. 2 v. 31—189.
——, The register of. Hazard, S. Phil.,
1828-35. 8 v. X.
——, votes and proceedings of the house
of representatives of the province of.
1682 to 1726. Phil., 1752-53. 2 v. D.
R.
—— pilgrim, and other poems. Illus.
Whittier, J. G. Bost., 1872. 16—09.
Pepys, Samuel, Diary and correspond-
ence of; with a life and notes, by Rich-
ard, Lord Baybrooke. Phil., 1855. 4 v.
27—160.
Percival Keene. Marryat, Capt. F. N.
Y., 1857. 5—30.
Percy, Thomas. Reliques of ancient
English poetry ; with a memoir and a
critical dissertation, by Rev. Geo. Gilfil-
lan. Edin., 1858. 3 v. 16—95.
Percy Effingham: a novel. Cockton, H.
Phil., n. d. 41—230.
Peregrine Pickle, The adventures of.
Smollett, T. Lond., 1872. 2 v. 41—
229.
Pericles, The age of. Lloyd, W. W.
Lond., 1875. 2 v. 40—225.
Perrier, Amelia. A good match. N.
Y., 1873. 6—38.
Perrin du Lac, F. M. Voyage dans
les deux Louisianes. Lyon, 1805. W.
Perry, Matthew C., Commodore. Narra-
tive of the expedition of an American
squadron to the China seas and Japan,
performed in the years 1852, '53, and
'54, by order of the government of the
United States. Compiled from the orig-
inal notes and journals of Commodore

Perry and his officers, at his request,
and under his supervision, by Francis
L. Hawks, D. D. LL. D., with numerous
illustrations. Published by order of the
congress of the United States. Wash.,
1856. 3 v. 8—47.
Perry, Commodore Oliver Hazard, The life
of. Mackenzie, A. S. N. Y., 1843. 2 v.
13—78.
Persia, An historical and descriptive account of. Fraser, J. B. Edin., 1834.
36—217.
Personal memoirs. Buckingham, J. T.
Bost., 1852. 2 v. 11—64.
—— reminiscences, by Chorley, Planche,
and Young. (Bric-a-brac series, vol. 1.)
Richard H. Stoddard, ed. N. Y., 1874.
11—61.
—— reminiscences, by Barham, Harness,
and Hodder. (Bric-a-brac series, vol. 4.)
N. Y., 1875. 11—61.
—— sketches of his own times. Barrington, Sir J. N. Y., 1853. 3—20.
Persuasion. Austen, J. Lond., 1870.
4—27.
Peru, History of the conquest of. Prescott, W. H. N. Y., 1841. 2 v. 36—216.
—— : incidents of travel and explora-
tion in the land of the Incas. Illus.
Squier, E. G. N. Y., 1877. 10—57.
• ——, The royal commentaries of.
La Vega, G. de. Lond., 1688. 35—209.
——, Travels in. Tschudi, J. J. von.
Lond., 1848. 10—58.
Peter Pilgrim. Bird, R. M. Phil., 1838.
2 v. in one. P—2.
—— Simple. Marryat, Capt. F. N. Y.,
1857. 5—30.
Petitot, Claude-Bernard. Mémoires du
cardinal de Richelieu, sur le règne de
Louis XIII, depuis 1610 jusqu'à 1619.
Paris, 1823. 10 v. D. R.
Petits poëtes Français. Poitevin, P.
Paris, 1864. 2 v. W.
Petrifactions and their teachings. Illus.
Mantell, G. A. Lond., 1851. 15—91.
Petronel: a novel. Marryat, Miss F.
Lond. and N. Y., n. d. 4—22.
Pettigrew, Thomas Joseph. Chroni-
cles of the tombs: a select collection of
epitaphs. Lond., 1857. 27—163.
Petzholdt, Alexander. Lectures to
farmers on agricultural chemistry.
(Farmers' library, vol. 1.) N.Y., 1846. 8.

Pickering, John. A vocabulary of words and phrases which have been supposed to be peculiar to the United States of America; with an essay on the present state of the English language in the United States. Bost., 1816. V.

Pickwick papers. Illus. Dickens, C. N. Y., 1868. 2 v. 2 copies. 3—15 and 16.

* **Pictorial** history of the American civil war. Leslie, F. N. Y., 1862. Vol. 1. V.

Pictures from Italy. Illus. Dickens, C. N. Y., 1868. 2 copies. 3—15 and 16.

Picturesque America; or, the land we live in; a delineation by pen and pencil of the mountains, rivers, lakes, forests, water-falls, shores, cañons, valleys, cities, and other picturesque features of our country. W. C. Bryant, ed. Illus. N. Y., 1872. 2 v. M.

Pidgin-English sing-song. Leland, C. G. Phil., 1876. 17—106.

Pieces of a broken-down critic, picked up by himself. Baden-Baden, 1858. 19—115.

Pierce, Edward M. The cottage cyclopædia of history and biography; with a chronological view of American history. Illus. Hartford, 1859. 23—138.

Pierce, Gilbert A. The Dickens dictionary: a key to the characters and principal incidents in the tales of Charles Dickens; with additions by W. A. Wheeler. Illus. Bost., 1872. 3—16.

Pierson, Hamilton W. Jefferson at Monticello; or, the private life of Thomas Jefferson from entirely new materials; with numerous fac-similes. N. Y., 1862. 24—142.

Piggot, A. Snowden. The chemistry and metallurgy of copper, with a description of the principal copper mines of the United States and other countries. Phil., 1858. V.

Pike, Frances West Atherton. A wife's story, and other tales. Lond., 1875. 3 v. 4—25.

Pike, Mary H., (*Mary Langdon.*) Ida May: a story of things actual and possible. Bost., 1854. 6—40.

Pike, Nicholas. Sub-tropical rambles in the land of the aphanapteryx: personal experiences, adventures, and wanderings in and around the island of Mauritius. Illus. N. Y., 1873. 10—56.

Pike, Zebulon M. An account of expeditions to the sources of the Mississippi, and through the western part of Louisiana to the sources of the Arkansas, Kansas, La Platte, and Pierre Jaun Rivers; performed by order of the Government of the United States during the years 1805-07. Phil., 1810. 10—56.

——, Life of. (Library of American biography, vol. 15.) 11—65.

Pike county ballads, and other pieces. Hay, J. Bost., 1873. 17—106.

Pilgrim and the shrine, The. Ainslie, H. Lond. and N. Y., 1871. 2—10.

Pilgrim's progress, The. Illus. Bunyan, J. N. Y., 1851. 23—167.

Pillar of fire, The. Ingraham, J. H. Phil., 1860. 4—25.

Pillars of the house, The. Yonge, C. M. Lond. and N. Y., 1874. 2 v. 5—30.

Pindar, Peter, *pseud.* See Wolcott, John.

Pink and white tyranny. Illus. Stowe, H. B. Bost., 1872. 6—35.

Pinkney, William, Life, writings, and speeches of. Wheaton, H. N. Y., 1826. 12—68.

——, Life of. (Library of American biography, vol. 6.) 11—65.

Pioneer mothers of the west. Illus. Frost, J. Bost., 1875. 40—221.

Pioneers, The. Illus. Cooper, J. F. N.Y., 1864. 3—14.

Pirate, The. Scott Sir W. Bost., 1868. 3—17.

——, The, and the three cutters. Illus. Marryat, Capt. F. N. Y., n. d. 5—30.

Pitkin, Timothy. A statistical view of the commerce of the United States of America: its connection with agriculture and manufactures; and an account of the public debt, revenues, and expenditures of the United States. N. Y., 1817. 18—109.

Pitt, William, The speeches of. Lond., 1846. 4 v. 27—161.

Plague in London, History of the. De Foe, D. Oxford, 1840. 27—162.

Plain talks on familiar subjects. Holland, J. G. N. Y., 1872. 3—18.

Plains of the great west, The. Illus. Dodge, R. I. N. Y., 1877. 10—57.

Planchette; or, the despair of science. Sargent, E. Bost., 1869. 15—93.

Planetary and stellar worlds. Mitchel, O. M. N. Y., 1868. 14—32.

Plantaganets, The early. (Epochs of history.) Stubbs, W. N. Y., n. d. 34—207.

Plato, Dialogues of. B. Jowett, tr. N. Y., 1872. 26—155.

Contents.

Vol. 1. Charmides; Lysis; Laches; Protagoras; Euthydemus; Ion; Meno; Euthyphro; Apology; Crito; Phædo; The symposium; Phædrus; Cratylus.

Vol. 2. The republic; Timæus; Critias.

Vol. 3. Gorgias; Philebus; Parmenides; Theætetus; Sophist; Statesman.

Vol. 4. Laws; Appendix; Lesser Hippias; First Alcibiades; Menexenus; Index of persons and places.

Plattner, Charles Frederick. The use of the blow-pipe in the examination of minerals, ores, furnace - products, and other metallic combinations. J. S. Muspratt, tr. Lond., 1845. T.

Play and profit in my garden. Roe, Rev. E. P. N. Y., 1873. 24—143.

Played out. . Thomas, A. N. Y., 1867. 5—28.

Playfair, John. Elements of geometry; containing the first six books of Euclid. N. Y., 1854. 15—88.

Playing for high stakes. Thomas, A. N. Y., 1868. 5—28.

—— the mischief: a novel. De Forrest, J. W. N. Y., 1875. 41—230.

Playing-cards, The history of. Illus. Taylor, E. S. Lond., 1865. 2—13.

Plays and puritans, and other historical essays. Kingsley, C. Lond., 1873. 23—166.

—— of Philip Massinger. N. Y., 1860. 16—100.

Pleadings with my mother, the church in Scotland. Carlyle, T. Edin., 1854· 27—161.

Plon, Eugene. Thorwaldsen: his life and works. Illus. I. M. Luyster, tr. Bost., 1874. 11—62.

Plough, the loom, and the anvil, The. Skinner, J. S. Phil., 1851· 3 v. T.

Plutarchus. (Plutarch's lives.) From the original Greek, with notes critical and historical; and a life of Plutarch, by J. and W. Langhorne. Lond., 1813. 6 v. 11—62.

Poacher, The. Marryat, *Capt. F.* N. Y., 1857. 5—30.

Poe, Edgar Allen, The works of. N. Y., 1868. 4 v. 2—12.

Poems, descriptive, dramatic, legendary, and contemplative. Simms, W. G. N. Y., 1853. 2 v. 16—96.

Poet at the breakfast-table, The. Holmes, O. W. Bost., 1872. 2—11.

*Poetical quotations from Chaucer to Tennyson. Allibone, S. A. Phil., 1874. 17—105.

Poetry, A treatise on. Aristotle. Lond., 1812. 2 v. R—2.

—— and song, A library of; being choice selections from the best poets. Illus. Bryant, W. C. N. Y., 1872. 16—94.

——, Humorous, of the English language. Parton, J. Bost., 1870. 16—95.

—— of the orient. Alger, W. R. Bost., 1866. 16—98.

——, The household book of. Dana, C. A. N. Y. and Lond., 1869. 16—94.

Poets and poetry of the west. Coggeshall, W. T. Columbus, *Ohio,* 1860. 16—94.

Poinsett, Joel R. Notes on Mexico; with a sketch of the revolution. Lond., 1825. 32—191.

Point of honor, A. Edwards, A. N. Y., 1870. 6—39.

Poitevin, Prosper. Petits poëtes Français, depuis Malherbe jusqu'à nos jours; avec des notices biographiques et littéraires sur chacun d'eux. Paris, 1864. 2 v. W.

Poland, History of. (Lardner's cabinet cyclopædia.) Lond., 1831. 36—217.

——, The history of. Fletcher, J. Lond., 1831. 36—217.

Polar sea, Journey to the shores of the. Illus. Franklin, *Sir* J. Lond., 1823. 9—51.

Political economy, The principles of. M'Culloch, J. R. Edin., 1825. 15—88.

—— economy, Principles of. Carey, H. C. Phil., 1837. 3 v. R—1.

—— economy, Some leading principles of. Cairnes, J. E. N. Y., 1874. 15—88.

—— economy, The principles of. Bowen, F. Bost., 1856. 15—88.

—— economy, A treatise on, in the form of a romaunt. Balt., 1824. 15—88.·

Political ethics, A manual of. Lieber, F. Phil., 1875. 2 v. 18—108.

—— grammar of the United States. Mansfield, E. D. Cin., 1846. 18—109.

—— history of the United States of North America during the great rebellion. McPherson, E. Wash., 1864. 30—178.

—— Same, second edition. 1865. 30—178.

—— history of the United States of America during the period of reconstruction. McPherson, E. Wash., 1871. 30—180.

—— parties in the United States. Van Buren, M. N. Y., 1867. 26—154.

—— philosophy. Brougham, H. Second edition. Lond., 1849. 3 v. 15—92.

*—— register, 1801-13. Cobbett, W. Lond. 21 v. S.

* Politics, A hand-book of. McPherson, E. Wash., 1872. 18—108.

—— for young Americans. Nordhoff, C. N. Y., 1875. 19—114.

Pollard, Eliza F. Hope deferred. N. Y., 1872. 5—28.

Pollok, Robert. The course of time. Bost., 1862. 16—96.

Polybius, The general history of. J. Hampton, tr. Lond., 1811. 35—209.

Polyglot of foreign proverbs, with English translations. Bohn, H. G. Lond., 1857. 16—96.

Pompeiana: the topography, edifices, and ornaments of Pompeii. Illus. Gell, Sir W., and J. P. Gandy. Lond., 1821. First series. 17—102.

——. Illus. Gell, Sir W. Lond., 1832. 2 v. 17—102.

Ponsonby, Lady Emily Charlotte Mary. A mother's trials. N. Y., 1860. P—1.

Ponton, Mungo. Earthquakes and volcanos; their history, phenomena, and probable causes. Illus. Lond., 1870. 15—89.

Poor, Henry V. Manual of the railroads in the United States, for 1868-69. N. Y., 1868. D. R.

Poor humanity. Robinson, F. W. N. Y., 1868. 5—29.

—— Jack. Illus. Marryat, Capt. F. N. Y., n. d. 5—30.

Poor Matt; or, the clouded intellect. Ingelow, J. Bost., 1869. 39.

—— Miss Finch. Illus. Collins, W. W. N. Y., 1869. 5—28.

Pope, Alexander. The works of; with notes and illustrations by himself and others; and a life of the author by Wm. Roscoe. Lond., 1847. 8 v. 16—95.

Contents.

Vol. 1. Life of the author.

Vol. 2. Early poems; Translations and imitations; Essay on criticism; Rape of the lock.

Vol. 3. Miscellaneous poems; The Dunciad.

Vol. 4. Essay on man; Moral epistles; Satires.

Vol. 5. Satires; Fragments and fugitive pieces.

Vols. 6, 7, and 8. Correspondence.

Popes, The history of the. Ranke, L. Lond., 1847. 3 v. 32—195.

Popular science monthly, The. Conducted by E. L. Youmans. Illus. N. Y., 1872-76. 9 v. 15—87.

Population, An essay on the principle of. Malthus, T. R. Lond., 1826. 2 v. 14—84.

——, An inquiry into the principle of. Grahame, J. Edin., 1816. 14—84.

Porcupine's works. Cobbett, W. Lond., 1801. 12 v. X.

Porter, George Richardson. The progress of the nation in its various social and economical relations, from the beginning of the nineteenth century to the present time. Lond., 1836-43. 3 v. 19—117.

Porter, Jane. The Scottish chiefs. Phil., 1871. 7—41.

—— Thaddeus of Warsaw. N. Y., 1856. 7—41.

Porter, Noah. The human intellect; with an introduction upon psychology and the soul. N. Y., 1869. 15—92.

Porter, Rose. Foundations; or, castles in the air. N. Y., n. d. 6—38.

—— The winter fire: a sequel to "Summer drift-wood." N. Y., n. d. 6—38.

—— Uplands and lowlands; or, three chapters in life. N. Y., n. d. 6—38.

* Portrait gallery of eminent men and women of Europe and America. Duyckinck, E. A. N. Y., n. d. 2 v. 153.

Portraits of eminent Americans. Livingston. N. Y., Lond., and Paris, 1854. 68.

Portugal. (L'Univers.) Denis. Paris, 1846. D. R.

Portugal, The revolutions of. Vertot D'Aubeuf, R. A. de. Lond., 1721. 36—217.

Posey, Thomas, Life of. (Library of American biography, vol. 19.) 11—65.

Potiphar papers, The. Illus. Curtis, G. W. N. Y., 1869. 5—34.

Poussin, Guillaume Tell. The United States: its power and progress. E. L. Du Barry, tr. Phil., 1851. 29—175.

Powell, J. W. Exploration of the Colorado river of the west and its tributaries, in 1869-72. Illus. Wash., 1875. L.

Power of the soul over the body, The. Moore, G. N. Y., 1845. E.

Power, Tyrone. Impressions of America during the years 1833-35. Phil., 1836. 2 v. in one. 9—53.

Powers, A practical treatise on. Sugden, Sir E. Phil., 1856. 2 v. T.

Poynter, Miss. Ersilia. N. Y., 1876. 41—228.

—— My little lady. N. Y. 7—44.

Practical assaying, Manual of. Mitchell, J. Lond., 1846. T.

—— builder and workman's companion. Illus. Nicholson, P. Lond., n. d. 3 v. T.

—— masonry. Illus. Shaw, E. Bost., 1846. T.

—— miner's guide. Budge, J. Lond., 1845. T.

—— receipts, A cyclopædia of six thousand. Cooley, A. J. N. Y., 1875. 40—225.

—— tunnelling. Illus. Simms, F. W. Lond., 1844. T.

Praed, Winthrop Mackworth, The poems of,—with a memoir by the Rev. Derwent Coleridge. N. Y., 1865. 2 v. 17—105.

Prairie, The. Illus. Cooper, J. F. N. Y., 1870. 3—14.

—— and forest. Illus. Gillmore, P. N. Y., 1874. 2—9.

Prayer-gauge debate, The, by Prof. Tyndall, Francis Galton, and others, against Dr. Littledale, President McCosh, the duke of Argyll, Canon Lyddon, and "The Spectator." Bost., 1876. 19—116.

Pre-Adamite earth. Harris, J. Bost., 1856. 14—81.

Preble, Edward, Life of. (Library of American biography, vol. 22.) 11—65.

Preble, George Henry. Our flag:—origin and progress of the flag of the United States of America, with an introductory account of the symbols, standards, banners, and flags of ancient and modern nations. Illus. Albany, 1872. 29—176.

Precaution. Illus. Cooper, J. F. N. Y., 1871. 3—14.

Pre-historic nations. Baldwin, J. D. N. Y., 1871. 14—81.

—— times. Illus. Lubbock, Sir J. N. Y., 1872. 14—81.

Premiums paid to experience. Illus. "Edward Garrett." N. Y., n. d. 3—15.

Prentice, George Dennison. Prenticeana; or, wit and humor in paragraphs; with a biographical sketch of the author, by G. W. Griffin. Phil., 1871. 2—10.

—— The poems of; edited, with a biographical sketch, by J. J. Piatt. Cin., 1876. 17—105.

Prenticeana; or, wit and humor in paragraphs. Prentice, G. D. Phil., 1871. 2—10.

Prentiss, Elizabeth. Fred, and Maria, and me. Illus. N. Y., 1872. 39.

—— Stepping heavenward. N. Y., n. d. 3—15.

Prentiss, Sergeant Smith, a memoir of; edited by his brother. N. Y., 1858. 2 v. 13—78.

Pre-Raphaelitism. Ruskin, J. N. Y., 1865. 26—158.

Prescott, Mary N. Matt's follies, and other stories. Illus. Bost., 1873. 39.

Prescott, William Hickling. History of the conquest of Mexico, with a preliminary view of the ancient Mexican civilization, and the life of the conqueror, Hernando Cortes. N. Y., 1841. 3 v. 2 copies. 32—191.

—— History of the conquest of Peru, with a preliminary view of the civilization of the Incas. N. Y., 1841. 2 v. 36—216.

—— History of the reign of Philip the second, king of Spain. Bost., 1855-58. 3 v. 36—213.

—— History of the reign of Ferdinand and Isabella, the catholic. N. Y., 1851. 3 v. 12—69.

——, Life of. Ticknor, G. Bost., 1864. 11—60.

Presidential counts, The : a complete record of the proceedings of Congress at the counting of the electoral votes in all the elections of president and vice-president of the United States, together with all congressional debates incident thereto, or to proposed legislation upon that subject; with an analytical intro- duction. N. Y., 1877. 40—225.

Presidents of the United States, Memoirs and administrations of the. Illus. Will- iams, E. N. Y., 1849. 24—141.

President's daughters, The. Bremer, F. Lond., 1852. P—1.

Pretenders and their adherents, The. Jesse, J. H. Lond., 1846. 2 v. 12—67.

Pretty Miss Bellew. "Theodore Gift." N. Y., 1876. 41—228.

—— Mrs. Gaston, and other stories. Illus. Cooke, J. E. N. Y., n. d. 4—26.

Prey of the gods, The. Marryat, Miss F. Lond. and N. Y., n. d. 4—22.

Prices, A history of. Tooke, T. Lond., 1848. L.

Prichard, James Cowles. The natural history of man; comprising inquiries into the modifying influence of physical and moral agencies on the different tribes of the human family. Illus. Lond. and Paris, 1848. 15—89.

—— Researches into the physical history of man. Lond., 1813. 15—89.

Pride of Britannia humbled, The. Cob- bett, W. N. Y., 1815. 33—201.

—— and prejudice: a novel. Austen, J. Lond., 1870. 4—27.

Prime, Edward Dore Griffin. Around the world: sketches of travel through many lands and over many seas. Illus. N. Y., 1872. 17—103.

Prime, Samuel Irenæus. The Alham- bra and the Kremlin : the south and the north of Europe. Illus. N. Y., 1873. 17—101.

Prime, William Cowper. Boat life in Egypt and Nubia. Illus. N. Y., 1872. 8—49.

—— Tent life in the Holy Land. Illus. N. Y., 1874. 8—49.

—— I go a-fishing. N. Y., 1874. 8—49.

—— The old house by the river. N. Y., 1868. 2—13.

—— Later years. N. Y., 1867. 2—13.

Prime minister, The. Trollope, A. Phil., n. d. 7—43.

Primitive man. Illus. Figuier, L. N.Y., 1871. 15—89.

Prince, L. Bradford. E pluribus unum:- the articles of confederation es. the con- stitution ; the progress of nationality among the people and in the govern- ment. N. Y., 1867. 26—155.

Prince and the page, The. Illus. Yonge, C. M. Lond., 1866. 38.

—— consort, The life of H. R. H. the. Illus. Martin, T. N. Y., 1875-77. Vols. 1 and 2. 40—222.

—— Eugene and his times. Illus. "Louise Mühlbach." N. Y., 1874. 4— 21.

—— of darkness, The. Southworth, E. D. E. N. Phil., 1869. 6—37.

—— of the house of David, The. Ingra- ham, J. H. Phil., 1860. 4—25.

—— Rupert and the cavaliers. Illus. Warburton, E. Lond., 1849. 3 v. 12— 67.

Princess and the goblin, The. Illus. MacDonald, G. N. Y., 1871. 7—45.

—— of Thule, A. Black, W. N.Y.,1874. 5—29.

*Printing, A history of the art of. Illus. Humphreys, H. N. Lond., 1868. 14—80.

——, The art of. Hansard, T. C. Edin., 1851. 14—80.

Prior, James. Memoir of the life and character of the Right. Hon. Edmund Burke; with specimens of his poetry and letters. Bost., 1854. 2 v. 13—77.

Prior, Matthew, Poetical works of; with a life, by the Rev. J. Mitford. Bost., 18—50. 2 v. 16—98.

Private land claims in the territory of N Mexico. House Report No. 457, 35 Congress, 1st session. X.

Privateersman, The. Illus. Marry Capt. F. N. Y., n. d. 5—30.

Problematic characters. Spielhagen, N. Y., 1871. 6—36.

Proceedings of the city council of Boston April 17, 1865, on occasion of the death of Abraham Lincoln. Bost., 1865. 27— 160.

Proctor, Adelaide Anne, Poems of Bost., 1869. 16—98.

Proctor, Richard Anthony. The sun ruler, fire, light, and life of the planetary system. Illus. Lond., 1871. 14—82.

Proctor, Richard Anthony. Other worlds than ours: the plurality of worlds studied under the light of recent scientific researches. Illus. N. Y., 1871. 14—82.

—— Half-hours with the stars: a plain and easy guide to the knowledge of the constellations. Lond., 1871. 14—80.

—— Light science for leisure hours: a series of familiar essays on scientific subjects, natural phenomena, etc. N. Y., 1871. 14—82.

—— The expanse of heaven: a series of essays on the wonders of the firmament. N. Y., 1874. 14—82.

—— The universe and the coming transits: presenting researches into, and new views respecting the constitution of the heavens; together with an investigation of the conditions of the coming transits of Venus, recently confirmed by a unanimous vote of the chief astronomers of Great Britain. Illus. Lond.,1874. 14—82.

—— The moon: her motions, aspect, scenery, and physical condition. Illus. N. Y., 1873. 14—82.

—— The borderland of science: a series of familiar dissertations on stars, planets, and meteors; sun and moon; earthquakes; flying-machines; coal; gambling; coincidences; ghosts, etc. Phil. and Lond., 1874. 14—82.

—— Essays on astronomy: a series of papers on planets and meteors, the sun and sun-surrounding space, stars and star cloudlets; and a dissertation on the approaching transits of Venus; preceded by a sketch of the life and work of Sir John Herschel. Illus. Lond. and N. Y., 1872. 14—82.

—— Science byways: a series of familiar dissertations on life in other worlds; comets, and the sun; the north pole; rain; danger from lightning; growth and decay of mind; the brain and mental feats; automata, etc.; to which is appended an essay entitled money for science. Lond., 1875. 14—82.

Professor at the breakfast-table, The. Holmes, O. W. 2—10.

——, The. "Currer Bell." N. Y., 1868. 2 copies. 7—45.

Progress of the nation, The. Porter, G. R. Lond., 1836-43. 3 v. 19—117.

11 I

Prolegomena logica. Mansel, H. L. Bost., 1860. 15—88.

Pronouncing handbook of words often misprouounced. Soule, R., and L. J. Campbell. Bost., 1873. 15—93.

Prose idylls, new and old. Kingsley, C. Lond., 1874. 28—166.

—— miscellanies from Heinrich Heine. Phil., 1876. 41—227.

Prosper: a novel. Cherbuliez, V. N. Y., 1874. 7—46.

Prosper Mérimée's letters to an incognita, with recollections by Lamartine and George Sand. (Bric-a-brac series, vol. 3.) Richard H. Stoddard, ed. N. Y., 1874. 19—114.

Prosser, *Mrs.* Original fables. Illus. Lond., n. d. 38.

Protestant revolution, The era of the. Seebohm, F. Bost., 1874. 36—215.

Proud, Robert. The history of Pennsylvania, from 1681 to 1742. Phil., 1797-98. 2 v. 31—189.

Prout, Father, *pseud.* See Mahony, F. S.

Provincial letters. Pascal, B. *Rev.* T. M'Crie, tr.; O. W. Wright, ed. N. Y., 1866. P—2.

Prudence Palfrey: a novel. Aldrich, T. B. Bost., 1874. 6—35.

Prue and I. Curtis, G. W. N. Y., 1867. O—1.

Psyche of to-day, A. Jenkin, C. N. Y., 1874. 6—38.

Psychology, The data of. Spencer, H. N. Y., 1869. 15—92.

Public and parlor readings, for the use of dramatic and reading clubs; and for public, social, and school entertainment. Dialogues and dramas, humorous and miscellaneous. Lewis B. Monroe, ed. 3 v. 19—114.

—— libraries in the United States of America; their history, condition, and management. Special report, Department of the Interior, Bureau of Education. Wash., 1876. X.

* —— library of Cincinnati, Catalogue of the. Cin., 1871. 1—1.

—— men of the revolution, The. Sullivan, W. Phil., 1847. 12—68.

Publicans and sinners: a novel. Braddon, M. E. N. Y., 1874. 5—29.

Puck. "Ouida." Phil., 1870. 7—44.

Pufendorf, Samuel von. The law of nature and nations. Oxford, *Eng.*, 1710. 26—153.

Pugin, Augustus, and John Britton. Illustrations of the public buildings of London; with historical and descriptive accounts of each edifice. Second edition, enlarged, by W. H. Leeds. Illus. Lond., 1838. 2 v. 15—87.

Puissant, L. Traité de géodésie; ou, exposition des méthodes trigonométriques et astronomiques applicables à la mesure de la terre, et à la construction du canevas des cartes topographiques. Paris, 1842. 2 v. W.

Pulaski, *Count,* Life of. (Library of American biography, vol. 14.) 11—65.

Pulszky, Francis. The tricolor on the Atlas; or, Algeria and the French conquest. Illus. N. Y., 1855. 35—213.

Puritan revolution, The first two Stuarts and the. (Epochs of history.) Gardiner, S. R. Bost., 1876. 34—207.

Puritans, The history of the. Neal, D. Bath, *Eng.*, 1793-97. 5 v. 32—195.

Purple and fine linen: a novel. Fawcett, E. N. Y. and Lond., 1873. 5—30.

Puss-cat mew, and other stories. Illus. Knatchbull-Hugessen, E. H. N. Y., 1871. 38.

Put yourself in his place. Reade, C. Bost., 1871. 7—42.

Putnam, Israel, Life of. (Library of American biography, vol. 7.) 11—65.

—— The life of. Illus. Cutter, W. N. Y., 1861. 11—64.

—— county, New York. The history of. Blake, W. J. N. Y., 1849. 31—189.

Putnam's monthly magazine of American literature, science, and art. N. Y. 10 v. 29—171.

Pyrenees, A tour through the. Taine, H. A. N. Y., 1874. 10—56.

Quantrill, Thomas H. The mechanic's calculator and tinman's guide; comprehending principles, rules, and tables adapted to the practical use of the trade. Illus. Wash., 1848. D. R.

Quatrefages, A. de. Metamorphoses of man and the lower animals. H. Lawson, *M. D.,* tr. Lond., 1864. 14—85.

Queechy. "Elizabeth Wetherell." Phil, 1873. 2 v. in one. 7—42.

Queen Hortense. Illus. "Louise Mühlbach." N. Y., 1871. 4—21.

—— Mary; a drama. Tennyson, A. Bost., 1875. 17—106.

—— of hearts, The. Collins, W. W. N. Y., 1874. 5—28.

—— of the county, The. Stretton, J. C. Bost., 1865. 6—38.

——, The. Carey, W. Lond., 1820. 34—208.

—— Mab. Kavanagh, J. N. Y., 1872. 7—41.

Queen's English, A plea for the. Alford, H. N. Y., n. d. 27—160.

—— necklace, The. Dumas, A. D. Lond. and Phil., 1875. 3—20.

—— revenge, and other stories. Collins, W. W. Phil., n. d. 5—28.

Queens of England, Lives of the. Illus. Strickland, A. Lond., 1871. 8 v. 13—76.

—— of Scotland, Lives of the. Strickland, A. N. Y., 1853-59. 8 v. 11—62.

—— of England of the house of Hanover, Lives of the. Doran, J. N. Y. 1865. 2 v. 11—60.

—— of society, The. Illus. "G. and P. Wharton." Lond., 1872. 40—222.

Queer little people. Illus. Stowe, H. B. Bost., 1873. 39.

Quentin Durward. Scott, *Sir* W. Bost., 1868. 3—17.

Question of honor, A. "Christian Reid." N. Y., 1875. 4—26.

Quiet life, Memorials of a. Hare, A. J. C. N. Y., n. d. 2 v. 41—229.

Quincy, Josiah. The history of Harvard university. Cambridge, 1840. 2 v. 29—175.

Quits: a novel. Tautphœus, J. M. P. Ball, 1872. 2 v. in one. 6—36.

Quixstar: a novel. Gardiner, M. P. N. Y. 1873. 7—41.

Quodlibet, Annals of. Kennedy, J. Phil., 1860. 6—39.

Rabelais. François. The works Illustrated by Gustave Doré. Lond., n 1—1.

Rachel Ray. Trollope, A. Lond., n. d. 7—43.

—— Gray. Kavanagh, J. N. Y., 1873. 7—41.

——, (Eliza Rachel Felix,) Memoirs of. A. de Barrera. N. Y., 1858. 11—60.

Racine, Jean, Œuvres de, précédées des mémoires sur sa vie, par Louis Racine. Paris, 1869. W.

Railroads of the United States, Manual of the. Poor, H. V. N. Y., 1868. D. R.

Rale, Sebastian, Life of. (Library of American biography, vol. 17.) 11—65.

Raleigh, *Sir* Walter. History of the world. Edin., 1820. 6 v. 32—194.

——, Works of; to which are prefixed the lives of the author, by Oldys and Birch. Oxford, 1829. 8 v. 27—159.

——, Memoirs of the life of. Thomson, K. B. Lond., 1830. 13—77.

——, and his time, with other papers. Kingsley, C. Boston., 1859. Q—2.

Ralph, the heir. Illus. Trollope, A. N. Y., 1871. 6—35.

—— Wilton's weird: a novel. Alexander, *Mrs*. N. Y., 1875. 7—44.

Ramage, Crauford Tait. Beautiful thoughts from Greek authors, with English translations. Liver., 1864. 16—96.

—— Same, from Latin authors. Liver., 1869. 16—96.

—— Same from French and Italian authors. Liver., 1866. 16—96.

—— Same, from German and Spanish authors. Liver., 1868. 16—96.

Rambling story, A. Clarke, M. C. Bost., 1875. 3—15.

Rameses the great. Illus. Lanoye, F. T. de. N. Y., 1872. 28—169.

Ramsay, David. The history of the revolution of South Carolina, from a British province to an independent state. Trenton, 1785. 2 v. 31—187.

Ramsey, J. G. M. The annals of Tennessee, to the end of the eighteenth century. Phil., 1860. 31—186.

Ranald Bannerman's boyhood. Illus. MacDonald, G. Phil., 1874. 39.

Randall, Henry S. Sheep husbandry in the south, in a series of letters. Phil., 1849. D. R.

—— The life of Thomas Jefferson. N. Y., 1858. 3 v. 12—66.

Randolph, *Mrs*. Wild Hyacinth: a novel. Phil., 1876. 41—228.

Randolph Gordon. "Ouida." Phil., 1867. 7—44.

Rangers; or, the tory's daughter. Thompson, D. P. Bost., 1871. 2 v. in one. O—1.

Ranke, Leopold. The Ottoman and the Spanish empires in the 16th and 17th centuries. Phil., 1845. 36—217.

—— The history of the popes, their church and state, and especially of their conflicts with protestantism in the 16th and 17th centuries. E. Foster, tr. Lond., 1847. 3 v. 32—195.

Ranlett, William H. The architect: a series of original designs for domestic and ornamental cottages and villas; connected with landscape gardening. Illus. N. Y., 1849. 2 v. V.

Rapids of Niagara, The. Illus. "Elizabeth Wetherell." N. Y., 1876. 7—42.

Rationalism in Europe, History of the rise and influence of the spirit of. Lecky, W. E. H. N. Y., 1870. 2 v. 27—161.

Rattlin, the reefer. Illus. Edited by *Capt.* Marryat. Lond. and N. Y., 1873. 5—30.

Rau, Charles. Early man in Europe. Illus. N. Y., 1876. 40—225.

Raumer, Friedrich Ludwig Georg *von*. America and the American people. W. Turner, tr. N. Y., 1846. 8—49.

Ravenshoe. Kingsley, H. Lond., 1864. 7—43.

Raynal, F. E. Wrecked on a reef; or, twenty months among the Auckland isles: a true story. Illus. Lond., 1874. 8—48.

Read, Thomas Buchanan, The poems of. Bost., 1860. 2 v. 16—96.

Reade, Charles. A terrible temptation. Illus. N. Y., 1871. 7—42.

—— A good fight, and other tales. Illus. N. Y., 1859. 7—42.

—— It is never too late to mend: a matter-of-fact romance. N. Y., 1873. 5—28.

—— Peg Woffington, Christie Johnstone, Clouds and sunshine, Art, Propria quæ maribus, The box-tunnel, and Jack of all trades. Bost., 1869. 7—42.

—— White lies: a novel. N. Y., 1873 5—28.

—— Love me little, love me long. Bost. 1872. 7—42.

Reade, Charles. Hard cash : a matter-of-fact romance. Illus. N. Y., 1873. 5—28.

—— Griffith Gaunt; or, jealousy. Bost., 1871. 7—42.

—— The cloister and the hearth; or, maid, wife, and widow. Bost., 1871. 7—42.

—— Put yourself in his place. Bost., 1871. 7—42.

——, and D. Boucicault. Foul play : a novel. Bost., 1872. 7—42.

—— The eighth commandment. Bost., 1860. 7—42.

—— A simpleton : a story of the day. N. Y., 1874. 5—28.

Reade, Winwood. The martyrdom of man. N. Y., 1874. 27—161.

—— The outcast. Lond., 1875. 3—17.

Real folks. Illus. Whitney, A. D. T. Bost., 1872. 7—44.

Realmah. Helps, Sir A. Lond., 1869. 3—18.

Rebel war clerk's diary, A. Jones, J. B. Phil., 1866. 2 v. 30—181.

Rebellion, Ambrose's letters on the. Kennedy, J. P. N. Y., 1865. 26—155.

——, An alphabetical list of battles in the war of the. Wells, J. W. Pamphlet. Wash., 1875. M.

——, History of the. Giddings, J. R. N. Y., 1864. 30—179.

* —— record : a diary of American events. Illus. Moore, F. N. Y., 1861-68. 12 v. 30—180.

Recherches historiques et politiques sur les États-Unis de l'Amérique septentrionale. Warden, D. B. Paris, 1788. 4 v. W.

Reclus, Jean Jaques Élisée. The earth : a descriptive history of the phenomena of the life of the globe. Illus. B. B. and H. Woodward, trs. N. Y., 1872. 14—83.

—— The ocean, atmosphere, and life; being the second series of a descriptive history of the life of the globe. Illus. N. Y., 1873. 14—83.

Recollections and suggestions, 1813-1873. Russell, Earl. Bost., 1875. 34—207.

—— of a busy life. Illus. Greeley, H. N. Y., 1868. 11—60.

Recreations of a country parson. Boyd, A. K. H. Bost., 1869. 2 v. 2—12.

Recreations of Christopher North. (Modern British essayists.) Wilson, J. Bost., 1854. 27—159.

Recueil de documents et mémoires originaux sur l'histoire des possessions espagnoles dans l'Amérique. Ternaux-Compans, H. Paris, 1840. W.

—— d'observations astronomiques. Humboldt, F. H. A. von. Paris, 1810. 2 v. W.

—— des éloges historiques. Cuvier, G. L. Paris, 1861. 3 v. W.

Red as a rose is she. Broughton, R. N. Y., 1872. 4—23.

—— Court farm, The. Wood, E. P. Phil., n. d. 41—229.

—— river of Louisiana, Exploration of the. Illus. Marcy, R. B. Wash., 1853. D. R.

—— rover, The. Illus. Cooper, J. F. N. Y., 1870. 3—14.

Red-Jacket, The life and times of. Stone, W. L. N. Y. and Lond., 1841. 12—63.

Redgauntlet. Scott, Sir W. Bost., 1868. 3—17.

Redskins, The. Illus. Cooper, J. F. N. Y., 1864. 3—14.

Red-tape and pigeon-hole generals, as seen from the ranks during a campaign in the army of the Potomac, by a citizen soldier. N. Y., 1864. 24—143.

Redwood : a tale. Sedgwick, C. M. N. Y., 1850. 6—39.

Reed, Joseph, Life of. (Library of American biography, vol. 18.) 11—65.

Rees, James. The life of Edwin Forrest, with reminiscences and personal recollections. Phil., 1874. 11—60. .-

Reformation of the church of England, The history of the. Burnet, G. Lond., 1850. 2 v. 32—196.

Reginald Archer. Seemüller, A. M. C. Bost., 1871. P—2.

—— Lyle. Pardoe, J. N. Y., 1864. 0—3.

Register of debates in Congress; from the second session, eighteenth, to the second session, twenty-second congress. 15 v. D. R.

* **Regulations** for the government of the United States navy. Wash., 1870. R—2.

Reid, Christian, pseud. See Fisher, F. C.

Reign of law, The. Illus. Argyll, *Duke of.* N. Y., 1873. 19—114.

Reindeer, dogs, and snow-shoes. Illus. Bush, R. J. N. Y., 1871. 17—103.

Rejected addresses, and other poems. Smith, H. and G. N. Y., 1871. 17—105.

Relacion historica de la vida y apostolicas Tareas, del venerable Padre Fray Junipero Serra. Palou, F. México, 1787. W.

Religion and science, History of the conflict between. Draper, J. W. N. Y., 1875. 15—88.

—— and the state; or, the Bible and the public schools. Spear, S. T., *D. D.* N. Y., 1876. 40—224.

Religious courtship. De Foe, D. Oxford, 1840. 27—163.

—— poems. Illus. Stowe, H. B. Bost., 1867. 16—100.

Reliques of ancient English poetry. Percy, T. Edin., 1858. 3 v. 16—95.

—— of father Prout, late P. P. of Watergrasshill, county Cork, Ireland. Mahony, F. S. Illus. Lond., 1873. 19—114.

Remembrancer; or impartial history of public events. Lond., 1775-78. 11 v. X.

Renan, Joseph Ernest. An essay on the age and antiquity of the book of the Nabathæan agriculture; to which is added an inaugural lecture on the position of the Shemitic nations in the history of civilization. Lond., 1862. V.

Renwick, James. Life of De Witt Clinton. N. Y., 1870. 13—79.

Reparation, and other tales. Fullerton, *Lady* G. Balt., 1875. 41—228.

Repertory of arts and manufactures. Illus. Lond., 1794-1802. 16 v. 18—111.

—— Same. Illus. 2d series. Lond., 1802-08. 12 v. 18—110 and 111.

Representative men. Emerson, R. W. Bost., 1861. 27—161.

Reptiles and birds. Illus. Figuier, L. N. Y., 1870. 14—82.

Republican court, The. Illus. Griswold, R. W. N. Y. and Lond., 1867. 2—9.

Researches into the physical history of man. Prichard, J. C. Lond., 1813. 15—89.

Retribution. Southworth, E. D. E. N. Phil., 1856. 6—36.

Reuter, Fritz. Seed-time and harvest; or, "During my apprenticeship." Phil., 1871. 6—35.

Revere, Joseph Warren. A tour of duty in California, including a description of the gold region; and an account of the voyage around Cape Horn; with notices of Lower California, the Gulf and Pacific coasts, and the principal events attending the conquest of the Californias. Illus. J. N. Balestier, ed. N. Y., 1849. 17—101.

Reveries of a bachelor. "Ik Marvel." N. Y., 1871. 3—20.

Revised regulations for the army of the United States, 1861. Phil., 1862. R—2.

Revolution in America, Principles and acts of the. Niles, H. Balt., 1822. 25—152.

——, The pictorial field-book of the. Lossing, B. J. N. Y., 1851-52. 2 v. 30—178.

Revolutionary war, Records of the. Saffell, W. T. R. Phil., 1860. X.

Révolutions du globe. Cuvier, G. L. Paris, 1864. W.

Reynard, the fox, The pleasant history of. Illus. Lond. and N. Y., 1873. 38.

Reynaud, Léonce. Memoir upon the illumination and beaconage of the coasts of France. Illus. P. C. Hains, tr. Wash., 1876. D. R.

Rhees, William J. Manual of public libraries, institutions, and societies in the United States and British provinces of North America. Phil., 1859. V.

Rhetoric and belles-lettres, Lectures on. Blair, H. Phil., 1860. 14—81.

Rhymes and jingles. Illus. Dodge, M. M. N. Y., 1875. 39.

Rhode Island and Providence plantations, Records of the colony of. Bartlett, J. R. Prov., 1856-62. 7 v. 32—182.

—— Historical Society, Collections of the. Prov., 1827-38. 4 v. 30—182.

Ribault, John, Life of. (Library of American biography, vol. 17.) 11—65.

Rice, George Edward. An old play in a new garb, (Hamlet, prince of Denmark,) in three acts. Illus. Bost., 1853. 16—100.

Rich, Obadiah. Bibliotheca Americana nova: a catalogue of books relating to America, in various languages. Lond., 1846. 2 v. D. R.

Richard Vandermarck : a novel. Harris, M. C. N. Y., 1871. 41—228.

Richardson, Albert Deane. Beyond the Mississippi; from the great river to the great ocean; life and adventure on the prairies, mountains, and Pacific coast. 1857-67. Illus. Hartford, 1867. 17—101.

Richardson, Charles. "A new dictionary of the English language. Phil., 1847. 2 v. 22—131.

Richardson, G. F. An introduction to geology, and its associate sciences, mineralogy, fossil botany, conchology, and palæontology. Lond., 1851. 15—91.

Richardson, Sir John. Arctic searching expedition: a journal of a boat-voyage through Rupert's Land and the Arctic sea in search of the discovery ships under command of Sir John Franklin; with an appendix on the physical geography of North America. Illus. 2 v. Lond., 1851. 9—51.

Richardson, Samuel. Clarissa; or, the history of a young lady : condensed by C. H. Jones. N. Y., 1874. 4—24.

Richter, Jean Paul Friedrich. Titan: a romance. C. T. Brooks, tr. Bost., 1871. 2 v. P—1.

—— Flower, fruit, and thorn pieces; or, the married life, death, and wedding of the advocate of the poor, Firmian Stanislaus Siebenkäs. E. H. Noel, tr. Bost., 1869. 2 v. 2—11.

—— Levana; or, the doctrine of education. Bost., 1866. P—1.

—— Hesperus; or, forty-five dog-post days: a biography. C. T. Brooks, tr. Bost., 1865. 2 v. 7—41.

——, Life of, with his autobiography. Eliza B. Lee, tr. Bost., 1842. 2 v. 12—72.

Ricketson, Daniel. The history of New Bedford, Bristol county, Massachusetts; including a history of the old township of Dartmouth and the present townships of Westport, Dartmouth, and Fairhaven, from their settlement to the present time. New Bedford, 1858. 3 182.

Riddell, Mrs. J. H., (F. G. Trafford.) The earl's promise: a novel. 2 v. in one. Leip., 1873. 41—226.

—— A life's assize: a novel. Lond., 1871. 3 v. 4—26.

—— Frank Sinclair's wife, and other stories. Lond., 1874. 3 v. 4—26.

Riddle, Albert G. Bart Ridgeley;—a story of Northern Ohio. Bost., 1873. 4—24.

—— Alice Brand: a romance of the Capital. N. Y., 1875. 4—24.

Riddle, Joseph Esmond, and Thomas K. Arnold. "A copious and critical English-Latin lexicon, founded on the German-Latin dictionary of Dr. Charles Ernest Georges. N. Y., 1849. 22—131.

Ridgely, David. Annals of Annapolis, from the period of the first settlements in its vicinity until the war of 1812. Balt., 1841. 31—189.

Ridpath, John Clark. A popular history of the United States of America, from the aboriginal times to the present day: embracing an account of the aborigines; the Norsemen in the new world; the discoveries by the Spaniards, English, and French; the planting of settlements; the growth of the colonies; the struggle for liberty in the revolution; the establishment of the union; the development of the nation; and the civil war. Illus. Cin.; 1876. 29—174.

Riedesel, Friederike Charlotte Louise von. Letters and journals relating to the war of the American revolution, and the capture of the German troops at Saratoga. Illus. W. L. Stone, tr. Albany, 1867. 12—69.

Riedesel, Major-General, Memoirs, letters, and journals of, during his residence in America. Illus. W. L. Stone, ed. Albany, 1868. 2 v. 40—224.

Rienzi, the last of the Roman tribunes. Bulwer-Lytton, Sir E. Phil., 1869. 5—33.

Right at last, and other tales. Gaskell, E. C. N. Y., 1860. 41—228.

—— one, The. Schwartz, M. S. Bost., 1871. 5—28.

Rights of war and peace. Grotius, H. Lond., 1738. N.

Riker, James, *jr.* The annals of New-town, in Queen's county, New York: containing its history from its first settlement, together with many interesting facts concerning the adjacent towns; also a particular account of numerous Long Island families now spread over this and various other states of the union. N. Y., 1852. 31—189.

Riley, Henry Thomas. *Dictionary of Latin quotations, proverbs, maxims, and mottos, classical and mediæval; with a selection of Greek quotations. Lond., 1856. 16—96.

Rinaldo : a poem. Tasso, T. Lond., 1792. 16—95.

Ring, Max. John Milton and his times: an historical novel. Illus. F. Jordan, tr. N. Y., 1868. 5—29.

Ring of Amasis, The. Bulwer-Lytton, *Sir* E. N. Y., 1863. 2—8.

Ripley, Roswell S. The war with Mexico. N. Y., 1849. 2 v. 30—179.

Rise and fall of the slave power in America, History of the. Wilson, H. Bost., 1874-77. 3 v. 30—181.

Ritch, John W. The American architect. Illus. N. Y., n. d. V.

Ritchie, Anna Cora Mowatt. The mute singer: a novel. N. Y., 1866. 4—26.

—— Autobiography of an actress; or, eight years on the stage. Bost., 1854. 11—64.

Ritchie, James S. Wisconsin and its resources; with Lake Superior, its commerce and navigation; including a trip up the Mississippi, and a canoe voyage on the St. Croix and Brule rivers to Lake Superior; to which are appended the constitution of the state, with the routes of the principal railroads, list of post-offices, etc.; with illustrations and authentic maps of Wisconsin and the region of Lake Superior. Illus. Phil., 1857. 31—186.

Ritchie, Leitch. (Romance of history.) France. Illus. Lond., n. d. 2—8.

Rittenhouse, David, Memoirs of the life of. Barton, W. Phil., 1813. 12—68.

——, Life of. (Library of American biography, vol. 7.) 11—65.

River legends. Illus. Knatchbull-Hugessen, E. H. Lond., 1875. 39.

Rives, William C. History of the life and times of James Madison. Bost., 1859. Vol. 1. 11—59.

Road-making, A manual of the principles and practice of. Gillespie, W. M. N. Y., 1853. T.

Roads, A treatise on. Parnell, *Sir* H. Lond., 1838. T.

——, A treatise on. Bloodgood, D. D. W. Albany, 1838. T.

——, The practice of making and repairing. Hughes, T. Lond., 1838. T.

Rob of the bowl. Kennedy, J. P. Phil., 1861. 6—39.

—— Roy. Scott, *Sir* W. Bost., 1868. 3—17.

—— Roy on the Baltic, The. Illus. Macgregor, J. Bost., n. d. 17—101.

—— Roy on the Jordan, Nile, Red sea, and Gennesareth. Illus. Macgregor, J. N. Y., 1870. 17—101.

Roba di Roma. Story, W. W. Lond., 1866. 2 v. 2—10.

Robert Falconer. MacDonald, G. Lond., n. d. 7—45.

Robertson, Margaret Murray. Janet's love and service. N. Y., n. d. 6—39.

Robertson, John P. and William P. Letters on Paraguay; comprising a four years' residence in that republic, under the government of the dictator, Francia. Lond., 1839. 3 v. 36—216.

Robertson, William. The history of the reign of the emperor Charles the fifth. N. Y., 1839. 36—218.

—— The history of the discovery and settlement of America. N. Y., 1839. 29—176.

—— The history of Scotland during the reigns of queen Mary and king James the sixth, till his accession to the crown of England. N. Y., 1836. 34—204.

Robin, M. Nouveau voyage dans l'Amérique septentrionale, en l'année 1781; et campagne de l'armée de M. le comte de Rochambeau. Phil. et Paris, 1782. W.

Robinson. A. Life in California during a residence of several years in that territory; comprising a description of the country and the missionary establishments, with incidents, observations, etc., etc.; to which is annexed a historical account of the origin, customs, and

·traditions of the Indians of Alta-California. Illus. N. Y., 1846. R—2.
Robinson, Frederick William. Poor humanity: a novel. N. Y., 1868. 5—29.
—— No man's friend: a novel. N. Y., 1867. 5—29.
—— Anne Judge, spinster. N. Y., n. d. 5—29.
—— Sweet nineteen; or, Woodleigh. N. Y., n. d. 5—29.
—— Stern necessity: a novel. N. Y., 1871. 5—29.
—— True to herself: a romance. N. Y., 1872. 5—29.
—— A girl's romance, and other tales. N. Y., 1872. 5—29.
—— A bridge of glass: a novel. N. Y., 1872. 5—29.
—— For her sake. Illus· N. Y., 1869. 5—29.
—— Mattie, a stray. N. Y., 1871. 5—29.
—— Carry's confession: a novel. N. Y., 1871. 5—29.
—— Christie's faith. N. Y., 1867. O—3.
—— A woman's ransom. Bost., n. d. 5—29.
—— Her face was her fortune: a novel. N. Y., 1875. 5—29.
Robinson, *Mrs,* H. A. Six months in Kansas. Bost., 1856. 17—101.
Robinson, Henry Crabb, Diary, reminiscences, and correspondence of. Sadler, T. Bost., 1869. 2 v. 27—161.
Robinson, Sara T. L. Kansas, its interior and exterior life; including a full view of its settlement, political history, social life, climate, soil, productions, scenery, etc. Illus. Bost. and Lond., 1857. 31—187.
Robinson Crusoe, The life and adventures of. Illus. De Foe, D. Lond., n. d. 38.
Robison, John. A system of mechanical philosophy; with notes by David Brewster. Illus. Edin., 1822. 4 v. 15—89.
Roche, Regina Maria. The children of the abbey: a tale. Phil., 1869. 6—38.
Rochefoucauld, F., *Duc de la.* See La Rochefoucauld, F., *Duc de.*
Rochefoucauld-Liancourt, F. A.· F., *Duc de la.* See La Rochefoucauld-Liancourt, F. A. F., *Duc de.*
Rocks ahead; or, the warnings of Cassandra. Greg, W. R. Bost., 1875. 40—222.

Rockwell, Charles. The Catskill mountains and the region around; their scenery, legends, and history; with sketches in prose and verse, by Cooper, Irving, Bryant, Cole, and others. Illus. N. Y., 1867. 17—102.
Rocky Mountain saints, The. Illus. Stenhouse, T. B. H. N. Y., 1873. 26—155.
Roderick Hudson. James, H. Bost., 1876. 41—228.
—— Random, The adventures of. Smollett, T. Lond., 1872. 41—229.
Roe, *Rev.* Edward Payson. Opening a chestnut burr. N. Y., n. d. 6—38.
—— What can she do? N. Y., 1873. 6—38.
—— Barriers burned away. N. Y., 1875. 6—38.
—— From jest to earnest. N. Y., 1875. 6—38.
—— Near to nature's heart. N. Y., n. d. 6—38.
—— Play and profit in my garden. N. Y., 1873. 24—143.
Roger *de Wendover.* Flowers of history: comprising the history of England from the descent of the Saxons to A. D. 1235. Formerly ascribed to Matthew Paris. J. A. Giles, tr. Lond., 1849. 2 v. 33—201.
Rogers, *Rev.* Henry. The superhuman origin of the Bible inferred from itself. N. Y., 1875. 40—224.
Rogers, Samuel, The complete poetical works of; with a biographical sketch, and notes. E. Sargent, ed. N. Y., 1871. 17—105.
Rogers, Thomas J. ·A new American biographical dictionary; or, remembrancer of the departed heroes, sages, and statesmen of America. Phil., 1829. 23—139.
Roget, Peter Mark. Thesaurus of English words and phrases, so classified and arranged as to facilitate the expression of ideas, and assist in literary composition. Bost., 1868. Q—2.
Rokeby. Scott, *Sir* W. N. Y., 1871. 17—105.
Roland Cashel. Illus. Lever, C. J. N.Y., n. d. 5—29.
—— Yorke: sequel to "The Chaunings." Wood, E. P. Phil., n. d. 41—230.

Rollin, Charles. Ancient history. Lond., 1851. 32—193.

Rolt, John. Essay on moral command. Lond., 1842. E.

Roman antiquities of Dionysius Halicarnassensis. Lond., 1758. 4 v. 34—203.

——— commonwealth, History of the later. Arnold, T. N. Y., 1846. 35—212.

——— empire; reflections on the causes of its rise and fall. Montesquieu, C. de S. Edin., 1775. 35—211.

——— empire, History of the decline and fall of the. Gibbon, E. N. Y., 1850. 4 v. 35—211.

——— history. Hooke, N. Lond., 1830. 6 v. 35—212.

——— history; the early empire. (Epochs of history.) Capes, W. W. N. Y., n. d. 35—212.

——— law, Introduction to. Hadley, J. N. Y., 1874. 19—114.

——— question, The. About, E. Bost., 1859. 40—222.

——— republic, History of the revolution that happened in the. Vertot D'Aubeuf, R. A. Lond., 1724. 2 v. 35—211.

——— republic, History of the progress and termination of the. Ferguson, A. Phil., 1841. 35—212.

——— republic of 1849, with accounts of the inquisition. Dwight, T. N. Y., 1851. 35—213.

——— world, The old. Lord, J. N. Y., 1873. 35—209.

Romance: (Little classics, vol. 7.) Bost., 1875. 5—33.

———, A view of the commencement and progress of. Smollett, T. Lond., 1872. 40—224.

——— of a poor young man, The. Feuillet, O. N. Y., 1875. 41—228.

——— of the peerage, The. Craik, G. L. Lond., 1848-50. 4 v. 11—63.

——— of the green seal, The. Warfield, C. A. N. Y., 1866. 6—35.

——— of the harem, The. Illus. Leonowens, A. H. Bost., 1873. 17—101.

——— of old court life in France. Illus. Elliot, F. N. Y., 1874. 5—28.

Romans under the empire, History of. Merivale, C. Lond., 1850. 3 v. 35—211.

Romantic biography of the age of Elizabeth. Taylor, W. C. Lond., 1842. 2 v. 12—67. ·

Romany Rye, The: sequel to "Lavengro." Borrow, G. N. Y., 1857. 5—28.

Rome, A general history of. Merivale, C. N. Y., 1875. 35—212.

——— and the newest fashions in religion. Gladstone, W. E. N. Y., 1875. 40—225.

——— and its vicinity, The topography of. Gell, Sir W. Lond., 1834. 2 v. 9—52.

———, Days near. Illus. Hare, A. J. C. Phil., 1875. 2 v. in one. 17—102.

———, History of. Arnold, T. N. Y., 1851. 35—212.

———, History of. Wachsmuth, Schlosser & Co. Phil., 1837. 35—212.

———, History of. Livius, T. G. Baker, tr. Phil., 1840. 2 v. 35—212.

———, History of. Goldsmith, O. Edin., 1812. 2 v. 35—211.

———, History of. Mommsen, T. N. Y., 1871-72. 4 v. 35—211.

———, The comic history of. Illus. Beckett, G. A. a'. Lond., n. d. 2—9.

Romola. "George Eliot." N. Y., 1876. 6—36.

Rooke, John. Geology as a science, applied to the reclamation of land from the sea, the construction of harbors, the formation of railroads, and the discovery of coal; seconded with a dissertation on geology. Lond., 1840. 15—91.

Roorbach, Orville A. Bibliotheca Americana: catalogue of American publications, including reprints and original works, from 1820 to 1852, inclusive; together with a list of periodicals published in the United States. N. Y., 1852. T.

——— Supplement to the Bibliotheca Americana. N. Y., 1855. T.

Rory O'More. Lover, S. Lond. and N. Y., n. d. 7—45.

Roscoe, William. The life of Lorenzo de Medici, called the magnificent. Phil., 1803. 3 v. 12—70.

——— The life and pontificate of Leo the tenth. Lond., 1846. 2 v. 11—65.

Rose, George. Observations on the historical work of the late Right Hon. Charles James Fox; with a narrative of the events which occurred in the enterprise of the earl of Argyle, in 1685, by Sir Patrick Hume. Lond., 1809. T.

Rose, Hugh James. A new general biographical dictionary. Lond., 1853. 12 v. 23—139.

Rose Clark. " Fanny Fern." N. Y., 1856. O—3.

—— garden, The. " S. B. A.`Moslih-Ed-din." Bost., 1872. 7—46.

—— in bloom : a sequel to " Eight Cousins." Alcott, L. M. Bost., 1876. 5—31.

—— in June, A. Illus. Oliphant, M. O. W. Bost., 1874. 41—230.

—— Leblanc. Fullerton, *Lady* G. N. Y., 1875. 41—228.

Rosenberg, C. G. Jenny Lind in America. N. Y., 1851. 8—50.

Ross, Joel H. What I saw in New York ; or, a bird's eye view of city life. Illus. Auburn, 1851. R—2.

Ross, *Sir* John. A voyage of discovery for the purpose of exploring Baffin's bay, and inquiring into the probability of a north-west passage. Illus. Lond., 1819. 9—51.

—— Narrative of a second voyage in search of a north-west passage, and of a residence in the arctic regions during the years 1829-33; including the discovery of the northern magnetic pole. Illus. Lond., 1835. 2 v. V.

Rossetti, Christina G. Poems. Illus. Bost., 1872. 17—105.

Rotteck, Charles *von.* A general history of the world, from the earliest times until the year 1831 ; translated from the German, and continued to 1840 by Frederick Jones. Illus. First American edition. Phil., 1840. 4 v. 32—194.

Rouge et noir. About, E. Phil., 1873. 6—40.

Roughing it. Illus. " Mark Twain." Hartford, 1872. 2—9.

Round, William M. F. Torn and mended : a Christmas story. Illus. Bost., 1877. 41—226.

Round my house. Hamerton, P. G. Bost., 1876. 40—222.

Roundabout papers. Illus. Thackeray, W. M. Lond., 1869. 5—32.

Rousseau, Jean Jacques, Œuvres complètes de; avec des notes historiques. Illus. Paris, 1864. 4 v. W.

——, The confessions of. Translated from the French. Illus. Lond., 1874. 20—122.

Routledge, James. Chapters in the history of popular progress, chiefly in relation to the freedom of the press a trial by jury—1660-1820, with an application to later years. Lond., 1876. 2 170.

Royal engineers, Papers on subjects connected with the duties of the corps Illus. Lond., 1844-49. 10 v. T.

—— kalendar, and court and city register for England, Scotland, Ireland, and the colonies. Lond., 1853-57. 4 v. D — R.

—— naval biography. Marshall, *Lieu.* Lond., 1823-30. 12 v. 13—75.

Rude stone monuments. Illus. Ferguson, J. Lond., 1872. 14—82.

Ruffini, Giovanni. Doctor Antonio : a tale of Italy. N. Y., 1867. 6—40.

—— Lorenzo Benoni; or, passages in the life of an Italian. Edited by a friend. N. Y., 1860. 6—40.

—— Vincenzo; or, sunken rocks. Lond., 1863. 3 v. in one. 6—35 and 40.

Rule, William Harris, *D. D.* History of the Inquisition, from its establishment in the twelfth century to its extinction in the nineteenth. Illus. Lond., 1874. 2 v. 32—192.

Ruling ideas in early ages, and their relation to old testament faith. Mozley, J. B. N. Y., 1877. 18—108.

Rumford, Benjamin Thompson, *count of.* Essays, political, economical, and philosophical. Lond., 1797-1802. 3 v. 27—159.

——, Life of. (Library of American biography, vol. 15.) 11—65.

Runaway match, The. Wood, E. P. Phil., n. d. 41—230.

Running the gauntlet. Yates, E. Lond. and N. Y., n. d. 7—45.

Rupert Godwin. Braddon, M. E. N — Y., n. d. 5—29.

Ruschenberger, William S. W. Elements of natural history; embracing zoology, botany, and geology. Illus. Phil., 1860. 2 v, 14—85.

Rush, James. The philosophy of the human voice; embracing its psychological history, etc. Phil., 1867. 15—3.

Ruskin, John. The stones of Venice. Illus. N. Y., 1864. 3 v. 26—158.

—— Same. Lond., 1851. 3 v. R—2.

Germantown and Valley Forge; with a list of distinguished prisoners of war; the time of their capture, exchange, etc.; to which is added the half-pay acts of the continental congress; the revolutionary pension laws; and a list of the officers of the continental army who acquired the right to half-pay, commutation, and lands. Phil., 1860. X.

Safford, James M. Geology of Tennessee: published by authority of the general assembly. Nashville, 1869. L.

Sailing on the Nile. Laporte, L. Bost., 1872. 17—103.

Saint Andrews as it was and as it is. Illus. Grierson, J. St. Andrews, 1838. 33—201.

—— Domingo, History and present condition of. Brown, J. Phil., 1837. 2 v. 36—217.

—— Elmo: a novel. Evans, A. J. N. Y. and Lond., 1874. 7—44.

Saintine, X. B., *pseud.* See Boniface, X.

St. George and St. Michael: a novel. Illus. MacDonald, G. N. Y., n. d. 7—45.

St. John, James Augustus. History of the manners and customs of ancient Greece. Lond., n. d. 3 v. in one. 35—209.

St. Martin's eve. Wood, E. P. Phil., n. d. 41—230.

Saint Mars, N. Cisterne de Courtiras, *viscomtesse de,* (*Countess Dash.*) Mademoiselle Fifty Millions; or, the adventures of Hortense Mancini. Adelaide De V. Chaudron, tr. N. Y., 1869. 5—28.

St. Pierre, Jacques Henri Bernardin de. Studies of nature. H. Hunter, tr. Phil., n. d. 15—92.

—— Paul and Virginia. Illus. N. Y., 1873. 7—42.

Saint Simon, Louis Rouvroy, *duke of.* Memoirs on the reign of Louis XIV, and the regency. Bayle St. John, tr. Lond., 1876. 3 v. 35—214.

St. Lawrence and Franklin counties, N. Y., A history of. Illus. Hough, F. B. Albany, 1853. 31—190.

—— Ronan's well. Scott, *Sir* W. Bost., 1868. 3—17.

—— Valentine's day; or, the fair maid of Perth. Scott, *Sir* W. Bost., 1868. 3—17.

Salad for the social. Saunders, F. N. Y. and Lond., 1856. 2—10.

Salem: a tale of the seventeenth century. Castleton, D. R. N. Y., 1874. P—2.

Sallustius, Caius Crispus. The history of the conspiracy of Catiline and the Jugurthine war. W. Rose, tr. Phil., 1837. 35—212.

Salverte, Anne Joseph Eusèbe Baconnière. The occult sciences: the philosophy of magic, prodigies, and apparent miracles; with notes, by A. T. Thomson. N. Y., n. d. 2 v. 14—85.

—— History of the names of men, nations, and places, in their connection with the progress of civilization. L. H. Mordacque, tr. Lond., 1864. 2 v. 26—156.

Sand, George, *pseud.* See Dudevant, A. L. A. D.

Sandford and Merton, The history of. Illus. Day, T. Phil., 1869. 39.

Santa Claus land. Illus. Douglas, A. M. Bost., 1874. 39.

—— Fé expedition, Narrative of the. Illus. Kendall, G. W. N. Y., 1850. 2 v. 8—50.

Sans Souci series. The life, letters, and table-talk of Benjamin Robert Haydon. Illus. R. H. Stoddard, ed. N. Y., 1876. 40—221.

—— Men and manners in America one hundred years ago. Illus. H. E. Scudder, ed. N. Y., 1876. 40—221.

—— Anecdote biography of Percy Bysshe Shelley. R. H. Stoddard, ed. N. Y., 1877. 40—221.

Sappho, Poetical works of. F. Fawkes, tr. Lond., 1832. 17—107.

Saracens, The history of the. Ockley, S. Lond., 1847. 36—217.

——, The history and conquests of the. Freeman, E. A. Lond., 1876. 36—217.

Sargent, Epes. Planchette; or, the despair of science: a full account of modern spiritualism, its phenomena, and the various theories regarding it; with a survey of French spiritism. Bost., 1869. 15—93.

—— Peculiar: a tale of the great transition. N. Y., 1864. 6—39.

Sargent, Winthrop. The history of an expedition against Fort du Quesne, in

1755, under Major-General Edward Braddock. Phil., 1855. 30—179.

Satanstoe. Illus. Cooper, J. F. N. Y., 1867. 3—14.

Saunders, Frederick. Salad for the social. N. Y. and Lond., 1856. 2—10.

Saunders, John. Abel Drake's wife: a novel. N. Y., 1863. 5—29.

—— Bound to the wheel: a novel. N. Y., 1866. 5—29.

—— Hirell: a novel. N. Y., 1870. 5—29.

—— Martin Pole: a novel. N. Y., 1863. 5—29.

—— Israel Mort, overman: a story of the mine. Illus. Phil., 1872. P—1.

Saunders, Katherine. The high mills. Illus. Phil., 1872. 5—28.

Sauzay, A. Wonders of glass-making in all ages. (Illustrated library of wonders.) N. Y., 1872. 28—169.

Saxe, John Godfrey, Poems by. Bost., 1869. 16—99.

—— Leisure-day rhymes. Bost., 1875. 17—105.

Saxe Holm's stories. N. Y., 1874. 5—31.

Saxon studies. Hawthorne, J. Bost., 1876. 10—57.

Say and seal. "Elizabeth Wetherell" and A. B. Warner. Phil., 1870. 2 v. in one. 7—42.

Scandinavia, History of. Sinding, P. C. N. Y., 1859. 36—217.

Scarlet letter, The. Illus. Hawthorne, N. Bost., 1876. 3—18.

Scenes and adventures in the Ozark mountains of Missouri and Arkansas. Illus. Schoolcraft, H. R. Phil., 1853. 17—101.

—— in the south. Creecy, J. R. Wash., 1860. 17—103.

—— of clerical life. Illus. "George Eliot." N. Y., 1874. 6—36.

Sceptres and crowns. Illus. "Elizabeth Wetherell." N. Y., 1875. 7—42.

Schellen, Thomas Joseph Heinrich. Spectrum analysis in its application to terrestrial substances, and the physical constitution of the heavenly bodies. Jane and Caroline Lassell, trs. W. Huggins, ed. Illus. N. Y., 1872. 14—82.

Schiller, Johann Christoph Friedrich von. History of the revolt of the Netherlands. Lond., 1847. 2 v. 36—218.

Schiller, Johann Christoff Freidrich, von. History of the thirty years' war. Rev. A. J. W. Morrison, tr. Lond., 1851. 36—218.

—— Revolt of the Netherlands, etc. Lond., 1870. 2—11.

—— early dramas and romances. H. G. Bohn, tr. Lond., 1867. 2—11.

Contents.

The robbers; Fiesco; Love and intrigue; Demetrius; The ghost seer; and The sport of destiny.

—— Historical dramas. Lond., 1870. 12—56.

Contents.

Don Carlos; Mary Stuart; The maid of Orleans; and The bride of Messina.

—— Historical and dramatic works. Rev. A. J. W. Morrison. tr. Lond., 1871. 2 v. 36—218.

Contents.

Revolt of the Netherlands; Thirty years' war; Wallenstein; William Tell.

——, The life of; comprehending an examination of his works. Lond., 1825. 12—69.

Schlegel, Carl Wilhelm Friedrich von. A course of lectures on modern history. L. Purcell and R. H. Whitelock, trs. Lond., 1849. 32—193.

Schliemann, Henry. Troy and its remains: a narrative of researches and discoveries made on the site of Ilium and in the Trojan plain. Illus. P. Smith, ed. Lond., 1875. 40—225.

Schlosser, Friedrich Christoph. History of the eighteenth century, and of the nineteenth, till the overthrow of the French empire. D. Davison, tr. Lond., 1843-52. 8 v. 32—194.

School and the army in Germany and France, The. Hazen, W. B. N. Y., 1872. 2—8.

—— days at Rugby, by an old boy. Illus. Hughes, T. Bost., 1869. 2—11.

School-houses. Illus. Johonnot, J. N. Y., 1871. 19—117.

Schoolcraft, Henry Rowe. Narrative journal of travels through the northwestern regions of the United States, extending from Detroit, through the great chain of American lakes, to the sources of the Mississippi river. Illus. Albany, 1821. 9—52.

—— Notes on the Iroquois. Albany, 1847. 30—178.

Schoolcraft, Henry Rowe. Personal memoirs of a residence of thirty years with the Indian tribes on the American frontiers. Phil., 1851. 8—48.

—— The Indian in his wigwam; or, characteristics of the red race of America. N. Y., 1848. 8—48.

—— * Historical and statistical information respecting the history, condition, and prospects of the Indian tribes of the United States; collected and prepared under the direction of the bureau of Indian affairs. Illus. Phil., 1851-57. 6 v. N.

—— Scenes and adventures in the semi-alpine region of the Ozark mountains of Missouri and Arkansas, which were first traversed by De Soto, in 1541. Illus. Phil., 1853. 17—101.

Schoolcraft, Mary Howard. The black gauntlet: a tale of plantation life in South Carolina. Phil., 1860. P—2.

Schools and schoolmasters, My. Miller, H. Bost., 1869. 2—11.

Schramke, T. Description of the N. Y. Croton aqueduct, in English, German, and French. Illus. N. Y. and Berlin, 1846. D. R.

Schuckers, J. W. The life and public services of Salmon Portland Chase; to which is added the eulogy on Mr. Chase, delivered by Wm. E. Evarts, before the alumni of Dartmouth college, June 24, 1874. N. Y., 1874. 11—59.

Schultes, Henry. An essay on aquatic rights. Lond., 1811. T.

Schurz, Carl, The speeches of: collected and revised by the author. Phil., 1865. 24—143.

Schuyler, Eugene, *Ph. D.* Turkistan: notes of a journey in Russian Turkistan, Khokand, Bukhara, and Kuldja. Illus. N. Y., 1876. 2 v. 40—225.

Schwartz, Marie Sophie. Birth and education. Selma Borg and Marie A. Brown, trs. Bost., 1871. 5—28.

—— Guilt and innocence. S. Borg and M. A. Brown, trs. Bost., 1871. 4—21.

—— The right one. S. Borg and M. A. Brown, trs. Bost., 1871. 5—28.

—— Gold and name. S. Borg and M. A. Brown, trs. Bost., 1872. 5—28.

—— Two family mothers. S. Borg and M. A. Brown, trs. Bost., 1872. 5—28.

Schwartz, Marie Sophie. The wife of a vain man. S. Borg and M. A. Brown, trs. Bost., 1872. 5—28.

—— Gerda; or, the children of work. Selma Borg and Marie A. Brown, tr. Phil., 1874. 6—38.

Schweinfurth, Georg. A. The heart of Africa: three years' travels and adventures in the unexplored regions of Central Africa, from 1868 to 1871; with an introduction by Winwood Reade. Ellen E. Frewer, tr. Illus. N. Y., 1874. 2 v. 10—56.

Science and art, Lectures on. Illus. Lardner, D. N. Y., 1850. Vol. 2. T.

—— byways. Proctor, R. A. Lond., 1875. 14—82.

—— for the young. Illus. Abbott, J. N. Y., 1872. 38.

—— of wealth, The. Walker, A. Bost., 1867. 15—89.

——, philosophy, and religion. Bascom, J. N. Y., 1872. 14—85.

Scientific American: an illustrated journal of art, science, and mechanics. V ol. 35. N. Y., 1876. U.

Scintillations from the prose works of Heinrich Heine. N. Y., 1873. 4—22.

Scotland, History of the rebellions in. Chambers, R. Edin. and Lond., 1827—29. 5 v. 33—201.

——, The history of. Robertson, W. N. Y., 1836. 34—204.

——, History of. Buchanan, G. Aberdeen, 1771. 2 v. 34—204.

——, Prehistoric annals of. Illus. Wilson, D. Lond., 1863. 2 v. 34—204.

Scott, Genio C. Fishing in American waters. Illus. N. Y., 1873. 19—115.

Scott, Winfield, *Lieutenant-General,* Memoirs of; written by himself. N. Y., 1864. 2 v. 12—72.

Scott, *Sir* Walter, The poetical works of. Illus. Complete in one volume, with all his introductions and notes; also, various readings and the editor's notes. N. Y., n. d. 16—94.

—— Tales of a grandfather: history of Scotland, with notes. Illus. 6 v. in three. Bost., 1861. 34—204.

—— Waverly novels. Illus. Bost., 1868-69. 25 v. 3—17.

Contents.

—— The lady of the lake : a poem. N. Y., 1873. 17—105.

—— The lay of the last minstrel. N. Y., 1871. 17—105.

—— Marmion. N. Y., 1871. 17—105.

—— Rokeby. N. Y., 1871. 17—105.

—— The lord of the isles. N. Y., 1871. 17—105.

—— The life of. Lockhart, J. G. Edin., 1871. 11—64.

—— The life of. Chambers, R. Lond., 1871. 13—76.

—— Ivanhoe : (Condensed classics.) N. Y., 1876. 5—33.

Scottish chiefs, The. Porter, J. Phil., 1871. 7—41.

—— Gael, The. Illus. Logan, J. Lond., 1831. 2 v. 34—204.

—— life, Curious storied traditions of. Leighton, A. Edin., 1860. 41—227.

Scouring of the white horse. Illus. Hughes, T. Lond., 1859. O—3.

Scudder, Horace Elisha. The dwellers in Five Sisters Court. N. Y., 1876. 41—226.

Sculpture, Wonders of. Illus. Viardot, L. N. Y., 1873. 28—169.

Sea lions, The. Illus. Cooper, J. F. N. Y., 1864. 3—14.

Seaboard parish, The : sequel to "Annals of a quiet neighbourhood." Illus. Mac-Donald, G. N. Y., 1873. 7—45.

—— slave states, A journey through the. Olmsted, F. L. N. Y., 1856. 8—49.

Sealed packet, The. Trollope, T. A. Phil., n. d. 7—43.

Seaman, Ezra C. Essays on the progress of nations in civilization, productive industry, wealth, and population. N. Y., 1852. 18—109.

Search for winter sunbeams. Illus. Cox, S. S. N. Y., 1870. 17—103.

Second war between the United States and Great Britain, History of. Ingersoll, C. J. Phil., 1852. Vol. 1. 31—186.

—— visit to the United States of North America. Lyell, Sir C. N. Y. and Lond., 1850. 2 v. 10—58.

—— wife, The. John, E. Phil., 1874. 7—42.

Secretary of the Interior, Reports of the, from 1849 to 1873. X.

Secrets of the sanctum. Hill, A. F. Phil., 1875. 40—222.

Sedgwick, Catherine Maria. Redwood : a tale. N. Y., 1850. 6—39.

—— A New England tale, and other miscellanies. N. Y., 1852. 6—39.

Sedgwick, Theodore, jr. A memoir of the life of William Livingston ; with extracts from his correspondence, and notices of various members of his family. N. Y., 1833. 12—70.

Seebohm, Frederic. The era of the protestant revolution. (Epochs of history.) Bost., 1874. 36—215.

Seed-time and harvest. Reuter, F. Phil., 1871. 6—35.

Seeley, John Robert. Ecce homo: a survey of the life and work of Jesus Christ. Bost., 1870. E.

Seemüller, Anne Moncure Crane. Emily Chester: a novel. Bost., 1870. P—2.

—— Reginald Archer: a novel. Bost. 1871. P—2.

—— Opportunity : a novel. Bost., 1871. 2 copies. P—2.

Self-help. Smiles, S. Bost., 1869. 2—13.

Self-raised ; or, from the depths : a sequel to "Ishmael ; or, in the depths." Southworth, E. D. E. N. Phil., 1876. 6—36.

Seminole war, Sketch of the; by a lieutenant of the left wing. Charleston, 1836 30—179.

Seneca nation of Indians, Proceedings of a joint committee of Friends for promoting the civilization of the. Balt., 1847. T.

—— Further proceedings of the same. Balt., 1850. T.

Sénégambie et Guinée, Tardieu; Nubie, Chérubini; Abyssinie, Desverges. (L'Univers.) Paris, 1847. D. R.

Sense and sensibility: a novel. Austen, J. Lond., 1870. 4—27.

Septimius Felton; or, the elixir of life. Hawthorne, N. Bost., 1872. 3—18.

Sermons out of church. Muloch, D. M. N. Y., 1875. 40—222.

—— preached before the University of Oxford. Mozley, J. B. N. Y., 1876. 18—108.

Servants of the stomach, The. Macé, J. N. Y., 1868. 15—88.

Settlers in Canada, The. Illus. Marryat, *Capt.* F. N. Y., n. d. 5—30.

Seven curses of London, The. Greenwood, J. Bost., 1869. 19—114.

—— golden candlesticks, The. Illus. Tristram, H. B. Lond., n. d. 28—165.

—— months' run, A. Brooks, J. N. Y., 1874. 10—57.

—— years, and other tales. Kavanagh, J. N. Y., 1872. 3 v. in one. 7—41.

Sevenoaks: a story of to-day. Illus. Holland, J. G. N. Y., 1875. 3—18.

Sévigné, Marie de Rabutin Chantal, *marquise,* The letters of, to her daughter and friends. *Mrs.* Hale, ed. Bost., 1874. 13—79.

Seville, William Penn. *A table of United States bounties and premiums for the enlistment of volunteers during the war of the rebellion. Wash., 1865. L.

Seward, William. Anecdotes of distinguished persons, chiefly of the present and two preceding centuries. Illus. Lond., 1798. 4 v. 11—63.

Seward, William Henry, The works of; George E. Baker, ed. N. Y., 1853. 3 v. 25—148.

—— Travels around the world. Illus. Olive Risley Seward, ed. N. Y., 1873. 17—101.

Seward, William Henry. Autobiography of; from 1801 to 1834; with a memoir of his life, and selections from his letters, from 1831 to 1846; by F. W. Seward. Illus. N. Y., 1877. 13—74.

Sex in education; or, a fair chance for girls. Clarke, E. H. Bost., 1874. 40—222.

Seymour's humorous sketches, comprising eighty-six caricature etchings, illustrated in prose and verse, by Alfred Crowquill. Lond., 1872. 2—7.

Shadow of Ashlydyat, The. Wood, E. P. Phil., n. d. 41—230.

Shairp, John Campbell. Culture and religion in some of their relations. N. Y., 1873. 19—114.

Shakespeare, William, The works of, containing his plays and poems, to which is added a glossary. Lond., 1797. 6 v. 16—94.

Contents.

Vol. 1. The tempest; The two gentlemen of Verona; The merry wives of Windsor; Twelfth night, or, what you will; Measure for measure; Much ado about nothing; Midsummer night's dream.

Vol. 2. Love's labor lost; The merchant of Venice; As you like it; All's well that ends well; The taming of the shrew; Winter's tale; Comedy of errors.

Vol. 3. Macbeth; King John; King Richard the second; King Henry the fourth; King Henry the fifth.

Vol. 4. King Henry the sixth; King Richard the third; King Henry the eighth; Troilus and Cressida.

Vol. 5. Timon of Athens; Coriolanus; Julius Cæsar; Antony and Cleopatra; Cymbeline; Titus Andronicus.

Vol. 6. Pericles; King Lear; Romeo and Juliet; Hamlet; Othello.

——, The works of. Edited by Howard Staunton. Illus. Lond. and N. Y., n. d. 3 v. 16—94.

—— Six old plays, on which Shakespeare founded his "Measure for measure;" "Comedy of errors;" "Taming the shrew;" "King John;" "King Henry the fourth," and "King Henry the fifth;" and "King Lear." Lond., 1779. 2 v. 16—100.

——, The. complete concordance to. Clarke, M. C. Bost., 1853. 16—94.

——, Memoirs of the life of. White, R. G. Bost., 1865. 13—76.

Sharpe, Samuel. The history of Egypt, from the earliest times till the conquest by the Arabs, A. D. 640. Lond., 1846. 36—216.

—— History of Egypt under the Ptolemies. Lond., 1838. 36—216.

Shattuck, Lemuel. Report to the committee of the city council, appointed to obtain the census of Boston, for the year 1845. Bost., 1846. D. R.

Shaw, Edward. Practical masonry; or, a theoretical and operative treatise of building. Illus. Bost., 1846. T.

Shaw, Thomas B. A complete manual of English literature: W. Smith, ed.; with a sketch of American literature, by H. H. Tuckerman. N. Y., 1870. 28—170.

Shawl-straps. (Aunt Jo's scrap-bag, vol. 2.) Alcott, L. M. Bost., 1872. 5—31.

Shen, John Gilmary. Discovery and exploration of the Mississippi valley. N. Y., 1852. 29—176.

Sheahan, James W. The universal historical atlas, genealogical, chronological, and geographical; exhibiting the rise and progress of all governments the origin, descent, and intermarriages of royal families and governing dynasties; the lives of historical personages, and the boundaries of the various countries during important periods; being a comprehensive history of the world from the latest recognized authorities. N. Y., 1873. R.

Sheep husbandry in the south. Illus. Randall, H. S. Phil., 1849. D. R.

Shelburne, William, earl of, Life of. Fitzmaurice. Lord E. Lond., 1875-76. 3 v. 40—224.

Shelley, Percy Bysshe, Poetical works of; edited by Mrs. Shelley, with a memoir. Bost., 1867. 4 v. 16—97.

Contents.

Vol. 1. Memoir, by Charles E. Norton; Queen Mab; Alastor, or, the spirit of solitude; The revolt of Islam.

Vol. 2. Prometheus unbound; The Cenci; Hellas.

Vol. 3. Œdipus Tyrannus, or, Swellfoot, the tyrant; Early poems; Poems written in 1816-20.

Vol. 4. Poems written in 1820-22; Translations; Hymns of Homer; Epigrams.

——, Poetical works of. Bound with Coleridge and Keats. 16—94.

12 I

Shelley, Percy Bysshe. Anecdote biography of. (Sans Souci series.) N. Y., 1877. 40—221.

Sherburne, John Henry. The life and character of John Paul Jones. N. Y., 1851. 12—66.

Sheridan, Richard Brinsley, The dramatic works of; with a memoir of his life. Lond., 1857. 27—160.

Contents.

Life of Richard Brinsley Sheridan; The rivals; St. Patrick's day; The duenna; The school for scandal; The critic; Trip to Scarborough; Pizarro; Verses to the memory of Garrick.

——, Memoirs of the life of. Moore, T. N. Y., 1853. 2 v. 13—78.

——, Speeches of; with a sketch of his life. Lond., 1842. 3 v. 25—152.

—— The works of, with a memoir by J. P. Browne, M. D.; containing extracts from the life, by Thomas Moore. Lond., 1874. 2 v. 24—142.

Sherman, Henry. The governmental history of the United States of America, from the earliest settlement to the adoption of the present federal constitution; in four parts. Hartford, 1860. 29—177.

Sherman, William Tecumseh. Memoirs of: by himself. N. Y., 1875. 2 v. 40—225.

Sherman's historical raid. Boynton, H. V. Cin., 1875. 40—224.

Shillaber, Benjamin Penhallow. Life and sayings of Mrs. Partington, and others of the family. Illus. N. Y., 1854. 2—8.

"Ship ahoy!" a yarn in thirty-six cable lengths. Illus. N. Y., 874. 5—29,

—— in the desert, The. "Joaquin Miller." Bost., 1875. 17—105.

Shirley. "Currer Bell." N. Y., 1868. 2 copies. 7—45.

Shoemakers' village. Holbeach, H. Lond., 1871. 2 v. in one. P—3.

Short studies on great subjects. Froude, J. A. N. Y., 1872-77. 3 v. O—2.

Shuckford, Samuel. The sacred and prophane history of the world connected. Lond., 1731-40. 4 v. 32—194.

Siamese twins, a satirical tale of the times, with other poems. Bulwer-Lytton, Sir E. N. Y., 1831. 17—105.

Sibly, Ebenezer. A new and complete illustration of the celestial science of astrology. Lond., 1784. 23—165.

Sibyl Huntington: a novel. Dorr, J. C. R. Phil., 1873. 5—30.

Siddons, *Mrs.*, Memoirs of. Boaden, J. Lond., 1831. 2 v. 11—60.

Sidney, Algernon, Life of. Van Santvoord, G. N. Y., 1853. 11—64.

Sidney, *Sir* Philip, The miscellaneous works of; with a life of the author. Gray, Wm. Bost., 1860. 27—159.

Sidonie. Daudet, A. Bost., 1877. 3—18.

Sierra Nevada, Mountaineering in the. King, C. Bost., 1872. 17—104.

Sights a-foot. Collins, W. W. Phil., n. d. 17—101.

—— and insights. Whitney, A. D. T. Bost., 1876. 2 v. 7—44.

Signa: a story. "Ouida." 3 v. in one. Leip., 1875. 41—226.

Sign-boards, The history of. Illus. "Jacob Larwood" and J. C. Hotten. Lond., 1866. 2—11.

Signers of the declaration of independence, A biography of the. Judson, L. C. Phil., 1839. 12—63.

—— Same. Illus. Phil., 1831. 5 v. 12—70.

Sikes, *Mrs.* Wirt. (Formerly Olive Logan.) They met by chance: a society novel. N. Y., 1873. 41—223.

—— Get thee behind me, Satan! a homeborn book of home-truths. N. Y., 1872. 41—223.

—— Before the footlights and behind the scenes: a book about the "show business" in all its branches. Illus. Phil., 1870. 2—9.

Silas Marner. "George Eliot." Bost., 1869. 6—36.

Silcote of Silcotes. Kingsley, H. Lond., 1869. 7—43.

Silent partner, The. Phelps, E. S. Bost. and Lond., 1871. 6—40.

—— witness, The. Yates, E. Bost., 1875. 7—45.

Silliman, Augustus E. A gallop among American scenery; or, sketches of American scenes and military adventure. N. Y., 1843. 8—50.

Silver cord, The. Illus. Brooks, C. S. N. Y., 1861. 6—35.

—— pitchers, and other stories. Alcott, L. M. Bost., 1876. 5—31.

Silvia: a novel. Kavanagh, J. N. Y., 1873. 7—41.

Simms, Frederick Walter. Practical tunnelling. Illus. Lond., 1844. T.

Simms, Jeptha Root. Trappers of New York; or, a biography of Nicholas Stoner and Nathaniel Foster, together with anecdotes of other celebrated hunters, and some account of Sir William Johnson and his style of living. Illus. Albany, 1871. 40—222.

Simms, William Gilmore. The history of South Carolina, from its first European discovery to its erection into a republic. Charleston, 1840. 31—187.

—— The Maroon: a legend of the Caribbees, and other tales. Phil., 1855. 6—39.

—— The wigwam and the cabin; or, tales of the south. Phil., 1853. 2—10.

—— Poems, descriptive, dramatic, legendary, and contemplative. N. Y., 1853. 2 v. 16—96.

—— The forayers; or, the raid of the dog-days. Illus. N. Y., 1855. 41—229.

—— Eutaw: a sequel to "The Forayers:" a tale of the revolution. Illus. N. Y., 1856. 41—229.

—— The Yemassee: a romance of Carolina. Illus. N. Y., 1853. 41—229.

—— Guy Rivers: a tale of Georgia. Ill. N. Y., 1855. 41—229.

—— Katharine Walton; or, the rebel of Dorchester. Illus. N. Y., 1854. 41—229.

—— The partisan: a romance of the revolution. Illus. N. Y., n. d. 41—229.

—— Woodcraft; or, hawks about the dovecote: a story of the south at the close of the revolution. Illus. N. Y., 1854. 41—229.

—— The scout; or, the black riders of Congaree. Illus. N. Y., 1854. 41—229.

—— Mellichampe: a legend of the Santee. N. Y., 1870. 41—229.

Simple story, A. Inchbald, E. N. Y., n. d. 5—23.

Simpleton, A. Reade, C. N. Y., 1874. 5—28.

Simpson, *Sir* George. Narrative of a journey round the world during the years 1841 and 1842. 2 v. Lond., 1847. 9—51.

Simpson, *Capt.* James H. Report of explorations across the great basin of

the territory of Utah. for a direct
wagon-route from Camp Floyd to Genoa,
in Carson valley, in 1859. Illus. Wash.,
1876. D. R.

Sinding, Paul C. History of Scandinavia, from the early times of the Norsemen and Vikings to the present day.
N. Y., 1859. 36—217.

Sir Brooke Fossbrooke. Lever. C. J. N.
Y., 1872. 5—29.

—— Jasper Carew. Int. Lever. C. J.
N. Y., 1872. 5—29.

—— Launcelot Greaves. and. Adventures
of an atom. Smollett, T. Lond., 1872.
41—220.

—— Harry Hotspur of Humblethwaite.
Illus. Trollope, A. N. Y., 1871. 5—25.
Siren. A. Trollope. T. A. N. Y., 1871.
5—25.

Sismondi, Jean Charles Léonard Si-
monde de. History of the Italian republics. (Lardner's cabinet cyclopædia.) Phil., 1832. 35—212.

—— Historical view of the literature of
the south of Europe. T. Roscoe, tr.
Lond., 1850. 2 v. 28—170.

Sister's bye-hours. Ingelow, J. Bost.,
1871. 38.

Six old plays. Shakespeare, W. Lond.,
1779. 2 v. 16—100.

—— of one by half a dozen of the other.
Mrs. Stowe, Mrs. Whitney, and others.
Bost., 1872. 2—13.

—— weeks in the saddle. Illus. Waller,
S. E. Lond., 1874. 17—102.

—— years later. Dumas, A. D. Phil.,
1875. 3—20.

Skelton, John, Poetical works of.
Bost., 1864. 3 v. 16—98.

Sketch-book of Geoffrey Crayon, gent.
Irving, W. Phil., 1871. 3—19.

—— Same: author's revised edition.
N. Y., 1864. 3—19.

Sketches by "Boz." Illus. Dickens, C.
Bost. and Lond., n. d. 3—15.

—— in France. Dumas, A. D. Phil.,
n. d. 3—20.

—— of art, literature, and character.
Jameson, A. M. Bost., 1866. 2—13.

—— of Irish character. Illus. Hall, A.
Lond., n. d. 2—10.

—— of the history of man. Kames,
Lord. Edin., 1778. 3 v. 15—89.

Skinner, John S. The plough, the

loom. and the anvil. Phil., 1851. 3 v.
T.

—— The monthly journal of agriculture.
Illus. N. Y., 1846-48. 3 v. S.

Skirmishing. Jenkin. C. N. Y., 1870.
6—38.

Slave power. The. Cairnes, J. E. N. Y.,
1862. 19—117.

Slip in the fens, A. Illus. N. Y., 1873.
5—31.

Small house at Allington, The. Illus.
Trollope, A. N. Y., 1865. 5—28.

Smart, Hawley. Breezie Langton : a
story of fifty-two to fifty-five. N. Y.,
1870. 5—25.

Smeaton, John. Reports made on various occasions in course of his employ-
ment as a civil engineer. Lond., 1812.
3 v. T.

——. Miscellaneous papers of. Illus.
Lond., 1814. T.

Smiles, Samuel. Character. N. Y., 1872.
0—3.

—— Self-help, with illustrations of character and conduct. Bost., 1869. 2—13.

—— The life of George Stephenson, railway engineer. Bost., 1868. 13—76.

—— The Huguenots in France, after the
revocation of the edict of Nantes : with
a visit to the country of the Vaudois.
N. Y., 1874. 35—213.

Smith, Alexander. A life-drama, and
other poems. Bost., 1859. 16—100.

Smith, Charles H., (Bill Arp.) Bill Arp,
so called: a side-show of the southern
side of the war. Illus. N. Y., 1866. 0—3.

Smith, Charles John. Synonyms dis-
criminated : a complete catalogue of
synonymous words in the English language: with descriptions of their various
shades of meaning, and illustrations of
their usages and specialties. N. Y., 1871.
14—81.

Smith, George. Assyrian discoveries :
an account of explorations and discoveries on the site of Nineveh, during 1873
and 1874. Illus. N. Y., 1875. 10—56.

Smith, Rev. Edward P. Incidents of the
United States Christian Commission.
Illus. Phil., 1871. 2—7.

Smith, Horace and James. Rejected
addresses, and other poems, with a biographical sketch. E. Sargent, ed. N. Y.,
1871. 17—105.

South Carolina, View of. Drayton, J. Charleston, 1802. 31—188.
—— meadows: a tale of long ago. Disosway, E. T. Phil., 1874. 3—15.
Southern and western songster. Grigg, J. Phil., 1856. 16—100.
—— and western states, The industrial resources of the. De Bow, J. D. B. N. O., 1853. 3 v. 18—110.
—— history of the war: official reports of battles. N. Y., 1863. 30—180.
Southey, Robert. History of the Peninsular war. Lond., 1828. 4 v. 33—199.
—— Early naval history of England. Phil., 1835. 33—199.
—— History of Brazil. Lond., 1822. 3 v. 35—209.
—— Select lives of Cromwell and Bunyan. Lond., 1849. 12—71.
—— Common-place book; edited by his son-in-law, John Wood Warter. N. Y., 1860. 2 v. 27—159.
—— Poetical works; with a memoir of the author. Bost., 1864. 10 v. 16—98.

Contents.

Vol. 1. Life of Southey; General preface; Joan of Arc; The vision of the maid of Orleans.
Vol. 2. Preface; Dedication to Edith Southey; The triumph of woman; Wat Tyler; Poems concerning the slave trade; Botany-Bay eclogues; Sonnets; Monodramas; The amatory poems of Abel Shufflebottom; Love elegies; Lyric poems; Songs of the American Indians; Occasional pieces; The retrospect; Hymn to the penates.
Vol. 3. Preface; English eclogues; Nondescripts; The devil's walk; Inscriptions; Carmen triumphale, for the commencement of the year 1814; Odes; Epistle to Allan Cunningham.
Vol. 4. Thalaba, the destroyer.
Vol. 5. Madoc; Madoc in Wales; Madoc in Aztlan.
Vol. 6. Ballads and metrical tales.
Vol. 7. Ballads and metrical tales; Advertisement; A tale of Paraguay; All for love, or, a sinner well saved; The pilgrim to Compostello.
Vol. 8. The curse of Kehama.
Vol. 9. Roderick, the last of the Goths.
Vol. 10. The poet's pilgrimage to Waterloo; Carmen nuptiale; The lay of the laureate; Funeral song for the Princess Charlotte of Wales; A vision of judgment; Oliver Newman, a New England tale; Miscellaneous poetical remains.

Southgate, Henry. Things a lady would like to know concerning domestic management and expenditure: arranged

for daily reference, with hints regarding the intellectual as well as the physical life. Fifth edition. Lond., 1877. 90—122.
South-sea idyls. Stoddard, C. W. Bost., 1873. 19—114.
Southworth, Alvan S. Four thousand miles of African travel: a personal record of a journey up the Nile and through the Soudan to the confines of Central Africa; embracing a discussion of the sources of the Nile, and an examination of the slave trade. Illus. N. Y. and Lond., 1875. 10—57.
Southworth, Emma Dorothy Eliza Nevitte. The curse of Clifton; same as "Fallen pride." Phil., 1852. 6—37.
—— The discarded daughter. Phil., 1852. 6—37.
—— The wife's victory, and other nouvelettes. Phil., 1854. 6—37.
—— The lost heiress. Phil., 1854. 6—37.
—— The deserted wife. Phil., 1855. 6—37.
—— The missing bride; or, Miriam, the avenger. Phil., 1855. 6—37.
—— Vivia; or, the secret of power. Phil., 1857. 6—37.
—— The three beauties. Phil., 1858. 6—37.
—— The two sisters. Phil., 1858. 6—37.
—— The lady of the isle: a romance of real life. Phil., 1859. 6—37.
—— The haunted homestead, and other nouvelettes; with an autobiography of the author. Phil., 1860. 6—37.
—— The mother-in-law: a tale of domestic life. Phil., 1860. 6—37.
—— The gipsy's prophecy; or, the bride of an evening. Phil., 1861. 6—36.
—— The fatal marriage. Phil., 1863. 6—37.
—— The bridal eve. Phil., 1864. 6—37.
—— Allworth abbey. Phil., 1865. 6—37.
—— The bride of Lewellyn. Phil., 1866. 6—37.
—— The fortune-seeker. Phil., 1866. 6—37.
—— The widow's son. Phil., 1867. 6—37.

Southworth, Emma Dorothy Eliza Nevitte. Fallen pride; or, the mountain girl's love: same as " Curse of Clifton." Phil., 1868. 6—37.

—— The changed brides. Phil., 1869. 6—37.

—— The bride's fate: a sequel to the "Changed brides." Phil., 1869. 6—36.

—— The prince of darkness: a romance of the Blue Ridge. Phil., 1869. 6—37.

—— The family doom ; or, the sin of a countess. Phil., 1869. 6—36.

—— The maiden widow : a sequel to the "Family doom." Phil., 1870. 6—36.

—— Cruel as the grave. Phil., 1871. 6—36.

—— Tried for her life: a sequel to "Cruel as the grave." Phil., 1871. 6—36.

—— Love's labor won. Phil., 1862. 6—36.

—— India; the pearl of Pearl river. Phil., 1857. 6—36.

—— Retribution: a tale of passion. Phil., 1856. 6—36.

——, and Frances Henshaw Baden. The Christmas guest: a collection of stories. Phil., 1870. 6—36.

—— Fair play ; or, the test of the Lone Isle. Phil., 1868. 6—36.

—— How he won her: a sequel to "Fair play." Phil., 1869. 6—36.

—— The mystery of Dark Hollow. Phil., 1875. 6—37.

—— Ishmael ; or, in the depths. Phil., 1876. 6—36.

—— Self-raised ; or, from the depths: a sequel to "Ishmael." Phil., 1876. 6—36.

—— A noble lord: sequel to "The lost heir." Phil., 1872. 6—36.

—— A beautiful fiend ; or, through the fire. Phil., 1873. 6—36.

—— Victor's triumph ; sequel to "A beautiful fiend." Phil., 1874. 6—36.

—— The spectre lover; and other stories by her sister, *Mrs. Frances Henshaw Baden.* Phil., 1875. 6—36.

Souvestre, Emile. An attic philosopher in Paris ; or, a peep at the world from a garret. N. Y., 1869. 2—9.

Spain, Ten days in. Illus. Field, Kate. Bost., 1875. 17—104.

—— and Portugal, The history of. (Lardner's cabinet cyclopædia.) Lond., 1832-33. 5 v. 36—217.

Spain. (Romance of history.) Illus. Trueba, T. de. Lond., n. d. 2—8.

——, The history of the revolutions in. Vertot D'Aubeuf, R. A. de. Lond., 1724. 36—217.

—— under Charles the second. Stanhope, A. Lond., 1840. 36—218.

Spalding, J. Willett. Japan and around the world : an account of three visits to the Japanese empire. Illus. N. Y., 1855. 10—57.

Spanish Americans, Four years among. Hassaurek, F. N. Y., 1868. 17—104.

—— gypsy: a poem. "George Eliot." Bost., 1868. 16—99.

Spare hours. Brown, J. Bost., 1869. 2 v. 2—13.

Sparks, Jared. The library of American biography. N. Y., 1834-48. 25 v. 11—65.

Contents.

proposed Honduras interoceanic railway. Illus. N. Y., 1855. 9—52.

—— Nicaragua: its people, scenery, monuments, and the proposed interoceanic canal. Illus. N. Y., 1852. Vol. 2. 10—56.

——, and E. H. Davis. Ancient monuments of the Mississippi valley. Illus. N. Y., 1848. 14—80.

—— Peru: incidents of travel and exploration in the land of the Incas. Illus. N. Y., 1877. 10—57.

Squire Trevlyn's heir. Wood, E. P. Phil., 1863. 6—35.

Staël-Holstein, Anne Louise Germaine Necker, *Baronne de*, Œuvres complètes de. Paris, 1861. 2 v. W.

——, Œuvres posthumes de; précédées d'une notice sur son caractère et ses écrits. Paris, 1861. W.

—— Corinne; or, Italy. Isabel Hill, tr. N. Y., n. d. 7—41.

Stanhope, Alexander. Spain under Charles the second; or, extracts from the correspondence of Hon. Alexander Stanhope, British minister at Madrid, 1690-99. Lond., 1840. 36—218.

Stanhope, Philip Henry; formerly *Lord* Mahon. History of the war of the succession in Spain. Lond., 1836. 36—218.

—— History of England, from the peace of Utrecht to the peace of Paris. H. Reed, ed. N. Y., 1849. 2 v. 34—207.

—— Historical essays. Lond., 1861. Q—2.

Stanley, Arthur Penrhyn. Lectures on the history of the Jewish church, from the captivity to the Christian era. Third series, with two maps. N. Y., 1877. 32—196.

—— The life and correspondence of Thomas Arnold, *D. D.* 2 v. in one. N. Y., 1877. 11—60.

Stanley, Henry M. How I found Livingstone: travels, adventures, and discoveries in Central Africa; including an account of four months' residence with Dr. Livingstone. Illus. N. Y., 1872. 10—56.

—— My Kalulu; prince, king, and slave; a story of Central Africa. Illus. N. Y., 1874. 17—101.

Stanley Thorn. Cockton, H. Lond. and N. Y., n. d. 6—40.

Star and a heart, A. Marryat, *Miss* F. Bost., n. d. 41—230.

—— out of Jacob, The. Illus. Warner, A. B. N. Y., 1873. 7—42.

Stark, John, Life of. (Library of American biography, vol. 1.) 11—65.

Stars, Catalogue of 2,381 principal fixed. Baily, F. Lond., 1825. T.

State of the union, The. A complete documentary history of the public affairs of the United States, foreign and domestic, for the year 1854. Wash., 1855. S.

Stately homes of England, The. Illus. Jewitt, L., and S. C. Hall. Phil., n. d. 40—225.

Statesman's manual. Illus. Williams, E., and B. J. Lossing. N. Y., 1858. 6 v. S.

—— year-book. Martin, F. Lond. and N. Y., 1872-77. 6 v. 18—109.

Statesmen of the time of George the third, Historical sketches of. Brougham, H. Lond., 1853. 3 v. 12—72.

Statutes at large of the Confederate States of America. James M. Matthews, ed. Richmond, 1862-64. 2 v. 19—113.

* —— (revised) in force in the District of Columbia. 21—128.

Stedman, Edmund Clarence, The poetical works of. Bost., 1873. 17—105.

—— Victorian poets. Bost., 1876. 19—116.

Steele, Ashbel. Chief of the pilgrims; or, the life and time of William Brewster. Illus. Phil., 1857. Q—2.

Steinmetz, Andrew. History of the Jesuits, from the foundation of their society to its suppression by Pope Clement fourteenth; their missions throughout the world; their educational system and literature, with their revival and present state. Lond., 1848. 3 v. 32—195.

Stenhouse, Thomas B. H. The Rocky Mountain saints; a full and complete history of the Mormons, from the first vision of Joseph Smith to the last courtship of Brigham Young; and the development of the great mineral wealth of the territory of Utah. Illus. N. Y., 1873. 26—155.

Stephen, *Sir* James. Lectures on the history of France. N. Y., 1852. 35—214.

Stone, William Leete. Life of Joseph Brant, (Thayendanegea;) including the border wars of the American revolution. N. Y., 1838. 2 v. 12—68.

—— The life and times of Sir William Johnson, bart. Albany, 1865. 2 v. 11—59.

—— Memoirs, and letters and journals of Major-General Reidesel, during his residence in America. Max ron Eelking, tr. Illus. Albany, 1868. 2 v. 40—224.

Stones of Venice, The. Illus. Ruskin, J. N. Y., 1864. 3 v. 2 copies. 15—87 and 26—158.

Stories and tales. Illus. Andersen, H. C. N. Y., 1875. 39.

—— for the household. Illus. Andersen, H. C. Lond., 1872. 38.

—— for children, by eleven sophomores. Bost., 1875. 38.

—— of bird life. Illus. Berthoud, H. Lond., 1875. 38.

—— of success. Cobb, J. F. Lond. and N. Y., n. d. 40—222.

—— of inventors and discoverers. Illus. Timbs, J. N. Y., 1860. 2—13.

—— told to a child. Illus. Ingelow, J. First and second series. Bost., 1866. 2 v. 39.

Storms, The philosophy of. Espy, J. J. Bost., 1841. 15—92.

Stormy life, A. Illus. Fullerton, *Lady* G. N. Y., 1874. 5—28.

Story, Joseph, Life and letters of; edited by his son, W. W. Story. Bost., 1851. 2 v. 13—74.

—— A discourse upon the life, character, and services of the Hon. John Marshall, LL. D., chief justice of the United States. Bost., 1835. 11—59.

——, The miscellaneous writings of; edited by his son, W. W. Story. Bost., 1852. 27—160.

Story, William Wetmore. Roba di Roma. Lond., 1866. 2 v. 2—10.

—— Life and letters of Joseph Story. Bost., 1851. 2 v. 13—74.

—— Nero: an historical play. Lond. and N. Y., 1875. 17—105.

Story of a millionaire, The. "Louise Mühlbach." N. Y., 1872. 7—41.

—— of Kennett, The. Taylor, J. B. N. Y., 1868. 5—34.

Story of my life. Anderson, H. C. N. Y., 1871. 13—76.

—— of the new priest in Conception bay, The. Illus. Lowell, R. T. S. N. Y., 1873. 2 v. in one. 7—43.

—— of Pauline, The. Clunes, G. C. Lond., 1870. 2 v. in one. P—3.

—— of Sibylle, The. Feuillet, O. Bost., 1872. 41—230.

Stowe, Harriet Beecher. Lady Byron vindicated: a history of the Byron controversy from its beginning, in 1816, to the present time. Bost., 1870. 2—9.

—— Uncle Tom's cabin; or, life among the lowly. Illus. Bost., 1871. 6—35.

—— The May Flower, and miscellaneous writings. Bost., 1871. 6—35.

—— The pearl of Orr's island: a story of the coast of Maine. Bost., 1869. 6—35.

—— Agnes of Sorrento. Bost., 1869. 6—35.

—— Nina Gordon: a tale of the great Dismal Swamp. Bost., 1871. 6—35.

—— The minister's wooing. Bost., 1872. 6—35.

—— My wife and I; or, Harry Henderson's history. Illus. N. Y., 1872. 6—35.

—— Oldtown fireside stories. Illus. Bost., 1872. 3—19.

—— The chimney-corner, by Christopher Crowfield. Bost., 1868. 6—35.

—— Religious poems. Illus. Bost., 1867. 16—100.

—— Queer little people. Illus. Bost., 1873. 39.

—— Pink and white tyranny: a society novel. Illus. Bost., 1872. 6—35.

—— Little pussy willow. Illus. Bost., 1870. 39.

—— Little foxes, by Christopher Crowfield. Bost., 1873. 39.

—— Palmetto-leaves. Illus. Bost., 1873. 17—102.

—— We and our neighbors; or, the records of an unfashionable street: a sequel to "My wife and I." Illus. N.Y., 1875. 6—35.

Strange adventures of a phaeton, The. Black, W. N. Y., 1876. 5—29.

—— story, A. Bulwer-Lytton, *Sir* E. Phil., 1869. 5—33.

Strange world, A. Braddon, M. E. N.Y., 1875. 5—29.

Strangers and pilgrims: a novel. Illus. Braddon, M. E. N. Y., 1874. 5—29.

Strathmore. "Ouida." Phil., 1871. 7—44.

Strength of materials. Tate, T. Lond., 1850. V.

—— of timber, cast and malleable iron, and other materials, A treatise on the. Illus. Barlow, P. Lond., 1851. 15—88.

—— and beauty: discussions for young men. Hopkins, M. N. Y., 1874. E.

Stretton: a novel. Illus. Kingsley, H. N. Y., 1869. 6—35.

Stretton, J. C. Margaret and her bridesmaids. Bost., 1864. 6—38.

—— Queen of the county. Bost., 1865. 6—38.

Strickland, Agnes. Lives of the queens of Scotland, and English princesses connected with the regal succession of Great Britain. N.Y., 1853-59. 8 v. 11—62.

—— Lives of the queens of England, from the Norman conquest. Illus. Lond., 1871. 8 v. 13—77.

Strickland, William P. Old Mackinaw; or, the fortress of the lakes, and its surroundings. Phil., 1860. 31—186.

Strother, David H., (Porte Crayon.) Virginia illustrated: containing a visit to the Virginian Canaan, and the adventures of Porte Crayon and his cousins. Illus. N. Y., 1857. 24—141.

—— Trips of Brown, Jones, and Robinson. Illus. N. Y., 1873. 5—28.

Stubbs, Rev. William. The early Plantagenets. (Epochs of history.) N. Y., n. d. 34—207.

Student, The. Bulwer-Lytton, Sir E. N. Y., 1860. 2 v. in one. 2—13.

Studies for stories. Illus. Ingelow, J. Bost., 1870. 38.

—— from life. Muloch, D. M. N. Y., 1861. 4—23.

—— of nature. St. Pierre, J. H. B. de. Phil., n. d. 15—92.

——, stories, and memoirs. Jameson, A. M. Bost., 1866. 2—13.

Study of words, On the. Trench, R. C. N. Y., 1868. 14—81.

Stumbling-blocks. "Gail Hamilton." Bost., 1868. E.

Subjection of women, The. Mill, J. S. N. Y., 1870. 3—19.

Subterranean world, The. Illus. Hartwig, G. N. Y., 1871. 14—83.

Subterraneous surveying, and the variation of the magnetic needle. Fenwick, T. Lond., 1822. T.

Sub-tropical rambles. Illus. Pike, N. N. Y., 1873. 10—56.

Suburban sketches. Illus. Howells, W. D. Bost., 1872. 2—8.

Success and its conditions. Whipple, E. P. Bost., 1875. 19—116.

Sue, Eugène, pseud. See Sue, M. J.

Sue, Marie Joseph, (Eugene Sue.) The mysteries of Paris. Illus. Lond., 1845. 3 v. 4—21.

—— The wandering Jew. Lond. and N. Y., n. d. 4—21.

Sugar and hydrometers, Reports on. McCulloh, R. S. Wash., 1848. S.

Sugden, Sir Edward. A practical treatise on powers. Phil., 1856. 2 v. T.

Sullivan, James. The history of the district of Maine. Bost., 1795. 30—183.

Sullivan, John, Life of. (Library of American biography, vol. 13.) 11—65.

Sullivan, William. The public men of the revolution; including events from the peace of 1783 to the peace of 1815; in a series of letters; with a biographical sketch of the author, by his son, John T. S. Sullivan. Phil., 1847. 12—68.

Sully, Maximilian de Bethune, duke of, Memoirs of; to which is added The trial of Ravaillac for the murder of Henry the great. Lond., 1761. 3 v. 13—73.

Summer in Leslie Goldthwaite's life. A. Illus. Whitney. A. D. T. Bost. 1872. 7—44.

. Summer's romance. A. Healy. M. Bost. 1872. P—3.

Summer, Charles. The works of. Bost. 1874. 12 v. 9—54.

* Sun pictures of Rocky Mountain scenery. Hayden. F. V. N. Y. 1870. 9—54.

——, The. Illus. Proctor. R. A. Lond. 1874. 14—32.

——, The. Illus. Guillemin. A. N. Y. 1872. 25—164.

Supply of water to London. The. Illus. Matthews. W. Lond. 1841. T.

—— of water to the metropolis. Report of the general board of health on the. Lond., 1850. D. R.

Surgeon's daughter. and Castle Dangerous. Scott. Sir W. Bost., 1868. 3—17.

Surtees, R. S. Jorrock's jaunts and jollities. Phil. 1838. 2 v. in one. 2—10.

—— Mr. Sponge's sporting tour. Illus. H. W. Herbert. ed. N. Y. 1856. 3—5.

Surrey, Henry Howard. earl of. Poetical works of: with a memoir. Bost. 1864. 16—99.

Surveying, A collection of tables and formulæ useful in. Lee. T. J. Wash., 1853. 15—87.

Survivors of the Chancellor. The. Illus. Verne. J. Bost., 1876. 5—31.

Susan Fielding: a novel. Illus. Edwards, A. N. Y., n. d. 6—30.

Sutro, Adolph. Mineral resources of the United States. Balt., 1868. D. R.

Swallow barn. Illus. Kennedy, J. P. N. Y., 1872. 6—39.

Swallow, G. C. Geological report of the country along the line of the southwestern branch of the Pacific railroad, state of Missouri. St. Louis, 1859. D. R.

Swan, James G. The north-west coast: or, three years' residence in Washington territory. Illus. N. Y., 1857. R—2.

Swedenborg, Emanuel. The true Christian religion: containing the universal theology of the new church, foretold by the Lord in Daniel vii, 13, 14, and in the Apocalypse, xxi, 1, 2. N. Y., 1873. 1—4.

—— Heaven and its wonders, the world of spirits, and Hell: from things heard and seen. Lat. S. Nobb. tr. N. Y., 1872. 1—4.

—— Angelic wisdom concerning the Divine Providence. N. Y. 1873. 1—8.

—— The four leading doctrines of the new church, signified by the New Jerusalem in the Revelation: being those concerning the Lord, the Sacred Scripture, faith, and life. N. Y. 1873. 1—8.

—— Angelic wisdom concerning the Divine Love and the Divine Wisdom. N. Y. 1872. 1—3.

—— Miscellaneous theological works: The New Jerusalem and its heavenly doctrine: Brief exposition: The intercourse between the soul and the body: The white horse mentioned in the Apocalypse, chap. xix: An appendix to the treatise on The white horse: On the earths in the universe: The last judgment: A continuation concerning The last judgment. N. Y. 1871. 1—8.

—— Conjugial love and its chaste delights: also. adulterous love and its sinful pleasures: being a translation of his " Delitiæ sapientiæ de amore conjugiali: post quas sequuntur voluptates insaniæ de amore scortatorio." N. Y., 1871. 1—8.

—— The Apocalypse revealed, wherein are disclosed the arcana there foretold, which have heretofore remained concealed. N. Y., 1873. 2 v. 1—3.

—— Arcana cœlestia: the heavenly arcana contained in the Holy Scriptures, or, Word of the Lord unfolded: beginning with the book of Genesis: together with wonderful things seen in the world of spirits and in the heaven of angels. N. Y., 1870-73. 10 v. 1—1 and 2.

Sweet nineteen: or, Woodleigh. Robinson, F. W. N. Y., n. d. 5—29.

Sweet, Robert. Flora Australasica: or, a selection of handsome or curious plants, natives of New Holland and the South Sea islands. Illus. Lond., 1827-28. R—2.

Swift, Jonathan. The works of. Lond., 1765-75. 25 v. 27—164.

Contents.

ton's lament; The village doctor; A singular letter from Southern Africa, etc. Vols. 7 and 8. My English acquaintance; The murderer's last night; Narration of certain uncommon things that did formerly happen to me; The ways; The wet wooing; Ben-na Groich, etc. Vols. 9 and 10. Rosaura, a tale of Madrid; Adventure in the North-west territory; Harry Bolton's curacy; The Florida pirate; The Pandour and his princess; The beauty draught, etc. Vols. 11 and 12. The Natolian story-teller; The first and last crime; John Rintoul; Major Moss; The premier and his wife, etc.

—— of the argonauts, and other sketches. Harte, F. B. Bost., 1875. 3—19.

—— of the borders and of Scotland. Wilson, J. M. Edin., n. d. 11 v. O—2.

—— of the good woman. Paulding, J. K. N. Y., 1867. 2—8.

—— of old travel. Illus. Kingsley, H. Lond. and N. Y., 1869. 2—10.

—— of the genii or, the delightful lessons of Horam the son of Asmar. *Sir* Charles Morell, tr. Illus. New edition, collated and edited by Philo-Juvenis, Lond., 1873. O—1.

—— of a traveller. Irving, W. N. Y., 1867. 3—19.

—— of a grandfather : history of Scotland. Scott, *Sir* W. Bost., 1861. 6 v. in three. 34—204.

Talfourd, Thomas Noon, Critical and miscellaneous writings of. (Modern British essayists.) Bost., 1854. 27—159.

Talisman, The two drovers, My aunt Margaret's mirror, The tapestried chamber, and The laird's Jock. Scott, *Sir* W. Bost., 1862. 3—17.

Talking to the children. Macleod, A. N. Y., 1872. 38.

Tallis's illustrated atlas, and modern history of the world. R. M. Martin, ed. Lond. and N. Y., 1851. X.

Tallyrand-Périgord, Charles Maurice de. Memoir concerning the commercial relations of the United States with England ; with an essay on new colonies. Lond., 1806. 29—177.

Tancred ; or, the new crusade. Disraeli, B. Lond., 1871. 4—24.

Tandon, Moquin. The world of the sea. Illus. *Rev.* H. Martyn Hart, tr. Lond., n. d. 14—83.

Taney; Roger Brooke, Memoir of. Tyler, S. Balt., 1872. 12—66.

Tanglewood tales. Illus. Hawthorne,N. Bost., 1868. 3—18.

Tappen, George. Professional observations on the architecture of the principal ancient and modern buildings in France and Italy ; with remarks on painting and sculpture. Lond., 1806. T.

Tartarie, Beloutchistan, Boutan, et Népal, (L'Univers.) Debeux et Valmont. Afghanistan. Raymond. Paris, 1848. D. R.

Tasso, Torquato. Jerusalem delivered : an heroic poem. J. Hoole, tr. Lond., 1802. 2 v. 16—95.

—— Rinaldo : a poem. J. Hoole, tr. Lond., 1792. 16—95.

Tate, Thomas. Strength of materials; containing various original and useful formulæ, specially applied to tubular bridges, wrought-iron and cast-iron beams, etc. Lond., 1850. V.

Tautphœus, Jemima Montgomery, *baroness.* Quits : a novel. Phil., 1872. 2 v. in one. 6—36.

—— At odds. Phil., 1872. 6—36.

—— The initials : a story of modern life. Phil., n. d. 6—36.

—— Cyrilla ; or, the mysterious engagement. Phil., n. d. 6—36.

Taylor, Edward S. The history of playing cards; with anecdotes of their use in conjuring, fortune-telling, and card-sharping. Illus. Lond., 1865. 2—13.

Taylor, Isaac. Words and places ; or, etymological illustrations of history, ethnology, and geography. Lond., 1873. 19—114.

Taylor, James Bayard. A journey to Central Africa ; or, life and landscapes from Egypt to the negro kingdoms of the White Nile. Illus. N. Y., 1869. 17—103.

—— Northern travel : summer and winter pictures : Sweden, Denmark, and Lapland. N. Y., 1869. 17—103.

—— The lands of the Saracen ; or, pictures of Palestine, Asia Minor, Sicily, and Spain. N. Y., 1869. 17—103.

—— Travels in Greece and Russia, with an excursion to Crete. N. Y., 1870. 17—103.

Taylor, James Bayard. At home and abroad: a sketch-book of life, scenery, and men. N. Y., 1869. 17—103.
—— Same. 2d series. N. Y., 1869. 17—103.
—— Views a-foot; or, Europe seen with knapsack and staff. N. Y., 1870. 17—103.
—— Eldorado; or, adventures in the path of empire; comprising a voyage to California, via Panama; life in San Francisco and Monterey; pictures of the gold region, and experiences of Mexican travel. N. Y., 1868. 17—103.
—— By-ways of Europe. N. Y., 1869. 17—103.
—— A visit to India, China, and Japan, in the year 1853. N. Y., 1869. 17—103.
—— Hannah Thurston: a story of American life. N. Y., 1868. 5—34.
—— John Godfrey's fortunes: related by himself. N. Y., 1865. 5—34.
—— The story of Kennett. N. Y., 1868. 5—34.
——, The poems of. Bost., 1866. 16—98.
—— Joseph and his friend: a story of Pennsylvania. N. Y. and Lond., 1870. 5—34.
—— Beauty and the beast, and tales of home. N. Y., 1872. 5—34.
—— Egypt and Iceland in the year 1874. N. Y., 1874. 40—222.

Taylor, Jeremy. The great exemplar; or, the life of Jesus Christ. N. Y., 1859. 2 v. 13—78.
——, Life of. Bonney, H. K. Lond., 1815. 12—70.

Taylor, Joseph. A fast life on the modern highway; being a glance into the railroad world from a new point of view. Illus. N. Y., 1874. 2—11.

Taylor, Richard Cowling. Statistics of coal: the geographical and geological distribution of mineral combustibles, or, fossil fuel; with the amounts of production, consumption, and commercial distribution in all parts of the world. Phil., 1848. 19—113.

Taylor, William Cooke. A manual of ancient and modern history. N. Y., 1852. 32—193.
—— History of the civil wars of Ireland, from the Anglo-Norman invasion till the

union of the country with Great Britain. Edin., 1831. 2 v. 34—205.
—— Modern British Plutarch; or, lives of men distinguished in the recent history of England for their talents, virtues, or achievements. N. Y., 1846. 11—63.
—— Romantic biography of the age of Elizabeth; or, sketches of life from the bye-ways of history, by the Benedictine Brethren of Glendalough. Lond., 184_. 2 v. 12—67.
—— The history of Mohammedanism and its sects; derived chiefly from oriental sources. Lond., 1834. 27—162.

Technical repository, The. Illns. Gill, Lond., 1822-27. 11 v. 18—110.
—— Same. 2d series. Lond., 1827-30. 6 v. 18—109.

Tegnér, Esaias. Frithiof's saga. W. L. Blackley, tr. Bayard Taylor, ed. N. Y., 1871. 17—106.

Tehuantepec railway, The: its location, features, and advantages, under the Sere grant of 1869. Illus. N. Y., 1869. 'I'.

Teignmouth, John Shore, lord. Memoirs of the life and correspondence of Sir William Jones. Lond., 1806. 12—70.

Telemachus, Adventures of. Fenelon. N. Y., 1872. 7—41.

Telford, Thomas, Life of, written by himself; containing a descriptive narrative of his professional labors, with a folio atlas of copper-plates. J. Rickman, ed. Lond., 1838. V.

Teller, George D. *American shippers' and express guide, traveller's direction, and official post-office and telegraph guide; showing the names, alphabetically arranged, of every city, town, and village in the United States and Canada. Buffalo, 1870. 23—137.

Tempest-tossed: a romance. Tilton, N. Y., 1874. 3—16.

Ten Brook, Andrew. American state universities; their origin and progress; a history of congressional university land-grants; a particular account of the rise and development of the university of Michigan, and hints toward the future of the American university system. Cin., 1875. 40—224.

Ten old maids: a novel. Smith, J. P. N. Y. and Lond., 1874. 5—30.

—— months in Brazil. Illus. Codman, J. Bost., 1867. 17—102.

—— times one is ten. Hale, E. E. Bost., 1872. 5—34.

—— thousand a year. Warren, S. Phil., n. d. 6—35.

Tenant of Wildfell Hall, The. "Acton Bell." N. Y., 1868. 7—45.

Tenants of Malory, The. Le Fanu, J. S. N. Y., 1871. 5—29.

Tennessee, The annals of. Ramsey, J. G. M. Phil., 1860. 31—186.

Tenney, Sanborn. Natural history : a manual of zoology. Illus. N. Y., 1866. 14—82.

Tennyson, Alfred, Poetical works of. Bost., 1869. 2 v. 16—99.

—— Gareth and Lynette. Illus. Bost., 1872. 16—99.

——, A concordance to the entire works of. Brightwell, D. B. Lond., 1869. 16—100.

—— Queen Mary: a drama. Bost., 1875. 17—106.

—— Harold : a drama. Author's edition from advance sheets. Bost., 1877. 17—106.

Tent life in the holy land. Illus. Prime, W. C. N. Y., 1874. 8—49.

Terhune, Mary Virginia, (*Marion Harland.*) True as steel: a novel. N. Y. and Lond., 1874. 7—44.

—— Jessamine : a novel. N. Y. and Lond., 1874. 7—44.

—— From my youth up. N. Y., 1875. 41—228.

Ternaux-Compans, Henri. Recueil de documents et mémoires originaux sur l'histoire des possessions Espagnoles dans l'Amérique, à diverses époques de la conquête. Paris, 1840. W.

—— Bibliothèque américaine ; ou, catalogue des ouvrages relatifs à l'Amérique. Paris, 1837. X.

Terrible temptation, A. Illus. Reade, C. N. Y., 1871. 7—42.

Territoire de l'Orégon, Exploration du. Illus. Duflot de Mofras. Paris, 1844. 2 v. W. Atlas, U.

Tested ; or, hope's fruition. Gardner, C. E. N. Y. and Lond., 1874. 7—43.

13 I

Testimony of the rocks, The. Miller, H. Bost., 1869. 15—91.

Texas journey, A. Olmsted, F. L. N. Y., 1857. 8—49.

—— and the gulf of Mexico. Illus. Houston, M. C. Lond., 1844. 2 v. 17—104.

——. Kennedy, W. Lond., 1841. 2 v. 31—187.

——, The history of the republic of. Maillard, N. D. Lond., 1842. 31—187.

——. Cordova, J. de. Phil., 1859. 31—187.

——, Information about. Braman, D. E. E. Phil., 1857. 31—187.

Texian expedition against Mier, The. Illus. Green, T. J. N. Y., 1845. 8—49.

Text-book of ecclesiastical history. Gieseler, J. C. L. Phil., 1836. 3 v. 32—196.

Thackeray, Anne Isabella. Old Kensington : a novel. Illus. N. Y., 1873. 4—21.

—— Miss Angel : a novel. Illus. N. Y., 1875. 4—21.

—— Bluebeard's keys, and other stories. N. Y. 1875. 4—21.

—— Toilers and spinsters, and other essays. Lond., 1874. 27—162.

Thackeray, William Makepeace. The adventures of Philip on his way through the world; to which is prefixed a shabby-genteel story. Illus. Lond., 1869. 2 v. 5—32.

—— Same. Household edition. Bost., 1869. 5—31.

—— The book of snobs; and sketches and travels in London. Illus. Lond., 1869. 5—32.

—— Ballads and tales. Illus. Lond., 1870. 5—32.

—— The memoirs of Barry Lyndon, esq , written by himself; with the history of Samuel Titmarsh, and the great Hoggarty diamond. Illus. Lond., 1869. 5—32.

—— Denis Duval; Lovel, the widower ; and other stories Illus. Lond., 1869. 5—32.

—— The Irish sketch-book ; and Notes of a journey from Cornhill to Grand Cairo. Illus. Lond., 1870. 5—32.

—— The history of Henry Esmond, esq., a colonel in the service of her majesty

Queen Anne; written by himself. Illus. Lond., 1869. 5—32.
—— Vanity Fair: a novel without a hero. Illus. Lond., 1869. 2 v. 5—32.
—— Same. N. Y., 1865. 5—32.
—— The Virginians: a tale of the last century. Illus. Lond., 1869. 2 v. 5—32.
—— Same. N. Y., 1859. 5—32.
—— Catherine, a story; Little travels; The Fitz-Boodle papers. Illus. Lond., 1869. 5—32.
—— The Paris sketch-book of Mr. M. A. Titmarsh; and The memoirs of Mr. Charles Yellowplush. Illus. Lond., 1869. 5—32.
—— Roundabout papers, (from the Cornhill magazine,) and The second funeral of Napoleon. Illus. Lond., 1869. 5—32.
—— The history of Pendennis: his fortunes and his misfortunes, his friends and his greatest enemy. Illus. Lond., 1868. 2 v. 5—32.
—— The Newcomes; or, the memoirs of a most respectable family. Edited by Arthur Pendennis, esq. Illus. Lond., 1869. 2 v. 5—32.
—— Same. Bost., 1870. 5—31.
—— Burlesques. Illus. Lond., 1869. 5—32.
—— The Christmas books of Mr. M. A. Titmarsh. Illus. Lond., 1871. 5—32.
—— The four Georges and the English humorists of the eighteenth century. Illus. Lond., 1869. 5—32.
Thaddeus of Warsaw. Porter, J. N. Y., 1856. 7—41.
Thalheimer, Mary Elsie. A manual of ancient history. Illue. Cin., 1872. 32—193.
That boy of Norcott's. Illus. Lever, C. J. N. Y., 1869. 5—29.
—— lass o' Lowrie's. Illus. Burnett, F. H. N. Y., 1877. 4—26.
—— queer girl. Illus. Townsend, V. F. Bost., 1875. 39.
Thatcher, Benjamin Bussey. Indian biography; or, an historical account of those individuals who have been distinguished among the North American natives as orators, warriors, statesmen, and other remarkable characters. N. Y., 1848. 2 v. 13—78.

Thaxter, Celia. Among the Isles of Shoals. Illus. Bost., 1873. 17—102.
Their wedding journey. Illus. Howells, W. D. Bost., 1874. 2—8.
Theo Leigh. Thomas, A. N. Y., 1870. 5—28.
Theologia Germanica. Susanna Winkworth, tr. Bost., 1860. E.
Theological essays. De Quincey, T. Bost., 1854. 2 v. 2—12.
Theology in the English poets. Brooke, S. A. N. Y., 1875. 28—166.
Thesaurus of English words and phrases. Roget, P. M. Bost., 1868. Q—2.
They met by chance: a society novel. Logan, O. N. Y., 1873. 41—228.
Thief in the night, The. Spofford, H. P. Bost., 1872. 4—22.
Thierry, Jacques Nicolas Augustin. History of the tiers état; or, third estate in France. Lond., 1859. 35—213.
—— History of the conquest of England by the Normans. Lond., 1847. 2 v. 34—205.
—— Historical essays, published under the title of "Dix ans d'études historiques," and Narratives of the Merovingian era; or, scenes of the sixth century. Phil., 1845. 27—159.
Thiers, Louis Adolphe. History of the French revolution. Lond., n. d. 35—214.
Things not generally known: a popular hand-book of facts not readily accessible in literature, history, and science. David A. Wells, ed. N. Y., 1873. 26—155.
Thirlwall, Connop. History of Greece. N. Y., 1848-51. 2 v. 35—209.
Thirty years in the harem. Melek-Hanum. N. Y., 1872. 2—10.
—— years in the United States senate. Benton, T. H. N. Y. and Lond., 1854. 2 v. 28—165.
—— years with the Indian tribes on the American frontiers. Personal memoirs of a residence of. Schoolcraft, H. R. Phil., 1851. 8—48.
—— years' war, History of the. Schiller, J. C. F. von. Phil., 1861. 36—218.
—— years' war, The. Gardiner, S. R. Lond., 1874. 36—215.

Thomas, George, *earl of Albemarle.* Fifty years of my life. N. Y., 1876. 40—224.

Thomas, Joseph. Universal pronouncing dictionary of biography and mythology. Phil., 1870. 2 v. 23—137.

——— 'A comprehensive medical dictionary, containing the pronunciation, etymology, and signification of the terms made use of in medicine and the kindred sciences; with an appendix, comprising a complete list of all the more important articles of the materia medica, arranged according to their medicinal properties. Phil., 1874. 23—138.

Thomas Wingfold, curate. MacDonald, G. N. Y., 1876. 7—45.

Thompson, Andrew. In the holy land. Illus. Lond., 1874. 17—101.

Thompson, Benjamin F. The history of Long Island, from its discovery and settlement to the present time. Illus. N. Y., 1843. 2 v. 31—139.

Thompson, Daniel Pierce. The rangers; or, the tory's daughter: a tale illustrative of the revolutionary history of Vermont, and the northern campaign of 1777. Bost., 1871. O—1.

——— The Green Mountain boys: a historical tale of the early settlement of Vermont. Bost., 1871. 2 v. in one. O—1.

Thompson, Richard W. The papacy and the civil power. N. Y., 1876. 18—108.

Thompson, Waddy. Recollections of Mexico. N. Y. and Lond., 1846. 8—49.

Thompson, Zadoc. History of Vermont, natural, civil, and statistical. Illus. Burlington, 1842. 30—183.

Thomson, C. Wyville. The depths of the sea: an account of the general results of the dredging cruises of H. M. SS. 'Porcupine' and 'Lightning,' during the summers of 1868, '69. and '70. Illus. N. Y. and Lond., 1873. 14—83.

Thomson, James, Poetical works of. Bost., 1865. 2 v. 16—97.

——— The seasons. Bost., 1862. 16—96.

Thomson, Katherine Byerly, (*Grace and Philip Wharton.*) Memoirs of Sarah, duchess of Marlborough, and of the court of Queen Anne. Lond., 1839. 2 v. 11—61.

Thomson, Katherine Byerly, (*Grace and Philip Wharton.*) Memoirs of the Jacobites of 1715 and 1745. Lond., 1845. 3 v. 11—62.

——— Memoirs of the life of Sir Walter Ralegh, with some account of the period in which he lived. Lond., 1830. 13—77.

——— The queens of society. Illustrated by Charles Altamont Doyle and the brothers Dalziel. Lond., 1872. 40—222.

——— The wits and beaux of society. Illustrated by H. K. Browne and James Godwin, and engraved by the brothers Dalziel. Lond., 1871. 40—222.

Thomson, Mortimer, (*Q. K. Philander Doesticks.*) Doesticks. Illus. N. Y., 1859. 2—11.

Thoreau, Henry David. The Maine woods. Bost., 1868. 17—104.

——— Cape Cod. Bost., 1865. 17—104.

——— Excursions. Bost., 1866. 17—104.

——— Letters to various persons. Bost., 1865. 19—115.

——— Walden. Bost., 1874. 9—53.

——— A Yankee in Canada; with anti-slavery and reform papers. Bost., 1874. 9—53.

——— A week on the Concord and Merrimack rivers. Bost., 1868. 9—53.

Thornton, J. Quinn. Oregon and California in 1848, with an appendix, including recent and authentic information on the subject of the gold-mines in California. Illus. N. Y., 1849. 2 v. 9—53.

Thorvaldsen : his life and works. Illus. Plon, E. Bost., 1874. 11—62.

Thoughts about art. Hamerton, P. G. Bost., 1874. 28—165.

———, letters, and opuscules of Blaise Pascal. N. Y., 1869. 2—11.

Thousand miles in the Rob Roy canoe, A. Illus. Macgregor, J. Bost., 1871. 17—101.

Three beauties, The. Southworth, E. D. E. N. Phil., 1858. 6—37.

——— books of song. Longfellow, H. W. Bost., 1872. 16—95.

——— brides, The. Yonge, C. M. N. Y., 1876. 5—30.

——— clerks, The. Trollope, A. N. Y., 1868. 7—43.

——— feathers. Illus. Black, W. N. Y., 1875. 5—29.

Three musketeers, The. Dumas, A. D. Lond. and N. Y., n. d. 5—31.

—— scouts, The. Trowbridge, J. T. Bost., 1874. 6—39.

—— sisters and three fortunes. Lewes, G. H. N.Y., n. d. 5—28.

—— thousand miles through the Rocky Mountains. Illus. McClure, A. K. Phil., 1869. 17—102.

—— years in California. Illus. Colton, W. N. Y., 1851. 17—103.

Throne of David, The. Illus. Ingraham, J. H. Phil., 1860. 4—25.

Throstlethwaite. Morley, S. Phil., 1876. 41—229.

Through night to light: sequel to "Problematic characters." Spielhagen, F. N. Y., 1871. 6—36.

—— Persia by caravan. Arnold, A. N. Y., 1877. 10—57.

Thucydides. History of the Peloponnesian war. W. Smith, tr. Phil., 1840. 35—209.

——, Life of. Lond.,1831. 3 v. 13—79.

Thunder and lightning. Illus. Fonvielle, W. de. N. Y.,1872. 28—169.

Tickell, Thomas, Poetical works of; with a life by Dr. Johnson. Bost., 1864. 16—97.

Ticknor, George. Life of William Hickling Prescott. Bost., 1864. 11—60.

—— Life, letters, and journals of. Bost., 1876. 2 v. 12—66.

Tiers état: or, third estate in France. Thierry, J. N. A. Lond., 1859. 35—213.

Tilton, Theodore. Tempest-tossed: a romance. N. Y., 1874. 3—16.

Timbs, John. Stories of inventors and discoverers in science and the useful arts. Illus. N. Y., 1860. 2—13.

—— The year-book of facts in science and art. Lond., 1853-57. 5 v. 15—93.

Timrod, Henry, The poems of; with a sketch of the poet's life. P. H. Hayne, ed. N. Y., 1873. 16—100.

Tit for tat: a novel. Smith, M. E. N. Y., 1856. 7—41.

Titan. Richter, J. P. Bost., 1871. 2 v. 1'—1..

Titcomb, Timothy, pseud. See Holland, J. G.

Tocqueville, Charles Alexis Henri Maurice Clérel de. The old régime and

the revolution. J. Bonner, tr. N. Y., 1856. 35—213.

——, Memoirs, letters, and remains of. Bost., 1862. 2 v. 12—72.

—— The republic of the United States of America, and its political institutions, reviewed and examined. H. Reeves, tr. N. Y., 1862. 29—177.

Toilers and spinsters, and other essays. Thackeray, A. I. Lond., 1874. 27—162.

Toinette: a tale of transition. Churton, H. N. Y., 1875. 3—16.

Tolla: a tale of modern Rome. About, E. Bost., 1856. 6—40.

Tom Brown at Oxford: a sequel to "School-days at Rugby." Hughes, T. Bost., 1869. 2 v. 2—11.

—— Burke "of Ours." Lever, C. J. Phil., n. d. 5—29.

—— Jones; or, the history of a foundling. Fielding, H. N. Y., 1861. 2 v. 5—34.

—— Pippin's wedding: a novel. Phil., 1871. P—3.

Tomo-chi-chi, Mico of the Yamacraws, Historical sketch of. Jones, C. C. Albany, 1868. 30—178.

To-morrow of death, The. Illus. Figuier, L. Bost., 1875. 15—89.

Tongue of fire, The. Arthur, W. Nashville, 1856. E.

Tony Butler. Lever, C. J. N. Y., 1872. 5—29.

"Too good for him." Marryat, Miss F. Lond. and N. Y., n. d. 4—22.

Too strange not to be true. Illus. Fullerton, Lady G. N. Y., 1872. 5—28.

Tooke, John Horne. The diversions of Purley, with the author's letter to John Dunning. New edition, by Richard Taylor. Lond., 1840. Q—1.

Tooke, Thomas. A history of prices, and of the state of the circulation, from 1839 to 1847; with a general review of the currency question. Lond., 1848. L.

Tooke, William. History of Russia, from the foundation of the monarchy by Rurik, to the accession of Catharine the second. Lond., 1800. 2 v. 36—220.

Torn and mended: a Christmas story. Illus. Round, W. M. F. Bost., 1877. 41—226.

Tour into the North-west territory. Harris, T. M. Bost., 1805. 10—58.
—— of the world in eighty days. A. Verne, J. Bost., 1874. 5—31.
Tourist's guide of the United States. Illus. Bachelder, J. B. Bost., 1873. 10—57.

Towner, Ausburn. Chedayne of Kotono : a story of the early days of the republic. N. Y., 1877. 3—17.

Townsend, George Alfred. The new world compared with the old : a description of the American government, institutions, and enterprises, and of those of our great rivals at the present time, particularly England and France. Illus. Hartford, 1870. 17—102.

Townsend, George H. * The manual of dates : a dictionary of reference to all the most important events in the history of mankind. Lond., 1862. 23—138.

Townsend, George Tyler. Three hundred of Æsop's fables, literally translated from the Greek. Illus. Lond., 1871. 38..

Townsend, Luther Tracy. Credo. Bost., 1869. E.
—— God-man ; or, search and manifestation. Bost., 1872. E.

Townsend, Virginia Frances. That queer girl. Illus. Bost., 1875. 39.

Tracts on mathematical and philosophical subjects. Hutton, C. Lond., 1812. 3 v. 15—87.

Trading : finishing the "House in town." Illus. "Elizabeth Wetherell." N. Y., 1873. 7—42.

Trafford, F. G., pseud. See Riddell, Mrs. J. H.

Trafton, Adeline. Katherine Earle. Illus. Bost., 1874. 41—229.
—— An American girl abroad. Illus. Bost., 1875. 40—222.

Tragedies of the wilderness. Drake, S. G. Bost., 1841. 2—13.

Tragedy of Brutus : or, the fall of Tarquin. Payne, J. H. Albany, 1875. 16—100.

Train, George Francis. An American merchant in Europe, Asia, and Australia : a series of letters from Java, Singapore, China, Bengal, Egypt, the Holy Land,

the Crimea and its battle-grounds, England, Melbourne, Sydney, etc., etc.; with an introduction by Freeman Hunt. N. Y., 1857. R—2.

Transcendentalism in New England. Frothingham, O. B. N. Y., 1876. 40—224.

Transformations of insects. Illus. Duncan; P. M. Phil., n. d. 14—83.

Transmission of life, The. Napheys, G. H. Phil., 1874. 1—4.

Trappers of New York : or, a biography of Nicholas Stoner and Nathaniel Foster. Illus. Simms, J. R. Albany, 1871. 40—222.

Travels among the northern and southern Indians. Illus. McKenney, T. L. N. Y., 1846. ' 2 v. in one. 30—178.
—— and adventures of Capt. John Smith. Richmond, 1819, 31—187.
—— and adventures of Monsieur Violet, The. Illus. Marryat, Capt. F. Lond. and N. Y., 1874. 5—30.
—— around the world. Illus. Seward, W. H. N. Y., 1873. 17—101.
—— in the west and Cuba. Turnbull, D. Lond., 1840. 8—49.
—— in North America ; with geological observations. Lyell, Sir C. N. Y., 1852. 10—58.
—— in North America. Murray, C. A. Lond., 1839. 2 v. 9—52.
—— in North and Central Africa. Illus. Barth, H. N. Y., 1857-59. 3 v. 10—56.
—— in the states of Ohio, Kentucky, Tennessee, and the Upper Carolinas. Michaux, F. A. Lond., 1805. 10—58.
—— of Anacharsis the younger in Greece. Barthélemy, J. J. Lond., 1794. 7 v. 8—48.-
—— maps, plans, views, and coins illustrative of the same. Lond., 1793. 9—51.
—— of Anna Bishop in Mexico, 1849. Phil., 1852. 8—50.
—— of an Irish gentleman in search of a religion. Moore, T. Balt., n. d. E.
—— through Louisiana. Bossu, J. A. Lond., 1771. 2 v. 10—58.
—— through the Canadas. Heriot, G. Lond., 1807. 8—47.
—— through the interior parts of North America. Carver, J. Lond., 1778. 8—49.

Travels to the equinoctial regions of America. Humboldt, F. H. A. *von.* Lond., 1852. 3 v. 8—50.
—— to the Pacific ocean. Lewis, M., and W. Clarke. Lond., 1815. 3 v. 10—58.

Treasury of thought. Ballou, M. M. Bost., 1872. 2—7.

Treaties and conventions made since July 4th, 1776. Senate ex. doc. No. 36, 41st Cong., 3d session. Wash., 1871. X.
——, declarations of war, manifestoes, and other public papers relating to peace and war among the potentates of Europe, from 1495 to the present time. Lond., 1710. 3 v. 33—201.
—— between the United States of America and the several Indian tribes, from 1778 to 1837 ; compiled and printed by the direction, and under the supervision, of the commissioner of Indian affairs. Wash., 1837. X.

Tredgold, Thomas. Principles of warming and ventilating public buildings, dwelling-houses, manufactories, etc. Lond., 1824. 15—88.
—— Elementary principles of carpentry. Illus. Phil., 1847. T.

Trench, Richard Chenevix. On the study of words: lectures. N. Y., 1868. 14—81.

Trenton falls. Illus. Willis, N. P. N. Y., 1851. 17—102.

Trevelyan, G. Otto. The life and letters of Lord Macaulay. N. Y., 1876. 2 v. 11—59.

Trial, The: sequel to the "Daisy chain." Illus. Yonge, C. M. Lond. and N. Y., 1871. 5—30.

*Tribune almanac; 1838 to 1868. N. Y., 1868. 2 v. 24—141.

Tricotrin. "Ouida." Phil., 1871. 7—44.

Tried for her life: a sequel to "Cruel as the grave." Southworth, E. D. E. N. Phil., 1871. 6—36.

Tristram, Henry Baker. The seven golden candlesticks. Illus. Lond., n. d. 28—165.

Trollope, Anthony. The vicar of Bullhampton: a novel. Illus. N. Y., 1870. 5—28.
—— The Claverings: a novel. N. Y., 1871. 5—28.

Trollope, Anthony. Last chronicle of Barset. Illus. N. Y., 1867. 5—28.
—— Can you forgive her ? Illus. N. Y., n. d. 5—28.
—— Orley farm: a novel. Illus. N. Y., 1871. 5—28.
—— Phineas Finn, the Irish member: a novel. Illus. N. Y., 1868. 5—28.
—— He knew he was right. Illus. N. Y., 1870. 5—28.
—— Ralph, the heir: a novel. Illus. N. Y., 1871. 6—35.
—— The small house at Allington: a novel. Illus. N. Y., 1868. 5—28.
—— The Eustace diamonds: a novel. N. Y., 1872. 5—28.
—— Doctor Thorne: a novel. N. Y., 1870. 7—43.
—— The three clerks: a novel. N. Y., 1868. 7—43.
—— The Belton estate. Phil., 1866. 7—43.
—— Barchester towers. Phil., n. d. 7—43.
—— The Bertrams: a novel. N. Y., 1871. 7—43. .
—— Castle Richmond: a novel. N. Y., 1862. 7—43.
—— Rachel Ray: a novel. Lond., n. d. 7—43.
—— Miss Mackenzie. Lond., n. d. 7—43.
—— The Kellys and the O'Kellys: a novel. N. Y., 1860. 7—43.
—— Framley parsonage: a novel. N. Y., 1871. 7—43.
—— North America. N. Y., 1863. 17—104.
—— The golden lion of Grandpère: a novel. Illus. N. Y., 1872. 5—28.
—— Harry Heathcote of Gangoil: a tale of Australian bush-life; and Lady Anna: a novel. N. Y., 1874. 5—28.
—— Sir Harry Hotspur of Humblethwaite. Illus. N. Y., 1871. 5—28.
—— The struggles of Brown, Jones, and Robinson, by one of the firm. N. Y., 1873. 5—28.
—— Phineas Redux: a novel. Illus. N. Y., 1874. 5—28.
—— The West Indies and the Spanish main. N. Y., n. d. 9—53.
—— The way we live now: a novel. Illus. N. Y., 1875. 5—28.

Tyndall, John. Heat considered as a mode of motion. Illus. N. Y., 1869. 15—88.

—— Sound : a course of eight lectures. Illus. N. Y., 1867. 15—39.

—— Fragments of science for unscientific people : a series of detached essays, lectures, and reviews. N. Y., 1872. 15—89.

—— The forms of water in clouds, rivers, ice, and glaciers. Illus. N. Y., 1872. 14—83.

—— Light and electricity : notes of two courses of lectures before the Royal Institution of Great Britain. N. Y., 1871. 15—89.

—— Faraday as a discoverer. N. Y., 1873. 11—64.

—— Hours of exercise in the Alps. Illus. N. Y., 1873. 15—89.

—— Contributions to molecular physics in the domain of radiant heat. Illus. N. Y., 1873. 15—88.

Types of mankind. Illus. Nott, J. C. and G. R. Gliddon. Phil., 1854. 14—80.

Tyson, George E. Arctic experiences. Illus. N. Y., 1874. 17—102.

Tytler, Alexander Fraser. Elements of general history, ancient and modern, with a history of the United States, by an American gentleman ; and a table of chronology, etc. Concord, *N. H.*, 1851. 32—193.

Tytler, Patrick Fraser. England under the reigns of Edward the sixth and Mary. Lond. 1839. 2 v. 34—207.

Tytler, Sarah. The Huguenot family. N. Y., 1868. P—2.

Unawares. "S. B. A. Moslih-Eddin." Bost., 1872. 7—46.

Uncivilized races of men. Illus. Wood, J. G. Hartford, 1871. 2 v. 26—153.

Uncle Silas: a novel. Le Fanu, J. S. N. Y., n. d. 5—29.

—— Tom's cabin. Illus. Stowe, H. B. Bost., 1871. 6—35.

Uncommercial traveller. Illus. Dickens, C. 2 copies. 3—15 and 16.

Under the greenwood tree. Hardy, T. N. Y., 1874. 5—30.

—— the willows, and other poems. Lowell, J. R. Bost., 1869. 17—106.

Under two flags. "Ouida." Phil., 1867. 2 copies. 7—44.

—— foot: a novel. Clyde, A. Illus. N. Y., 1870. 6—35.

Underwood, Francis Henry. Lord of himself: a novel. Bost., 1874. 5—30.

Undine and other tales. Illus. La Motte-Fouqué, F. de. N. Y., 1871. 38.

Ungewitter, Francis H. Europe, past and present ; a comprehensive manual of European geography and history ; with separate descriptions and statistics of each state, and a copious index, facilitating reference to every fact in the history and present state of Europe. N. Y. and Lond., 1850. 32—192.

Union Pacific Rail-Road Company, Affairs of the. House report No. 78, 42d Congress, 3d session. V.

United colonies, Political annals of the present. Chalmers, G. Lond., 1780. 33—197.

—— Netherlands, History of the. Motley, J. L. N. Y., 1868. 4 v. 36—218.

—— States, The ; its power and progress. Poussin, G. T. Phil., 1851. 29—175.

—— States and Mexican boundary survey, Report on the. Illus. Emory, W. H. Wash., 1859. 3 v. X.

—— States, Army and navy journal, and gazette of the regular and volunteer forces of the. 1863-65. N.Y. 2 v. D. R.

—— States fiscal department. Mayo, R. Wash., 1847. 2 v. D. R.

—— States, History of the. Bancroft, G. Bost., 1850-74. 10 v. 2 copies. 29—174.

—— States, History of the. Hildreth, R. N. Y., 1851-60. 1st and 2d series. 6 v. 29—174.

—— States of America, The. Illus. Murray, H. Edin., 1844. 3 v. 29—177.

—— States of America, History of the. Illus. Hinton, J. H. Lond., n. d. 6 v. 29—175.

—— States of North America, History of the. Grahame, J. Phil, 1850. 2 v. 29—176.

—— States of North America. Warden, D. B. Edin., 1819. 3 v. 29—175.

* —— States bounties and premiums, A table of. Seville, W. P. Wash., 1865. L.

—— States, A comic history of the. Illus. Hopkins, L. N. Y., 1876. 41—227.

United States, A popular history of the. Illus. Ridpath, J. C. Cin., 1876. 29—174.

—— States, The foundations of civil order and political life in the. Mulford, E. N. Y., 1875. 40—224.

*—— States during its first century, Biographical annals of the civil government of the. Lanman, C. Wash., 1876. 22—132.

—— States, The constitutional and political history of the :—1750-1833. Holtz, H. von. Chic., 1876. 40—224.

—— States of America, The governmental history of the. Sherman, H. Hartford, 1860. 29—177.

Unity of law, The. Cary, H. C. Phil., 1872. 15—87.

*Universal exhibition, Illustrated catalogue of the, published with the Art journal. Lond., 1867. 26—153.

—— geography, The London atlas of. Arrowsmith, J. Lond., 1842. U.

—— history. Müller, J. von. Bost., 1837. 4 v. 32—193.

—— progress, Illustrations of. Spencer, H. N. Y., 1868. 14—84.

Universe and the coming transits, The. Illus. Proctor, R. A. Lond., 1874. 14—82.

Unkind word, The; and other stories. Muloch, D. M. N. Y., 1872. 4—23.

Unknown river, The. Illus. Hamerton, P. G. Bost., 1872. 28—165.

Unseen universe; or, physical speculations on a future state. N. Y., 1875. 14—81.

—— world, The. Fiske, J. Bost., 1876. 40—222.

Unto this last. Ruskin, J. N. Y., 1866. 15—89.

Uplands and lowlands. Porter, R. N. Y., n. d. 6—38.

Upper Mississippi. Gale, G. Illus. Chicago, 1867. 9—53.

—— Rhine, The. Illus. Mayhew, H. Lond., 1858. 17—102.

Ups and downs. Hale, E. E. Bost., 1873. 5—34.

Ure, Andrew. *A dictionary of arts, manufactures, and mines; containing a clear exposition of their principles and practice. Illus. N. Y., 1848. 22—133.

Ure, Andrew. A new system of geology, in which the great revolutions of the earth and animated nature are reconciled at once to modern science and sacred history. Illus. Lond., 1829. 15—91.

—— The philosophy of manufactures; or, an exposition of the scientific, moral, and commercial economy of the factory system of Great Britain. Lond., 1835. T.

—— The cotton manufacture of Great Britain systematically investigated. Illus. Lond., 1836. 2 v. T.

Use of the body in relation to the mind, On the. Moore, G. N. Y., 1849. E.

Useful and entertaining tracts, A miscellany of. Chambers, W. and R. Edin., 1847. 10 v. 27—162.

Utah, Report of explorations across the great basin of the territory of. Illus. Simpson, Capt. J. H. Wash., 1876. D. R.

Vagabond adventures. Keeler, R. Bost., 1870. 17—104.

—— heroine, A. Edwards, A. N. Y., 1873. 7—46.

Vagabonds, The. Trowbridge, J. T. Bost., 1871. 17—106.

Vale of cedars, The. Aguilar, G. N. Y., 1872. 5—34.

Valentine, the countess. "Carl Detlef." Phil., 1874. 5—30.

—— Vox, the ventriloquist. Cockton, H. Phil., n. d. 6—35.

Valerie, an autobiography. Illus. Marryat, Capt. F. Lond. and N. Y., n. d. 5—30.

—— Aylmer: a novel. "Christian Reid." N. Y., 1872. 5—23.

Valley of the Mississippi, History of the discovery and settlement of the. Monette, J. W. N. Y., 1848. 2 v. 29—176.

Van Buren, Martin. Inquiry into the origin and course of political parties in the United States. N. Y., 1867. 26—154.

—— , The life and political opinions of. Holland, W. M. Hartford, 1835. 11—64.

Van Dewall, M. A great lady: a romance. Illus. M. S., tr. Phil., 1874. 5—28.

Van Rensselaer, Jeremiah. Lectures on geology, delivered in the New York atheneum in the year 1825. N. Y., 1825. 15—91.

Van Santvoord, George. Life of Algernon Sidney; with sketches of some of his contemporaries, and extracts from his correspondence and political writings. N. Y., 1853. 11—64.

—— Sketches of the lives and judicial services of the chief justices of the supreme court of the United States. N.Y., 1854. 12—69.

Van Walrée, E. C. W. See Walrée, E. C. W., *van.*

Vane, *Sir* Henry, Life of. (Library of American biography, vol. 4.) 11—65.

Vanity fair. Illus. Thackeray, W. M. Lond., 1869. 2 v. 2 copies. 5—32.

Vashti; or, until death do us part. Evans, A. J. N. Y., 1874. 7—44.

Vattel, Emmeric de. *The law of nations; or, principles of the law of nature applied to the conduct and affairs of nations and sovereigns. J. Chitty, tr. Phil., 1849. 21—128.

Vaughan, Henry, the sacred poems and private ejaculations of; with a memoir by the *Rev.* H. F. Lyte. Bost., 1854. 16—98.

Vegetable world, The. Illus. Figuier, L. Lond. and N. Y., n. d. 14—82.

Vegetation, First forms of. Illus. Macmillan, H. Lond., 1874. 14—85.

——, The wonders of. Illus. Marion, F. N. Y., 1874. 28—169.

Venegas, Miguel. A natural and civil history of California. Lond., 1759. 2 v. 31—187.

Venetia. Disraeli, B. Lond., 1871. 4—24.

Venetian history, Sketches from. Illus. Lond., 1846. 2 v. 35—212.

—— life. Howells, W. D. N. Y., 1867. 17—104.

Ventilation and lighting of the house, Report from the select committee on. Lond., 1852. D. R.

Vergennes, Charles Gravier de. Mémoire historique et politique sur la Louisiane. Paris, 1802. W.

Vermont, History of. Illus. Thompson, Z. Burlington, 1842. 30—183.

——, The natural and civil history of. Williams, S. Burlington, *Vt.*, 1809. 2 v. 30—183.

Verne, Jules. The fur country; or, seventy degrees north latitude. Illus. N. D'Anvers, tr. Bost., 1874. 5—31.

Verne, Jules. Twenty thousand leagues under the seas; or, the marvellous and exciting adventures of Pierre Aronnax, Conseil, his servant, and Ned Land, a Canadian harpooner. Illus. Bost., 1874. 5—31.

—— A floating city, and the blockade runners. Illus. N. Y., 1874. 5—31.

—— From the earth to the moon direct in ninety-seven hours and twenty minutes; and a trip round it. Illus. L. Mercier and Eleanor E. King, trs. N. Y., 1874. 5—31.

—— Meridiana: the adventures of three Englishmen and three Russians in South Africa. Illus. N. Y., 1874. 5—31.

—— A journey to the north pole. Illus. Lond. and N. Y., 1875. 5—31.

—— A journey to the center of the earth; containing a complete account of the wonderful and thrilling adventures of the intrepid subterranean explorers, Prof. von Hardwigg, his nephew Harry, and their Icelandic guide, Hans Bjelke. Illus. Bost., n. d. 5—31.

—— From the clouds to the mountains; comprising narratives of strange adventures by air, land, and water; with a chapter by Paul Verne, brother of Jules Verne. A. L. Alger, tr. Illus. Bost., 1874. 5—31.

—— A tour of the world in eighty days. G. M. Towle, tr. Bost., 1874. 5—31.

—— The mysterious island: the modern Robinson Crusoe. Illus. W. H. G. Kingston, tr. N. Y., 1876. 5—31.

—— Doctor Ox's experiment, and other stories. G. M. Towle, tr. Bost., 1874. 5—31.

—— The field of ice. Illus. Lond. and N. Y., 1875. 5—31.

—— The wreck of the Chancellor. G. M. Towle, tr. Bost., 1875. 5—31.

—— The survivors of the Chancellor: diary of J. R. Kazallon, passenger. Ellen Frewer, tr. Illus. Bost., 1876. 5—31.

—— Voyages and adventures of Captain Hatteras: the English at the north pole. Lond., n. d. 5—31.

—— Michael Strogoff, the courier of the Czar. Illus. W. H. G. Kingston, tr. N. Y., 1877. 5—31.

Verner's pride: a tale of domestic life. Wood, E. P. Phil., n. d. 41—230.

Véronique: a romance. Marryat, *Miss* F. Bost., n. d. 6—35.

Vertot D'Aubeuf, René Aubert de. The history of the revolutions that happened in the government of the Roman republic. Lond., 1724. 2 v. 35—211.
—— The revolutions of Portugal. Lond., 1721. 36—217.
—— The history of the revolutions in Spain. Lond., 1724. 36—217.
—— The history of the knights hospitallers of St. John of Jerusalem ; styled afterwards the knights of Rhodes, and, at present, the knights of Malta. Edin., 1757. 5 v. 30—184.

Vestiges of the natural history of creation, with a sequel. Chambers, R. N. Y., 1846. 28—170.

Viardot, Louis. Wonders of European art. (Illustrated library of wonders.) N. Y., 1874. 28—169.
—— Wonders of Italian art. (Illustrated library of wonders.) N. Y., 1872. 28—169.
—— Wonders of sculpture. (Illustrated library of wonders.) N. Y., 1873. 28—169.

Vicar of Bullhampton, The. Illus. Trollope, A. N. Y., 1870. 5—28.
—— of Wakefield, The. Illus. Goldsmith, O. Lond. and N. Y., n. d. 2—7.
—— Same, with a memoir by the *Rev.* R. A. Willmott. Lond., n. d. 5—33.

Vicar's daughter, The : sequel to "Annals of a quiet neighbourhood." Illus. MacDonald, G. Bost., 1872. 7—45.

Vicat, Louis Joseph. A practical and scientific treatise on calcareous mortars and cements, artificial and natural. *Capt.* J. T. Smith, tr. Lond., 1837. T.

Vicomte de Bragelonne, The. Dumas, A. D. N. Y., and Lond., n. d. 2 v. 5—31.

Victor Norman, rector. Denison, M. A. Phil., 1873. O—2.

Victorian poets. Stedman, E. C. Bost., 1876. 19—116.

Victories of love, The. Patmore, C. Lond., 1863. 16—100.

Victor's triumph : sequel to "A beautiful fiend." Southworth, E. D. E. N. Phil., 1874. 6—36.

Victory of the vanquished, The. Charles, E. N. Y., n. d. 3—20.

Vienna international exhibition in 1873, Reports of the commissioners of the United States to the. Illus. Robert H. Thurston, ed. Wash., 1876. 4 v. 24—141.

Contents.

Vol. 1. Introduction ; Executive commission ; Agriculture ; The exhibition, its antecedents, inception, organization, and results ; Abstracts of foreign reports on exhibits from the United States ; Report of Hon. H. Garretson ; Report on forestry, by J. A. Warder ; Sheep and wool, by J. R. Dodge.
Vol. 2. Science ; Education :—Report on chemicals, by J. L. Smith ; on Vienna bread, by E. N. Horsford ; on commercial fertilizers, by P. Collier ; on photography, by C. A. Doremus ; on medicine and surgery, by A. Ruppaner ; on physical apparatus, by W. Gibbs ; on instruments of precision, by C. F. Carpenter and R. D. Cutts ; on telegraphy, by R. B. Lines ; on telegraphs and apparatus, by D. Brooks ; on education, by E. Seguin and J. W. Hoyt ; on deaf-mute instruction and governmental patronage of art, by E. M. Gallaudet ; on printing, by G. W. Silcox and A. H. Brown.
Vol. 3. Engineering :—Manufactures and machinery, R. H. Thurston ; Sewing-machines, G. A. Fairfield ; Civil engineering and architecture, W. Watson ; Hydraulic engineering, C. Davis.
Vol. 4. Architecture ; Metallurgy ; General index :—Construction of dwellings in Vienna, J. R. Niernsee ; Architecture and materials, N. L. Derby ; Wood industries, N. M. Lowe ; Working of stone and artificial stone, L. J. Hinton ; Metallurgy of iron and steel, W. P. Blake ; Metallurgy of lead, silver, copper, and zinc, H. Painter ; General index.

Views a-foot. Taylor, J. B. N. Y., 1870. 17—103.
—— along the boundary between the United States and Mexico. Q—1.

Vikram and the vampire. Illus. Burton, R. F. N. Y., n. d. P—2.

Villa Eden. Auerbach, B. Bost., 1870. 6—35.
—— on the Rhine, The. Auerbach, B. N. Y., 1874. 2 v. 41—226.
NOTE.—"The villa on the Rhine" is the tale "Villa Eden," republished under another title.

Villes anséatiques. (L'Univers.) Rochelle. Paris, 1844. D. R.

Villette. "Currer Bell." N. Y., n. d. 2 copies. 7—45.

Vincent, Frank, *jr.* The land of the white elephant : sights and scenes in South-Eastern Asia : a personal narrative of travel and adventure in Farther India, embracing the countries of Burma, Siam, Cambodia, and Cochin-China; 1871-74. Illus. N. Y., 1874. 17—101.

Vincenzo; or, sunken rocks. Ruffini, G. Lond. 1863. 3 v. in one. 2 copies. 6—35 and 40.

Viollet-le-Duc, Eugene Emmanuel. The habitations of men in all ages. Illus. B. Bucknall, tr. Bost., 1876. 14—80.

Virgilius Maro, Publius, (Virgil,) Works of. Wrangham, Sotheby, and Dryden, trs. Lond., 1830. 2 v. 17—107.

Contents.
Vol. 1. Biographical sketch of Virgil; The eclogues; The Georgics; The Æneid.
Vol. 2. The Æneid, concluded.

——, Æneid of. J. Conington, tr. N. Y., 1867. 16—95.

—— Same; with English notes. Bowen, F. Bost., 1860. T.

—— The Æneids of, done into English verse by William Morris. Bost., 1876. 17—105.

Virginia, Acts of assembly passed in the colony of, 1662 to 1715. Lond., 1727. D. R.

——, A history of. Howison, R. R. Phil., 1846-48. 2 v. 31—188.

—— illustrated. "Porte Crayon." N.Y., 1857. 24—141.

——, Introduction to the history of the colony and ancient dominion of. Campbell, C. Richmond, 1847. 31—188.

——, Notes on the state of. Jefferson, T. Trenton, 1803. 31—188.

——, Old churches, ministers, and families of. Illus. Meade, W. Phil., 1857. 2 v. 31—188.

——, Sketches of. Foote, W. H. Phil., 1850. 1st and 2d series. 2 v. 31—188.

——, The history of. Burk, J. Petersburgh, 1804-05. 3 v. 31—188.

——, History of. Illus. Richmond, 1819. 31—188.

——, History of, commenced by John Burk, and continued by Skelton Jones and Louis Hue Girardin. Petersburgh, 1816. 31—188.

Virginians, The. Illus. Thackeray, W. M. Lond., 1869. 2 v. 2 copies. 5—32.

Vision, The. Dante Alighieri. Lond., 1819. 3 v. 16—95.

Vivia; or, the secret of power. Southworth, E. D. E. N. Phil., 1857. 6—37.

Vivian Grey, and other tales. Disraeli, B. Lond. and N. Y., n. d. 4—24.

Vocabulary; or, collection of words and phrases which have been supposed to be peculiar to the United States of America. Pickering, J. Bost., 1816. V.

Volcanos, active and extinct, earthquakes, and thermal springs. Daubeny, C. Lond., 1848. 15—89.

Volckhausen, Ad. von. Why did he not die ? or, the child from the Ebräergang. Mrs. A. L. Wister, tr. Phil., 1872. 0—1.

Voltaire, François-Marie Arouet. Œuvres complètes de. Illus. Paris, 1864. 13 v. W.

—— History of the Russian empire, under Peter the great. Aberdeen, 1777. 13—78.

—— A discourse on the history of Charles the twelfth, king of Sweden. Lond., 1732. 11—60.

—— The age of Louis the fourteenth. Lond., 1752. 2 v. 12—72.

Von Auer, Adelheid. See Auer, A. von.

Von Borcke, Heros. See Borcke, Heros von.

Von Hillern, Wilhelmine. See Hillern, W. von.

Von Volckhausen, Ad. See Volckhausen, A. von.

Voyage dans les États-Unis d'Amérique, fait en 1795-97. La Rochefoucauld-Liancourt, F. A. F. Paris, n. d. 8 v. W.

—— dans les deux Louisianes. Perrin du Lac, F. M. Lyon, 1805. W.

—— round the world. Illus. Belcher, *Sir* E. Lond., 1843. 2 v. 8—49.

—— to the Pacific and Beering's strait. Beechey, F. W. Phil., 1832. 2 copies. 8—47.

—— up the Amazon river. Edwards, W. H. N. Y., 1847. 9—53.

—— of the Jamestown on her errand of mercy. Bost., 1847. L.

Voyages and adventures of Captain Hatteras : the English at the north pole. Verne, J. Lond., n. d. 5—31.

—— and travels of Captains Lewis and Clarke, A journal of the. Gass, P. Phil., 1810. 9—50.

Voyages and travels, A collection of; with an account of the progress of navigation from its first beginning. Illus. Lond., 1732-45. 8 v. 10—55.

——— du sieur de Champlain ; ou, journal òs decouvertes de la Nouvelle France. Paris, 1830. 2 v. W.

——— from China to America. Meares, J. Lond., 1791. 2 v. 8—48.

——— to the frozen ocean. Mackenzie, A. Lond., 1801. 9—55.

Vue de la colonie espagnole du Missisipi, ou des provinces de Louisiane et Floride occidentale, en l'année 1802. Berguin-Duvallon. Paris, 1804. W.

Wade, John. British history chronologically arranged; comprehending a classified analysis of events and occurrences in church and state, and of the constitutional, political, commercial, intellectual, and social progress of the united kingdom, from the first invasion by the Romans to A. D. 1847. Lond., 1848, 32—192.

Wager of battle: a tale of Saxon slavery in Sherwood forest. Herbert, W. H. N. Y., 1855. P—3.

Wages question, The. Walker, F. A. N. Y., 1876. 40—225.

Waiting for the verdict. Illus. Davis, R. H. N. Y., 1868. 6—39.

Walden. Thoreau, H. D. Bost., 1874. 9—53.

Waldfried: a novel. Auerbach, B. S. A. Stern, tr. N. Y., 1874. 7—46.

Walford, L. B. Mr. Smith; a part of his life. N. Y., 1875. 41—228.

Walker, Amasa. The science of wealth: a manual of political economy, embracing the laws of trade, currency, and finance. Bost., 1867. 15—89.

Walker, Francis Amasa. The Indian question. Bost., 1874. 28—166.

——— The wages question : a treatise on wages and the wages class. N. Y., 1876. 40—225.

Walker, Joseph Cooper. Historical memoir on Italian tragedy, from the earliest period to the present time; illustrated with specimens and analysis of the most celebrated tragedies; and in-

terspersed with occasional observations on the Italian theatres ; and biographical notices of the principal tragic writers of Italy. Illus. Lond., 1799. 25—152.

Walker. William. The war in Nicaragua. Mobile, 1860. 36—217.

Walks from Eden. Illus. "Elizabeth Wetherell." N. Y., 1873. 7—42.

Wallace, Alfred Russel. The geographical distribution of animals; with a study of the relations of living and extinct faunas as elucidating the past changes of the earth's surface. Illus. N. Y., 1876. 2 v. 24—141.

——— The Malay archipelago; the land of the orang-utan, and the bird of paradise: a narrative of travel, with studies of man and nature. Illus. N. Y., 1869. 24—141.

Wallace, D. Mackenzie. Russia. N. Y., 1877. 40—225.

Wallace, Lew. The fair god; or, the last of the 'Tzins: a tale of the conquest of Mexico. Bost., 1873. O—1.

Waller, S. E. Six weeks in the saddle: a painter's journal in Iceland. Illus. Lond., 1874. 17—102.

Waln, Robert, jr. The hermit in Philadelphia, by Peter Atall. Phil., 1821. 2—12.

Walpole, Horace. Memoirs of the reign of King George the third. Lond., 1851. 4 v. 34—206.

——— Memoirs of the reign of King George the second. Lond., 1847. 3 v. 34—206.

——— The letters of Horace Walpole, earl of Orford. Illus. P. Cunningham, ed. Lond., 1861-66. 9 v. 40—223.

Walrée, E. C. W. van, (Christine Müller.) The burgomaster's family; or, weal and woe in a little world. Sir John Shaw Lefevre, tr. Lond., 1872. 6—39.

Walter Goring. Thomas, A. N. Y., 1866. 5—28.

Wanderer, The. Burney, F. Lond., 1814. 5 v. 7—46.

Wandering Jew, The. "Eugene Sue." Lond. and N. Y., n. d. 4—21.

War in the southern department of the United States, Memoirs of the. Lee, H. Wash., 1827. 30—181.

——— in West Florida and Louisiana, Historical memoir of the. Latour, A. L. Phil., 1816. 30—179.

War of the rebellion, The pictorial book of anecdotes and incidents of the. Kirkland, F. Hartford, 1866. 2—7.

—— of the independence of the United States of America, History of the. Botta, C. New Haven, 1838. 2 v. 30—179.

—— of 1812, The pictorial field-book of the. Lossing, B. J.⸱ N. Y., 1868. 30—178.

—— of the succession in Spain, History of the. Mahon, *Lord.* Lond., 1836. 36—218.

—— with America, France, Spain, and Holland, History of the. Illus. Andrews, J. Lond., 1785-86. 4 v. 33—199.

—— with Great Britain, Official letters of the military and naval officers of the United States during the. Brannan, J. Wash., 1823. 30—179.

—— with Mexico, The. Ripley, R. S. N. Y., 1849. 2 v. 30—179.

Warburton, Eliot. Memoirs of Prince Rupert and the cavaliers; including their private correspondence. Illus. Lond., 1849. 3 v. 12—67.

Ward, Artemus, *pseud.* See Browne, C. F.

Ward, Artemus: the genial showman. Illus. Hingston, E. P. Lond., 1870. 11—60.

Ward, James H. A manual of naval tactics; with a brief critical analysis of the principal modern naval battles. N. Y., 1859. R—2.

Ward, *Sir* Henry George. Mexico in 1827. Lond., 1828. 2 v. 32—191.

Ward, Robert Plumer. Fielding, or, society; Atticus, or, the retired statesman; and St. Lawrence. Phil., 1837. 3 v. in one. O—3.

Ward, Samuel, Life of. (Library of American biography, vol. 19.) 11—65.

Ward, Thomas. England's reformation: a poem. Balt., n. d. 17—107.

Warden, David Baillie. Recherches historiques et politiques sur les États-Unis de l'Amérique septentrionale; par un citoyen de Virginie. Paris, 1788. 4 v. W.

—— L'art de vérifier les dates: chronologie historique de l'Amérique. Paris, 1826-44. 10 v. D. R.

—— United States of North America: a statistical, political, and historical account, from the period of their first colonization to the present day. Edin., 1819. 3 v. 29—175.

Warden, Robert B. An account of the private life and public services of Salmon Portland Chase. Cin., 1874. 11—59.

Warfield, Catherine Anne. The household of Bouverie; or, the elixir of gold: a romance. N. Y., 1860. 2 v. 7—41.

—— The romance of the green seal. N. Y., 1866. 6—35.

—— Hester Howard's temptation: a soul's story. Phil., 1875. 7—41.

Waring, George Edwin, *jr.* A farmer's vacation. ⸱Illus. Bost., 1876. 10—56.

Warming and ventilating. Arnott, N. Lond., 1838. T.

—— and ventilating, Principles of. Tredgold, T. Lond., 1824. 15—88.

—— and ventilating, On the history and art of. Illus. Bernan, W. Lond., 1845. R—2.

Warner, Anna B. Dollars and cents. Phil., 1871. 7—43.

—— My brother's keeper. Phil., 1873. 7—42.

—— The star out of Jacob. Illus. N. Y., 1873. 7—42.

Warner, Charles Dudley. My winter on the Nile, among the mummies and Moslems. Illus. Hartford, 1876. 10—56.

—— In the Levant. Bost., 1877. 10—56.

Warner, Oliver. Twenty-third report to the legislature of Massachusetts, relating to the registration of births, marriages, and deaths in the commonwealth for the year ending Dec. 31, 1864. Bost., 1866. D. R.

Warner, Susan, (*Elizabeth Wetherell.*) Queechy. Phil., 1871. 2 v. in one. 7—42.

—— The house in town: a sequel to "Opportunities." N. Y., 1872. 7—42.

—— Trading: finishing the story of the "House in town." Illus. N. Y., 1873. 7—42.

—— " What she could :" first of a series consisting of " What she could," " Opportunities," " The house in town," and " Trading." Illus. N. Y., 1872. 7—42.

—— Opportunities: a sequel to "What she could." Illus. N. Y., 1871. 7—42.

Warner, Susan, (*Elizabeth Wetherell.*)
The old helmet. N. Y., 1874. 7—42.

—— The hills of the Shatemuc. Phil.,
1873. 7—42.

—— Daisy. Phil., 1873. 2 v. in one.
7—42.

—— Melbourne house. Illus. N. Y.,
1874. 2 v. in one. 7—42.

—— The wide, wide world. Phil., 1876.
2 v. in one. 7—42.

—— The house of Israel. Illus. N. Y.,
1872. 7—42.

—— Walks from Eden. Illus. N. Y.,
1873. 7—42.

—— Sceptres and crowns. Illus. N.
Y., 1875. 7—42.

—— and Anna. Say and seal. Phil.,
1870. 2 v. in one. 7—42.

—— The rapids of Niagara. Illus. N.
Y., 1876. 7—42.

Warren, Joseph. An oration delivered
March 6, 1775, to commemorate the
bloody tragedy of the 5th of March, 1770.
Bost., 1775. 27—160.

——, The life of. (Library of American
biography, vol. 10.) 11—65.

Warren, Samuel. Passages from the
diary of a late physician. N. Y., 1871.
3 v. in one. 7—45.

—— Ten thousand a year: a novel.
Phil., n. d. 6—35.

—— Now and then :—" through a glass,
darkly." N. Y., 1843. 7—45.

Warwick, *Sir* Philip. Memoirs of the
reigne of King Charles the first, with a
continuation to the happy restauration
of King Charles the second. Lond.,
1701. 11—65.

Was he successful? Kimball, R. B. N.
Y. and Leipsic, 1864. 4—25.

Washburn, Katharine Sedgwick. The
Italian girl. Bost., 1874. 41—227.

Washington, George. Farewell address to the people of the United States.
Phil., 1858. V.

——, The writings of, with a life of the
author. Sparks, J. N. Y., 1847-48. 12
v. 25—149.

——, Life of. Irving, W. N. Y., 1855-59.
5 v. 13—74.

——, Life of, during the war and the
presidency. Marshall, J. Phil., 1850.
2 v. 13—74.

Washington and his generals. Headley,
J. T. N. Y., 1875. 2 v. in one. Q—2.

——, The house of; or, Mount Vernon
and its associations. Illus. Lossing, B.
J. N. Y., 1870. 26—155.

Water-babies, The. Kingsley, C. Bost.,
1869. 38.

Waterloo: a sequel to " The conscript of
1813." Illus. Erckmann, E., and A.
Chatrian. N. Y., 1872. 5—31.

Waterston, William. *A cyclopædia
of commerce, mercantile law, finance,
commercial geography, and navigation;
with an essay on commerce, by J. R. Mc-
Culloch. Lond., 1843. 21—128.

Water-witch, The. Illus. Cooper, J. F.
N. Y., 1871. 3—14.

Watson, Elkanah. Men and times of
the revolution. W. C. Watson, ed. N.
Y., 1856. 12—68.

Watson, John F. Annals and occurrences of New York city and state in the
olden time. Phil., 1846. 31—190.

—— Annals of Philadelphia and Pennsylvania in the olden time. Illus. Phil.,
1845. 2 v. 31—189.

Watson, Robert. The history of the
reign of Philip the second, king of Spain,
and of Philip the third, king of Spain.
N. Y., 1818. 2 v. in one. 12—68.

Watts, Isaac. Horæ lyricæ; with a life
of the author, by Robert Southey. Bost.,
1864. 16—97.

Waverly. Scott, *Sir* W. Bost., 1868.
3—17.

Way we live now, The: a novel. Illus.
Trollope, A. N. Y., 1875. 5—28.

Wayne, Anthony, Life and services of.
Illus. Moore, H. N. Phil., 1845. 13—79.

——, Life of. (Library of American biography, vol. 4.) 11—65.

Ways of the hour, The. Illus. Cooper,
J. F. N. Y., 1870. 3—14.

We and our neighbors: sequel to "My
wife and I." Illus. Stowe, H. B. N. Y.,
1875. 6—35.

—— boys: written by one of us for the
amusement of pa's and ma's in general,
aunt Lovisa in particular. Bost., 1876.
39.

—— girls. Illus. Whitney, A. D. T.
Bost., 1872. 7—44.

Weale, John. London, exhibited in 1851; elucidating its natural and physical characteristics, its antiquity and architecture, its arts, manufactures, trade, and organization, etc. Illus. Lond., n. d. 27—160.

———— Rudimentary dictionary of terms used in civil and naval architecture, building and construction, early and ecclesiastical art, civil and mechanical engineering, fine art, mining and surveying. Lond., 1849-50. 21—128.

———— Bridges: in theory, practice, and architecture. Lond., 1839. 2 v. T.

———— Portfolio of ancient capital letters, monograms, quaint designs, etc., etc., colored and tinted. Illus. Lond., 1858-59. V.

Webster, Daniel, The works of. Bost., 1851. 6 v. 25—148.

————, Life of. Curtis, G. T. N. Y., 1870. 2 v. 12—66.

————, The diplomatic and official papers of, while secretary of state. N. Y., 1848. 18—109.

Webster, Leland A. Present status of the philosophy of society: a treatise designed to show the insufficiency of existing systems of thought concerning the phenomena of society, and the tendencies toward a larger system; being part of a series comprising a complete review, historical and critical, of the progress of thought in social philosophy: which review is itself intended as a general introduction to a complete and exhaustive inquiry into the causes which determine the social condition of mankind; embodying the outlines of a thorough philosophy of society, and a complete science of sociology. N. Y., 1866. 14—84.

Webster, Noah. *An American dictionary of the English language. Springfield, Mass., 1872. 22—131.

Wedding garments; or, Bessie Morris's diary. McLain, M. W. N. Y., 1875. P—1.

Wedding-day in all ages and countries, The. Wood, E. J. N. Y., 1869. 28—169.

*Weekly register. Niles, H. Balt. and Phil., 1811-49. 76 v. D. R.

Weil, Gustav. The Bible, the Koran, and the Talmud; or, biblical legends of the Mussulmans. N. Y., 1846. E.

Wellington, Arthur, *duke of,* Life and campaigns of. Wright, G. N. Lond., 1839-41. 4 v. 11—62.

Wells, David Ames. The year-book of agriculture. Illus. Phil., 1856. D. R.

Wells, J. W. An alphabetical list of the battles (with dates) of the war of the rebellion. Pamphlet. Wash., 1875. M.

Wells, William Vincent. Explorations and adventures in Honduras, comprising sketches of travel in the gold regions of Olancho, and a review of the history and general resources of Central America. Illus. N. Y., 1857. 9—51.

Wenderholme: a story of Lancashire and Yorkshire. Hamerton, P. G. Bost., 1876. 41—227.

Wept of the Wish-ton-wish, The. Illus. Cooper, J. F. N. Y., 1864. 3—14.

Weppner, Margaretha. The north star and the southern cross: being the personal experiences, impressions, and observations, in a two years' journey round the world. Lond., 1876. 2 v. 40—222.

Werner, Ernest, *pseud.* At the altar. Phil., 1872. O—1.

———— "Good luck!" Frances A. Shaw, tr. Bost., 1874. 4—21.

———— Broken chains. F. A. Shaw, tr. Bost., 1875. 41—230.

———— A hero of the pen. F. A. Shaw, tr. Bost., 1875. 41—230.

Wesley, *Rev.* John, The life and times of the. Tyerman, L. N. Y., 1872. 3 v. 12—69.

West Indies and the Spanish main, The. Trollope, A. N. Y., n. d. 9—53.

———— Lawn and the rector of St. Mark's. Holmes, M. J. N. Y. and Lond., 1874. 7—42.

Western Africa. Illus. Wilson, J. L. N. Y., 1856. 36—215.

———— states, Notes on the. Hall, J. Phil., 1838. 29—177.

———— territory of North America, A topographical description of the. Imlay, G. Lond., 1797. 29—177.

———— Virginia, History of the early settlement and Indian wars of. Illus. De Hass, W. Wheeling, 1851. 31—188.

Western world; or, travels in the United States. Mackay, A. Phil., 1849. 2 v. 8—50.

Westminster review, The. 1839-60. 2 v. X.

Westward ho! Kingsley, C. Lond. and N. Y., 1871. 7—43.

Wetherell, Elizabeth, pseud. See Warner, Susan.

Wetmore, Alphonso. A gazetteer of the state of Missouri, with frontier sketches, and illustrations of Indian character. St. Louis, 1837. 31—186.

Wharton, Grace and Philip, pseud. See Thomson, K. B.

What answer? Dickinson, A. Bost., 1869. 2—13.

—— can she do? Roe, Rev. E. P. N. Y., 1873. 6—38.

—— I saw in California. Bryant, E. N. Y., 1848. 17—103.

—— I saw in New York. Illus. Ross, J. H. Auburn, 1851. R—2.

—— Katy did: a story. Illus. Coolidge, S. Bost., 1873. 38.

—— Katy did at school. Illus. Coolidge, S. Bost., 1874. 38.

"—— she could:" first of a series, consisting of "What she could," "Opportunities," "The house in town," and "Trading." Illus. "Elizabeth Wetherell." N. Y., 1872. 7—42.

—— the moon saw, and other tales. Illus. Andersen, H. C. Lond., 1871. 38.

—— the swallows sang: a novel. Spielhagen, F. N. Y., 1873. 6—36.

—— will he do with it? by Pisistratus Caxton. Bulwer-Lytton, Sir E. Phil., 1869. 2 v. 5—33.

Wheaton, Henry. *Elements of international law. Bost., 1855. 21—123.

—— Some account of the life, writings, and speeches of William Pinkney. N. Y., 1826. 12—68.

Wheeler, George M., lieut. U. S. A. Geographical and geological explorations and surveys west of the one hundredth meridian. Illus. Wash., 1875. Vols. 3 and 5. D. R.

—— Preliminary report, principally in Nevada and Arizona. Wash., 1872. D. R.

—— Same in Utah, Nevada, and Arizona, with a map. D. R.

Wheeler, George M., lieut. U. S. A. Report upon the determination of the astronomical co-ordinates of the primary stations at Cheyenne, Wyoming Territory, and Colorado Springs, Colorado Territory, made during the years 1872-73. Wash., 1874. D. R.

—— Report upon ornithological specimens collected in the years 1871, 1872, and 1873. Wash., 1874. D. R.

—— Progress report upon geographical and geological explorations and surveys in 1872, with illustrations and maps. Wash., 1874. D. R.

—— Catalogue of plants collected in the years 1871, 1872, and 1873, with descriptions of new species. Wash., 1874. D. R.

—— Appendix FF of the annual report of the chief of engineers for 1874. Pamphlet. Wash., 1874. D. R.

—— Preliminary report upon invertebrate fossils collected by the expeditions of 1871, 1872, and 1873, with descriptions of new species. Pamphlet. Wash., 1874. D. R.

—— Systematic catalogue of vertebrata of the eocene of New Mexico, collected in 1874. Wash., 1875. D. R.

—— Preliminary report upon a reconnaissance through Southern and Southeastern Nevada, made in 1869. Wash., 1875. D. R.

—— Appendix LL of the annual report of the chief of engineers for 1875, upon the geographical explorations and surveys west of the one hundredth meridian, with illustrations and maps. Wash., 1875. D. R.

—— Geological atlas projected to illustrate the explorations and surveys. Wash., 1874. D. R.

—— Topographical atlas, accompanying the reports. Wash., 1874. D. R.

Wheeler, Gervase. Homes for the people, in suburb and country; adapted to American climate and wants. Illus. N. Y., 1868. 15—90.

Wheeler, Henry G. Biographical and political history of congress. N. Y., 1848. 31—186.

Wheeler, J. Talboys. An analysis and summary of Herodotus. Lond., 1852. 35—210.

Wheeler, John H. Historical sketches of North Carolina, from 1584 to 1851. Illus. Phil., 1851. 2 v. in one. 31—188.

Wheeler, William A. An explanatory and pronouncing dictionary of the noted names of fiction; including familiar pseudonyms, surnames bestowed on eminent men, and analogous popular appellations often referred to in literature and conversation. Bost., 1872. 28—165.

Wheelock, Julia S. The boys in white: the experience of a hospital agent in and around Washington. N. Y., 1870. 2—13.

Whewell, William. History of the inductive sciences, from the earliest to the present time. N. Y., 1858. 2 v. 15—92.

—— The elements of morality, including polity. N. Y., 1845. 2 v. E.

Which shall it be? a novel. Alexander, *Mrs.* N. Y., 1874. 7—44.

Whipple, Edwin Percy. The literature of the age of Elizabeth. Bost., 1869. 28—166.

—— Character and characteristic men. Bost., 1871. 41—228.

—— Success and its conditions. Bost., 1875. 19—116.

Whispers from fairy land. Illus. Knatchbull-Hugessen, E. H. N. Y., 1875. 39.

Whitcher, Frances Miriam. The widow Bedott papers. Illus. N. Y., 1875. 2—8.

White, Andrew Dickson. The warfare of science. N. Y., 1876. 40—221.

White, Charles A. Report of the geological survey of the state of Iowa. Illus. Des Moines, 1870. 2 v. L.

White, Henry Kirke, Poetical works of; with a memoir by *Sir* Harry Nicolas. Bost., 1864. 16—97.

White, James. History of France, from the earliest times to 1848. N. Y., 1849. 35—214.

White, Richard Grant. Memoirs of the life of William Shakespeare; with an essay toward the expression of his genius, and an account of the rise and progress of the English drama. Bost., 1865. 13—76.

—— Words and their uses, past and present: a study of the English language. N. Y., 1871. 14—81.

White as snow. "Garrett, E. and R." N. Y., n. d. 3—15.

—— lies. Reade, C. N. Y., 1873. 5—28.

White phantom, The. Braddon, M. E. N. Y., 1868. 5—29.

Whitefield, *Rev.* George, Life of. Harsha, D. A. Albany, 1866. 13—76.

Whiteladies: a novel. Oliphant, M. O. W. N. Y., 1875. 41—227.

Whitney, Adeline Dutton Train. A summer in Leslie Goldthwaite's life. Illus. Bost., 1872. 7—44.

—— Real folks. Illus. Bost., 1872. 7—44.

—— We girls: a home story. Illus. Bost., 1872. 7—44.

—— The other girls. Illus. Bost., 1873. 7—44.

—— Hitherto: a story of yesterdays. Bost., 1869. 7—44.

—— Sights and insights: Patience Strong's story of over the way. Bost., 1876. 2 v. 7—44.

Whitney, Josiah Dwight. The metallic wealth of the United States, compared with that of other countries. Illus. Phil., 1854. T.

Whittaker, Frederick. A complete life of General George A. Custer. Illus. N. Y., n. d. 40—224.

Whittier, John Greenleaf. Old portraits and modern sketches. Bost., 1850. 2—13.

—— Leaves from Margaret Smith's journal in the province of Massachusetts bay; 1678-79. Bost., 1849. 27—162.

——, Poetical works of. Bost., 1872. 2 v. 16—99.

—— The Pennsylvania pilgrim, and other poems. Illus. Bost., 1872. 16—99.

—— Hazel-blossoms. Bost., 1875. 17—106.

Whittlesey, Charles. Early history of Cleveland, Ohio; including original papers and other matter relating to the adjacent country; with biographical notices of the pioneers and surveyors. Illus. Cleveland, 1867. 31—186.

"**Who** breaks—pays." Jenkin, C. N. Y., 1873. 6—38.

*"**Who's** who. C. H. Oakes, ed. Lond., 1850-55. 3 v. 18—112.

Why did he not die? Volckhausen, A. von. Phil., 1872. O—1.

—— we laugh. Cox, S. S. N. Y., 1876. 19—116.

Whymper, Frederick. Travel and adventure in the territory of Alaska, formerly Russian America, now ceded to the United States, and in various other parts of the North Pacific. Illus. N. Y., 1871. 17—102.

Wichert, Ernst. The green gate: a romance. *Mrs.* A. L. Wister, tr. Phil., 1875. 41—229.

Wicliff, The life of. Le Bas, C. W. Lond., 1832. 13—78.

Wide, wide world, The. "Elizabeth Wetherell." Phil., 1876. 2 v. in one. 7—42.

Widow Bedott papers, The. Illus. Whitcher, F. M. N. Y., 1875. 2—8.

—— Goldsmith's daughter. Smith, J. P. N. Y., 1872. 5—30.

Widower, The. Smith, J. P. N. Y., 1872. 5—30.

Widow's son, The. Southworth, E. D. E. N. Phil., 1867. 6—37.

Wife of a vain man, The. Schwartz, M. S. Bost., 1873. 5—28.

Wife's story, and other tales. Pike, F. W. A. Lond., 1875. 3 v. 4—25.

—— victory, The. Southworth, E. D. E. N. Phil., 1854. 6—37.

Wiffin, Jeremiah Holme. Historical memoirs of the house of Russell, from the time of the Norman conquest. Illus. Lond., 1833. 2 v. 33—200.

Wigwam and the cabin, The. Simms, W. G. Phil., 1853. 2—10.

Wikoff, Henry. My courtship and its consequences. N. Y., 1855. 2—12.

—— the adventures of a roving diplomatist. N. Y., 1857. O—3.

Wild Hyacinth: a novel. Randolph, *Mrs.* Phil., 1876. 41—228.

—— North land, The. Illus. Butler, W. F. Phil., 1874. 17—101.

—— scenes of a hunter's life. Illus. Frost. J. Bost., 1875. 10—57.

Wilfrid, Cumbermede. Illus. MacDonald, G. N. Y., 1872. 7—45.

Wilhelm Meister's apprenticeship. Goethe, J. W. *von.* Lond., 1870. 6—40.

Wilkes, Charles. Narrative of the United States exploring expedition during the years 1838—42. Illus. N. Y., 1851. 5 v. 9—51.

Wilkinson, James. Memoirs of my own times. Phil., 1816. 3 v. 29—177.

Wilkinson, Sir John Gardner. Manners and customs of the ancient Egyptians. Illus. 1st and 2d series. Lond., 1837-41. 6 v. 36—216.

Wille, Elizabeth de. Johannes Olaf: a novel. F. E. Bunnett, tr, Bost., 1873. P—2.

Williams, Edwin. The presidents of the United States, their memoirs and administrations, etc. Illus. N. Y., 1849. 24—141.

—— and B. J. Lossing. The statesman's manual: addresses and messages of the presidents of the United States. Illus. N. Y., 1858. 6 v. 8.

Williams, John Lee. The territory of Florida, from the first discovery to the present time. N. Y., 1837. 31—185.

Williams, Roger, Life of. (Library of American biography, vol. 14.) 11—65.

Williams, Samuel. The natural and civil history of Vermont. Burlington, Vt., 1809. 2 v. 30—183.

Williamson, William D. The history of the state of Maine, from its first discovery, A. D. 1602, to the separation, A. D. 1820. Hallowell, 1832. 2 v. 30—183.

Willis, Nathaniel Parker. Canadian scenery; illustrated by W. H. Bartlett. Lond., 1842. 2 v. 17—101.

—— Paul Fane ; or, parts of a life else untold. N. Y., 1857. O—3.

—— Out-doors at Idlewild ; or, the shaping of a home on the banks of the Hudson. N. Y., 1855. P—2.

——, The poems of ;—sacred, passionate, and humorous. N. Y., 1873. 17—106.

—— Health trip to the tropics. N. Y., 1853. 17—102.

—— Trenton falls, picturesque and descriptive ; embracing the original essay of John Sherman, the first proprietor and resident. Illus. N. Y., 1851. 17—102.

Willis, the pilot ; or, the after adventures of the Swiss family Robinson. Illus. Lond., n. d. 38.

Wilson, Alexander, Life of. (Library of American biography, vol. 2.) 11—65.

Wilson, Andrew. The abode of snow: observations on a tour from Chinese Thibet to the Indian Caucasus through the upper valleys of the Himalaya. N. Y., 1875. 10—57.

Wilson, Augusta J., (formerly Miss A. J. Evans.) Vashti; or, until death do us part: a novel. N. Y., 1874. 7—44.

—— Beulah: a novel. N. Y. and Lond., 1874. 7—44.

—— Macaria: a novel. N. Y. and Lond., 1874. 7—44.

—— Inez: a tale of the Alamo. N. Y., 1876. 7—44.

—— St. Elmo: a novel. N. Y. and Lond., 1874. 7—44.

—— Infelice: a novel. N. Y. and Lond., 1876. 7—44.

Wilson, Daniel. Prehistoric annals of Scotland. Illus. Lond., 1863. 2 v. 34—204.

Wilson, Henry. History of the rise and fall of the slave power in America. Bost., 1874-77. 3 v. 31—181.

Wilson, Henry, and James Caulfield. The book of wonderful characters: memoirs and anecdotes of remarkable and eccentric persons in all ages and countries. Illus. Lond., n. d. 2—8.

Wilson, James Grant. The life and letters of Fitz-Greene Halleck. N. Y., 1869. 12—66.

Wilson, Rev. John Leighton. Western Africa: its history, condition, and prospects. Illus. N. Y., 1866. 36—215.

Wilson, John. The elements of punctuation; with rules on the use of capital letters. Bost., 1856. 14—85.

Wilson, John, Prof., (Christopher North.) "Christopher North;" a memoir of John Wilson, compiled from family papers and other sources, by his daughter, Mrs. Gordon. Illus. N. Y., 1863. 13—74.

—— The recreations of Christopher North. (Modern British essayists.) Bost., 1854. 27—159.

—— Lights and shadows of Scottish life. Phil., 1871. 2—13.

——, and W. Maginn, J. G. Lockhart, J. Hogg, and R. Shelton Mackenzie. Noctes ambrosianæ. N. Y., n. d. 5 v. 2—10.

—— The genius and character of Burns. N. Y., 1845. 11—63.

Wilson, John Mackay. Tales of the borders and of Scotland; historical, traditionary, and imaginative. Edin., n. d. 11 v. 3—18.

Wilson, Sir Robert. Brief remarks on the character and composition of the Russian army; and a sketch of the campaigns in Poland, in the years 1806-07. Lond., 1810. T.

Wilson, Robert Anderson. Mexico and its religion; with incidents of travel in that country, during parts of the years 1851-54. Illus. N. Y., 1855. 17—104.

Winchell, Alexander. Sketches of creation: a popular view of some of the grand conclusions of the sciences in reference to the history of matter and of life; together with a statement of the intimations of science respecting the primordial condition and the ultimate destiny of the earth and the solar system. Illus. N. Y., 1874. 14—85.

Winchendon, History of the town of. Illus. Marvin, A. P. Winchendon, 1868. 30—182.

Winds of the globe; or, the laws of atmospheric circulation over the surface of the earth. Coffin, J. H. Wash., 1875. D. R.

Wing and wing. Illus. Cooper, J. F. N. Y., 1864. 3—14.

Winifred Bertram. Charles, E. N. Y., n. d. 3—20.

Winning his way. Coffin, C. C. Bost., 1866. 7—46.

Winsor, Justin. A history of the town of Duxbury, Mass.; with genealogical registers. Bost., 1849. 30—182.

Winter fire, The: a sequel to "Summer driftwood." Porter, R. N. Y., n. d. 6—38.

Winthrop, Theodore. John Brent. Bost., 1862. 4—24.

—— Edwin Brothertoft. Bost., 1862. 4—24.

—— Cecil Dreeme; with a portrait and biographical sketch of the author, by G. W. Curtis. N. Y., 1876. 4—24.

Wirt, William. Sketches of the life and character of Patrick Henry. N. Y., 1860. 13—76.

——, Memoirs of the life of. Kennedy, J. P. Phil., 1850. 2 v. 11—59.

Wisconsin, Collections of the State Historical Society of, 1856. Madison, 1857. Vol. 3. 31—186.

——, The history of. Smith, W. R. Madison, 1854. Vol. 3. 31—186.

Wisconsin and its resources. Illus. Ritchie, J. S. Phil., 1857. 31—186.

Wise, Henry Augustus, *lieut., U. S. N.* Los gringos; or, an inside view of Mexico and California; with wanderings in Peru, Chili, and Polynesia. N. Y., 1850. 9—53.

—— Captain Brand of the "Centipede:" a pirate of eminence in the West Indies, his loves and exploits; together with some account of the singular manner by which he departed this life. Illus. N. Y., 1871. 5—28.

Wit and humor, Cyclopædia of. Illus. Burton, W. H. N. Y., 1872. 2—7.

Within an ace. Jenkin, C. N. Y., 1875. 6—38.

—— and without. MacDonald, G. N. Y., 1872. 17—106.

—— the maze: a novel. Wood, E. P. Phil., n. d. 41—230.

Witt, *Madame* Pauline Guizot de. A French country family. Illus. *Mrs.* D. M. Craik, tr. N. Y., 1868. O—3.

Wits and beaux of society, The. Illus. Thomson, K. B. Lond., 1871. 40—222.

Wives and daughters. Illus. Gaskell, E. C. N. Y., 1866. 6—35.

Wolcott, John, (*Peter Pindar,*) Poetical works of; with memoirs and anecdotes of the author. Dublin, 1788. 16—100.

Wolfert's roost and other papers. Irving, W. N. Y., 1855. 3—19.

Woman against woman. Marryat, *Miss* F. Bost., n. d. 6—35.

—— in her various relations. Abell, L. G. N. Y., 1860. P—2.

—— in white, The. Illus. Collins, W. W. N. Y., 1873. 6—38.

—— in the nineteenth century. Ossoli, M. F. Bost., 1855. 2—8.

Womankind in Western Europe. Illus. Wright, T. Lond., 1869. 28—165.

Woman's friendship. Aguilar, G. N. Y., 1871. 5—34.

—— kingdom, The. Illus. Muloch, D. M. N. Y., 1870. 5—28.

—— ransom, A. Robinson, F. W. Bost., n. d. 5—29.

—— worth and worthlessness. "Gail Hamilton." N. Y., 1872. 2—10.

Women of Israel, The. Aguilar, G. N. Y., 1871. 2 v. 5—34.

Wonder stories told for children. Illus. Andersen, H. C. N. Y., 1875. 39.

Wonderful characters, The book of. Illus. Wilson, H., and J. Caulfield. Lond., n. d. 2—8.

—— balloon ascents. Illus. Marion, F. N. Y., 1870. P—2.

—— escapes. Illus. Bernard, F. N. Y., 1871. O—3.

Wood, Edward J. Giants and dwarfs. Lond., 1868. 2—8.

—— The wedding-day in all ages and countries. N. Y., 1869. 28—169.

Wood, *Lady* Emma. Below the salt: a novel. Lond., 1876. 3 v. 4—27.

Wood, Ella Price, (*Mrs.* Henry Wood.) Squire Trevelyn's heir: a novel of domestic life. Phil., 1863. 6—35.

—— Mrs. Halliburton's troubles: a novel. N. Y., n. d. 5—29.

—— East Lynne; or, the earl's daughter. N. Y., n. d. 5—29.

—— Castle Wafer; or, the plain gold ring. N. Y., n. d. 5—29.

—— The heir to Ashley. N. Y., n. d. 5—29.

—— St. Martin's eve. Phil., n. d. 41—230.

—— Roland Yorke: sequel to "The Channings." Phil., n. d. 41—230.

—— Elster's folly. Phil., n. d. 41—230.

—— The castle's heir; or, lady Adelaide's oath. Illus. Phil., n. d. 41—230.

—— Dene Hollow: a novel. Phil., n. d. 41—230.

—— Oswald Cray. Phil., n. d. 41—230.

—— The master of Greylands: a novel. Phil., n. d. 41—130.

—— The Channings: a domestic novel in real life. Phil., n. d. 41—230.

—— Verner's pride: a tale of domestic life. Phil., n. d. 41—230.

—— George Canterbury's will. Phil., n. d. 41—230.

—— The shadow of Ashlydyat. Phil., n. d. 41—230.

—— Lord Oakburn's daughters. Phil., n. d. 41—230.

—— The runaway match. Phil., n. d. 41—230.

—— The haunted tower. Phil., n. d. 41—230.

Wood, Ella Price, (*Mrs.* Henry Wood.) The lost bank note. Phil., n. d. 41—230.

—— The mystery. Phil., n. d. 41—230.

—— Within the maze: a novel. Phil., n. d. 41—230.

—— Bessy Rane: a novel. Phil., n. d. 41——230.

—— The Red Court farm: a new novel. Phil., n. d. 41—229.

—— Mildred Arkell. Phil., 1865· 41—229.

—— Parkwater; or, told in the twilight. Phil., n. d. 41—230.

Wood, John George. The uncivilized races of men in all countries of the world. Illus. Hartford, 1871. 2 v. 26—153.

—— Homes without hands; being a description of the habitations of animals, classed according to the principle of their construction. Illus. N. Y., 1874. 15—90.

—— Man and beast, here and hereafter; illustrated by more than three hundred original anecdotes. N. Y., n. d. 19—116.

—— Insects at home: a popular account of all those insects which are useful or destructive, and minutely describing their structure, habits, and transformations. Illus. Phil., 1873. 19—116.

—— **Woodcraft;** or, hawks about the dovecote. Illus. Simms, W. G. N. Y., 1854. 41—229.

Woods, Daniel B. Sixteen months at the gold diggings. N. Y., 1851. 9—50.

Woods and by-ways of New England, The. Illus. Flagg, W. Bost., 1872. 19—115.

Woodstock. Scott, *Sir* W. Bost., 1868. 3—17.

Wooing o't, The. Alexander, *Mrs.* N. Y., 1873. 7—44.

Woolman, John, A journal of the life, gospel labors, and Christian experiences of. N. Y., 1845. E.

Woolrych, Humphry W. The life of the Right Honourable Sir Edward Coke, lord chief justice of the king's bench. Lond., 1826. 11—62.

Woolsey, *Rev.* Theodore, and others. The first century of the republic: a review of American progress. Illus. N. Y., 1876. 40—225.

Woolworth, James M. Nebraska in 1857. Omaha, 1857. 31—187.

Worcester, Joseph E. *A dictionary of the English language. Bost., 1860. 22—131.

Words and places. Taylor, I. Lond., 1873. 19—114.

—— and their uses, past and present. White, R. G. N. Y., 1871. 14—81.

—— : their use and abuse. Mathews, W. Chic., 1876. 40—223.

Wordsworth, William, Poetical works of. Bost., 1864. 7 v. 16—97.

Contents.

Vol. 1. Sketch of Wordsworth's life; Poems written in youth; Poems referring to the period of childhood; Poems founded on the affections; Notes.

Vol. 2. Poems on the naming of places; Poems of the fancy; Miscellaneous sonnets; Notes.

Vol. 3. Memorials of a tour in Scotland, 1803; Same, in 1814; Poems dedicated to national independence and liberty; Memorials of a tour on the continent; Memorials of a tour in Italy, 1837; The river Duddon; Yarrow revisited, and other poems; Notes.

Vol. 4. The white doe of Rylstone; Ecclesiastical sonnets; Evening voluntaries; Poems composed or suggested during a tour in the summer of 1833; Poems of sentiment and reflection; Sonnets dedicated to liberty and order; Sonnets upon the punishment of death; Notes.

Vol. 5. Miscellaneous poems; Inscriptions; Selections from Chaucer modernized; Poems referring to the period of old age; Epitaphs and elegiac pieces; Appendix, Prefaces, &c.

Vol. 6. The excursion.

Vol. 7. The prelude; or, growth of a poet's mind.

Work: a story of experience. Illus. Alcott, L. M. Bost., 1873. 5—31.

Workingmen's homes. Hale, E. E. Bost., 1874. 27—162.

World at home, The. Illus. Kirby, M. and E. Lond. and N. Y., 1872. 38.

—— before the deluge, The. Illus. Figuier, L. N. Y., 1869. 14—83.

——, History of the. Illus. Smith, P. N. Y., 1865–66. 3 v. 32—194.

——, History of the. Rotteck, C. *von.* Phil., 1840. 4 v. 32—194.

——, History of the. Raleigh, *Sir* W. Edin., 1820. 6 v. 32—194.

—— of the sea. Illus. Tandon, M. Lond., n. d. 14—83.

——, Sacred and prophane history of the. Shuckford, S. Lond., 1731-40. 4 v. 32—194.

——, The sacred history of the. Turner, S. Lond., 1833-37. 3 v. 32—194.

World-noted women. Illus. Clarke, M. C. N. Y., 1857. 11—59.

Worthies of England, The history of the. Fuller, T. Lond., 1840. 3 v. 13—75.

Wrangham, Francis. The British Plutarch: containing the lives of the most eminent divines, patriots, statesmen, warriors, philosophers, poets, and artists of Great Britain and Ireland, from the accession of Henry the eighth to the present time. Lond., 1816. 6 v. 11—63.

Wraxall, Sir Nathaniel William. Historical memoirs of my own time, from 1772 to 1784. Lond., 1815. 2 v. 36—220.

—— Memoirs of the courts of Berlin, Dresden, Warsaw, and Vienna, from 1777 to 1779. Lond., 1800. 2 v. 36—220.

Wreck of the Chancellor, The. Verne, J. Bost., 1875. 5—31.

Wrecked in port: a novel. Yates, E. N. Y., 1869. 5—28.

—— on a reef. Illus. Raynal, F. E. Lond., 1874. 8—48.

Wright, George Newnham. Life and campaigns of Arthur, duke of Wellington. Lond., 1839-41. 11—62.

Wright, Thomas. Womankind in Western Europe, from the earliest times to the seventeenth century. Illus. Lond., 1869. 28—165.

—— A history of caricature and grotesque in literature and art. Illustrated by F. W. Fairholt. Lond., 1875. 2—7.

Writing, reading, and speaking, The arts of. Cox, E. W. N. Y. and Lond., 1873. 19—114.

Wuthering heights and Agnes Grey. "Ellis" and "Acton Bell." Lond., 1870. 7—45.

Wyandotte. Illus. Cooper, J. F. N.Y., 1864. 3—14.

Wyatt, Sir Thomas. Poetical works of; with a memoir. Bost., 1864. 16—97.

Wyoming. A sketch of the history of. Chapman, I. A. Wilkesbarre, 1830. 31—189.

——, History of. Miner, C. Phil., 1845. 31—189.

Wyss, Johann Rudolph rev. The Swiss family Robinson; or, adventures of a father, mother, and four sons in a desert island. Illus. N. Y., 1872. 38.

Xenophon, The whole works of. Phil., 1845. 35—209.

——, Works of. E. Spelman, tr. Lond., 1830. 2 v. 17—107.

Yankee in Canada, A. Thoreau, H. D. Bost., 1874. 9—53.

Yates, Edmund. The forlorn hope. Lond. and N. Y., n. d. 7—45.

—— Land at last. Lond. and N. Y., n. d. 7—45.

—— Kissing the rod. Lond. and N. Y., n. d. 7—45.

—— Running the gauntlet. Lond. and N. Y., n. d. 7—45.

—— Wrecked in port: a novel. N. Y., 1869. 5—28.

—— The silent witness: a novel. Bost., 1875. 7—45.

—— A dangerous game. Bost., 1874. 7—45.

Year-book of facts in science and art. Timbs, J. Lond., 1853-57. 5 v. 15—93.

Yellow fever, The cause and prevention of. Barton, E. H. N. Y., 1857. L.

Yellowstone, Wonders of the. Illus. James Richardson, ed. N. Y., 1874. 17—101.

Yelverton, Thérèse, viscountess Avonmore. Teresina in America. Lond., 1875. 2 v. 10—57.

Yemassee, The. Illus. Simms, W. G. N. Y., 1853. 41—229.

Yesterday, to-day, and forever: a poem in twelve books. Bickersteth, E. H. N. Y., 1876. 17—105.

Yesterdays with authors. Fields, J. T. Bost., 1872. 2—11.

Yonge, Charles Duke. Three centuries of English literature. N. Y., 1872. 28—169.

—— The life of Marie Antoinette, queen of France. Lond., 1876. 2 v. 40—223.

Yonge, Charlotte Mary. The dove in the eagle's nest. N. Y., 1872. 5—30.

—— The heir of Redclyffe. N. Y., 1871. 2 v. 5—30.

—— The prince and the page: a story of the last crusade. Illus. Lond., 1866. 38.

Yonge, Charlotte Mary. A book of worthies gathered from the old histories, and now written anew. Lond., 1869. 39.

—— The little duke, Richard the fearless. Illus. Lond., 1869. 38.

—— The Danvers papers : an invention. Lond., 1867. 2—13.

—— The clever woman of the family. Lond. and N. Y., 1871. 5—30.

—— Hopes and fears; or, scenes from the life of a spinster. Lond., 1864. 5—30.

—— Heartsease; or, the brother's wife. Illus. Lond. and N. Y., 1871. 5—30.

—— Dynevor terrace; or, the clue of life. Lond. and N. Y., 1871. 5—30.

—— History of Christian names. Lond., 1863. 2 v. 26—156.

—— The young step-mother; or, a chronicle of mistakes. Lond. and N. Y., 1871. 5—30.

—— The daisy chain; or, aspirations: a family chronicle. Illus. Lond. and N. Y., 1871. 5—30.

—— The trial; or, more links of the daisy chain: sequel to the "Daisy chain." Illus. Lond. and N. Y., 1871. 5—30.

—— Beechcroft. N. Y., 1871. 5—30.

—— The chaplet of pearls; or, the white and black Ribaumont. Lond., 1868. 5—30.

—— The lances of Lynwood. Illus. Lond., 1868. 38.

—— A book of golden deeds of all times and all lands. Bost., 1871. 39.

—— P's and Q's; or, the question of putting upon. Illus. Lond., 1872. 39.

—— Lady Hester; or, Ursula's narrative. Lond., 1874. 5—30.

—— The pillars of the house; or, under wode, under rode. Lond. and N. Y., 1874. 2 v. 5—30.

—— My young Alcides: a faded photograph. N. Y., 1876. 5—30.

—— The three brides. N. Y., 1876. 5—30.

Youmans, Edward Livingstone. The correlation and conservation of forces:

15 ɪ

a series of expositions by *Prof.* Grove, *Prof.* Helmholtz, *Dr.* Mayer, *Dr.* Faraday, *Prof.* Liebig, and *Dr.* Carpenter. N. Y., 1868. 15—88.

Young, Edward. Poetical works of. Bost., 1864. 2 v. 16—98.

Young, Edward, (*statistician.*) Labor in Europe and America: a special report on the rates of wages, the cost of subsistence, and the condition of the working classes in Great Britain, Germany, France, Belgium, and other countries of Europe; also in the United States and British America. Wash., 1875. X.

Young, George R. The British North American colonies. Lond., 1834. 33—200.

Young duke, and Coningsby. Disraeli, B. Lond. and N. Y., n. d. 4—24.

—— step-mother, The. Yonge, C. M. Lond. and N. Y., 1871. 5—30.

—— surveyor, The. Illus. Trowbridge, J. T. Bost., 1875. 39.

Yucatan, Incidents of travel in. Illus. Stephens, J. L. N. Y., 1847. 2 v. 9—52.

Yusef; or, the journey of the Frangi. Illus. Browne, J. R. N. Y., 1872. 17—104.

Zanoni. Bulwer-Lytton, *Sir* E. Phil., 1867. 5—33.

Zeisberger, David. Grammar of the language of the Lenni Lenape, or, Delaware Indians. P. S. Du Ponceau, tr. Phil., 1827. L.

Zell's popular encyclopedia: a universal dictionary of English language, science, literature, and art. Illus. Colange, L. 2 v. Phil., 1876. 36—215.

Zirkel, Ferdinand. Microscopical petrography. Vol. 6, Geological exploration of the fortieth parallel, by Clarence King. Illus. Wash., 1876. D. R.

Zoonomia ; or, the laws of organic life. Darwin, E. Lond., 1801. 4 v. 14—83.

O

Warner, Susan, (*Elizabeth Wetherell*.) The old helmet. N. Y., 1874. 7—42.

—— The hills of the Shatemuc. Phil., 1873. 7—42.

—— Daisy. Phil., 1873. 2 v. in one. 7—42.

—— Melbourne house. Illus. N. Y., 1874. 2 v. in one. 7—42.

—— The wide, wide world. Phil., 1876. 2 v. in one. 7—42.

—— The house of Israel. Illus. N. Y., 1872. 7—42.

—— Walks from Eden. Illus. N. Y., 1873. 7—42.

—— Sceptres and crowns. Illus. N. Y., 1875. 7—42.

—— and Anna. Say and seal. Phil., 1870. 2 v. in one. 7—42.

—— The rapids of Niagara. Illus. N. Y., 1876. 7—42.

Warren, Joseph. An oration delivered March 6, 1775, to commemorate the bloody tragedy of the 5th of March, 1770. Bost., 1775. 27—160.

——, The life of. (Library of American biography, vol. 10.) 11—65.

Warren, Samuel. Passages from the diary of a late physician. N. Y., 1871. 3 v. in one. 7—45.

—— Ten thousand a year: a novel. Phil., n. d. 6—35.

—— Now and then :—" through a glass, darkly." N. Y., 1848. 7—45.

Warwick, *Sir* Philip. Memoirs of the reigne of King Charles the first, with a continuation to the happy restauration of King Charles the second. Lond., 1701. 11—65.

Was he successful? Kimball, R. B. N. Y. and Leipsic, 1864. 4—25.

Washburn, Katharine Sedgwick. The Italian girl. Bost., 1874. 41—227.

Washington, George. Farewell address to the people of the United States. Phil., 1858. V.

——, The writings of, with a life of the author. Sparks, J. N. Y., 1847-48. 12 v. 25—149.

——, Life of. Irving, W. N. Y., 1855-59. 5 v. 13—74.

——, Life of, during the war and the presidency. Marshall, J. Phil., 1850. 2 v. 13—74.

Washington and his generals. Headley, J. T. N. Y., 1875. 2 v. in one. Q—2.

——, The home of; or, Mount Vernon and its associations. Illus. Lossing, B. J. N. Y., 1870. 26—155.

Water-babies, The. Kingsley, C. Bost., 1869. 38.

Waterloo : a sequel to " The conscript of 1813." Illus. Erckmann, E., and A. Chatrian. N. Y., 1872. 5—31.

Waterston, William. 'A cyclopædia of commerce, mercantile law, finance, commercial geography, and navigation ; with an essay on commerce, by J. R. McCulloch. Lond., 1843. 21—128.

Water-witch, The. Illus. Cooper, J. F. N. Y., 1871. 3—14.

Watson, Elkanah. Men and times of the revolution. W. C. Watson, ed. N. Y., 1856. 12—68.

Watson, John F. Annals and occurrences of New York city and state in the olden time. Phil., 1846. 31—190.

—— Annals of Philadelphia and Pennsylvania in the olden time. Illus. Phil., 1845. 2 v. 31—189.

Watson, Robert. The history of the reign of Philip the second, king of Spain, and of Philip the third, king of Spain. N. Y., 1818. 2 v. in one. 12—68.

Watts, Isaac. Horæ lyricæ ; with a life of the author, by Robert Southey. Bost., 1864. 16—97.

Waverly. Scott, *Sir* W. Bost., 1868. 3—17.

Way we live now, The: a novel. Illus. Trollope, A. N. Y., 1875. 5—28.

Wayne, Anthony, Life and services of. Illus. Moore, H. N. Phil., 1845. 13—79.

——, Life of. (Library of American biography, vol. 4.) 11—65.

Ways of the hour, The. Illus. Cooper, J. F. N. Y., 1870. 3—14.

We and our neighbors: sequel to " My wife and I." Illus. Stowe, H. B. N. Y., 1875. 6—35.

—— boys: written by one of us for the amusement of pa's and ma's in general, aunt Lovisa in particular. Bost., 1876. 39.

—— girls. Illus. Whitney, A. D. T· Bost., 1872. 7—44.

Weale, John. London, exhibited in 1851; elucidating its natural and physical characteristics, its antiquity and architecture, its arts, manufactures, trade, and organization, etc. Illus. Lond., n. d. 27—160.

―――― Rudimentary dictionary of terms used in civil and naval architecture, building and construction, early and ecclesiastical art, civil and mechanical engineering, fine art, mining and surveying. Lond., 1849-50. 21—128.

―――― Bridges: in theory, practice, and architecture. Lond., 1839. 2 v. T.

―――― Portfolio of ancient capital letters, monograms, quaint designs, etc., etc., colored and tinted. Illus. Lond., 1858-59. V.

Webster, Daniel, The works of. Bost., 1851. 6 v. 25—148.

――――, Life of. Curtis, G. T. N. Y., 1870. 2 v. 12—66.

――――, The diplomatic and official papers of, while secretary of state. N. Y., 1848. 18—109.

Webster, Leland A. Present status of the philosophy of society: a treatise designed to show the insufficiency of existing systems of thought concerning the phenomena of society, and the tendencies toward a larger system; being part of a series comprising a complete review, historical and critical, of the progress of thought in social philosophy: which review is itself intended as a general introduction to a complete and exhaustive inquiry into the causes which determine the social condition of mankind; embodying the outlines of a thorough philosophy of society, and a complete science of sociology. N. Y., 1866. 14—84.

Webster, Noah. *An American dictionary of the English language. Springfield, *Mass.*, 1872. 22—131.

Wedding garments; or, Bessie Morris's diary. McLain, M. W. N. Y., 1875. P—1.

Wedding-day in all ages and countries, The. Wood, E. J. N. Y., 1869. 28—169.

* **Weekly** register. Niles, H. Balt. and Phil., 1811-49. 76 v. D. R.

Weil, Gustav. The Bible, the Koran, and the Talmud; or, biblical legends of the Mussulmans. N. Y., 1846. E.

Wellington, Arthur, *duke of*, Life and campaigns of. Wright, G. N. Lond., 1839-41. 4 v. 11—62.

Wells, David Ames. The year-book of agriculture. Illus. Phil., 1856. D. R.

Wells, J. W. An alphabetical list of the battles (with dates) of the war of the rebellion. Pamphlet. Wash., 1875. M.

Wells, William Vincent. Explorations and adventures in Honduras, comprising sketches of travel in the gold regions of Olancho, and a review of the history and general resources of Central America. Illus. N. Y., 1857. 9—51.

Wenderholme : a story of Lancashire and Yorkshire. Hamerton, P. G. Bost., 1876. 41—227.

Wept of the Wish-ton-wish, The. Illus. Cooper, J. F. N. Y., 1864. 3—14.

Weppner, Margaretha. The north star and the southern cross : being the personal experiences, impressions, and observations, in a two years' journey round the world. Lond., 1876. 2 v. 40—222.

Werner, Ernest, *pseud.* At the altar. Phil., 1872. O—1.

―――― "Good luck!" Frances A. Shaw, tr. Bost., 1874. 4—21.

―――― Broken chains. F. A. Shaw, tr. Bost., 1875. 41—230.

―――― A hero of the pen. F. A. Shaw, tr. Bost., 1875. 41—230.

Wesley, *Rev.* John, The life and times of the. Tyerman, L. N. Y., 1872. 3 v. 12—69.

West Indies and the Spanish main, The. Trollope, A. N. Y., n. d. 9—53.

―――― Lawn and the rector of St. Mark's. Holmes, M. J. N. Y. and Lond., 1874. 7—42.

Western Africa. Illus. Wilson, J. L. N. Y., 1856. 36—215.

―――― states, Notes on the. Hall, J. Phil., 1838. 29—177.

―――― territory of North America, A topographical description of the. Imlay, G. Lond., 1797. 29—177.

―――― Virginia, History of the early settlement and Indian wars of. Illus. De Hass, W. Wheeling, 1851. 31—188.

14 I